AF361568

The Christology of Erasmus

The Christology of Erasmus

Christ, Humanity, and Peace

Terence J. Martin

The Catholic University of America Press  Washington, D.C.

Copyright © 2024
The Catholic University of America Press
All rights reserved

The paper used in this publication meets the minimum requirements of
American National Standards for Information Science—Permanence
of Paper for Printed Materials, ANSI Z39,48-1992.
∞

Interior and cover design by Reflective Book Design

Cataloging-in-Publication Data is available from the Library of Congress
ISBN: 978-0-8132-3802-9
eISBN: 978-0-8132-3803-6

Peace and joy,
For Herold Weiss

CONTENTS

ACKNOWLEDGMENTS

Nothing of scholarly value is accomplished alone, even during the Covid pandemic, when many of us retreated to the solitude of our studies, wherein we might discover the time and space for fruitful reading and writing. Even then, I certainly was not alone, as no scholar can be who habitually feasts on the rich fare of books that keep us company. Nor was I without the valuable input of scholarly friends. In this regard, I am grateful to Phyllis Kaminski, whose interest and insights many times helped me sort through some of the most perplexing questions dealt with in theological materials. My long-time friend and colleague Herold Weiss read and commented on every page of this book, and I have greatly benefitted from his observations and questions. Conversations with Charles Wilson, William Schweiker, and Richard B. Miller on the overall design of this project proved to be—as always—enjoyable and enriching. I appreciate, as well, the feedback provided by Willis Goth Regier on selected chapters of this book.

ABBREVIATIONS

ASD   *Opera omnia Desiderii Erasmi Roterdami.* Amsterdam, 1969–.

COE   *Contemporaries of Erasmus: A Biographical Register of the Renaissance and Reformation.* 2 vols. Edited by Peter G. Bietenholz. Toronto: University of Toronto Press, 1987.

CWE   *The Collected Works of Erasmus.* Toronto: University of Toronto Press, 1974–.

NRSV   *The New Oxford Annotated Bible: New Revised Standard Version.* Fourth edition. Edited by Michael D. Coogan. Oxford: Oxford University Press, 2010.

The Christology of Erasmus

Introduction

Erasmus of Rotterdam never wrote a formal work in Christology, though it remains true that nothing is more central to his religious thinking than the reality of Christ—in his eyes, not only the supreme revelation of divine mercy embodied in the life of Jesus of Nazareth to which Christian scriptures variously testify but, equally, the divine presence undergirding that life-centering ethic of love and peace (what Erasmus calls the "philosophy of Christ"), which calls for resolute opposition to the ever-prevailing forces of ignorance, arrogance, and brutality. Again and again, therefore, we find Erasmus striking Christological notes, though it is not his manner to pull those points together and present them in a systematic fashion.

With that in mind, this book gathers the various Christological reflections widely scattered across the writings of Erasmus, thereby distilling his tacit concerns and explicit claims regarding the biblical figure of Jesus and the enduring reality of Christ. Such an undertaking involves—among other things—consideration of Erasmus's philological and critical work on biblical materials, and with that, the often-heated controversies over Christological doctrine that ensued. It mandates attention to his interpretive labor on both Hebrew and Christian scriptures, the former giving rise to some sprightly allegorical readings with Christological significance and the latter in the form of biblical paraphrases, where the voice of Erasmus subtly speaks through the ostensibly straightforward retelling of the text. It also invites engagement with the many letters, adages, homilies, and treatises of various sorts wherein Erasmus imaginatively depicts the ironic power of divine revelation and creatively sharpens the ethical and political edge to the philosophy of Christ. My design is to distill the Christological elements from these varied sources in a manner that shows both the range and the coherence of Erasmus's thinking on Christological matters.

What emerges—in a nutshell—is a Christology that arises from personal piety steadfastly respectful of Catholic teaching. It takes its start by way of critical exegesis of biblical texts informed with skills in ancient languages, frequently crafted in dialogue with patristic commentaries, and often defended in controversies with various adversaries of the day. It also consistently involves his singular creativity and dialectical dexterity to address the kind of conundrums so common in Christological debates, and while duly attentive to questions of doctrine, it ultimately proceeds in the service of ethical and political goods. While Erasmus carefully works within the broad parameters of orthodox teaching—something wrongly doubted by some theologians of his day—his critical skills with languages, accent on rhetoric in theology, keen sense of irony, appreciation for the limits of human knowledge, and passionate defense of peace give his work a distinctive stamp and thereby make a singular contribution to the history of Christology. It is the purpose of this book to take up and discuss the many and varied things Erasmus has to say when addressing Christological questions, and to do so in a manner that highlights precisely these defining characteristics that shape his reflections and give them lasting value.

Before jumping directly into the heart of the Erasmian materials pertaining to Christology, it will be helpful to consider a number of factors that—in one way or another—give shape to everything that follows, but which may also generate some confusions when encountered in the context of Christological reflections without prior discussion. Addressing these matters from the start, in other words, will offer some helpful guidance in traversing the landscape of the Christology of Erasmus.

Erasmus as Theologian

To begin with, an initial question must be faced and resolved, and that is, whether, and in what sense, it can be said that Erasmus had or wrote a Christology. Certainly, he did not draft a formal treatise addressing the nature and function of Christ, as Christian theologians often have done. Nor has it been clear to many whether Erasmus should be considered a theologian at all, so the first question really is two-fold. Was Erasmus a theologian, and if so, in what sense? Further, with some clarity gained on that question, do his reflections on Christ constitute a theological project: if so, in what sense?

His many theological critics of the day—eminent professionals from universities in Louvain, Paris, and beyond, but also some leading reformers eventually outside the Roman Catholic fold—had few doubts. For them, Erasmus was a theological pretender at best, and he had no business treading on their turf. Erasmus is merely a "theologizing humanist," French theologian Noël Béda declared along these lines,[1] by which he means—in the words taken from the conclusion of the censures of Erasmus spearheaded by Béda—that Erasmus is one who thinks "that perfect and peerless theology consists in knowing Greek and Hebrew writings," even while he lacks training in the "discipline of theology."[2] Interestingly enough, Martin Luther—every bit the heretic in the eyes of Béda—thought much the same thing about Erasmus. As Luther

1. Erasmus, *Supputatio errorum in censuris Natalis Beddae*, ed. Edwin Rabbie, in *Opera omnia Desiderii Erasmi Roterodami*, IX - V (Leiden: Brill, 2013), 222, where Erasmus mentions Béda's slur. On Erasmus's controversy with Béda, see Erika Rummel, *Erasmus and His Catholic Critics, 1523–1536*, vol. 2 (Nieuwkoop: De Graaf Publishers, 1989), 29–59; James K. Farge, "Noël Béda and the Defense of the Tradition," in *Biblical Humanism and Scholasticism in the Age of Erasmus*, ed. Erika Rummel (Leiden: Brill, 2008), 143–64. First references to individual works of Erasmus and to specific volumes of the *Opera omnia Desiderii Erasmi Roterodami* give complete bibliographic information. Thereafter, all references to individual works are given with a shortened title, followed by ASD with volume and page number.

2. Erasmus, *Clarifications Concerning the Censures Published at Paris in the Name of the Theology Faculty There*, ed. and trans. Clarence H. Miller, in *Collected Works of Erasmus: Controversies*, vol. 82 (Toronto: University of Toronto Press, 2012), 255. On the conflict between humanist scholars and scholastic theologians, see Erika Rummel, *The Humanist-Scholastic Debate in the Renaissance and Reformation* (Cambridge, MA: Harvard University Press, 1995), 96–125. First references to specific works of Erasmus and to individual volumes of the *Collected Works of Erasmus* give complete bibliographic information. Thereafter, all references to individual works are given with a shortened title, followed by CWE with volume and page number.

saw it, Erasmus was "equipped with languages and the arts" and "wrote many excellent things," but—being "without God"—he never wrote "a line about Christ."[3] Even fellow humanist Jacques Lefèvre, whose work we will encounter in chapter 6, considered Erasmus more learned and eloquent than theological, thus branding him a "would-be theologian."[4]

Shifting now to the perspective of Erasmus on these questions, it is safe to say that he was ambivalent at best in his attitude toward theologians and their profession. He regularly lampoons their "vain talking" (*mataiologia*), "frivolous arguments," and "quarrels without end,"[5] thereby distancing himself from what he calls that "squalid mob of carping theologues,"[6] even while he respectfully grants that not all theologians deserve such criticism[7] and admits that he once took a degree in

3. *Luther's Works: Table Talk*, vol. 54, trans. Theodore G. Tappert (Philadelphia: Fortress Press, 1967), 71, 312, and 69. Thus, Luther writes, "Erasmus sticks to his own affairs, that is, to heathen business. He doesn't care about ours, that is, theological affairs" (77). Luther thereby reduced Erasmus to "the status of a literary dilettante," as Marjorie O'Rourke Boyle puts it in *Rhetoric and Reform: Erasmus's Civil Dispute with Luther* (Cambridge, MA: Harvard University Press, 1983), 98. Luther similarly slams Erasmus as another Lucian and Epicurus, thereby deriding him as a mocker and an atheist. See Luther, *The Bondage of the Will*, trans. Philip S. Watson, in *Luther's Works: Career of the Reformer*, vol. 33, ed. Philip S. Watson (Philadelphia: Fortress Press, 1972), 24, 29. Erasmus notes that the adherents of Luther had praised Erasmus as "the prince of theologians," though he was suddenly regarded as "entirely ignorant of theology" as soon as he spoke against Luther. See Erasmus, *A Warrior Shielding a Discussion of Free Will, Book One* (*Hyperaspistes*), trans. Peter Macardle and Clarence H. Miller, in *Collected Works of Erasmus: Controversies*, vol. 76, ed. Charles Trinkaus (Toronto: University of Toronto Press, 1999), 109.

4. Erasmus, *Apology against Jacques Lefèvre D'Étaples*, trans. Howard Jones, in *Collected Works of Erasmus: Controversies*, vol. 83 (Toronto: University of Toronto Press, 1998), 106. "Erasmus wants to be known as a theologian," Lefèvre observes (n. 430).

5. Thus, Erasmus warns, scholars "must take care not to pursue theology in such a manner as to fall into *mataiologia*, fighting endlessly about frivolous claptrap." See Erasmus, *Annotation on 1 Timothy 1*, n. 13, translation taken from Erika Rummel, *Erasmus's Annotations on the New Testament: From Philologist to Theologian* (Toronto: University of Toronto Press, 1986), 143–44. See also Erasmus, *A Response to the Annotations of Edward Lee*, trans. Erika Rummel, in *Collected Works of Erasmus: Controversies*, vol. 72 (Toronto: University of Toronto Press, 2005), 309; Erasmus, *A System or Method of Arriving by a Short cut at True Theology*, trans. Robert D. Sider, in *Collected Works of Erasmus: New Testament Scholarship*, vol. 41 (Toronto: University of Toronto Press, 2019), 705, n. 1117. Consider also the satirical sketch of theologians in Erasmus, *Praise of Folly*, trans. Betty Radice, in *Collected Works of Erasmus: Literary and Educational Writings*, vol. 27, ed. A. H. T. Levi (Toronto: University of Toronto Press, 1986), 107, 126–30.

6. Erasmus to John Colet, letter 108, in *Collected Works of Erasmus: Correspondence*, vol. 1, trans. R. A. B. Mynors and D. F. S. Thomson (Toronto: University of Toronto Press, 1974), 204.

7. Alongside his many criticisms of scholastic theologians, Erasmus is quick to acknowledge that good theologians are not his intended target. See, among many examples, Erasmus to Maarten Van Dorp, letter 337, in *Collected Works of Erasmus: Correspondence*, vol. 3, trans. R. A. B. Mynors and D. F. S. Thomson (Toronto: University of Toronto Press, 1976), 149–54; Erasmus, *An Apologia Concerning Three Passages Which the Theologian Sancho Carranza Had Defended as*

theology.[8] It is true, as well, that Erasmus denies to Lefèvre that he ever claimed for himself the title of theologian, even though—in the opposite vein—he in turn complains that Béda failed to address him as "your fellow theologian."[9] And there are times when Erasmus sets his modesty aside and proudly includes himself among theologians.[10] Clearly, there is plenty of waffling from Erasmus with respect to his status as a theologian. Suffice it to say that any clarity on these questions depends entirely on how one construes the task and purpose of theology.

As Erasmus describes it, "the chief goal of theologians is to explain prudently divine literature," which means that theology is first and foremost an interpretive discipline dedicated to understanding the meaning and message of biblical texts. Along with this interpretive task, Erasmus declares in a manner that is both quite traditional and yet clearly critical of many professional theologians of his day, theologians are "to give an account of the faith and not of frivolous questions," by which

Rightly Criticized by Zúñiga, trans. Charles Fantazzi, in _Collected Works of Erasmus: Controversies_, vol. 74, ed. Jan Bloemendal (Toronto: University of Toronto Press, 2022), 223.

8. Erasmus reports from Florence in 1506 that he received "a doctorate in theology, against my own inclinations, which were overborne by my friends' insistence." See Erasmus to Jan Obrecht, letter 201, in _Collected Works of Erasmus: Correspondence_, vol. 2, trans. R. A. B. Myors and D. F. S. Thomson (Toronto: University of Toronto Press, 1975), 124. Erasmus evidently received the degree in around fifteen days from the University in Turin. See Paul F. Grendler, "How to Get a Degree in Fifteen Days: Erasmus' Doctorate in Theology from the University of Turin," _Erasmus of Rotterdam Society Yearbook_ 18 (1998): 40–69; Jan Van Herwaarden, "Erasmus's Doctorate in Turin, Free Thought and Rotterdam, 1506–1876," in _Between Saint James and Erasmus: Studies in Late-Medieval Religious Life: Devotions and Pilgrimage in the Netherlands_, trans. Wendie Shaffer and Donald Gardner (Leiden and Boston: Brill, 2003), 637–62.

9. "There is nothing I would claim for myself less than the profession of theologian," Erasmus says to Lefèvre, "even though at the insistence of certain of my friends I long ago took that rank. Where in my writings do I boast of being a theologian? Who has ever heard me at any time congratulate myself on that title, even in casual conversation?" (Erasmus, _Apology against Lefèvre_, CWE 83: 106). Along the same line, see Erasmus, To the Reader, letter 1309, in _Collected Works of Erasmus: Correspondence_, vol. 9, trans. R. A. B. Mynors (Toronto: University of Toronto Press, 1989), 170–71; Erasmus, _Warrior Shielding a Discussion 1_, CWE 76: 144, where Erasmus speaks tongue in cheek when referring to himself as "an old man like me who knows nothing of theology." Regarding Béda's failure to acknowledge Erasmus as a fellow theologian, see Erasmus to Noël Béda, letter 1581, in _Collected Works of Erasmus: Correspondence_, vol. 11, trans. Alexander Dalzell (Toronto: University of Toronto Press 1994), 131. See also Manfred Hoffmann, _Rhetoric and Theology: The Hermeneutic of Erasmus_ (Toronto: University of Toronto Press, 1994), 18–21.

10. See, for instance, Erasmus to Adrian VI, letter 1352, CWE 9: 435–36, where Erasmus recalls how he was called a "bulwark of a more genuine theology." See also Erasmus, _A Warrior Shielding a Discussion of Free Will, Book Two (Hyperaspistes)_, trans. Clarence H. Miller, in _Collected Works of Erasmus: Controversies_, vol. 77, ed. Charles Trinkaus (Toronto: University of Toronto Press, 2000), 390, where Erasmus casually includes himself among "we theologians."

Erasmus intends to distinguish sound inquiry into essential matters of Christian faith and life from the ridiculous topics often addressed by scholastic theologians. Then again, for Erasmus, theologians should work to "discourse seriously and effectually on godliness," and, in fact, "to elicit tears, to set our souls aflame for heavenly things."[11] With these three points, we get a glimpse of how Erasmus conceives the task and purpose of theology, and thus we get an idea of the criteria he would have us use to judge in what sense his work is theological, and if so, whether or not, and in what sense, he may be said to be a theologian.

For theology to adequately fulfill its interpretive charge requires a "pure heart," Erasmus piously writes, but it also requires skill in ancient languages and knowledge of grammar and rhetoric—precisely the humanist resources Erasmus brought to bear in his *Annotations* on biblical books, and exactly those things that unnerved scholastic theologians who were primarily trained in logic and philosophy.[12] In this regard, Erasmus declares that he is writing "annotations not doctrines," by which he modestly indicates that he has assumed the "smaller share in theology" by working to lay the critical foundation designed "to help" others pursue full-fledged exegesis, though, as will be evident in the chapters to follow, he also offers his own readings of biblical literature in an array of genres.[13]

When theologians turn to "give an account of the faith," therefore, Erasmus counsels "pious inquiry and inquisitive piety."[14] With this couplet, he indicates that theological investigations should arise from, and serve, the life of piety, while at the same time, he affirms that piety itself should be freely and resolutely inquisitive.[15] The result, we are told in

11. Erasmus, *System of True Theology*, CWE 41: 517.

12. On the personal and intellectual requirements for sound theology, see Erasmus, *System of True Theology*, 491–92, 496–507.

13. For the claim that Erasmus is writing "annotations not doctrine," see the *Apology against Lefèvre*, CWE 83: 16, 30, and 73. For the same assertions, see Erasmus, *An Apologia in Response to the Two Invectives of Edward Lee*, CWE 72: 48, where he insists that "no one has ever claimed a smaller share in theology than I, who have chosen for myself the lowliest part of all, that is grammar, and have left more sublime matters to more talented men." For the claim that Erasmus has worked on biblical materials with "the pure and godly desire to help," see "The *Apologia* of Desiderius Erasmus of Rotterdam," trans. John M. Ross, CWE 41: 459.

14. Erasmus, "To the Pious Reader," which serves as a preface to the *Paraphrase on Matthew*, in *Collected Works of Erasmus: New Testament Scholarship*, vol. 45, trans. Dean Simpson (Toronto: University of Toronto Press, 2008), 14–15, n. 53.

15. See Erasmus, "To the Pious Reader," CWE 45:10, where Erasmus asserts that "everyone

what is, in fact, a description of theology itself, will be "pious learning and learned piety"[16]—a second couplet used by Erasmus to emphasize the necessary fusion of faith with the resources of intelligent life for the development of sound theology. With this phrase, however, Erasmus also moves to distinguish his standard for good theology from what he deems the spurious questions eagerly pursued by scholastic theologians given over to "the subtleties of dialectic and to Aristotelian philosophy,"[17] and it is meant as well to check the presumption of authors who rely on "bare assertion and unilateral judgment" to authorize their religious opinions.[18] Neither learning divorced from the service of faith nor faith that is willfully insulated from the resources of the learned, Erasmus concludes, is adequate for sound theological investigation.

Finally, we are told, theologians are to speak "seriously and effectually" on the pious and virtuous life, by which Erasmus means that theology requires well-practiced rhetorical skill in order to inspire and support the rejuvenation of faith and the renewal of ethical life. The ultimate purpose of theological work, as Erasmus sees it, is the effective communication of the insights garnered by skillful interpretation of biblical literature and learned explanations of Christian faith, and to do so in a manner that has a transformative impact on the recipients' lives. In fact, Erasmus declares with astounding idealism, "to persuade

---

must be allowed 'inquiry'—one that is sober and godly—especially into those things that render life better."

16. Erasmus to Paul Volz, letter 858, in *Collected Works of Erasmus: Correspondence*, vol. 6, trans. R. A. B. Mynors and D. F. S. Thomson (Toronto: University of Toronto Press, 1982), 73. On the notion of piety in the work of Erasmus, see John W. O'Malley, "Introduction," in *Collected Works of Erasmus: Spiritualia*, vol. 66, ed. John W. O'Malley (Toronto: University of Toronto Press, 1988), xi. As O'Malley writes, the word piety for Erasmus includes "godliness, holiness, charitable living, virtuous or devout life, and genuine piety." Depending on the context, it can refer to the life of faith alone or the larger fusion of faith and virtue.

17. Erasmus, *System of True Theology*, CWE 41: 699. The complaints of Erasmus about the attention to frivolous questions by theologians trained in philosophy are ubiquitous; for a fine discussion with examples, see 513–16, 699–704. "What is the profit," Erasmus wonders, "if I torture myself about whether God is able to create a person without sin ... whether the soul of Christ could have been duped or could have been deceived; whether the proposition, 'God is a beetle,' is as possible as this one, 'God is a man,' and so on?" Consider also the satirical account of the absurd questions of theologians in *Praise of Folly*, CWE 27: 126–27.

18. Boyle, *Rhetoric and Reform*, 60. Many might fit this bill, but Erasmus certainly includes Luther among those who claim to be the "sole interpreter" of scripture. See Erasmus, *Hyperaspistes 1*, CWE 76: 205. Erasmus cautions Luther that the word of God is not the same as "your interpretations and assertions," and he challenges him to "show us by what arguments we can be sure that you have the Spirit as your master" (195, 239).

human beings that in this world we should live like angels, pure from all stain of sin, that alone is the duty of a Christian theologian."[19] To be sure, such a statement must have shocked theologians of his period, just as it would stun many professional theologians of our day. What Erasmus has in mind, it is true, points to the very highest ideals of what he calls the "philosophy of Christ"—that vital compendium of what may look like "crude precepts" but which ultimately are life-ennobling virtues taught by Christ, embodied in his life, and proclaimed in Christian scriptures.[20]

As will become clear in the course of this book, this philosophy is a religious ethic focused on faith, mercy, kindness, tolerance, and peace; rather than being a set of abstract ideals or principles, however, it entails a way of being human that is embodied in Christ, audible in Scriptures, and thus set before human beings as an ultimate target and measure (*scopus*) of redeemed life. It is, as Erasmus puts it, "a way of life rather than a form of argument," and thus it concerns basic "inclinations and intentions of the heart" rather than the extent of one's learning or prowess in argumentation.[21] As an ethic in the very richest sense of that word, he continues, the philosophy of Christ opens the way for the "transformation" of the twisted and corrupted condition of human life. It promises, in other words, the "restoration of nature, which was created whole and sound," and, as we will see in the final chapter of this book, it signals the redeemed life of personal and social peace.[22]

Quite simply, there is nothing more central to Erasmus's reflections on Christ, nor more theological, than his efforts to convey the philosophy of Christ with all the persuasive power he can muster. A theologian

---

19. "The *Paraclesis* of Erasmus of Rotterdam to the Pious Reader," trans. Ann Dalzell, CWE 41: 413.

20. For a list of the biblically based precepts that are to shape authentic Christian life, see Erasmus, *Paraclesis*, CWE 41: 412–13, where Erasmus includes "that wealth is to be scorned; that a Christian must not trust in worldly supports but must depend solely on heaven; that he must not avenge a wrong; that he must bless them that curse him, do good to them that abuse him; that all good people are to be loved and cherished equally as members of the same body; that the wicked are to be tolerated if they cannot be corrected; that those who are despoiled of their goods, those who are deprived of their possessions, those who mourn are to be counted happy, not to be pitied; [and] that death is to be desired by the godly, for it is none other than the passage to immortality." For similar lists, see "The *Methodus* of Erasmus of Rotterdam," trans. Robert D. Sider, CWE 41: 440–42; *System of True Theology*, CWE 41: 517–19.

21. Erasmus, *Paraclesis*, CWE 41: 415.

22. Erasmus, *Paraclesis*, CWE 41: 415.

is a teacher and orator, in short, one who "urges, invites, and inspires" others to absorb this philosophy into the fabric of their lives,[23] thereby equipping people with the joy and tranquility proper to a Christian life.[24] That is the goal to which Erasmus strives, so that his many efforts toward this end—both exegetical and rhetorical, but also educational and political—qualify in the richest sense of the word as theological. It follows, naturally enough, that his reflections on Christ and his teaching fully constitute a Christology, even if they do not always fit neatly into the categories favored by professional theologians.

As Erasmus undertakes his theological reflections—sometimes independently, at other times through controversy with critics—certain recurring methodological features make their appearance, and as one might expect, these same factors are at play at most every step in his thinking about Christ. To begin with, Erasmus often underscores that he is engaging in a discussion rather than issuing doctrinal assertions or making pronouncements.[25] "In every area of discussion," he writes to Lefèvre, "there has always been room for disagreement," at least, he cautiously adds, in "those matters which do not properly bear upon articles of faith."[26] Because there exists a plurality of views on textual questions and matters of translation, it is the role of the "annotator" to "place before the reader a variety of material for him to consider."[27] But the same is true for theological interpreters, he observes, as sound exegesis and intelligent judgment on disputed questions must squarely

23. Erasmus, *Paraclesis*, CWE 41: 413. See also Erasmus, *System of True Theology*, CWE 41: 494–95. There is no reason to dismiss Erasmus from the task of theology simply because he embraces rhetoric and grammar, though critics in his own day and some scholars in our own make exactly that judgment. See, for instance, the discussion in Ross Dealy, *The Stoic Origins of Erasmus' Philosophy of Christ* (Toronto: University of Toronto Press, 2017), 55, n. 39.

24. See Erasmus to Paul Volz, letter 858, CWE 6: 74–75.

25. Erasmus, *Warrior Shielding a Discussion 1*, CWE 76: 101, 227. See also Erasmus, *A Discussion of Free Will*, trans. Peter Macardle, CWE 76: 88. Regarding his *Annotations*, Erasmus similarly insists that "I write annotations, not laws; I propose points to be considered, not immediately to be taken as certain." See Erasmus, *The Chief Points in the Arguments Answering Some Crabby and Ignorant Critics*, trans. Clarence Miller, CWE 41: 801. Then again, Erasmus writes to Edward Lee, "even in matters of grammar I make no pronouncements. I call my remarks annotations, not doctrines. And I offer them for discussion, I do not bring them forth as oracles" (Erasmus, *Apologia*, CWE 72: 48; see also 33). Erasmus similarly contrasts discussion from confrontation when describing the three dialogues written on "the question of Martin Luther." See Erasmus to Johann von Botzheim, letter 1341a, CWE 9: 347.

26. Erasmus, *Apology against Lefèvre*, CWE 83: 7.

27. Erasmus, *Apology against Lefèvre*, CWE 83: 76; along the same lines, see 16.

face the *de facto* plurality of readings and opinions, and this is precisely why Erasmus so regularly proceeds by gathering a variety of "alternative readings," often culled from the commentaries of church fathers and sometimes collated from ongoing debates.[28] Underlying this variety, however, is the simple but intractable fact that disagreements arise from differences of interpretation, and interpretation is required because scriptural texts and "articles of faith" (including Christological ones) are less than absolutely clear.[29]

Erasmus responds to this situation—perhaps surprisingly, but very sensibly—by imitating the stance of the Academic Skeptics of ancient Greece and Rome, whereby—with a certain neutrality still keen on discovering the truth—he "out of courtesy" considers sympathetically both sides of a dispute, "vacillating in the middle," so to speak, by suspending complete and final judgment in order to fairly weigh the strengths and weaknesses of both views, and only then giving preference to the most relatively adequate position.[30] This posture and procedure is explicitly

28. See, for instance, Erasmus, *Warrior Shielding a Discussion 1*, CWE 76: 117, where Erasmus describes his method in *Discussion of Free Will*. See, similarly, Erasmus, *Warrior Shielding a Discussion 2*, CWE 77: 466. It is perfectly correct, therefore, to say that "his view on grace and freedom was also that there are *several* views on grace and freedom." See B. A. Gerrish, "*De Libero Arbitrio* (1524): Erasmus on Piety, Theology, and the Lutheran Dogma," *Essays on the Works of Erasmus*, ed. Richard L. DeMolen (New Haven, CT: Yale University Press, 1978), 198. For another statement on the legitimacy of "alternative readings" in exegetical discussions, see Erasmus, *Apology against Lefèvre*, CWE 83: 69.

29. On the debate with Luther over the obscurity of biblical passages, and hence on the need for interpretation and the inevitable variety of interpretations, see Erasmus, *Warrior Shielding a Discussion 1*, CWE 76: 132, 216–24, and 244. Where difficulties are found and disputes over meaning arise, he continues, the debate turns to the differing quality of rival interpretations (180, 204, and 244). Claims to certitude in understanding scripture do not remove doubts, Erasmus argues, or "we would have to have faith in all the fanatics who boast … about having the Spirit" (215). On variation in the clarity of "articles of faith," see Eramus, *Warrior Shielding a Discussion 1*, CWE 76: 227–28.

30. See Erasmus, *Warrior Shielding a Discussion 1*, CWE 76: 127–28, 226–27. By reviving the "posture of modified Skepticism," Boyle writes, Erasmus "imitates the virtuosity of the Academics in arguing on both sides of the question, and of summarizing in favor of the most probable opinion, while yet suspending a judgment of certainty" (Boyle, *Rhetoric and Reform*, 20). For a classical expression of the Academic method, see Cicero's *Academica* and assorted dialogues. On familiarity with these sources in the Renaissance, see Charles B. Schmitt, *Cicero Scepticus: A Study of the Academica in the Renaissance* (The Hague, 1972). Erasmus's retrieval of the Academic method, Boyle notes, is primarily aimed against the "presumption of dogmatism" among theologians, though it ultimately seeks to clear the way for making truth "more manifest" (Boyle, *Rhetoric and Reform*, 17–19, 27). The suspension of judgment also is the mark of scholarly prudence, Erasmus writes, for "in the case of some things, greater erudition is revealed by being doubtful, and, with the Academics, by withholding judgment than by making a pronouncement"

present in Erasmus's exchange with Luther, though it is very much at work throughout the religious writings of Erasmus, as will be apparent in the chapters to follow. The best that can be done, Erasmus advises, given the relative obscurity of the questions and the inherent limitations of the human mind, is to make it possible for individuals to arrive at their preferred judgment in a manner that is well-informed with the evidence garnered from engagement with a variety of views. "Everyone is free to make up his own mind," Erasmus asserts with a decidedly modern ring, as a "certain license" is allowed to scholars.[31] At the same time, however, he typically and sincerely adds his deference to the church's authority on essential doctrines, though, as is so often the case with Erasmus, he does not say this without qualification.[32] In this manner, Erasmus sets out with his own theological inquiry by means of open yet measured discussion amid a variety of alternative views, and it is exactly that approach which he brings to bear in his Christological reflections.

An Erasmian Christology

As Marjorie O'Rourke Boyle puts it, the Christology of Erasmus is "as protean as the apostolic witness of the New Testament which accommodated divine revelation to human myopia," shifting with great variety

---

(Erasmus, *System of True Theology*, CWE 41: 699). What is more, Erasmus adds in what amounts to a philosophical principle, "in human affairs nothing has ever been so well done, nor will anything be done so well in this world, that it does not leave many things that ought to be corrected" (Erasmus, *Warrior Shielding a Discussion 2*, CWE 77: 634).

31. Erasmus, *Chief Points*, CWE 41: 801; *Apology against Lefèvre*, CWE 83: 73, 87. Regarding questions that are "useful" but not worth fighting "so fiercely as to break asunder the harmony of Christendom," Erasmus advises, it is "better to let everyone fully enjoy his own opinion" (*Warrior Shielding a Discussion 1*, CWE 76: 124).

32. Deference to the church's authority is hedged with the caveat that it is not always so clear "who" the church is; and with that, as well, "sometimes it is none too clear where the church is to be found," as the "visible" church—the institution of the day with all its warts and wens—may not always seem worthy of being called the church of Christ. See Erasmus to Wolfgang Faber Capito, letter 734, in *Collected Works of Erasmus: Correspondence*, vol. 5, trans. R. A. B. Mynors and D. F. S. Thomson (Toronto: University of Toronto Press, 1979), 233. On the "invisible" church held in hope and "perceived ... with the eyes of faith" and the "visible" church directly encountered in "its outer appearance," often worthy of "scorn or even aversion and hatred," see Erasmus, *On Mending the Peace of the Church*, trans. Emily Kearns, in *Collected Works of Erasmus: Expositions of the Psalms*, vol. 65, ed. Dominic Baker-Smith (Toronto: University of Toronto Press, 2010), 152–59. See also Margaret Mann Phillips, "Some Last Words of Erasmus," in *Luther, Erasmus and the Reformation: A Catholic-Protestant Reappraisal*, ed. John C. Olin, James D. Smart, and Robert E. McNally (New York: Fordham University Press, 1969), 105–10.

from one image to the next: "Christ the envoy, Christ the teacher, Christ the visage, Christ the discourse."[33] Indeed, Erasmus adds for good measure, Christ is Proteus as well, thereby signaling his appreciation for the richness and variability of traditional language for Christ.[34] It is understandable, consequently, to find an abundance of tropes used for Christ in the works of Erasmus. As John W. O'Malley observes, however, Christ is for Erasmus "first and foremost a teacher," and that certainly is true, as far as it goes, that is, as long as one does not stop with that image alone.[35] For Erasmus, the "heavenly philosophy" transmitted by Jesus and conveyed through scriptures are not simply a set of lessons and conclusions but a transformative address meant for the orientation and practice of life. As Erasmus puts it in the *Paraclesis*, the philosophy of Christ promotes, or certainly is designed to promote, "human happiness" and sound living before God and with others.[36]

Though Erasmus also speaks in traditional terms of redemption by the death of Jesus on the cross,[37] there remains a "decidedly sapiential cast to Erasmus' Christology," as O'Malley puts it.[38] It is not surprising, consequently, to find Erasmus—in the *Paraphrase on Luke*, for instance—casting the salvific work of Christ as the "heavenly Physician,"

33. Marjorie O'Rourke Boyle, *Erasmus on Language and Method in Theology* (Toronto: University of Toronto Press, 1977), 25–26.

34. Thus, Erasmus observes, "though nothing is more straightforward than our Christ, yet with some hidden intent he represents a kind of Proteus by the variety of his life and teaching" (Erasmus, *System of True Theology*, CWE 41: 557, n. 351). For examples, see Erasmus, *System of True Theology*, CWE 41: 552–58, 594–95. On the proverbial background of this title, see Erasmus, "As many shapes as Proteus," adage II. ii. 74, in *Collected Works of Erasmus: Adages*, vol. 33, trans. R. A. B. Mynors (Toronto: University of Toronto Press, 1991), 113–14. On "acting the part of Proteus," see Erasmus, "Adopt the outlook of the polyp," adage I. i. 93, in *Collected Works of Erasmus: Adages*, vol. 31, trans. Margaret Mann Phillips (Toronto: University of Toronto Press, 1982), 133–36. On Erasmus's application of this image to Christ, see Boyle, *Erasmus on Language and Method in Theology*, 122–23. The same language is used to describe Paul in Erasmus to Erard de la Marck, letter 916, CWE 6: 248–49.

35. John W. O'Malley, "Introduction," CWE 66: xxii–xxiii. Erasmus calls Jesus an "extraordinary and mighty teacher," to cite just one of many examples. See Erasmus, *Paraphrase on Luke 1–10*, trans. Jane E. Phillips, in *Collected Works of Erasmus: New Testament Scholarship*, vol. 47 (Toronto: University of Toronto Press, 2016), 144. On Erasmus's account of Jesus as a master of "good pedagogy," see Robert D. Sider and Dean Simpson, preface, *Paraphrase on Matthew*, CWE 45: xi.

36. Erasmus, *Paraclesis*, CWE 41: 417.

37. See, for example, Erasmus to Maarten Van Dorp, letter 337, CWE 3: 129; see also passages throughout the *Paraphrases*. On Christ as redeemer in the works of Erasmus, see John B. Payne, *Erasmus: His Theology of the Sacraments* (M. E. Bratcher, 1970), 64–65.

38. O'Malley, "Introduction," CWE 66: xxii.

whose wise and healing words "free men one and all by heavenly medicine from all diseases of the spirit." "To a sick spirit speech is a physician," the Greek adage says, and for Erasmus, this applies perfectly to Christ—the "Father's living word"—since the "medicine of the gospel" bequeathed by Christ is that "remedy that brings eternal health."[39] And that, in sum, is the enduring point and ultimate profit of the philosophy of Christ for Erasmus: the rebirth or regeneration (*renascentia*) of human life before God and with others.

While Erasmus can be found speaking to the "highest" questions in Christology, namely, the sublime transcendence of Christ and the place of Christ in the triune life of God, he more typically attends to the "lower" side of things by focusing on the incarnation of Christ in human form and life. Thinking about Christ through the lens of the incarnation, of course, allows Erasmus the opportunity to highlight the immense and unbounded love of God that assumes embodied life in Jesus of Nazareth, as it is above all the "extreme lowliness" of Christ incarnate, Erasmus writes, that testifies to the "unspeakable love" that God had for humanity.[40] In this regard, Erasmus shows exceptional dialectical finesse when speaking of the incarnation as a loving inversion of divine status in which the "Lord and creator of heaven and earth" is born in "complete lowliness."[41] With this inversion, however, Christ incarnate confronts the twisted inversions of the existing social world, where, for instance, those who are considered religious insiders are so often godless, while those who are deemed "strangers to religion" are, in fact, "nearer to true religion."[42]

---

39. Erasmus, *Paraphrase on Luke*, CWE 47: 7–8. For the comments of Erasmus on the classical adage, see "To a sick spirit speech is a physician," adage III. i. 100, in *Collected Works of Erasmus: Adages*, vol. 34, trans. R. A. B. Mynors (Toronto: University of Toronto Press, 1992), 223–24. On Christ as "supreme Physician," see Erasmus to Henry VIII, letter 1381, in *Collected Works of Erasmus: Correspondence*, vol. 10, trans. R. A. B. Mynors and Alexander Dalzell (Toronto: University of Toronto Press, 1992), 66.

40. Erasmus, *Apology against Lefèvre*, CWE 83: 33–34.

41. Erasmus, *Paraphrase on Luke*, CWE 47: 71. There is "more sublimity, more power, [and] more majesty in the quite humble birth of Christ," Erasmus states paradoxically, "than in all the pomps and triumphs of all the Caesars" (70). What is more, he continues with an eye on the suffering of Jesus, Christ claims for himself "the height of glory among humankind," but he does so—with a startling inversion of expectation—"by means of shame and humiliation." See Erasmus, *Paraphrase on Luke 11–24*, trans. Jane E. Phillips, in *Collected Works of Erasmus: New Testament Scholarship*, vol. 48 (Toronto: University of Toronto Press, 2003), 145.

42. Erasmus, *Paraphrase on Luke*, CWE 47: 86–87; see also 222.

In his teachings and actions, Erasmus tells us quite dramatically, Christ puts forth a radically new way of being in the world that signals a thorough-going inversion of existing human relations. What is revealed, thereby, is an alternative possibility—"the world turned upside down," as Erasmus calls it—where for example, the mighty are "dragged down," while the "estranged are "made children of God."[43] Such "an amazing reversal of human affairs," Erasmus exclaims, when sinners, who "in joy and gladness" welcome Jesus into their houses, turn out to be "more pleasing to God than people who are swollen-headed with the false conviction of their own righteousness."[44] Again and again, therefore, we find Erasmus emphasizing that the incarnation proceeds by a radical accommodation to human lowliness by means of divine love, which thereby introduces into the world an embodied expression of inclusive love and kindness to the lowly and outcast, which in turn challenges the twisted social order with a living representation of a new way of being human. The strong affirmation of the humanity of Christ by Erasmus, in the end, signals an equally strong affirmation of humanity at large—one that turns a topsy-turvy world on its head.

The central point of focus in the Christology of Erasmus is the redemptive function of Christ for human existence. Though Erasmus can be found considering the classical question of the two natures and one person of Christ, most often when pressed by one or another critic in controversy, he places far greater weight on the salvific fruits of Christ's life and death. To convey this transformative power, Erasmus often speaks in terms of the restoration or renewal of human life, and for

---

43. Erasmus, *Paraphrase on Luke*, CWE 47: 55. Erasmus relishes the surprising reversals of expectation found throughout Christian scriptures, and consequently, they come to play a regular role in his accounts of revelation and redemption in Christ. "Often those who are most scorned by the world are prized most highly by Christ," Erasmus writes, "and those whom the world takes to be most learned are simpletons in Christ's judgment" ("To the Pious Reader," CWE 45: 9). In keeping with this point, Erasmus paraphrases the words of Jesus in Matthew 11: 25–27, to say that the Father has "concealed this heavenly philosophy from those who are swollen with pride and haughty in the conviction that they possess worldly wisdom and prudence," while he has "opened it to those who are insignificant, lowly, and, according to the estimation of the world, foolish" (*Paraphrase on Matthew*, CWE 45: 189). Erasmus is well aware, of course, that while "human wisdom has its own arrogance," it also is the case that "the ignorance (no less haughty) of the uneducated has its arrogance, too" ("To the Pious Reader," CWE 45: 9).

44. Erasmus, *Paraphrase on Luke*, CWE 48: 137–39. Erasmus here recounts the story of Zacchaeus, a chief tax collector in Jericho, from Luke 19:1–10.

this purpose, language of healing is prominent. Christ brings the "medicine of his salvific word [*sermo*]," we are told, as "his whole person breathed nothing but a divine force for healing humankind."[45] It is true, of course, that Erasmus sometimes speaks of salvation in eschatological terms, especially when working with sources where such language is found, though his standard point of emphasis falls on the transformation of actual life. For that purpose, as will be evident throughout this book, he often speaks of Christ as a "pattern for living."[46] Indeed, he writes, Christ is a "perfect pattern of perfect love, humility, patient endurance, mercy, and gentleness."[47]

Erasmus is neither the first nor the last theologian to use such language for Christ, though this manner of speaking has met with significant criticism. Not only is it "unbiblical" (and hence, "dissonant with the gospel"), James M. Gustafson contends, but this approach seems to turn Christ into an ideal goal—perhaps "moral or spiritual perfection" or "individual peace and happiness"—to be "actualized" through "human striving." But the "personal center of the Christian life," Gustafson continues, is not "the goal of individual peace and happiness," which is "severely egocentric," but God's "work, will, and love in Jesus Christ."[48] In response, Erasmus surely agrees that Christ is the personal embodiment of God's reconciling love, and he too rejects the idea of personal peace as some kind of individual fulfilment, though it also is true that Erasmus is not so allergic to human striving as some of his contemporaries. When he speaks of Christ as a pattern, therefore, he refers to the "personal example of a holy life" offered by Christ,[49] and he above all stresses the causal agency of this example, for Christ is—in the apt

---

45. Erasmus, *Paraphrase on Luke*, CWE 48: 60; *Paraphrase on Luke*, CWE 47: 174–75. Not unexpectedly, Erasmus often introduces more variety in his accounts of Christ's salvific function. Thus, for instance, Christ is said to bring "complete and freely given forgiveness, freedom, sight, health, and wholeness" (146).

46. Erasmus, *Paraphrase on Luke*, CWE 47: 173.

47. Erasmus, "On Gospel Philosophy," trans. Ann Dalzell, CWE 41: 735. See also Erasmus to Paul Volz, letter 858, CWE 6: 77, where Erasmus speaks of "Christ our pattern."

48. James M. Gustafson, *Christ and the Moral Life* (Chicago: University of Chicago Press, 1968; Midway reprint, 1976), 152–87.

49. Erasmus, *An Explanation of the Apostles' Creed*, trans. Louis A. Perraud, in *Collected Works of Erasmus: Spiritualia and Pastoralia*, vol. 70, ed. John W. O'Malley (Toronto: University of Toronto Press, 1998), 357. See also Erasmus, *An Exposition of Psalm 38*, trans. Carolinne White, CWE 65: 14.

words of Erasmus—a most "compelling inviter," to whom people are called to turn with humility and love.[50] The same thing holds when Erasmus speaks of Christ as target (*scopus*), spring, anchor, cynosure, pillar, and foundation, as these things are meant not as something to be sought for personal advantage but as expressions of redemptive agency, where each term signals something done for the transformation of human existence.[51] They are terms of divine action, in other words, for the gracious making of "a holy and happy life," as Erasmus puts it.[52]

Again and again, as will be evident in several chapters to follow, Erasmus emphasizes the ethical responsibility to imitate Christ's transformative love for others, and thus to advance the cause of peace in the social worlds in which we live. The "new sort of people" established by Christ cling to the faith and virtues of Christ's heavenly philosophy by living "according to the example of Christ." This is "the target point (*scopum*) set out by Christ," Erasmus continues, to which this people are to respond with resolute imitation.[53] In this regard, as Jaroslav Pelikan observes, Erasmus offers us "a Christology of life and praxis rather than principally a Christology of doctrine."[54] Which is to say, the Christology of Erasmus culminates in a religious ethic centered on

50. Erasmus, *Paraphrase on Luke*, CWE 48: 137.

51. Erasmus, *System of True Theology*, CWE 41: 537–38.

52. Erasmus, *Explanation of the Creed*, CWE 70: 276

53. Erasmus, *System of True Theology*, CWE 41: 517–19. The emphasis on imitation in one's way of life, to which we will return in the first chapter, has led some scholars to underscore the influence on Erasmus from the *devotio moderna* of the Brethren of the Common Life, a form of simple and Christ-centered piety Erasmus encountered in his early years. See, for instance, R. J. Schoeck, *Erasmus of Europe: The Making of a Humanist, 1467–1500* (Edinburgh: Edinburgh University Press, 1990), 42–52; Richard L. DeMolen, *The Spirituality of Erasmus of Rotterdam* (Nieuwkoop: De Graaf Publishers, 1987), 35–52; Lewis E. Spitz, *The Religious Renaissance of the German Humanists* (Cambridge, MA: Harvard University Press, 1963), 199–200; and, more recently, Ann Dalzell, who describes this movement as "foundational for Erasmus' intellectual formation" (Dalzell, introduction, *Paraclesis*, CWE 41: 400–401). See also Dalzell, introduction, CWE 41: 408, n. 24; 422, n. 103; and 730–31, nn. 10, 11, and 15. In opposition to this view, Boyle argues that the "theological method of imitation which Erasmus advocates is grounded in the pedagogy of classical rhetoric more probably than in the piety of the Modern Devotion" (Boyle, *Erasmus on Language and Method in Theology*, 101, 233, nn. 244–45). For his part, Manfred Hoffmann observes that "the relation between the rhetorical concept of imitation and the theological concept of *imitatio Christi* has not yet been explored," thereby leaving the door nicely ajar for the acknowledgment that—as with so many things Erasmian—both views have merit, without either sufficing when taken alone (Hoffmann, *Rhetoric and Theology*, 267, n. 19). The chapters in this book follow the suggestion of Hoffmann.

54. Jaroslav Pelikan, *Jesus Through the Centuries: His Place in the History of Culture* (New York: Harper and Row, 1985), 176.

humility, patience, kindness, and peace—an ethic that is emblazoned with Christ's redemptive love and thus expressive of a transformed way of being human.

Of course, some scholars have objected to this emphasis on ethics, seeing it as a reduction of Erasmus's religious thinking to a merely moral plane, where he would be "more concerned with life than with doctrine."[55] Perhaps there is some truth to this complaint, for instance, when Lucien Febvre baldly declares that for Erasmus, "Christ was a precept, a moral doctrine, nothing else but the virtues he preached—charity, simplicity, patience, purity."[56] And yet, as overstated as this declaration may be, it certainly is the case that for Erasmus, religious life is intimately intertwined with ethical practice in imitation of Christ's virtuous actions. The "living reality of Christianity," as Augustin Renaudet describes it, centers in the ongoing imitation of Christ, which for Erasmus means living in accord with the virtues of the philosophy of Christ.[57] This is the hallmark of the Christology of Erasmus, where Christ lives and breathes (so to speak) in the virtuous lives of his followers, where they strive to "serve as a guide and a measuring stick of right living" for all who observe them.[58] The chapters that comprise this book are designed—from a variety of angles—to elucidate this very point.

Interpreting Erasmus

One might think, at first glance, that understanding Erasmus would be a relatively straight-forward business, as his writing is famously natural and wonderfully elegant. The French philologist Guillaume Budé, for instance, observes how Erasmus writes in a manner that is "so clear" and "at the same time so eloquent" as to be both readily accessible and easy "to digest." And yet, Budé continues astutely, Erasmus is so "marvelously clever"—a "witty and practiced ironist" he must be—as he

55. Manfred Hoffmann, "Erasmus and Religious Toleration," *Erasmus of Rotterdam Society Yearbook* 2, no. 1 (January 1980): 80, 83.

56. Lucien Febvre, *The Problem of Unbelief in the Sixteenth Century: The Religion of Rabelais*, trans. Beatrice Gottlieb (Cambridge, MA: Harvard University Press, 1982), 324.

57. Augustin Renaudet, *Études Érasmiennes (1521–1529)* (Paris: Librairie E. Droz, 1939), 125–48, 171–74.

58. Erasmus, *Paraphrase on Matthew*, CWE 45: 94, in paraphrase of Matthew 5:14–16. See also Erasmus, *System of True Theology*, CWE 41: 519.

reveals never-imagined "aspects of life" before the reader's "astonished gaze" through his "well-known middling level of style."[59] There is so often more than meets the eye in the works of Erasmus, so on second thought, it seems that interpreting Erasmus is not so simple after all, and the centuries-long conflict of interpretation over his work provides abundant evidence of this.[60]

Some difficulties are not specific to Erasmus, like shifts in judgment from early to later works, or changes in expression for different types of writings, though other hurdles pertain to him more directly, like the peculiar task of reading his *Paraphrases* of Christian scriptures, in which he subtly weaves his own voice into the retelling of the original text.[61] More trying problems arise in his religious writings, as we will see, largely because—as he so often proceeds exegetically—most everything from tradition finds a place in his thinking, so the challenge is to discern where Erasmus places his own emphasis, without gainsaying what he dutifully includes as part of Christian tradition. It is true as well, as Febvre comments, that Erasmus's manner of handling the "burning issues" of his day—so often reflecting his sense of complexity and aptitude for nuance—left his words "susceptible of two interpretations thoroughly different in spirit." This led readers to find "what is in themselves," Febvre notes, so that "the orthodox found their orthodoxy, the Reformed found their Reformation, [and] the skeptics found their irony."[62] In point of fact, things are even more complicated than that, as the orthodox often found a heretic, reformers found a Catholic, and skeptics found a very religious man. All of this holds true for interpreting the Christology of Erasmus, as we will see presently, where the challenge is to preserve the capacious quality of his thinking while tending to the distinctive points of emphasis in a manner that features

---

59. Guillaume Budé to Erasmus, letter 493, in *Collected Works of Erasmus: Correspondence*, vol. 4, trans. R. A. B. Mynors and D. F. S. Thomson (Toronto: University of Toronto Press, 1977), 148, 139, and 145.

60. Consult, above all, Bruce Mansfield, *Phoenix of His Age: Interpretations of Erasmus, c. 1550–1750* (Toronto: University of Toronto Press, 1979); *Man on His Own: Interpretations of Erasmus, C. 1750–1920* (Toronto: University of Toronto Press, 1992); and *Erasmus in the Twentieth Century: Interpretations c. 1920–2000* (Toronto: University of Toronto Press, 2003).

61. On the art and purposes of the *Paraphrases* of Erasmus, see Jan Bloemendal, "Erasmus' *Paraphrases on the New Testament*: Introduction," and "Exegesis and Hermeneutics in Erasmus' Paraphrases on Luke," *Erasmus Studies* 36 (2016): 105–22, and 148–62, respectively.

62. Febvre, *The Problem of Unbelief in the Sixteenth Century*, 325.

the delicate but surprising juxtapositions or fusions that appear so regularly in his theological reflections.

We have already encountered the conflict of interpretation over Erasmus's status as a theologian. That conflict persists today, with some scholars affirming that Erasmus was a theologian and others denying it.[63] But, of course, as we have seen earlier, so much of this debate pivots around the varying criteria used to define the nature of theology. Those who deny that Erasmus was a theologian largely do so because he does not fit their expectation for the kind of doctrinal work that they think should be produced by professional theologians in the service of ecclesial interests. Those espousing this view—curiously enough—have included conventional theologians who lament the prominence Erasmus gives to scholarly pursuits aside from traditional religious questions, but it also includes secular scholars from our own day who seem to celebrate the very same fact. The former regret the extent of Erasmus's interest in classical languages and literature, for example, since that seems to diminish what they consider to be the proper religious concerns of a theologian, while the latter concentrate their attention on precisely those scholarly interests, downplaying, or at least quietly side-stepping, the religious dimension of Erasmus's work. Those who affirm that Erasmus was a theologian, alternatively, tend to proceed with more broadly defined assumptions about the nature of theology, in which the critical and constructive input of other disciplines is integrated into the interpretive, explanatory, and rhetorical tasks which Erasmus assigns to theology.

When the task of theology is characterized as "pious inquiry and inquisitive piety," for instance, Erasmus signals his insistence that heartfelt piety and learned inquiry should be fused together in the pursuit of theological insight. Saying this, of course, is hardly novel, as many Christian theologians have sought to wed faith and reason in the service of good theology, though, it is important to note, not all have accepted

---

63. C. J. de Vogel affirms that Erasmus was "primarily a theologian" in "Erasmus and His Attitude Towards Church Dogma," in *Scrinium Erasmianum*, vol. 2, ed. J. Coppens (Leiden: E. J. Brill, 1969), 103–6, while Craig R. Thompson counters that regarding Erasmus "as primarily or essentially a theologian is going too far." See Craig R. Thompson, "Introduction," in *Collected Works of Erasmus: Literary and Educational Writings*, vol. 23, ed. Craig R. Thompson (Toronto: University of Toronto Press, 1978), xxiv.

such a working synthesis. What is new is the wide array of forms of knowledge that Erasmus integrates into the service of theological inquiry and communication, so that, for instance, the study of languages, rhetoric and literature; theory and practice of education; and a certain political advocacy on behalf of peace, replace the philosophical reasoning typically employed in the various forms of scholastic theology. That Erasmus also addresses these forms of learning, independently of religious questions, goes to show that he is far more than a theologian and never just a theologian; that these forms of knowledge so regularly find their unifying purpose in his reflections on Christ and the philosophy of Christ, as will be evident in the chapters that follow, illustrates the range and richness of his theological program. Sound interpretation of the Christology of Erasmus, therefore, requires a ready appreciation for the variety of ways in which Erasmus weds critical inquiry with religious commitments for the sake of theological judgment.

Perhaps the most interesting fusion introduced by Erasmus, and one that spans his religious works, concerns the way in which he handles traditional resources with what must appear to later readers to be decidedly modern sensibilities. Of course, Erasmus is not modern in any robust sense of that word, though it is fair to say that he anticipates and sometimes inaugurates exactly these sensibilities. It is true, for instance, that Erasmus piously regards biblical texts as divinely inspired, and thus because they are said to be uniquely free from error, they are held to possess "inviolable authority." Yet he knows full well from his editing and annotating of Christian scriptures that these texts have been corrupted by the "ignorance, carelessness, and indiscretion" of errant translators and drowsy scribes, and that further corruptions were "inserted by factions" to combat one heresy or another.[64] So the authority of sacred literature—the very sources to which appeal is made in Christology—bears the mark of fallible human life. As the product of human labor in particular historical contexts over time, these sources

---

64. Erasmus, "The *Apologia* of Desiderius Erasmus of Rotterdam," CWE 41: 462. That the canonical scriptures are "free from error," see Erasmus to Lorenzo Campeggi, letter 1167, in *Collected Works of Erasmus: Correspondence*, vol. 8, trans. R. A. B. Mynors (Toronto: University of Toronto Press, 1988), 116; *System of True Theology*, CWE 41: 696; and *Exposition of Psalm 38*, CWE 65: 42. On Erasmus's treatment of inspiration and error in biblical texts, see Erika Rummel, *Erasmus' Annotations on the New Testament*, 136–42.

have been subject to change and variation "for a thousand years," Erasmus observes.[65]

The same emphasis on the human character of theological sources appears when Erasmus speaks of the church fathers, many of whom played a vital part in the formation of Christological doctrine. Of great theologians generally, he notes, "they were very great men, but men after all," and hence, they must be read carefully and with a certain indulgence, as they can err.[66] And then again, finally, Erasmus advises readers to recognize the human fallibility and historical fluidity of church authority, even as he sincerely gives "the judgment of the church everywhere the reverence and authority which are its due."[67] With each of these examples, a traditional respect for religious authority is wed together—smoothly enough but by no means free from tension—with the critical sensibilities of a modern scholar.[68] Such fusions and the resulting tensions give a distinctive cast to his theological reflections, as will often be apparent in the chapters to follow. As a result, they mandate both attention to complexity and appreciation for nuance on the part of the interpreter of Erasmus's Christological reflections.

A pivotal example of the complexities at work in the theological writings of Erasmus, and with that, a recurring point where the good interpreter must pause to heed the underlying nuances in what Erasmus has to say, appears in what might be called his theological humanism. Though Erasmus is steeped in biblical sources and framed by Christian

65. Erasmus, "The *Apologia* of Desiderius Erasmus of Rotterdam," CWE 41: 462–63. For Erasmus, the biblical message may be "timeless," as Christine Christ-von Wedel puts it, but what is transmitted is a "time-sensitive historical report" that requires linguistic skill, historical knowledge, and imaginative interpretation. See Christine Christ-von Wedel, *Erasmus of Rotterdam: Advocate for a New Christianity* (Toronto: University of Toronto Press, 2013), 104. As she observes, Erasmus approached biblical literature with a "degree of historical awareness that was astonishing for his time" (105).

66. Erasmus to Henry Bullock, letter 456, CWE 4: 48. See also Erasmus to Jean de Carondelet, letter 1334, CWE 9: 248; "A Response by Desiderius Erasmus to the Discussions of a Certain 'Youth Who Would Teach his Elders,'" in *Collected Works of Erasmus: Controversies*, vol. 73, trans. Denis L. Drysdall (Toronto: University of Toronto Press, 2015), 144. See especially the lengthy and detailed review of the errors of church fathers—from Origen and Cyprian to Jerome and Augustine—in *Exposition of Psalm 38*, CWE 65: 43–51.

67. Erasmus to Jacob of Hoogstraten, letter 1006, in *Collected Works of Erasmus: Correspondence*, vol. 7, trans. R. A. B. Mynors (Toronto: University of Toronto Press, 1987), 52.

68. On the Erasmian ambivalence regarding tradition and modernity, see Spitz, *Religious Renaissance of the German Humanists*, 235. See also Terence J. Martin, "Heresy and Humanity: Erasmian Retrievals and Overtures," *Erasmus Studies* 41 (April 2021): 1–28.

tradition, as we will see, his theological writings often are linked by scholars with humanistic sensibilities. Boyle, for instance, calls his work an example of "evangelical humanism," and Charles Trinkaus speaks of the "humanist exegetical theology" of Erasmus.[69] Such designations are entirely appropriate, as will be evident throughout this book, as they speak nicely to the fusion of religious and humanistic commitments in his work. At the same time, however, the word "humanism" carries multiple meanings, and though the various senses are conceptually related in their focus on human capacities and their resulting fruits, it is important to keep these differences in mind when examining the Christology of Erasmus.[70]

For Erasmus himself, the term refers to the study of classical languages and literature, or what he calls "humane letters," and historians who study the sixteenth century usually use the term to refer to the broad intellectual movement throughout the European Renaissance that dedicated itself to this "new learning." A second sense of "humanism," one familiar in Renaissance literature but with roots in classical Greek and Roman philosophy, involves the affirmation of the natural capacities of human intelligence. This sense of humanism appears wherever Erasmus affirms the wisdom and virtues of ancient philosophers and Jewish tradition.[71] A third sense of humanism takes theological form when Erasmus insists that some cooperative openness on the part of the individual—comprised of a "contrite heart," a readiness to change, and habitual "service" for others— is needed to receive the redemptive love offered in Christ.[72] Though "all our sufficiency is

69. Boyle, *Rhetoric and Reform*, 13, 28. Emily Kearns similarly speaks of "the evangelical nature of Erasmian humanism" in the "Introduction" to Erasmus, *Homily on the Child Jesus*, trans. Emily Kearns, in *Collected Works of Erasmus: Literary and Educational Writings*, vol. 29, ed. Elaine Fantham and Erika Rummel (Toronto: University of Toronto, 1989), 54. See also Charles Trinkaus, "Introduction," CWE 76: xi.

70. For a discussion of the complex currents at play in the idea of humanism, see Augustin Renaudet, "Autour d'une définition de l'humanisme," in *Humanisme et Renaissance* (Genève: Librairie E. Droz, 1958), 32–53.

71. On the "not inconsiderable seeds of virtue and piety" in the "histories of the pagans" (by the "law of nature") and in the history of the Jews (by "the law of Moses"), see Erasmus, *Warrior Shielding a Discussion 2*, CWE 77: 734–38.

72. Erasmus, *Sermon on the Immense Mercy of God*, trans. Michael J. Heath, CWE 70: 126, 132–33. As Boyle writes, "cooperation in his self-making was fundamental to evangelical humanism" (Boyle, *Rhetoric and Reform*, 13, 28, 113). See also the second section of chapter 8 in this work.

from God," Erasmus piously affirms, some degree of human resolve and effort, no matter how small, is both required and possible for the redeemed life.[73] And then, finally, a fourth sense of humanism fits the Gospel ethic of humility, love, patience, and tolerance, as that ethic poses an ideal pattern for a new way of being human, and with that, it also prompts resolve and action that will enrich and enhance the character of human life.[74] With this sense, Erasmus puts forward a theologically based humanistic ethic designed to promote authentic peace in the world, which as we will see in chapter 8 includes both personal serenity and friendship between nations. What is important to keep in mind is that the humanistic tenor of Erasmus's theological reflections involves each of these senses of the term; so that once again, especially given the central part played by the "human" in his Christological reflections, sound interpretation demands careful attention to the complex and varying nuances of the humanistic tenor of his theological work.

There is much of interest and a great deal of value to be found in the Christology of Erasmus, and it is the purpose of this book to draw forth and render clear the significant contributions found in the works of Erasmus. His Christology is important, in the first place, for what it contributes to the range of Christian thought in the Renaissance and Reformation. Erasmus was truly unique for his time: steadfastly Christian in the Roman Catholic tradition, steeped in the humanistic methods of Renaissance scholarship, resolutely evangelical in his theological proposals, and passionately committed to the cause of peace. This singular position meant, of course, that he regularly found himself in the crossfire of religious disputes, though it also meant, in a more positive vein, that he was exceptionally conversant with leading scholars, churchmen, and reformers across the European landscape. The theological vision that emerged from this environment is distinctive and

---

73. "Free will does something good" when joined "with grace," Erasmus contends, even if "only the tiniest bit of power" is ascribed to freedom of choice (Erasmus, *Warrior Shielding a Discussion 1*, CWE 76: 190–92). It is better to "attribute something to free will," he repeats, "but only a little" (*Warrior Shielding a Discussion 2*, CWE 77: 399). See also 623 and 743 on the "minuscule" part played by natural human effort when compared with God's grace.

74. On the enhancement of life as the focus of theological humanism, see William Schweiker, "Humanity and the Global Future," in *Responsibility and the Enhancement of Life: Essays in Honor of William Schweiker*, ed. Günter Thomas and Heike Springhart (Leipzig: Evangelische Verlagsanstalt, 2017), 13–33.

creative, as we will see, since it brings forth an accounting of Christian faith and life that is anchored in biblical sources, conversant with the classics of Christian tradition, engaged with literary and philosophical literature of the classical world, and with those resources in hand, bent on the transformation of human life in keeping with the philosophy of Christ. The Christology of Erasmus provides a perfect lens with which to examine this contribution to religious thought of the period, so one purpose of this book is to augment the understanding of this historical significance.

At the same time, however, Erasmus's Christological reflections are important for theology itself—in part, certainly, for the history of theology, where attention to the works of Erasmus has been unduly restricted to his debate with Luther on grace and free will, but also for the history of Christology, where his writings rarely receive much attention. Since theologians necessarily work in the shadow of their traditions—reflecting even as they creatively amend what they inherit—they will profit from the insights and challenges found in the humanistic Christology of Erasmus. A second purpose of this book, therefore, is to fill the lacuna in theological understanding by offering a close reading of this insightful, challenging, but often overlooked resource.

Outline of Chapters

Erasmus does not deliver his Christological reflections in a systematic fashion, at least as might satisfy the organizational standards of professional theologians in his day or in ours. Nonetheless, as this book will show, what he offers us in the way of Christology is both a well-focused and coherent line of thinking. His many and diverse reflections hang together, in short, and they culminate in claims that are both theologically suggestive and ethically compelling. To clarify these values, the chapters that follow proceed according to thematic structures often employed in the history of Christology, when adjusted for the distinctive emphases of Erasmus.

The first and last chapters constitute bookends, so to speak, as they both address the sinful condition of human existence, while pointing toward the redemption offered in Christ. The sorry human condition and its ideal restoration, in short, provides Erasmus with the broad frame for his reflections, marking the conceptual starting point and its ultimate point of resolution. When tending to the twisted and corrupt character of social life, for instance, he accents how Christ is the ultimate goal (*scopus*), effective pattern, and enduring measure for the good and full life together (chapter 1), and where dwelling on the conflict and violence so regularly plaguing humanity, he shows how the redemptive peace offered in Christ issues in an enduring responsibility for advancing peace in the world (chapter 8). In both cases, therefore, Christ is the divine reality that from an abundance of mercy bestows the personal serenity and social guidance required to transform the broken and factious condition of human existence.

Erasmus is fully cognizant, of course, that Christ is never what people expect, but always something other and certainly something more. With this in mind, consequently, Erasmus instructs his readers how to think of divine revelation not as a simple and clear communication but rather as a manifestation under the cover of simplicity and humility; thus, he tutors these same readers in the demands of interpreting the words and actions of a figure who may appear ordinary or even insignificant, but who—on closer look and peering beneath the surface—turns out to harbor the greatest of wisdom and incomparable love. Though Erasmus begins his accounts of Jesus in the gospel narratives with the literal sense of biblical texts, therefore, at key moments, he lets loose with a keen sense of ironic surprise (chapter 2) and a playful attunement to divine transcendence by way of allegory (chapter 3). What he manages in the first case is a provocative reversal of the world's inverted habits of mind, so that what is revealed in Christ is something only gleaned by an ironic sensibility attuned to the reversal of appearance and reality, and what emerges in the second is an imaginative prompting to turn one's attention from immediate concerns to ultimate realities and thereby to think beyond the pale of the obvious and the mundane.

Christology has always concerned itself with questions of the divinity of Christ. As Erasmus often reminds us, however, the human capacity to understand the sublime truth revealed in Christ remains limited and muddled, so, in response, he pursues a cautious yet still daring blend of metaphysical modesty and rhetorical creativity when speaking of things divine. When addressing something as lofty as the intradivine relations of Father and Son, for instance, he counsels epistemic restraint, and this theological posture in turn allows for a striking degree of sympathy for the reasoning of heretics like Arius and his followers (chapter 4). When speaking of the creative and redemptive work of God through the Son, however, he advances an imaginative, though not entirely novel, reading of the Word of God as the copious eloquence of the Father (chapter 5). In both examples, we encounter the broad and free quality Erasmus brings to bear on such lofty, if not inscrutable, questions. What Erasmus contributes to discussions of the divinity of Christ, finally, is a counsel of restraint in metaphysical speculation, an accent on the revelatory breadth of the eternal Word (*sermo*) of God, and an invitation to think of Christ incarnate as the eloquent oration of God who conveys a transformative ethic for authentic human life.

The central impulse of the Christology of Erasmus, in the end, is the affirmation of the full incarnation of Christ in human existence (chapter 6), eschewing—as much as is possible for anyone working in Christology—lasting traces of docetic insulation of the divine from the struggles and agony of human experience (chapter 7). For Erasmus, it is "Christ's incarnation and passion" and not his transcendent sublimity, as Guy Bedouelle rightly observes, that serve as "the very source of [human] redemption."[75] In fact, Erasmus explains with great emphasis, the "extreme lowliness of Christ" in human form and life "redound[s] to the glory of Christ," just as it serves as living "testimony to the unspeakable love which he had for us."[76] Ultimately, for Erasmus, Christ embodies the merciful and healing embrace of humanity by God and a compelling model of reconciling love for those willing to live according to the Gospel philosophy. The strong affirmation of the humanity of Christ, therefore, naturally supports the ethic of peace that stands as the culmination of the Christology of Erasmus (chapter 8).

---

75. Guy Bedouelle, "Introduction," CWE 83: xxi.
76. Erasmus, *Apology against Lefèvre*, CWE 83: 33–34.

CHAPTER 1

Christ as *Scopus*

The Christology of Erasmus begins, surprisingly enough, not with the texts of Christian scriptures and early church commentaries, both of which constitute a central and abiding focus of his scholarly work, but with his take on the twisted and corrupted condition of the human world. This is true in two senses, one arising from the inherent dynamics of interpretation, the other stemming from one of the root dyads (sin and grace) shaping theological inquiry. As an interpretive discipline, theology proceeds by way of conversation between readers and certain texts historically granted authoritative status as in some way sacred and revelatory.[1] When readers approach such materials, however, they do so in a manner that is framed by all sorts of assumptions, some regarding the text and what it may or may not be able to offer, but others about human life and the condition of the world, in particular, what they deem to be the fundamental problems about the world as they find it. Understanding the Christology of Erasmus, therefore, requires close attention both to his critical regard for biblical texts, which he piously respects as the Word of God, albeit in words crafted and transmitted

---

1. On interpretation as conversation, see David Tracy, *Plurality and Ambiguity: Hermeneutics, Religion, Hope* (San Francisco: Harper and Row, 1987), 1–27.

by admittedly fallible traditions, and to his assessment of the condition of human life, especially its corruption and distortions, since—now in theological terms—it is this sorry and sinful state of existence that shapes his construal of the redemptive significance of the Christ figure.

Two writings by Erasmus are particularly important in this regard—the first, a letter written by Erasmus to Paul Volz (August 14, 1518) that served as the preface to a new edition of *The Handbook of the Christian Soldier*, and the second, the *System of True Theology*, an expanded outline for "method in theology" prepared for the second edition of Erasmus's New Testament in 1519.[2] Though written for different purposes—the letter to Volz as a trenchant call for the reformation of Christian life and the *System of True Theology* as a humanistic guide for the renaissance of true theology—they share a common device for diagnosing the inversions and distortions infecting human endeavors and for reorienting life and thought according to the ideal measure offered in the philosophy of Christ. In both pieces, Erasmus proposes that readers imagine human life as three concentric circles, each representing different rings of society—clergy, nobility, and common folk—with their distinctive statuses and specific responsibilities, though, he insists emphatically, all people are called in common to the center represented by Christ and his teachings.[3]

In their ideal condition, Erasmus suggests, clergy and nobility have their higher functions: offering prayer to God for the former and the preservation of "public peace" for the latter, though both also have a duty to offer accommodating service to those below them—the clergy giving counsel shaped by "the purity and light of Christ" to princes,

2. Erasmus, *The Handbook of the Christian Soldier* (*Enchiridion*), trans. Charles Fantazzi, CWE 66: 24–127. For the prefatory letter to Volz, see Erasmus to Paul Volz, letter 858, CWE 6: 72–91. Paul Volz was a Benedictine abbot and literary scholar of Sélestat and Strasbourg whose friendship with Erasmus survived Volz' turn to the Reformation. On Volz's life and work, see Miriam U. Chrisman, "Paul Volz," in *Contemporaries of Erasmus: A Biographical Register of the Renaissance and Reformation*, vol. 3, ed. Peter G. Bietenholz (Toronto: University of Toronto Press, 1987), 417–18. Further references to entries in *Contemporaries of Erasmus* will be given with author, entry title, and the abbreviation COE. See also Erasmus, *System of True Theology*, CWE 41: 481–713. On the *System of True Theology*, see Robert D. Sider, "The New Testament Scholarship of Erasmus: An Introduction," CWE 41: 114–19, 186–89; Mark Vessey, "The *Ratio* in Erasmus' Life and Work to 1519," in *Erasmus on Literature: His Ratio or "System" of 1518/1519*, ed. Mark Vessey (Toronto: University of Toronto Press, 2021), 21–47.

3. Erasmus to Paul Volz, CWE 6: 79–86; *System of True Theology*, CWE 41: 532–38.

and both clergy and rulers bestowing justice and guidance on the people.[4] In point of fact, however, the social order as Erasmus finds it is anything but ideal, and he shows himself to have an especially keen eye for spotting the corruption and distortions infecting these spheres. The letter to Volz, for instance, offers a stark diagnosis of the human world as twisted, corrupted, and generally askew, while the *System of True Theology* forwards a sustained critique of biblical ignorance, theological obscurantism, and twisted readings of scripture. In contrast and as a remedy, Erasmus highlights the reality of Christ and all his teachings as the ultimate goal (*scopus*) and living measure for authentic Christian life and thought.

The purpose of this chapter is to explore the meaning and significance of this first dimension of the Christology of Erasmus. To begin with, it is important to take a close look at the image of life as three concentric circles with Christ at the center, since it is there that we find Erasmus squarely facing up to the ways in which the social system of his day failed miserably when measured against two essential features of his Christology—ensuring universal accessibility to the Gospel of love embodied in the Christ figure, and with that, enabling the cultivation of godly and virtuous lives across the social spectrum. What emerges here, starkly and severely, is a bold indictment of the clerical world of Catholic orthodoxy, the privileged realm of noblemen and princes, and the reigning form of theology in the scholasticism of the Catholic universities. In a word, the spheres of human power are found to be seriously twisted and inverted, something that Erasmus notes in many of his writings in which he observes again and again how human life is topsy-turvy, inside-out, and in any case, far from how it should be.

It is this condition of life, consequently, that underscores the desperate need for a reliable guide and measure for the restoration of life and the rebirth of sound theology. Against this backdrop, therefore, Erasmus proposes that we conceive of Christ as "*scopus*," a term rich in meaning that signifies an ultimate goal to pursue, a reliable sighting by which to find orientation, and an ultimate measure by which to determine progress in living a godly and virtuous life.[5] In the letter to Paul

---

4. Erasmus, *System of True Theology*, CWE 41: 533.

5. For the general idea of *scopus* as target, see Erasmus, "To hit the target (*scopum*)," adage

Volz, for instance, Erasmus speaks of "Christ our pattern," by which he means not a *mere* pattern to be copied blithely by rote but rather the complete personal embodiment of the life of virtue, and thereby a transformative force—at once, prompting, inviting, and guiding a reversal of the twisted inversions endemic to the world in which we live.[6] In the *System of True Theology*, similarly, he depicts Christ as an interpretive *scopus* for good theology and a rhetorical model for the effective preacher; on both counts, for Erasmus, Christ is very much a present reality, accessible and inviting for all through the living words of scripture when interpreted and conveyed by theologians and preachers toward the end of godly and virtuous lives.

"A Single Centre, Jesus Christ"

Imagine the world as three concentric circles of social life, Erasmus suggests, with Christ residing preeminently at the center. While it has been suggested that the germ for this image may have come to Erasmus from a commentary on Paul by the English educator and churchman John Colet, it is more likely the original design of Erasmus.[7] For his part, Peter G. Bietenholz cites the work of mid-twentieth century biblical scholar Oscar Cullmann to claim that this image of the circles with Christ in the center "rests firmly on early Christian views," though there appears to be no support for this claim.[8] In fact, Cullmann is explain-

---

I. x. 30, in *Collected Works of Erasmus: Adages*, vol. 32, trans. R. A. B. Mynors (Toronto: University of Toronto Press, 1989), 247. The religious usage of Erasmus (using the Latinized version of the Greek *scopos*) is rooted in Philippians 3:14—"I press on toward the goal (*scopos*) for the prize of the heavenly call of God in Christ Jesus"—where *scopos* is interpreted as the "gospel target" in Erasmus's *Paraphrase on Philippians*, in *Collected Works of Erasmus: New Testament Scholarship*, vol. 43, ed. Robert D. Sider and trans. Mechtilde O'Mara and Edward A. Phillips, Jr. (Toronto: University of Toronto Press, 2009), 384–86. On the grammatical richness of this term, see Boyle, *Erasmus on Language and Method in Theology*, 74–81.

6. Erasmus to Paul Volz, CWE 6: 77.

7. See Boyle, *Erasmus on Language and Method in Theology*, 108–10; Georges Chantraine, SJ, *"Mystère" et "Philosophie du Christ" selon Erasme* (Namur: Secrétariat des Publications, 1971), 123–24. Colet's elaborate discussion of the "orbs and heavenly spheres" rotating around Christ is vastly different from the simple sketch of Erasmus. See *John Colet's Commentary on First Corinthians*, trans. Bernard O'Kelly and Catherine A. L. Jarrott (Binghamton, NY: Medieval and Renaissance Studies, 1985), 242–44. Colet earlier speaks about the imitation of Christ's life as "aiming arrows at life, that they may win the prize of Life itself" (163). The date of Colet's composition remains uncertain (19).

8. See Peter G. Bietenholz, *History and Biography in the Work of Erasmus of Rotterdam*

ing how Christ can be Lord over the world and the church in a manner that will avoid conflating or separating the world and the church, but his description of the "two concentric circles, whose common center is Christ"—proposed without any direct biblical or patristic citations— appears to be Cullmann's own theological construction.[9]

In a different vein, there is no reason in principle to rule out the possibility that Erasmus was influenced by broader social and literary currents. With this in mind, Boyle observes that Erasmus's treatment of the circles mirrors the literature of the feudal "estates" that was current before and during the sixteenth century, so it is possible that he was informed by these literary currents, or at least by the broadly felt sentiments they embody. She also suggests, reasonably enough, that the "radio-centric system" of "urban plans" in European fortifications and towns offers Erasmus a "second matrix" for his "concentric diagram."[10] As she notes, however, Erasmus's "diagrammatic allegory" is distinctive, and hence most likely original from his pen, in placing Christ, rather than the institutional church or the prince's castle, at the center of the circular design. His rendering of the image of the circles of social life likewise differs from mystically inclined hierarchies, like that of Dionysius (Denys) the Areopagite, for instance, in being neither graphically hierarchical nor theocentric.[11] In contrast to these sketches of the human world, therefore, the imagery of Erasmus is decidedly and distinctively Christocentric.[12]

Representing "the three estates of clergy, nobility, and common

---

(Genève: Librairie Droz, 1966), 85, n. 134. Georges Chantraine follows the lead of Bietenholz without critical scrutiny. See Chantraine,*"Mystère" et "Philosophie du Christ" selon Erasme*, 125, n. 114.

9. See Oscar Cullmann, *Christ and Time: The Primitive Christian Conception of Time and History*, revised edition, trans. Floyd V. Filson (Philadelphia: Westminster Press, 1964), 186–89. Cullmann defends his explanation of how Christ is lord of both the state and the church against both Emil Brunner, the Swiss Reformed theologian who warns against the "fanatical intermixture of Church and State" implied in Cullmann's model of two concentric circles; and Gerhard Kittel, the German Lutheran scholar, famous for his *Theological Dictionary of the New Testament* but infamous for his complicity in Nazi anti-Semitic propaganda, who complains that Cullmann introduces "a dualistic separation of the two" (206–8).

10. See Boyle, *Erasmus on Language and Method in Theology*, 98–107.

11. See Boyle, *Erasmus on Language and Method in Theology*, 107–11. See also Chantraine,*"Mystère" et "Philosophie du Christ" selon Erasme*, 123–24.

12. On the Christocentric character of Erasmian theology, see J. Coppens, "Où en est le portrait d'Érasme théologien?" *Scrinium Erasmianum*, vol. 2, 584.

people," Bietenholz suggests, these spheres form "the universe of Christendom" as Erasmus knew it.[13] The first circle, and hence the one closest to Christ, is comprised of "priests, bishops, cardinals, [and] popes," we are told, and it is their double duty, as Erasmus describes their station, to "embrace the intense purity of the centre and pass on as much as they can to those next to them." Standing "nearest Christ," and hence purified from "all earthly contagion," they nonetheless are said to bear the enormous responsibility to encourage princes to settle conflict peacefully, with a minimum of destruction, and to tolerate and foster the spiritual growth of ordinary people with "paternal indulgence." The greatest of responsibilities, therefore, is incumbent on their privileged status.

In the second sphere, one finds "lay princes," who "with their armies and laws serve Christ after a fashion," Erasmus asserts, primarily in defeating enemies in "necessary and just wars and keeping public peace." Though they "handle a certain amount of worldly business" of practical importance, they have, strictly speaking, "no part at all in Christian purity," as their work reflects only a "subdued image, a shadow rather, of divine justice." Besides, Erasmus adds with a strong dose of realism, they all too frequently pursue their "own advantage" rather than the "public good," they apply justice with "severity" in place of mercy, and they "pillage the people whose interest it was their duty to protect." How easily

13. Bietenholz, *History and Biography*, 85. Given the discussion of the Turks in the letter to Paul Volz, however—who Erasmus boldly characterizes as "at least human beings," and thus as perfect candidates for evangelical preaching—it seems that the image of the three circles might be conceived more broadly still. Erasmus does not pursue that possibility in the letter to Volz, though he does elsewhere, calling the Turks "in large part half-Christian and perhaps nearer to true Christianity than most of our own folk." See Erasmus to Paul Volz, CWE 6: 75–77; "War is a treat for those who have not tried it," adage IV. i. 1, in *Collected Works of Erasmus: Adages*, vol. 35, trans. Denis L. Drysdall (Toronto: University of Toronto Press, 2005), 432–33; and *A Most Useful Discussion Concerning Proposals for War against the Turks, Including an Exposition of Psalm 28*, trans. Michael J. Heath, in *Collected Works of Erasmus; Exposition of the Psalms*, vol. 64, ed. Dominic Baker-Smith (Toronto: University of Toronto, 2005), 232–33. Moving in the opposite direction, Georges Chantraine speaks of the image of three circles as comprising Christ's "church," as does James McConica, who characterizes the image as a "portrait of the Church." See Georges G. Chantraine, SJ, "The *Ratio verae theologiae* (1518)," in *Essays on the Works of Erasmus*, ed. Richard L. DeMolen (New Haven, CT: Yale University Press, 1978), 182; James Kelsey McConica, "Erasmus and the Grammar of Consent," *Scrinium Erasmianum*, vol. 2, 83. While Erasmus does speak of the circles as the "people of Christ" (*System of True Theology*, CWE 41: 532–33), it is too constrictive to identify this image with the church alone, as a great deal that lies outside the church is included in each sphere of life. Using the broadest language, Augustin Renaudet speaks of the three circles as describing "human society" (Renaudet, *Études Érasmiennes*, 151).

their legal and military power gives way to excess and harm, Erasmus observes. The third circle, finally, is populated by "common people"—the "undiscriminating crowd," as he calls them rather negatively—and though they are "the most earthly portion of this world," he adds with a quick shift of metaphor and a positive turn of meaning, they are "not so earthly that they are not members of Christ's body just the same."[14]

What we have in the image of the three circles, then, is a sketch of the existing social hierarchy of Erasmus's world, though the varying stations in life are ranked religiously by their proximity or distance from Christ at the center. It cannot go unnoticed, however, that while his description of princely power sounds a realistic note, his initial account of the clergy is clearly idealized, focusing entirely on their superior sanctity matched with their enormous responsibility. Despite this stock account of clerical rank, however, Erasmus's imagery, in fact, is designed to cut across privilege and hierarchy by emphasizing that all three spheres share "a single centre, Jesus Christ," to whom "all must strive with all the power each person has."[15] The ultimate center of life, in short, is a goal (*scopus*) to which all people are called to aspire, including powerful princes, even though they are sullied by the sordid affairs of the secular world, and ordinary folk as well, "the most stolid and untutored" of people, as Erasmus casts them. What seems at first glance to be a sketch of social division marked by clerical privilege, therefore, is actually a symbol of religious inclusion that Erasmus firmly grounds in the common center of Christ's teaching. There is "only one goal (*scopus*): Christ, and his teaching in all its purity," Erasmus insists again, and his supreme philosophy "must be set before everyone, that at least we may achieve something halfway."[16]

As God's eloquent wisdom in Christ accommodated itself to the weakness of humanity, Erasmus argues, so too "Christ would frequently

14. Erasmus to Paul Volz, CWE 6: 80–82; *System of True Theology*, CWE 41: 533. In this passage, one can glean the ambiguity in Erasmus's views of common people. Though he often reflects a rather pejorative view of commoners, important countercurrents appear throughout his writings, occasionally in the charming portraits found in the *Colloquies*, but most certainly in the sympathy he shows to the peasantry who suffer the carnage unleashed by the capricious military campaigns of princes, as well as, as we will see shortly, in his support for vernacular translations of the Bible.

15. Erasmus, *System of True Theology*, CWE 41: 533; Erasmus to Paul Volz, CWE 6: 82.

16. Erasmus to Paul Volz, CWE 6: 82. This inclusive exhortation is repeated in Erasmus to Paul Volz, CWE 6: 90.

accommodate himself to the frailties of the disciples."[17] And, in turn, evangelical philosophy is to continue to "accommodate itself equally to all"—to infants ("adjusting to their need") and to the experienced (who will find it "utterly demanding")—so that, Erasmus reasons, it is incumbent on scholars and churchmen to translate "divine literature" into "the vernacular tongues" so that it also can be "read by ordinary people." To that end, Erasmus happily imagines that the "farmer at his plough would chant some passage from these books, that the weaver at his shuttles would sing something from them," and, too, "that the traveller would relieve the tedium of his journey with stories of this kind."[18] For the very same reason, moreover—that Christ and his teaching be accessible to everyone—it is the proper aim of good theology and sound preaching, Erasmus advises, to convey Christ's message in a manner that is "easy and open to all" while still being "conducive to a good life."[19] What bold proposals for a society marked by rigid divisions of rank and for a hierarchical church organized around professionally defined levels of sanctity, and, too, what a startling suggestion for the scholastic theologians of the day—the "sons of Scotus," as Erasmus calls them, with their "exceedingly acute subtleties"—who certainly did not prize accessibility in what they wrote.[20] Toward the same end, once again, Erasmus appeals to the Pauline image of the body of Christ and its diverse but integral members to supplement the idea of Christ as a reality that includes and unifies great variety.[21]

---

17. See Erasmus, *Handbook of the Christian Soldier*, CWE 66: 35 on divine accommodation; *System of True Theology*, CWE 41: 535, 570 on Christ's adaptation "to those he was eager to attract."

18. Erasmus, *Paraclesis*, CWE 41: 410–11. On Erasmus's later qualification of his endorsement of vernacular translations of the Bible in response to criticism from Pierre Cousturier (Sutor), see Robert D. Sider, "General Introduction," CWE 41: 277. The apparent retraction from Erasmus is, to say the least, hedged and possibly ironic, as he denies only having said that "anyone at all should translate the sacred books into the vernacular," which nicely sidesteps the key issue of whether vernacular translations should be available to the laity, and though he confesses that it is best if "the common people learn through the spoken word," he then adds a truly difficult condition: "if a good teacher is available." See also Erasmus, "To the Pious Reader," CWE 45: 7–28. In this preface to the *Paraphrase on Matthew*, Erasmus echoes his call for the "books of Christ" to be "translated into all the languages of the nations," so that everyone, "the farmer, the smith, [and] stone-cutter will read him, prostitutes and pimps will read him, [and] even the Turks will read him" (17, 10).

19. Erasmus to Paul Volz, CWE 6: 74–75.

20. Erasmus, *System of True Theology*, CWE 41: 676. For Erasmus's oft-repeated complaints against the obscure and difficult writing of the theologians of his day, see 699–713.

21. Though understandable that Erasmus would tap into this Pauline image from 1 Corinthians

As much as the image of the circles illustrates the ideal of a common life modeled in Christ, it also serves Erasmus well for the purposes of religious and social criticism. In the world as it has come to be, the circles of life are frequently corrupted and sometimes completely reversed. To make this point, Erasmus introduces a realm of vices, comprised of "love of money, lechery, anger, revenge, jealousy, slander, and the other plagues," that is said to exist, oddly enough, "outside the third circle."[22] It turns out, however, that he is not proposing a fourth sphere of social life but rather is referring to the very worst of human existence—the subhuman, as it were, or what Erasmus calls simply "abominable"—marked by centrifugal vices that pull people away from the center. That condition, as he puts it, "becomes incurable" only when these vices "make themselves respectable under a mask of religion and duty and worm their way into higher circles." But this is precisely what happens, Erasmus tells us, when a prince exercises "tyrannical power under a pretext of justice and right," when a priest makes "religion an excuse for personal gain," or when a bishop seeks "worldly rule in the name of defending the church" by laying down laws "which purport to serve Christ's cause and in fact are poles apart from the teaching of Christ."[23]

How corrupt clerical and princely life become when their vices masquerade as virtue and merely apparent virtues are adorned with the "mask of piety without its genuine force."[24] At that point, Erasmus

---

12:12–31, it fits awkwardly when—as Boyle puts its—"the organic metaphor of the human body is superimposed upon the geometric model of concentric circles" (Boyle, *Erasmus on Language and Method in Theology*, 85). Interestingly, and with a richly speculative imagination, Boyle suggests that Christ as "centre geometrically" and "head organically" are held together graphically as "an armillary sphere with its concentric bands rotating around a central axis." For Boyle's interpretation of the "sacred geometry of the Erasmian circles"—at once Trinitarian, natural, and social—all "rotating on the axial Christ," see 87–90. It also is possible, and I think more likely, that Erasmus had no interest in unifying these diverse symbols, but rather was satisfied, as Boyle also notes, with the richly protean imagery for Christ available in Christian sources. For Erasmus's handling of 1 Corinthians 12:12–31, see Erasmus, *Paraphrase on 1 Corinthians*, CWE 43: 153–57.

22. Erasmus to Paul Volz, CWE 6: 82. Pierre Mesnard suggests that beyond the third circle is the "world" with "its vices and prestige, its pomp and its works." See Pierre Mesnard, "Un texte important d'Erasme touchant sa 'Philosophie chrétienne,'" *Revue Thomiste* 47: 3 (1947): 529. Mesnard may be correct, though Erasmus does not say as much. While Erasmus continues to refer to the "world" and "earthly things" as a life given over to lower passions and vices, and hence as centrifugal forces pulling people away from Christ, his entire focus rests on life within the three circles—what people today would call the social worlds—and his efforts are dedicated to exposing and countering all the ways that these vicious forces infect and distort these very social spheres.

23. Erasmus to Paul Volz, CWE 6: 82.

24. Erasmus to Paul Volz, CWE 6: 86.

notes, everything is twisted and contorted. And in that condition, he observes, one will find monks so worldly that they are "barely included in the outermost circle," while conversely and completely flipped, among those lay people who have twice married, "there are some whom Christ thinks worthy of the first circle."[25] In the same vein, Erasmus adds without hesitation, no one will get an argument from him should they think that—given the corrupted character of the nobility—the third circle is the proper abode for princes.[26] The estates of the world, in short, are corrupted and all mixed up, as the nominal residents of each sphere end up dwelling (at worst) below or (at best) above their normally designated domain.[27] With this account of the social worlds of his day, Erasmus offers us a first glimpse of the twisted inversions that infect the human world, and, as we will see, it is precisely that sad and sinful condition that cries out for the remedy of Christ proposed by Erasmus.

"A Topsy-Turvy World"

"What a topsy-turvy world we live in," Erasmus writes to John Colet in October of 1518. "Out of men we make gods and turn priesthood into tyranny," he complains, while princes, the pope, and even the "Grand Turk" conspire with their wars to destroy the "well-being of the common people." In a word, he concludes, "Christ is out of date," and the world is turned on its head.[28] These are familiar sentiments in the work of Erasmus, certainly in their clerical and political targets; then again with the diagnosis voiced in the grammar of inversion;[29] and finally in the lament about the willful ignorance of Christ. It is precisely this kind

25. Erasmus to Paul Volz, CWE 6: 83. Lacking biblical evidence for the inclusion of the twice married, Bietenholz suggests that Erasmus is alluding to Thomas More.

26. Erasmus to Paul Volz, CWE 6: 82.

27. As Ruth Mohl points out, "lament over the shortcomings of these various estates," including "an outspoken account of specific faults," were "well-defined traits" in the history of the literature of the estates. See Ruth Mohl, *The Three Estates in Medieval and Renaissance Literature* (New York: Columbia University Press, 1933), 6–7.

28. Erasmus to John Colet, letter 891, CWE 6: 168.

29. Erasmus frequently uses one or another form of *"praepostere"* to signify when something is inverted, reversed, backwards, upside down, inside out, absurd, preposterous, and so on, though he also uses *"absurdum"* and variations on *"verto"* and *"inverto."*

of world, Erasmus argues, that cries out with need for the renaissance of peace and the restoration of order offered in Christ.

The world has gone mad, Erasmus declares with lament, though as one adage puts it, "not everyone is mad in the same way," as one person suffers "from avarice, another from lust, one from ambition, another from envy."[30] Thankfully, Erasmus provides an extended catalogue of this condition in the *Praise of Folly*, in which—aside from many innocent and relatively harmless forms of folly and some rather odd but saintly forms of craziness—he takes satiric aim at those treacherous madmen, including powerful princes and illustrious clerics of many ranks and stations, who turn life upside down and inside out for their own gain or prestige.[31] There are theologians whose arrogance is so complete that they "fashion and refashion Holy Scriptures at will," while demanding that their far-fetched conclusions should "carry more weight than ... papal decrees." There are princes whose lives are so dissolute and whose policies are so rapacious and self-serving, that—when adorned with the regal symbols of virtue and justice—still manage to fool everyone into forgetting that a true prince is just the reverse, as a prince is called to be a "public servant" bound to serve the "well-being of his people." And there are bishops who—though decked out with the splendid accouterments indicating their innocence, knowledge, and purity—in fact, devote themselves expertly to increasing their revenues.[32] In sum, we are told, the world is inverted: what is valuable and virtuous is shunned, and what is worthless and vile is embraced, and to mask these distortions, the powerful skillfully manipulate their appearances to seem the opposite of what they are. In a world turned on its head, things simply are not what they appear to be.

30. Erasmus, "Not everyone is mad in the same way," adage III. x. 97, CWE 35: 396–97.

31. See Erasmus, *Praise of Folly*, CWE 27: 120–42, where Erasmus laughs critically at a rich assortment of professional fools. On the different types of folly in discrete sections of the *Praise of Folly*, see Clarence H. Miller's "Introduction" to his translation of Erasmus, *Praise of Folly* (New Haven, CT: Yale University Press, 1979), xxi–xxv. While it is true that Erasmus later deemed the *Praise of Folly* a mere "trifle," this is an ironic feint of minimization, which he also uses for his *Adages*, his work on the New Testament, and the famous response to Luther on free will. The complaint of Erasmus against the inversions committed by the powerful, therefore, is a serious indictment of their intentionally and viciously twisted lives. On the *Adages* and his work on scripture as "trivial," see Erasmus to Guillaume Budé, letter 480, CWE 4: 104; on his drafting a "trifling piece about the freedom of the will," see Erasmus to Ludwig Baer, letter 1419, CWE 10: 180.

32. Erasmus, *Praise of Folly*, CWE 27: 129, 135–36, and 137.

One finds a similarly capacious yet equally critical take on the world's inversions in the *Adages*, that massive collection of proverbs drawn from the literature of antiquity and presented to readers with comments of varying length and depth from Erasmus. Indeed, the *Adages* are a gold mine of materials for reflecting on the many ways in which life is so often turned backwards and topsy-turvy. Some of these cases, clearly enough, are simply ridiculous, mostly harmless, though the sentiments are familiar, even today. When "one who is far less learned disputes with an accomplished scholar," for example, it is "turning things upside down" (*praepostero*), just as it is a ridiculous inversion when someone entirely ignorant seeks to teach a person in the know.[33] Adages like this indicate the confusion of an existing or expected order, though it is equally absurd, Erasmus muses, to "try in vain to achieve the impossible" by reversing natural opposites ("To fish in the air, to hunt in the sea");[34] by confusing the natural sequence of cause and effect ("You lend light to the sun");[35] or by twisting the order of irreversible events ("To drag the clothes off a naked man").[36]

Then again, Erasmus observes with language that is still proverbial today, there are wrong-headed—and hence, preposterous (*praepostere*)—ways of getting something done, as when someone puts "the cart

33. Erasmus, "A fawn against a lion," adage I. iii. 49, CWE 31: 276–77. Along the same lines, see also Erasmus, "The sow (teaches) Minerva," adage I. i. 40; "A sow competed with Minerva," adage I. i. 41, CWE 31: 88–91. Roughly the same point is made in another proverb, in which Erasmus observes that "something is upside down" (*praepostere fieri*) when a mere boy dares to admonish an old man, or again, he notes—interestingly enough, given today's more flexible standards—when "the original order of things is reversed" (*pristinum rerum ordinem inuerti*), where men and women switch gender roles. See Erasmus, "The springs of the sacred rivers flow backwards," adage I. iii. 15, CWE 31: 247–48. See also Erasmus, "The steed is in pursuit of the tortoise," adage IV. iv. 68, in *Collected Works of Erasmus: Adages*, vol. 36, trans. John N. Grant and Betty I. Knott (Toronto: University of Toronto Press, 2006), 107, which is said when "something is being done in a quite absurd and unnatural (*praepostere et absurde*) way."

34. Erasmus, "To fish in the air, to hunt in the sea," adage I. iv. 74, CWE 31: 369; along the same lines, see Erasmus, "To whiten ivory with ink" adage I. iii. 70, CWE 31: 293. See also Erasmus, "The stag drags off the hounds," adage IV. iv. 11, CWE 36: 67–68, which signifies "a reversal (*praeposterum*) of nature or what is impossible."

35. Erasmus, "You lend light to the sun," adage I. vii. 58, CWE 32: 102. See also "To carry wood to the forest," adage I. vii. 57, CWE 32: 101.

36. Erasmus, "To drag the clothes off a naked man," adage I. iv. 76, CWE 31: 370; similarly, see "To cut a dead man's throat," adage I. ii. 54, CWE 31: 194–95, which can be used for someone who attacks "a book which all condemn"; Erasmus, "To reopen a closed subject," adage I. iv. 70, CWE 31: 365, where Erasmus quotes Cicero lamenting that "we put things back to front (*praeposteris*), and go over things already settled."

before the horse."[37] It is equally "topsy-turvy behavior" (*cum res prae-postere genitur*), he observes—like trying "to split logs with a key and open the door with an axe"—when someone uses "philosophical arguments to convince uneducated people and in learned company tries to win the day by shamelessly shouting them down."[38] The world is distorted, as well, when something essential is omitted or removed, as if someone were to try "to remove spring from the year," which is exactly what Erasmus thinks theologians have done by removing "the knowledge of languages and literature from the schools."[39] Things are, once again, commonly twisted out of proportion when someone inflates the importance of something that is entirely insignificant.[40]

While these adages illustrate the ridiculous inversions of common life, others point out the treacherous and devious subversions perpetrated by corrupt religious and political figures. Truly, the world is turned topsy-turvy, Erasmus insists in "The Sileni of Alcibiades"—his most thorough-going treatment of this type of reversal—when a king forsakes wise and virtuous governance for a life dominated by pleasure and luxury; when bishops abandon their calling as the "guardian" of the church to embrace "wordly wealth"; when popes turn from battling "simony, pride, lust, ambition, anger, [and] impiety " to undertake savage military campaigns; and, finally, when priests—whose "principal duty"

37. Erasmus, "The cart before the horse," adage I. vii. 28, CWE 32: 83. In such cases, things are "done the wrong way round (*praepostere*)," he adds elsewhere, as "when theory is accommodated to fact and not fact to theory, [and] when law is suited to conduct, not conduct corrected by law" ("By the Lesbian rule," adage I. v. 93, CWE 31: 465). See also "Back to front (*Praepostere*)," adage V. i. 30, CWE 36: 559, where Erasmus cites a "figure of style" called "hindermost first" or "latter first"; "The she-goat has not yet given birth, but the kid is playing on the roof," adage II. vi. 10, CWE 33: 295, a proverb said of those "who attack something in the wrong order (*praepostere*)"; and "You flay the beast before you've killed it," adage III. iii. 13, CWE 34: 286–87, also said for things "done in the wrong order (*praeposteris*)."

38. See Erasmus, "To split logs with a key and open the door with an axe," adage II. vi. 81, CWE 33: 330. See also "You are giving chaff to the dog and bones to the ass," adage III. v. 14, CWE 35: 74, which is "said when things are distributed the wrong way (*praepostere*)"; "To hunt a hare with an ox," adage IV. iv. 44, which refers to "those who undertake something that is ridiculous (*absurdam*), foolish (*stultam*), and absurd (*praeposteram*)."

39. "To remove spring from the year," adage IV. v. 60, CWE 36: 182–83.

40. See Erasmus, "Wondrous words about a lentil," adage IV. v. 30, CWE 36: 162. See also "You make of a fly an elephant," adage I. ix. 67, CWE 32: 219. Consider also "Straining at a gnat," adage III. x. 91, CWE 35: 392–93. Attributed by Erasmus to Jesus (Matt. 23:24), it refers to "absurdly punctilious people (*praeposter meticulosos*)," or those who are "delighted or alarmed in turn by trifles," while being "unconcerned with the most important things."

is "to scatter the seed of the divine word"—hurl themselves into a whirl of "vulgar cares."[41] Though Erasmus gladly grants that not everyone in these roles is corrupt, far too often, he complains, the world is stood on its head through their self-serving machinations.[42] The key to this plot of corruption and perversion, however, is that these inversions are concealed by a complementary reversal of appearances and reality, so that things are turned inside out (*praeposterum silenum*) in order to mask the inversion of ideals and realities.

Princes, for example, appear almost more than human when seen with "the sceptre, the insignia, [and] the bodyguards," though for those who peer behind the regal facade, they turn out to be "a despot, sometimes an enemy of his citizens, one who hates the public peace, and is skilled in sowing the seeds of discord." Bishops, too, might be taken for "heavenly character[s], even "more than human," when seen in their robes, "the mitre glittering with jewels and gold and the crozier equally studded with gems," though, in fact, when one peels away the costume, they are "nothing but a man of war, a merchant, even a despot." And monks, as well, always a target for Erasmian satire, could be taken for some desert fathers, though for the one who looks behind their austere appearance, they are found to be "mere buffoons, squanderers, impostors, [and] gluttons."[43] In these and similar examples, the ideal order of things is inverted, while appearances and reality are reversed to camouflage the inversion. "Many pretend to be what they are not," Erasmus observes in yet another adage, and it is exactly this kind of subterfuge that allows those with power to turn the world upside down, consistently to their benefit and inevitably to the harm of many.[44]

Roughly the same critical take on life turned upside down and inside out appears in the *Paraphrase on Matthew*, where Erasmus highlights the corruption and deception attributed to the scribes and Pharisees in

41. Erasmus, "The Sileni of Alcibiades," CWE: 34: 273–77.

42. Erasmus, "The Sileni of Alcibiades," CWE: 34: 267, 268.

43. Erasmus, "The Sileni of Alcibiades," CWE: 34: 267–68.

44. Erasmus, "Few men can plough, though many ply the goad," adage I. vii. 9, CWE 32: 71. Erasmus, similarly, notes in "Many bear the wand, few feel the god," adage I. vii. 6, CWE 32: 69–70, that "many mortals enjoy the outward signs and even the reputation of virtue, who lack virtue itself," and this applies, he wryly observes, to theologians, poets, monks, Christians, noblemen, virgins, kings, bishops, popes, and emperors. See also "An ape in purple," adage I. vii. 10, CWE 32: 71; "An ape is an ape, though clad in gold," adage I. vii. 11, CWE 32: 72.

the Gospel of Matthew. Their judgments are "distorted" (*praeposterum judicium*), Erasmus writes in paraphrase of Matthew 7:1–5, as they exaggerate "what is trivial" and judge others' faults harshly, all the while concealing their own faults with "the appearance of holiness."[45] "There is nothing more harmful than ungodliness," Erasmus declares with one eye on the biblical Pharisees and the other on religious officials of his own day, "to which the false appearance of sanctity adds credibility and authority."[46] Here again, we find Erasmus keen to emphasize the manner in which corrupt religious authorities turn the world on its head for their own benefit, all the while concealing their "inverted judgment" (*praepostero judicio*) with a false "appearance of godliness."[47] As he renders elements of Matthew 15:1–20, therefore, these religious officials place "the essence of godliness in external things"—the "choice of foods," for instance—while "they neglect the things that are of the heart." But "what kind of inverted holiness (*praeposterum sanctimoniae*) is this," he exclaims, "to have hands that are washed and a mind as well as a tongue polluted with so many crimes."[48] While the main purpose of the *Paraphrase on Matthew* is constructive—to elucidate the "heavenly philosophy" revealed in the teaching ministry of Jesus—it is part and parcel of this very Gospel philosophy to expose and castigate the treacherous inversion of value perpetrated by a corrupt clerical elite under the mask of piety (*praepostere religiosi*), especially where—as depicted in the Gospel of Matthew—this party resolutely sought the death of its "master teacher."[49]

The Letter to Paul Volz and the *System of True Theology* reflect exactly these familiar Erasmian judgments about the inversion of value in Christian life, and they do so, once again, with a sharply critical eye on the contributions of church leaders and theologians. What must the

45. CWE 45: 129–30, 136. See, similarly, Erasmus, "The good or ill that's wrought in our own halls," adage I. vi. 85, CWE 32: 56–57, concerning those who "make an inverted (*praepostere*) use of their sight" by harping on the faults of others, while being blind to those in their own home. On the use of "*praeposterus*" to depict the corruption and hypocrisy of the religious establishment in *Paraphrase on Matthew*, see the preface by Dean Simpson and Robert D. Sider, CWE 45: xii.

46. Erasmus, *Paraphrase on Matthew*, CWE 45: 136.

47. Erasmus, *Paraphrase on Matthew*, CWE 45: 232–33.

48. Erasmus, *Paraphrase on Matthew*, CWE 45: 233, 236.

49. Erasmus, *Paraphrase on Matthew*, CWE 45: 72, 362–63.

Turks think—Erasmus wonders with ironic empathy for this formidable enemy of Christian Europe—when they hear those "thorny and impenetrable thickets of arguments" of Christian theologians and see "eminent religious leaders" fighting each other "until they are pale with fury and reduced to insults and spitting?" What will they conclude, Erasmus wonders, when they discover just "how greedy and profligate and cruel" Christians are, even while "Christ's teaching" is "so infinitely different from all this?"[50] How incongruous and twisted this is, he muses, when impiety masquerades in "the form of piety" and the ungodly appear "under the cloak of godliness."[51]

But that is precisely what happens, Erasmus complains, when emphasis is placed on words rather than deeds, when priority is given to "external appearance" over "internal disposition, and when "ceremonies" take the place of faith and obedience.[52] "The goal of all of Christ's teaching," Erasmus writes, is "that we ourselves should live our lives in a godly and holy manner," and this mandates, in brief, a life rooted in faith (that "we place all our trust in God") and active in love (which "urges us to do good to all").[53] And yet, Erasmus laments, a greater weight has come to be given to obligatory ceremonies, distinctive dress, and dietary rules—though you will not "find any precept relating to ceremonies" in the "whole New Testament"—and the "duties of love" are subverted to secondary importance.[54] So here, once again, we find Christian life turned upside down, and this state of affairs, Erasmus suggests with pointed criticism, largely stems from degenerate monks

---

50. Erasmus to Paul Volz, CWE 6: 75–76. Erasmus pursues the same line of questioning—profiting from the critical vantage of the alien—in *The Education of a Christian Prince* (*Institutio*), trans. Neil M. Cheshire and Michael J. Heath, CWE 27: 286. There, Erasmus asks, "what do we imagine the Turks and Saracens say about us" when they see Christian princes in endless conflict and war, or that there are fewer "upheavals among the pagans than among those who preach perfect concord according to the doctrine of Christ?" On Erasmus's ironic use of the Turks for critique of Christian corruption, see Michael J. Heath, "Twelfth Annual Bainton Lecture: Erasmus and the Infidel," *Erasmus of Rotterdam Society Yearbook* 16 (1996): 22–23; Norman Housley, *Religious Warfare in Europe, 1400–1536* (Oxford: Oxford University Press, 2002), 137–49; and Terence J. Martin, "The Prospects for Holy War: A Reading of a 'Consultation' from Erasmus," *Erasmus Studies* 36, no. 2 (October 2016), 216.

51. Erasmus, *System of True Theology*, CWE 41: 620, 627.

52. Erasmus, *System of True Theology*, CWE 41: 620. While not condemning ceremonies in principle, Erasmus warns that "nothing is more deadly than counterfeit holiness (*simulata sanctimonia*)," and there is "no mask through which this more deceives than ceremonies" (615).

53. Erasmus, *System of True Theology*, CWE 41: 599.

54. Erasmus, *System of True Theology*, CWE 41: 598–99.

who "think their rule more important than the Gospel" and from self-serving priests who "love to hear themselves called fathers" while converting "the obedience of others into tyranny for themselves."[55] Little wonder, therefore, that ordinary folk would suffer confusion about religious and moral life.[56]

The world of Christian theology likewise has been turned topsy-turvy, Erasmus contends, by that "pharisaical breed" of professional theologians who fancy themselves the "pillars of the Christian religion."[57] Everything in theology has been flipped and distorted, he complains, starting with the simple and accessible eloquence of Christ giving way to the obtuse and impenetrable styles of "recent theology."[58] How "discordant" are the approaches of "those who follow Thomas and Scotus" on "divine things" compared with "the style of the prophets, Christ, and the apostles."[59] And how "flat" they are, indeed, "how frigid, how lifeless" when compared with the works of early Christian theologians who were trained in the liberal arts.[60] The problem, Erasmus declares, is that "the entire discipline" of theology has been swamped with the "subtleties of dialectic" and "Aristotelian philosophy."[61] But how "utterly absurd" ("*vehementer absurdum*"), he insists, to defend dogmas of religion by "the determinations and demonstrations" of philosophers. Doing so adulterates the "philosophy of Christ,"[62] Erasmus insists, by replacing the "oracles of eternal truth" (Erasmus mentions Origen, Basil, Chrysostom, and Jerome as examples) with "the trifling fabrications of men."[63]

What is more, Erasmus suggests, many of the questions addressed are "not really pious to investigate," others are not necessary for salvation, and some are so obscure as to deserve to be doubted, including, interestingly enough, speculating on exactly how to explain anything about the

55. Erasmus to Paul Volz, CWE 6: 86–87. On the degeneration of monasticism, see 86–90.

56. On the "topsy-turvy judgment of the public" (*praeposterum vulgi judicium*) on moral questions, see Erasmus to Paul Volz, CWE 6: 84–86.

57. Erasmus, *System of True Theology*, CWE 41: 713. On Erasmus's views of scholastic theology of his day, see Craig Thompson, CWE 39: 227–31, n. 190.

58. Erasmus to Paul Volz, CWE 6: 74.

59. Erasmus, *System of True Theology*, CWE 41: 514.

60. Erasmus, *System of True Theology*, CWE 41: 507.

61. Erasmus, *System of True Theology*, CWE 41: 699.

62. Erasmus, *System of True Theology*, CWE 41: 515–16.

63. Erasmus, *System of True Theology*, CWE 41: 510.

"ineffable bonding" of the divine and human natures of Christ, or for that matter, "rashly to define anything about the nativity of Christ according to the flesh."[64] It is even more preposterous, Erasmus notes, when theologians twist scripture to fit their "doctrinal formulations," taking "from the sacred books … only those bits that tend to justify their own inclinations."[65] All of this culminates in what is, for Erasmus, the consummate perversion of the philosophy of Christ: that theologians would be so intensely concerned with precise definition of the smallest doctrinal detail, producing countless volumes of competing and conflicting works, while contributing nothing to the "tranquility proper to a Christian" and failing to "teach us how to live" a virtuous life.[66]

All of these inversions and distortions, from the commonplace examples of twisted life to the many cases of treacherous corruption, mean that the social worlds of human life—those three concentric spheres of life described by Erasmus—are seriously disordered and dysfunctional. In short, the designated residents of the respective spheres are shifted to different spheres, and that usually means to a lower sphere for those with power and privilege. As mentioned earlier, for instance, it is likely that princes actually reside in the third sphere, given their self-serving and aggressive character.[67] Then, too, there are monks "who are barely included in the outermost circle," and yet—the one positive shift mentioned by Erasmus—there are "good men" among the laity who "Christ thinks worthy of the first circle."[68] So, in these cases, their social estates, measured by their piety and virtue, are actually reversed, with Erasmus bemoaning the decadence of those who fancy themselves close to Christ, while affirming the inclusion of common folk in the "body of Christ."[69]

Along the same line of thinking, Erasmus adds, how completely

64. Erasmus, *System of True Theology*, CWE 41: 700–701. "It seems not only superfluous," Erasmus adds, "but also dangerous so anxiously to investigate with human argumentation things that belong to matters of faith" (702).

65. Erasmus, *System of True Theology*, CWE 41: 679–80. See also Erasmus to Paul Volz, CWE 6: 78–79, 85. Erasmus readily admits that "nearly every one of the ancients [church fathers] sometimes twist the Scriptures whenever they contend with an adversary," including both Jerome and Ambrose. See Erasmus, *System of True Theology*, CWE 41: 683–90.

66. Erasmus to Paul Volz, CWE 6: 74.

67. Erasmus to Paul Volz, CWE 6: 82.

68. Erasmus to Paul Volz, CWE 6: 83. Given the degeneration of monasticism, Erasmus adds, "there is no question that laymen are preferable" in virtue and are, in fact, "more truly religious" (89–90).

69. Erasmus to Paul Volz, CWE 6: 534; see 81–82.

twisted it is to "misuse the words of Divine Scripture" by wrongly identifying the church with priests and the world with laity.[70] It is simply preposterous, Erasmus declares, when "we place in the world those whom Christ chose out of the world," while elevating priests to the first rank despite their well-known vices.[71] When priests neglect the "welfare of the flock" and cater to the "inclinations of princes," he concludes, then "they are moving on the outside boundary of their circle."[72] The same can be said of popes, Erasmus adds, who certainly are "not moving in the highest part of their circle" when encouraging "those who are slothful" with "pardons and indulgences."[73] The "common aim" of all is Christ, Erasmus reminds his readers, but people have turned away, corrupted by "ambition and greed," adrift in a world where "iniquity" abounds and "charity" grows cold and generally disoriented without anything to give direction or to provide stability.[74] Human life, in sum, is in need of renaissance and reorientation. It is against this dark and dismal background, therefore, that Erasmus sets the image of Christ as the central aim (*scopus*) and measure of Christian life.

"Christ Our Pattern"

"When all is dark, when the world is in tumult and men's opinions differ so widely, where can we take refuge," Erasmus asks, "if not upon the sheet-anchor of the Gospel teaching?"[75] The answer Erasmus gives to

70. Erasmus, *System of True Theology*, CWE 41: 679.

71. Erasmus, *System of True Theology*, CWE 41: 679. See also Erasmus, "The Sileni of Alcibiades," CWE 34: 271, where Erasmus identifies the church with the people and speaks of the bishops as the servants of the people.

72. Erasmus, *System of True Theology*, CWE 41: 534.

73. Erasmus, *System of True Theology*, CWE 41: 535; see 535, n. 237 for references regarding indulgences. What is more, "no one would say that they are engaged in what is peculiar to the heavenly philosophy," with their financial extortions and military ventures (535–36). Erasmus is less critical of popes in the *System of True Theology* than in the letter to Paul Volz, granting that it is "perhaps" impossible that the laws of popes "would correspond in every respect to the precepts of Christ," as "popes are men and prescribe ... what seems helpful for people who are weak." It is inevitable that one may miss "the innocence of Christ" in their "prescriptions" (536). This concession to the humanity of popes, however, harbors a potent criticism, as one cannot expect certitude, much less, infallibility, from such human beings. See 541 for the doubt of Erasmus regarding the notion that the "Roman pontiff ... cannot err whenever he makes a pronouncement on faith or morals."

74. Erasmus to Paul Volz, CWE 6: 78.

75. Erasmus to Paul Volz, CWE 6: 77. On the image of the "sheet-anchor," see Boyle, *Erasmus on Language and Method in Theology*, 59–60, 78.

his own question points to the "heavenly philosophy of Christ"—that integral ethic of godly and virtuous life—conveyed by Jesus, the "master teacher" who both embodies and conveys the ultimate target (*scopus*) for human existence.[76] In a corrupted and disordered world, as Erasmus tells it, Christ represents the goal, and hence also the source, for life that is stable and well-oriented because it is pious and virtuous.

Erasmus finds a scriptural basis for this notion in Philippians 3:14, where Paul declares that he will "press on toward the goal (*scopos*) for the prize of the heavenly call of God in Christ Jesus." In his paraphrase of this passage, Erasmus underscores the dynamic quality of the life that presses on toward Christ as goal. As André Godin puts it, the Pauline scheme adopted by Erasmus fuses the "profound desire" of the one "constantly moving" toward the goal, with the "irresistible appeal" that the goal exerts on the aspirations of the seeker.[77] Much as a racer is spurred on with great effort by the power of the finish line to attract and stimulate the pace, so Christ the *scopus*—at the center of the three circles—draws people toward himself with a kind of final causality that is divine love.[78]

Erasmus also emphasizes that Christ as *scopus* gives unity to Christian life. Of all the things one might pursue in life, Erasmus tells us, one should "attend to this one objective"—"that evangelical goal set before us"—as the primary and exclusive end of all effort and activity. It is exactly this unity that Erasmus stresses in the letter to Paul Volz, when he insists that it "must be impressed upon all men that there is a goal towards which they must strive. And there is only one goal (*scopus*): Christ, and his teaching in all its purity."[79] This "sign set up in advance,"

76. Erasmus, *Paraphrase on Matthew*, CWE 45: 79, 82.

77. André Godin, *Érasme, lecteur d'Origène* (Genève: Librairie Droz, 1982), 151.

78. On Christ as "a source of eternal fire [that] draws the order of priests close to him," and through the clergy, "summon[s] princes, as far as they can to themselves," see Erasmus to Paul Volz, CWE 6: 80. Georges G. Chantraine speaks a bit more broadly of the "image of Christ attracting to him all men through the three circles of his church" (Chantraine, "The *Ratio Verae Theologiae* (1518)," 182). Chantraine, similarly, writes that "Christ is the center of attraction of Christian people," and that is not only for priests and princes but also for the "Christian people" (Chantraine, *"Mystère" et "Philosophie du Christ" selon Érasme*, 124). See also Pierre Mesnard, who speaks of the center as the "principle of love that attracts all to him" ("Un texte important d'Érasme touchant sa 'Philosophie chrétienne,'" 528).

79. Erasmus to Paul Volz, CWE 6: 82. Having "only one master," Erasmus writes in paraphrase of Paul's first letter to the Corinthians, "we have the same doctrines, the same target (*scopus*)"

as Erasmus translates Paul, in turn yields a moral unity of purpose that subordinates other desires to their appropriate but secondary status. "Considering everything else secondary," he adds, "we set for ourselves nothing except the gospel target."[80] Christ as *scopus*, finally, is that mark or sign—akin to a "navigational sighting," as Boyle observes—by which people can take their bearings, measure their progress, and determine the course yet to be completed.[81] When Erasmus speaks of Christ as the center of a disordered and disoriented world, therefore, he refers to that divine sighting—and with that, the "truly salvific and efficacious philosophy" he transmitted—as the spiritual guidance and moral orientation needed to "attain true godliness and true happiness."[82]

Erasmus touches on the function of Christ as *scopus* for Christian life as early as 1503 in the *Handbook of the Christian Soldier*. Echoing Philippians 3:14, at least initially, Erasmus begins the fourth rule with this familiar counsel: "in order that you may press forward towards happiness on a surer course," it is important to "place Christ before you as the only goal (*unicum scopus praefigas*) of your life, and direct to him alone all your pursuits [and] all your endeavours."[83] Here again, Eras-

---

(*Paraphrase on 1 Corinthians*, CWE 43: 34). Then again, in the *System of True Theology*, Erasmus speaks of a "single center, Jesus Christ, towards whose absolutely unstained purity all must strive with all the power each person has" (533).

80. Erasmus, *Paraphrase on Philippians*, CWE 43: 384. On the image of the target as a "unifying principle" for Christian life, see Godin, *Érasme, lecteur d'Origène*, 44. Erasmus translates Philippians 3:14: "*iuxta praefixum signum*" as "according to the sign set up in advance." See *Paraphrase on Philippians*, CWE 43: 384–85, n. 43; *Opera omnia Desiderii Erasmi Roterdami*, VI - 3, ed. Andrew Brown (Amsterdam: Elsivier, 2004), 577, note on Phil 3:14.

81. Boyle, *Erasmus on Language and Method in Theology*, 78. Manfred Hoffmann regards Boyle's rendering of *scopus* as a "navigational sighting" for determining the proper course as "farfetched," insisting instead that "*scopus* is for Erasmus originally a rhetorical term" signifying "the essential point of a case or a question on which the speaker focuses everything" (Hoffmann, *Rhetoric and Theology*, 252, n. 104). Erasmus speaks in such terms when describing how a preacher should relate "everything towards the essential point as though towards a target." Erasmus adds, however, that such a target will assist the speaker in "not stray[ing] from the subject in pointless digressions or wandering in his speech like a madman," thereby playing the exact role Boyle depicts for a "sighting" at sea. See Erasmus, *The Evangelical Preacher* (*Ecclesiastes*)," in *Collected Works of Erasmus: Spiritualia and Pastoralia*, vol. 68, trans. James L. P. Butrica (Toronto: University of Toronto Press, 2015), 581–82. Elsewhere, Erasmus gives support to Boyle's reading by speaking of the pattern of Paul as a "target" (*scopum*) for bishops to keep before their eyes, "like an experienced navigator who, though he may be forced to deviate somewhat from his true course, will never take his eyes from the pole-star." See Erasmus to Philip of Burgundy, letter 1043, CWE 7: 133, lines 59–64.

82. Erasmus, *Paraphrase on Matthew*, CWE 45: 30.

83. Erasmus, *Handbook of the Christian Soldier*, CWE 66: 61. Erasmus echoes Paul's language

mus lays stress on the central points that later will resound in the letter to Paul Volz and the *System of True Theology*: first, that "Christ alone is the sole and highest good," and therefore, second, that Christ should be held up before us as the "sole target" for life's pursuits. One should, in other words, "love nothing, admire nothing, [and] hope for nothing save Christ or because of Christ."[84]

The latter clause, "because of Christ," leaves practical room for the use of the many goods of life, as Augustine would have it, though it also provides a measure for framing their use.[85] So many things in life, after all, are simply neutral—being neither "intrinsically good" nor inherently evil—so that, as Erasmus puts it, any such a thing should not be "sought after on its own account nor made use of to a greater or lesser extent except in so far as it leads to the supreme goal." The goods found in life, consequently, have their legitimate but relative value, and that value is determined, as Erasmus sees it, by their "usefulness or lack of usefulness" in guidance toward Christ. In the words of Erasmus, "as you hasten on a direct course towards the goal of the highest good, whatever you encounter on the way should be rejected or accepted according as it either facilitates or impedes your progress." Christ as *scopus*, therefore, serves as the true measure for the value of worldly "actions and ambitions," and in so doing, it also provides a reliable guide for finding and persisting on the "true path," a sighting for orientation for the one who presses forward in life in search of happiness.[86]

In the midst of this early discussion of Christ as *scopus*, Erasmus pauses to counsel his readers that they are "not to think of 'Christ' as an empty word." This is an unexpected thought, to say the least, and it is not entirely clear what Erasmus has in mind; it seems to refer to the idea that Christ, as a divine reality, may seem to be cut off from actual living. Quite the contrary, Erasmus continues, 'Christ' is rich in content,

---

in a letter to Justus Jonas in which he announces the new edition of the *Handbook of the Christian Soldier* with the letter to "Abbot Volz" as the preface. Despite the "evil report" (of his foes) and the "good report" (from his friends), Erasmus says, he will "fight on with all my might towards the goal of Christ (*Christi scopum*)" (Erasmus to Justus Jonas, letter 876, CWE 6: 145).

84. Erasmus, *Handbook of the Christian Soldier*, CWE 66: 61.

85. See Augustine, *The City of God against the Pagans*, trans. R. W. Dyson (Cambridge: Cambridge University Press, 1998), bk. 19, chap. 10, 930; chap. 13, 938; chap. 14, 938; and chap. 17, 943–45.

86. Erasmus, *Handbook of the Christian Soldier*, CWE 66: 61–65.

as "it stands for charity, simplicity, patience, purity, in brief all that he has taught." Christ, therefore, is identified with gospel virtues, and thus, Erasmus adds, "whoever strives after virtue alone directs his course to Christ."[87] Roughly the same sentiment appears later in the letter to Paul Volz, in which Erasmus refers to "Christ our pattern (*archetypo Christo*)" for the godly life, and he echoes this in the *System of True Theology* when he speaks of "Christ's teaching" as "the example and pattern for all the actions of our lives."[88]

This way of describing Christ—as the pattern for virtuous life— has given rise to a prominent line of interpretation that celebrates the ethical dimension of Erasmus's thinking about Christ, divorced from institutional dogma and severed from ceremonial practice. As P.-B. Pineau writes, for instance, "Erasmian Christianity seems in this way to detach itself from the very person of Christ, and is boiled down to a morality." Of Christ, Pineau declares, his role is principally "moral and exemplary."[89] Along the same lines, but with a richer sense of ethics and drawing from a wider array of Erasmian texts, Renaudet argues that Erasmus promoted a "religion of pure spirit," by which he means a life freed from "rigid dogmas and sterile theologies" and saturated with the "religious and moral teaching of Jesus, where the supreme truth about man and God expresses itself in familiar terms."[90] The "spirit of Erasmian theology," Renaudet says, promotes the "imitation of Christ"—an active life conformed to and transformed by what Erasmus calls the "philosophy of Christ"—and that, we are told, amounts to "a humanist ethic, reviewed and corrected according to the Gospel."[91]

Though these readings fairly reflect an important dimension of Erasmus's thinking, they have met with some determined criticism from more traditionally minded interpreters, in part for downplaying the mystery and transcendence of the person of Christ and in part for overlooking other materials in which Erasmus is more attentive to the doctrines of Catholic orthodoxy.[92] In speaking of Christ as the pattern

87. Erasmus, *Handbook of the Christian Soldier*, CWE 66: 61.

88. Erasmus to Paul Volz, CWE 6: 77; Erasmus, *System of True Theology*, CWE 41: 594–95.

89. P.-B. Pineau, *Érasme: Sa pensée religieuse* (Paris: Les Presses Universitaires de France, 1924), 116–18. See also Febvre, *The Problem of Unbelief in the Sixteenth Century*, 324–25.

90. Renaudet, *Études Érasmiennes*, 174–75.

91. Renaudet, *Études Érasmiennes*, 146–47.

92. See, for instance, Louis Bouyer, *Erasmus and the Humanist Experiment*, trans. Francis X.

for a godly and virtuous life, however, Erasmus is not diminishing the person of Christ, as these critics have suggested, but rather valorizing the ideal life at the center of gospel teaching. If Christ is identified with virtue, after all, such that someone who aspires to virtue can be said to be searching for Christ, this is not reducing Christ to ethical matters but broadening—even potentially universalizing—the power of Christ as *scopus*.

This is surely what Erasmus had in mind in "The Godly Feast," for instance, when he has Eusebius proffer the idea that, while sacred scripture is "the basic authority in everything," he cannot help but think that "some divine power" animated the hearts of pagan authors, so much so, in fact, that "perhaps the spirit of Christ is more widespread than we understand, and the company of saints includes many not in our calendar." With that in mind, Nephalius "can hardly help exclaiming, 'St Socrates, pray for us!'" and Chrysoglottus similarly hopes "that the souls of Virgil and Horace are sanctified."[93] These admirable pagans, in short, appear to have gleaned something of the wisdom of Christ, which would mean, of course, that the guiding and orienting power of Christ as *scopus* functions well beyond the confines of the Christian world.[94] If this is true—and Erasmus carefully and typically hedges his points with qualifications—then the power of Christ as *scopus* is extended beyond the confines of ecclesial Christianity so that it presumably can play the same guiding and attracting role for good people everywhere.

Besides universalizing the range of Christ as *scopus*, however, the

---

Murphy (London: Geoffrey Chapman, 1959), 138–75, who levels an aggressive assault on the work of Renaudet; Hoffmann, "Erasmus and Religious Toleration," 80, 83, where Renaudet is again the likely target; and Spitz, *The Religious Renaissance of the German Humanists*, 226–27.

93. Erasmus, "The Godly Feast," *Collected Works of Erasmus: Colloquies*, vol. 39, trans. Craig R. Thompson (Toronto: University of Toronto Press, 1997), 192–94. On the uses and meaning of these kinds of statements in the writings of Erasmus, see the extended comments of Thompson in CWE 39: 226–27, n. 187, 233–35, n. 215. See also Erasmus, *Explanation of the Apostles' Creed*, CWE 70: 338, where Erasmus imagines that there "may possibly be some land, some islands, or some continents in the universe that have not yet been discovered by sailors or geographers," "whether it be among the Indians, the Phoenicians, the Hyperboreans, or the Africans," "but in which Christian faith may flourish."

94. It may seem anachronistic to suggest that Erasmus was pondering what Catholic theologian Karl Rahner later came to affirm as the salvific "presence of Christ in non-Christian religions," though the idea of the universal presence of Christ is not without currency from the early days of Christian tradition. See Karl Rahner, *Foundations of Christian Faith: An Introduction to the Idea of Christianity*, trans. William V. Dych (New York: Seabury Press, 1978), 148–52, 311–21.

identification of Christ with the virtues he taught also serves to amplify the sense in which Christ as *scopus* is a full and living presence in Christian life. Erasmus goes to great lengths, in the first place, to express just how completely and perfectly Christ embodied the virtues he taught. Unlike other teachers, Erasmus tells us, Christ alone "exemplified completely all that he ever taught."[95] What is "distinctive in him," therefore, is that "his whole life was nothing but a perfect pattern of perfect love, humility, patient endurance, mercy, and gentleness."[96] Magnified as this point is, Erasmus sharpens it yet further, when he claims that "whatever was formerly sought from so many books, from so many holy men, can now be taken compendiously from Christ alone more clearly."[97] Anything but a mere pattern, therefore, and certainly not a simple role model in the ordinary sense of the word, Christ is said to be an entirely unique and full-blooded incarnation of perfect wisdom and virtue.

What is more, Erasmus continues, this personal compendium of wisdom and virtue is fully present in the gospel philosophy recorded in scripture. "He lives even now," Erasmus writes, and "breathes and speaks to us, I might almost say more effectively than when he lived among men."[98] Erasmus hesitates a bit in making this comparison, since he is well aware of the difficulties of interpreting these texts, though he confidently declares that "these books show you the living image of his holy mind and Christ himself" far "more vividly than any little statue" that may decorate a home or church. It is in the books of Christian scriptures, Erasmus argues, that the incarnate word is still heard, not as an abstract lesson but with a "living presence." Indeed, he asserts again, now without

95. Erasmus, *Paraclesis*, CWE 41: 408, 416.
96. Erasmus, "On the Gospel Philosophy," CWE 41: 735.
97. Erasmus, "On the Gospel Philosophy," CWE 41: 735–36.
98. Erasmus, *Paraclesis*, CWE 41: 417. See also Erasmus to Leo X, letter 384, CWE 3: 222. On the "living presence" of Christ in scripture, see Godin, *Érasme, lecteur d'Origène*, 48–49; Renaudet, *Études Érasmiennes*, 136; Boyle, *Erasmus on Language and Method in Theology*, 82–83; and Jacques Étienne, "La mediation des écritures selon Érasme," *Scrinium Erasmianum*, vol. 2: 4–5. Referring to the force of the gospel text as a "living word," Étienne speaks of the gospels in Erasmus as "the sacrament of the divine Word." Erasmus says much the same thing, interestingly enough, of classical authors like Cicero, who by means of their books "live on in such a fashion that they speak to more people and more effectively dead than alive" (Erasmus to William Warham, letter 396, CWE 3: 256). On this interesting, though extraordinary, suggestion, see William Barker, *Erasmus of Rotterdam: The Spirit of a Scholar* (London: Reaktion Books, 2021), 13.

any hesitation, the books of scripture "restore Christ to us so completely and so vividly that you would see him less clearly should you behold him standing before your very eyes."[99]

With these remarkable statements on the living presence of Christ in the written word, Erasmus underscores the degree to which Christ as *scopus* provides a living measure for the transformation of human life in accord with the target virtues proclaimed in the philosophy of Christ. Christ as *scopus*, therefore, as the ultimate target and perfect measure from the living words of the philosophy of Christ, abides in the proclamation that is Christian scriptures, Erasmus tells us, provided, of course, that these texts are interpreted soundly and preached effectively, and also provided that the faithful "bring eyes and ears by which he can be seen and heard."[100] As we will see in the final section of this chapter, however, these are no small conditions; consequently, they constitute formidable tasks for Christian theology and preaching.

Thinking about Christ as the ultimate *scopus* for human life offers some first glimpses of the meaning of redemption in the Christology of Erasmus. As a "teacher of heavenly philosophy," Erasmus writes initially, Christ puts forth "a truly salvific and efficacious philosophy" by which people can "attain godliness and true happiness."[101] When Erasmus speaks of Christ teaching a philosophy, of course, he is not referring to a theory about the world to be considered and debated but a "way of salvation" that is made known through his words and actions.[102] What Christ teaches, in essence, is a new way of being in the world, a new and richer way of living out human life. Indeed, Erasmus says more boldly, Christ actually creates "a new sort of people," where happiness is found not in the things admired by the "common crowd" but in a life of wisdom and virtue.[103] The redemptive function

99. Erasmus, *Paraclesis*, CWE 41: 422. Erasmus earlier used the same language to convey the biblical presence of Christ, noting that "the heavenly Word which once came down to us from the heart of the Father still lives and breathes for us and acts and speaks with more immediate efficacy, in my opinion, than in any other way" (Erasmus to Leo X, letter 384, CWE: 3: 222). Compare with the much later statement that "the gospel account places [Christ] before our eyes, as if in a theatre" (*Explanation of the Apostles' Creed*, CWE 70: 240).

100. Erasmus, *Paraclesis*, CWE 41: 417.

101. Erasmus, *Paraphrase on Matthew*, CWE 45: 83, 30.

102. Erasmus, "On Gospel Philosophy," CWE 41: 730.

103. Erasmus, *System of True Theology*, CWE 41: 517–19.

of Christ, on these terms, inaugurates a transformation of human life, and to this end, Christ's manner of teaching—far from simply teaching about virtue or merely offering lessons—transforms those who absorb his message with a kind of ethical causality. As Erasmus says of the virtues taught by Christ, he "implanted them, instilled them, so imprinted them in the hearts of all by his varied parables that they cannot be erased."[104] So what Erasmus has in mind is a truly unusual and remarkable form of ethical education, one that packs the power to fundamentally change the shape of human existence, directing those who absorb Christ's words to a full and happy existence because it is godly and virtuous.

The transformative force present in the living words of scripture, Erasmus says, prompts, invites, and guides a reversal of the twisted reversals endemic to human life. The twisted and corrupted state of life, as we saw earlier, is the starting point for the Christology of Erasmus, since it is this sorry and sinful state of life that cries out for something better, richer, and fuller. The meaning of "redemption" in any theology, after all, depends upon the condition that stands in need of remediation, whether that means that human life is sick, broken, corrupted, or captive. As we will see in other chapters of this book, Erasmus varies his language to capture some of the complexity and nuance of the human condition. In the present context, however, where Christ is talked of as the unique and universal *scopus* for human life, the condition that requires rectification is one, as we saw earlier, where life is turned upside down and inside out, not just in a ridiculous manner but through the treacherous agency and for the personal advantage of those with some form of power. Human life is twisted and corrupted, in short, where what is valuable and virtuous is shunned and what is worthless and vile is embraced, and the spheres of social life are seriously disordered, as well, leaving their residents religiously and morally disoriented, resulting in habitually inverted piety and twisted moral judgment.

With this condition in mind, the redemptive force of Christ as *scopus*—embodied in the philosophy of Christ—functions as an ideal

---

104. Erasmus, "On Gospel Philosophy," CWE 41: 735. From Christ, Erasmus similarly writes, "we acquire most properly the seeds and elements, as it were, of piety; through him we advance and grow; through him we attain perfection" (736).

point of reference against which to critically expose and measure the treacherous inversions of value infecting human life, and upon that critical challenge, Christ serves as a constructive force in attracting and drawing people toward himself and the life he embodies. As we have seen in this section, Christ as *scopus* constitutes a unique, universally available, and unifying target for a godly and virtuous life, and as such, it offers the possibility for the restoration of rightly ordered life and a redirecting of a misdirected life. In this sense, the redemptive agency of Christ as *scopus* stirs and guides the reversal of the twisted reversals plaguing human existence.

In the letter to Paul Volz, Erasmus augments this account of redemption by broadening his choice of imagery, some of which complements the meaning of salvation embedded in Christ as *scopus* by expanding upon the redemptive agency of Christ, and some of which display Erasmus's taste for greater rhetorical variety to convey the fullness of what is involved. Erasmus writes, to begin with, that what Christ offers above all is "the sheet-anchor of gospel teaching," signifying with that image the stability and security available in the teachings of Christ.[105] If human life is tossed about by the "horrible," "pestilent," and "ruinous" winds of ambition, greed, and love of pleasure, Erasmus writes, then that "truly sacred anchor of gospel teaching" provides an essential recourse for safety and refuge.[106] Continuing with nautical imagery, Erasmus also speaks of Christ as "cynosure"—that pole star by which sailors can take their bearing and find their way safely to their destination—now once again indicating the salvific function of Christ as guiding *scopus*. Other imagery echoes Christ's function as a source of support or stability, though without reference to nautical themes, as when Erasmus speaks of Christ as "pillar" (for support) and "foundation" (signaling stability).[107]

Elsewhere, Erasmus turns to natural elements and processes to depict the redemptive agency of Christ, and though this move may seem unusual, and a bit confusing as well, it helps to fill out with fresh

---

105. Erasmus to Paul Volz, CWE 6: 77. On the "sheet-anchor" as the "large anchor employed in emergency," see Boyle, *Erasmus on Language and Method in Theology*, 59–60.

106. Erasmus, "To the Pious Reader," CWE 45: 25–27; *System of True Theology*, CWE 41: 537. On Christ and stormy waters, see also *Paraphrase on Matthew*, CWE 45: 228–30.

107. Erasmus, *System of True Theology*, CWE 41: 537.

imagery the kind of restorative causality stemming from Christ at the center of the circles of human society. Though we are lost in a corrupted world, Erasmus writes, "Christ left us some live coals of his teaching, some living rivulets from the springs of his mind." Here we find, curiously enough, Erasmus speaking of Christ's work as both burning coal and living water, as we are encouraged to "blow up those coals of his into flame" and to "follow up those rivulets until we find the living water that springs up to life eternal." What Erasmus gets from these mixed metaphors is variety of expression: as he puts it, "Christ is our Rock, and this rock has in it the seeds of heavenly fire and veins of living water." To be sure, this is a strange thing to say—what a strange rock that would be—but it allows Erasmus to amplify the senses in which Christ offers human beings something rich and remedial, in response to which, Erasmus advises, we are to ceaselessly "mine the rich lodes of Christ," "rekindle" the "fire of charity" from "the flint," and never "cease to dig" for the "pure source" of divine waters.[108] In any case, and however it is expressed, Erasmus wishes to underscore and amplify the redemptive power of Christ, now augmenting the idea of Christ as *scopus* with natural imagery to express the causal agency by which Christ transforms life.

"Teach Us How to Live"

The philosophy of Christ—for Erasmus, that living, breathing, and speaking embodiment of Christ found in scriptural texts—indicates a "way of life rather than a form of argument. It is inspiration rather than erudition. It is transformation rather than argumentation." Far from being an academic exercise, therefore, what Christ puts forth primarily signals a "rebirth," meaning a "restoration of nature, which was created whole and sound."[109] It teaches an ideal way of being before God and living with others, as we saw in the previous section, that packs the

---

108. Erasmus to Paul Volz, CWE 6: 78. Working broadly with the correspondence of Erasmus, Chantraine argues that these assorted metaphors for the redemptive power of Christ are conceived by Erasmus with a systematic coherence designed to depict the outward movement of divine love intent on bringing others from the exterior to the center of the circles of life (Chantraine, *"Mystere" et "Philosophie du Christ,"* 114–23).

109. Erasmus, *Paraclesis,* CWE 41: 415.

power to redirect, guide, and attract human life, and, what is more, Erasmus emphasizes, it is "simple and available to everyone."[110] This salvific force, in other words, is bestowed on everyone through the words of Christ embodied in scripture, and yet, *with these rigorous conditions,* that this heavenly message must be recovered through sound interpretation and conveyed effectively to listeners who themselves must be capable of hearing and embracing its force. These are huge conditions, to say the least, as this places enormous responsibility on human intelligence and communication. Though Erasmus is never explicit in saying this, the redemptive words of Christ remain ink on paper without sound interpretation, effective preaching, and the capacity for hearing; which is why he places so much emphasis on the quality of theological interpretation, the skills of effective preaching, and the readiness of the faithful for transformation.

"The chief goal of theologians," as we heard earlier in the introduction, "is to explain prudently divine literature."[111] Toward this end, therefore, Erasmus goes to great length to explain the requirements and the procedures for quality interpretation of biblical texts, including, in particular, facility with biblical languages, knowledge of all sorts of natural and cultural things, and careful attention to the differences in persons and times portrayed in the texts.[112] Equipped with these tools, Erasmus continues, theologians are to "give an account of the faith and not of frivolous questions," which means, in essence, that they are "to discourse seriously and effectually on godliness" rather than squander their time on "certain tenets" that are not necessary for the "integrity of the Christian religion."[113] What Erasmus has in mind, clearly enough, is that theologians are to focus squarely on the godly and virtuous life at the heart of the philosophy of Christ, as their primary task is to draw

---

110. Erasmus, *Paraclesis*, CWE 41: 409.

111. Erasmus, *System of True Theology*, CWE 41: 517.

112. Erasmus, *System of True Theology*, CWE 41: 496–507. Erasmus here echoes Augustine's insistence on the value of competency in languages, broad knowledge of natural things and cultural signs, and close familiarity with disciplines of reason. See Augustine, *On Christian Doctrine*, trans. D. W. Robertson, Jr. (Indianapolis, IN: Bobbs-Merrill, 1958), 43–78.

113. Erasmus, *System of True Theology*, CWE 41: 517, 539–45. Erasmus speaks, for instance, of the "new and increasingly impudent dogmas" preached by theologians. Even the "unlettered" could not "stomach" what they said of "indulgences," he adds (Erasmus to Albert of Brandenburg, letter 1033, CWE 7: 112).

forth this divine target and measure from biblical texts and make it clear and compelling for readers and listeners.[114] All other considerations—those arcane speculations on doctrinal matters far and away beyond human understanding, but also the dubious inventions designed for profit or fancy—are simply frivolous and irrelevant to the theologian's work.

What is more, as we also heard in the introduction, in speaking about this ideal life, theologians and preachers are "to set our souls aflame for heavenly things."[115] They are, in other words, to allow the message to "penetrate into the very affections," such that they themselves and their readers and listeners will yearn for something richer and nobler and thereby become a "different person."[116] Such an expectation may startle academic theologians of our day, since many consider their discipline to be largely an intellectual enterprise, even if it is packed with religious and ethical implications. For Erasmus, however, the "first and only goal" of theology is to be "transformed into what you are learning."[117] In this sense, once again, theologians and preachers play a significant role in the redemptive work of Christ, since the publicity and the efficacy of the philosophy of Christ depends very much on their services.[118]

The aim and measure of good theology, in sum, is to "teach us how to live," and the constant and reliable measure of good living, as we saw in the previous section, is fidelity to "Christ our pattern."[119] Here, in a nutshell, we find the religious and ethical motivations of Erasmus for his critical and interpretive work on Christian scriptures, as the labor of theologians and preachers should be intent on transmitting the

114. See Erasmus to Paul Volz, CWE 6: 77.

115. Erasmus, *System of True Theology*, CWE 41: 517.

116. Erasmus, *System of True Theology*, CWE 41: 495. On the "affections of the heart" in the transformation of the one who imitates Christ, see Brian Cummings, "Erasmus, Sacred Literature, and Literary Theory," *Erasmus on Literature*, 57–62.

117. Erasmus, *System of True Theology*, CWE 41: 494. On the almost mystical sense of transformation, see Renaudet, *Études Érasmiennes*, 176.

118. As Boyle puts it, for Erasmus, the theologian's task is "the faithful transmission of creative Speech for the rebirth of civilization" (Boyle, *Erasmus on Language and Method in Theology*, 126). It is the task of theologians and preachers, she adds, to promote "the same transforming movement [as Christ] of human elements from a lower to a higher, purer region of the estate." Thus, they must speak with a "fiery tongue" in order "to seize, to transform, to convert" (113–14).

119. Erasmus to Paul Volz, CWE 6: 74, 77.

transformational message of Christ as *scopus*. In this sense, therefore, the heart of the theology of Erasmus is Christocentric,[120] and its agenda and value are consistently ethical in the very richest sense of that word.[121] However, because the ultimate pattern for good living is embodied in scriptural texts, these materials must be read well and conveyed persuasively if they are to have any transforming effect in life. Toward that end, Erasmus tells us, Christ also serves as the hermeneutical *scopus* for theologians and the rhetorical *scopus* for preachers.[122] Discerning and eliciting Christ in biblical texts, in other words, is the goal, guide, and measure for good theology, and projecting and persuading others to embrace the possibility of a godly and virtuous life is the shared goal and measure of theology and preaching.

Too many readings of biblical texts are willfully twisted, Erasmus complains, where someone takes "from the sacred books … only those bits that tend to justify their own inclinations," though such twisted manipulations of meaning are untwisted and set straight, we are told, if the interpretation is made to "conform to the life of Christ."[123] "The goal of all Christ's teachings," Erasmus writes emphatically, "is that we ourselves should live our lives in a godly and holy manner"; to that end, he advises, theologians are to read scripture in a manner that centers on precisely the "example and pattern" displayed by Christ.[124] Above all, that means highlighting the life of faith and love—the transforming ethical message of Christ—as opposed to those who insist upon

120. On the "christocentrism of Erasmus," see André Godin, *Érasme, lecteur d'Origène*, 49. See also John W. O'Malley, "Introduction," CWE 66: xxii; Barker, *Erasmus of Rotterdam*, 51.

121. By "ethics," I refer not merely to moral codes for governing behavior but to the principles that shape and direct a person's way of being in the world with others. Renaudet speaks of ethics in this sense when accenting the ethical meaning of the Christology of Erasmus. In his words, the "spirit of Erasmian theology" centers on the active practice of the "imitation of Christ," now rejuvenated and modernized with a focus on the virtues of Christ (Renaudet, *Études Érasmiennes*, 146–48).

122. On the life of Christ as model for the preparation of the preacher, see *System of True Theology*, CWE 41: 579–81. In imitation of the apostles, Erasmus advises, preachers are to neither provoke nor reproach, but to "invite to Christ, to newness of life, to salvation," and thus "accommodate themselves to all, as far as permitted, to entice more people to Christ" (593).

123. Erasmus, *System of True Theology*, CWE 41: 680. As Erasmus writes elsewhere, one is "not to twist Scripture to your own desires and resolutions. Rather temper your opinions and way of life to its rule" (Erasmus, *Paraphrase on Matthew*, CWE 45: 15).

124. Erasmus, *System of True Theology*, CWE 41: 594–95. Indeed, Erasmus writes, "no teaching is more effective than Christ's own life" (583).

ceremonies and regulations on food and dress as the core of religious life, and in stark contrast to so much of "scholastic theology" with its "superfluous" doctrinal inventions and prattling "exhibitionism" in public disputations.[125] The goal and measure of sound theology and good preaching is to facilitate the effective presence of Christ's healing restoration and orientation for life, a charge that is, for Erasmus, very much reliant on human intelligence and fervor, and hence, a task that inevitably remains as fragile and incomplete as it is vital and important.

125. On the duties of love in contrast with precepts on ceremonies, food, and clothing, see Erasmus, *System of True Theology*, 597–99; for a sharp criticism of the "superfluous" concerns and empty "word battles" of scholastic theologians, see *System of True Theology*, CWE 41: 699–713. For a more nuanced challenge to theologians of his day, see Erasmus, *Paraclesis*, CWE 41: 412–13, 420–21.

CHAPTER 2

Christ as Silenus

What a wild and daring suggestion it is when Erasmus wonders in print whether Christ was not "a marvellous Silenus," though he adds cautiously, "if one may be allowed to use such language of Him."[1] There is reason to be cautious, to be sure, as the classical accounts of the legendary Silenus are filled with material that—at first glance—must be unseemly, if not simply scandalous, as a portrayal of Christ. Said to be "the son of a nymph, less illustrious than a god, but superior to a man,"[2] the earliest images of Silenus are raw and racy: a sixth-century BCE Laconian cup with inscription, for instance, shows him with an "erect penis … equine tail and ears, and a shaggy head," while being offered wine by an apparent captor.[3] More often, however, we later find Silenus

1. Erasmus, "The Sileni of Alcibiades," adage III. iii. 1, CWE 34: 264.

2. Aelian, *Historical Miscellany*, trans. N. G. Wilson (Cambridge, MA: Harvard University Press, 1997), 3.18. Erasmus was familiar with many (but not all) of the classical sources listed in these pages, either directly or through collections. On the vast range of sources used in the *Adages*, see John N. Grant, "Erasmus' Adages," in *Collected Works of Erasmus: Prolegomena to the Adages*, vol. 30, trans. John N. Grant (Toronto: University of Toronto Press, 2017), 38–77; Margaret Mann Phillips, *The "Adages" of Erasmus: A Study with Translations* (Cambridge: Cambridge University Press, 1964), 393–403. On his long career as a translator of classical literature, see Erika Rummel, *Erasmus as a Translator of the Classics* (Toronto: University of Toronto Press, 1985).

3. *Encyclopedia of Comparative Iconography*, vol. 1, ed. Helene E. Roberts (Chicago: Fitzroy Dearborn, 1998), 264.

depicted as a plump old man with a great fondness for wine, often perched upon a donkey. As the "personal attendant and caretaker" of Dionysus and, in fact, his "adviser and instructor in the most excellent pursuits,"[4] Silenus is a regular in the entourage of Bacchus, and thus he enjoys the festive company of satyrs (famously "given to love"),[5] Sileni (apparently the sons of Silenus),[6] and maenads (women bacchants who share "the satyr's love of wine and sexual abandon").[7] Given this company, Silenus bears a reputation for sexual intensity—Ovid calls him an "insatiate lecher" who burns for the nymphs[8]—though he more often is cast as an unbridled lush and a wild dancer.[9]

These two attributes come together in the spectacular dance contest between Maron and Silenus for the prize golden "bowl of Bacchos" filled with "the oldest wine and the finest stuff." After Maron dances, Silenus takes his turn—"over the floor he twirled dancing round and round, upright upon his heels, and spun in circling sweep." With acrobatic moves and artful contortions, he moved restlessly "round and round in his wild caperings." But then "his knees failed him" and he "slipt to the ground and rolled over on his back," at which point he suddenly became a river, with his body "flowing with natural ripples all

4. Diodorus of Sicily, *Library of History*, vol. 2, trans. C. H. Oldfather (Cambridge, MA: Harvard University Press, 1961), 4.4.3–4.

5. Philostratus (the Elder), *Imagines*, trans. Arthur Fairbanks (Cambridge, MA: Harvard University Press, 1960), 1.22.25.

6. Nonnus, *Dionysiaca*, vol. 1, trans. W. H. D. Rouse (Cambridge, MA: Harvard University Press, 1956), 1.14.96–104. See also Nonnus, *Dionysiaca*, vol. 1, 13.43–45, where Nonnus speaks of Silenus and "his phalanx of Seilenoi"; vol. 2, 29.258, which refers to "three sons of shaggy haired Seilonos."

7. *Encyclopedia of Comparative Iconography*, vol. 1, 265.

8. Ovid, *Fasti*, trans. James George Frazer (Cambridge, MA: Harvard University Press, 1931), 1.393ff. In the *Metamorphoses*, Ovid similarly speaks of the tricks played by the satyrs and "that old rake, Silenus" to win the love of Pomono. See Ovid, *Metamorphoses*, trans. A. D. Melville (Oxford: Oxford University Press, 1986), 14.635–39.

9. See Pausanias, *Descriptions of Greece*, trans. W. H. S. Jones (Cambridge, MA: Harvard University Press, 1960), "Laconia" 25, 3.159, for a reference to Silenus as "the dancer." For his part, Lucian refers to Silenus having "danced the can-can [*cordaka* or cordax]" in "Icaromenippus, or the Sky-Man," in *Lucian*, vol. 2, trans. A. M. Harmon (Cambridge, MA: Harvard University Press, 1988), 27, 315. The *cordax* was an acrobatic and provocative dance associated with Greek drama. See Bernard Gredley, "Dance and Greek Drama," in *Themes in Drama*, vol. 3, *Drama, Dance, and Music*, ed. James Redmond (Cambridge: Cambridge University Press, 1981), 25–30. For his part, Erasmus has Silenus "obscenely dancing the *cordax* along with Polyphemus stamping his ratatan, and the nymphs dancing a barefoot ballet" (Erasmus, *Praise of Folly*, CWE 27: 94); see n. 131 in *Collected Works of Erasmus: Literary and Educational Writings*, vol. 28, ed. A. H. T. Levi (Toronto: University of Toronto Press, 1986), 471.

over." In honor of his efforts, Maron hurls the cup of wine into the river, "where it intoxicated the currents of the dancing river." "Tippler never satisfied," Maron cries out to Silenus, accept "the [lesser] silver bowl of Bacchos," as now you can "really make the grapes to grow."[10]

Silenus truly is a strange figure—merry and joyous, yet equally grotesque, as conveyed in Aimé-Jules Dalou's "The Triumph of Silenus" prominently displayed in the Luxembourg gardens of Paris;[11] languid and pathetic because he is completely sotted and bloated, something well captured in "The Drunkenness of Silenus" by Jean-François Legendre-Héral;[12] and yet comical because quite laughable, something at play in his pitiful plight after being stung by the bees whose honey he craved, an occasion where even Bacchus laughs at poor old Silenus.[13] The most intriguing thing about Silenus, however, is the wisdom he carefully conceals beneath this odd exterior. Who would ever dream, in fact, that such a rough, untamed, and lascivious character would be the bearer of profound wisdom on the meaning of life? But that is exactly what the shepherd boys of Virgil's sixth *Eclogue* discover when they come across "Silenus lying asleep in a cave, his veins swollen, as ever, with the wine of yesterday." Casting him into "fetters made from his own garlands," they force him to sing his songs of wisdom—the first about the creation of the world and the second concerning the gods.[14] Another account—this one in a fragment from Aristotle's *Eudemus* quoted in Plutarch's "A Letter to Apollonius"—tells of Midas pressing the captive Silenus to tell him "what is the best thing for mankind and what is the most preferable of all things." Forced to speak, Silenus proclaims that it is "utterly impossible" for human beings to "obtain the best thing of all," since what is best for them is "not to be born," and "the second best is, after being born, to die as quickly as possible."[15] Behind his ragged exterior, therefore, Silenus

10. See Nonnus, *Dionysiaca*, vol. 2, 19.136–345. Ovid also speaks of Silenus as "that old drunkard, whose staff supports his tottering steps, who sits so insecure upon his sagging ass" (*Metamorphoses*, 4.25–27).

11. Jules Dalou, "Le triomphe de Silène," (1885), Jardin de Luxembourg, Paris. See http://archeologue.over-blog.com/article-34827367.html.

12. Jean-François Legendre-Héral, "L'Ivresse de Silène," (1831), Musée des beaux arts de Lyon. Compare Antoine Laurent Dantan, "L'Ivresse de Silène" (marble, 1831), Louvre, Paris.

13. See Ovid, *Fasti*, 3.735ff.

14. *Virgil*, trans. H. Rushton Fairclough (Cambridge, MA: Harvard University Press, 1942), vol. 1, eclogue 6.13–17.

15. Plutarch, "A Letter to Apollonius," in *Plutarch's Moralia*, trans. Frank Cole Babbitt

turns out to be a figure capable of revealing profound, even if truly disquieting, wisdom.

Intriguing as the character of Silenus is, especially in the contrast of an unseemly exterior matched with surprising interior wisdom, it is little wonder that some would be aghast at the suggestion by Erasmus that Christ himself was a "marvellous Silenus." Certainly the mothers of Paris were shocked when Dalou's "The Triumph of Silenus" was placed in the Luxembourg gardens—indeed, they hoped and pleaded that the prefect would "remove these horrors from a garden frequented above all by children."[16] With equal reason, Erasmus must have understood that theologians of his day would not take kindly to comparing Christ with Silenus, which is why he defends the comparison in a letter to Maarten Van Dorp in 1515, even though Dorp himself had not explicitly mentioned this comparison. What Dorp challenges—aside from the "astringent pleasantries" aimed at theologians in *The Praise of Folly*, and besides what he takes to be the threat to the "integrity of Scriptures" stemming from Erasmus's focus on "Greek copies" of New Testament books—is the ascription of "foolishness" to Christ.[17]

The lengthy response of Erasmus, written, in fact, as a reply to those unnamed detractors who Erasmus is convinced are behind Dorp's challenge, aims to deflect the broader objections, but he also takes time to defend his use of daring Christological terms. If someone were to speak of Christ as a "drunkard" or a "heretic," for instance, it surely would sound offensive to pious sorts. But if it was explained, Erasmus

---

(Cambridge, MA: Harvard University Press, 1962), 115 D-E. On the importance of this dark piece of proverbial wisdom for the genesis of "Apollonian illusion," see Friedrich Nietzsche, *The Birth of Tragedy and The Genealogy of Morals*, trans. Francis Golffing (Garden City, NY: Doubleday and Company, 1956), 28–32. Werner Jaeger argues, however, that in this early dialogue, Aristotle cleverly "introduces into Silenus' words the fundamental conception of Plato's metaphysics." As Jaeger puts it, "in the absolute Good no earthly activity can share. [Thus] we must get back as quickly as possible out of the realm of Becoming and Imperfection into the unseen world of Being." See Werner Jaeger, *Aristotle: Fundamentals of the History of His Development*, trans. Richard Robinson, 2nd ed. (London: Oxford University Press, 1962), 48–49. On this claim in ancient literature, see Erasmus, "Not to be born is best," adage II. iii. 48, CWE 33: 160–62.

16. See Antoinette Le Normand, "Le triomphe de Silène de Jules Dalou," *La revue du Louvre et des musées de France* 30, no. 3 (1980): 166–67.

17. Maarten Van Dorp to Erasmus, letter 304, CWE 3: 17–23. Dorp is referring to the late section of the *Praise of Folly* where Erasmus has Folly say that "Christ too, though he was the wisdom of the Father, was made something of a fool himself in order to help the folly of mankind" (Erasmus, *Praise of Folly*, CWE 27: 148).

continues, that Christ "was intoxicated with the new wine of charity" and that "he brought a new kind of teaching" to his day, then "who could be offended," he asks, when the apparently scandalous term is rendered in a sound and rich sense? When Erasmus calls "Christ himself a sort of Silenus," similarly, he insists that a "pious and fair-minded man" will "find the allegory acceptable," though he knows that a "prejudiced interpreter" will find such words "intolerable."[18] The key to understanding this language correctly, as we will see in this chapter, is to persistently peer behind the veil of appearances, for as Erasmus tells us, only things that are of lesser or little value are "most fully open to perception," while "what is excellent is least conspicuous," so that "the real truth of [such] things is always most profoundly concealed."[19]

My aim in this chapter is to examine this ironic pattern of appearance and reality at work in the traditions about Silenus, focusing initially on its presence throughout the work of Erasmus but addressing especially its pivotal role in his Christological reflections. By calling this pattern "ironic," I mean to highlight the unexpected and often surprising manner by which what appears and what is hidden are inverted or reversed. Irony, in this sense, is both a state of affairs, as things are topsy-turvy or turned round-about and a way of seeing through the world's inversions while absorbing the surprising disclosures about matters of great importance to our lives.[20] This is the Silenus factor, if I may so label it, and it is at once a positive principle of revelation—the

18. Erasmus to Maarten Van Dorp, letter 337, CWE 3: 128–29. Erasmus later defends this comparison of Christ with "those Silenus figures spoken of by Alcibiades" in responding to criticisms from an unnamed critic, the identity of whom remains to be discovered (Erasmus to Maarten Lips, letter 843, CWE 6: 10, articles 21–22). That the critic was not Edward Lee, as some scholars have surmised, see Erika Rummel, *Erasmus and His Catholic Critics, 1515–1522*, vol. 1 (Nieuwkoop: De Graaf Publishers, 1989), 115–20; Rummel, "Introduction," CWE 72: xxi–xxii. In this letter, Erasmus clearly is irritated and testy, though he again defends himself by noting that "the same view is held in different language by every orthodox theologian." On the use of "base imagery" for Christ—robber, adulterer, thief, for instance—"meant to prod the soul to reach beyond the humble, earthen reality towards the heavenly," see Walter M. Gordon, *Humanist Play and Belief: The Seriocomic Art of Desiderius Erasmus* (Toronto: University of Toronto Press, 1990), 205–10.

19. Erasmus, "Sileni of Alcibiades," CWE 34: 266–67.

20. On irony, see Jonathan Lear, *A Case for Irony* (Cambridge, MA: Harvard University Press, 2011), 9–39, 119; on irony in the work of Erasmus, see Terence J. Martin, *Truth and Irony: Philosophical Meditations on Erasmus* (Washington, DC: The Catholic University of America Press, 2015), 223–37.

truly valuable and ultimately rich things of life often come to us in un-assuming, unimpressive, or possibly even repulsive, guises. But it is also a counsel for interpretation—one ought not to be taken in by appearances but rather should probe carefully and remain open to the startling discoveries resting beneath the surface.

Assorted examples of this factor are retrieved by Erasmus from classical tradition and duly recorded in the *Adages*, and, as we will see shortly, most of these repeat the pattern without an explicit reference to Silenus. It is important to note, in this regard, just how widely Erasmus applies the Silenus factor, and though many of his examples are negative cases—what he calls the "Silenus inside-out," those scoundrels who appear noble and impressive, but in fact are vicious and worthless[21]—there are abundant and significant cases of authentic Sileni that Erasmus puts to the service of ethical discovery. In a word, these Sileni show us a good deal about who we are and who we might be. In this regard, the figure of Socrates is an important and prominent example; as will be evident in due course, it is from the description of Socrates as a Silenus that Erasmus moves to speak of Christ in roughly the same richly ironic terms. An interesting and little-studied instance of this approach appears in the *Homily on the Child Jesus*, a short piece written by Erasmus in 1510 to endorse and embody the "spirit of devout learning" central to the educational program of a new school founded by John Colet.[22] As we will see in the final section of this chapter, this brief work is a simple but vivid exercise in ironic Christology.

"Though in Rustic Dress"

Early in "The Godly Feast," when Eusebius is giving his guests a tour of his gardens, Timothy is surprised to be told that the small channel carrying water and the pillars supporting the building are in fact not marble—though they appear that way—but cement with a "white coating." "An artistic deception," he exclaims, "I'd have sworn they were marble." "Let that be a warning to you," Eusebius says with an echo

---

21. Erasmus, "The Sileni of Alcibiades," CWE 34: 265.
22. Erasmus, *Homily on the Child Jesus*, CWE 29: 52–70.

of Seneca but on behalf of Erasmus, "appearances often deceive."[23] In this case, of course, we have the negative version of the Silenus factor, as something plain and ordinary is made to look fine and precious with a bit of paint, though the dissemblance is entirely innocent in that the change is motivated purely by taste and frugality. Often enough, however, things fall in line entirely with the pattern of Silenus, where something simple, small, or ordinary harbors something unexpectedly rich, large, or exceptional. A "thin drizzle," for example, may give birth "to a rainstorm," Erasmus notes, so "it behooves us to be watchful about small things," lest we be caught by an unwelcome surprise.[24] Roughly the same point becomes a political warning to the mighty, when Erasmus advises the young prince Charles that a prince should never "look down on anybody," even "the humblest of the common people," for "no one is so weak but that he may at some time be a friend who can help you," and then again, that "not even the most powerful prince can afford to provoke or disregard even the humblest enemy," as "often those who can do no harm physically can do so by guile."[25]

Speaking again with reference to natural things, Erasmus observes that the "flowers and leaves" of a tree "appeal to every eye," as "their great bulk is inescapable." The "seed," on the other hand, "what a tiny thing it is, how well concealed, how far from appealing to the eye, how little given to self-advertizement," and yet—as time and growth make

---

23. Erasmus, "The Godly Feast," CWE 39: 178–79. See Seneca, "De beneficiis," bk. 4. 34. 1, *Seneca: Moral Essays*, vol. 3, trans. John W. Basore (Cambridge, MA: Harvard University Press, 1935), 275.

24. Erasmus, "A tiny rain gives birth to a rainstorm," adage I. iii. 2, CWE 31: 236.

25. See Erasmus, *Education of a Christian Prince*, CWE 27: 211–12. That insignificant people may turn out to be helpful allies is conveyed through Aesop's fables of the lion saved by the mouse and the dove shielded by the ant. On the potential for devastating assaults arising from even the smallest of enemy, see Erasmus, "A dung-beetle hunting an eagle," adage III. vii. 1, CWE 35: 200–201, where Erasmus describes the lowly dung-beetle, a disgusting and despised little creature who lives in piles of dung, as a Silenus, who, if opened up, will be seen to have "so many uncommon gifts that, all things well considered, he will almost prefer to be a scarab rather than an eagle." Those gifts include "heroic mental powers" and "amazing energy in attack," qualities the dung beetle deploys in his clandestine attacks against the mighty eagle as revenge for the eagle's savage assault on the defenseless hare. On "A dung-beetle hunting an eagle," see Denis L. Drysdall, "Erasmus on Tyranny and Terrorism: *Scarabaeus aquilam quaerit* and the *Institutio principis christiani*," *Erasmus of Rotterdam Society Yearbook* 29 (2009), 89–102; Terence J. Martin, "The Intractable Dialectic of Tyranny and Terror: A Reading of an Erasmian Adage," *Soundings: An Interdisciplinary Journal* 98, no. 2 (May, 2015), 163–91. On the same points, see also Erasmus, "Even ant and gnat have their gall," adage II. v. 31, CWE 33: 256.

clear—it "contains the vital force of the whole."[26] So many of the treasures of nature, "gold and jewels," for instance, are hidden "in the deepest bowels of the earth," so here again one should not rest content with what sits on the surface and is visible to the eye alone, or things of the greatest value will be missed. Even with respect to the "physical makeup" of the human body, Erasmus continues, "that which makes the largest contribution to life [the breath] is by no means visible," so here once again we are told, one must look beneath the material appearance (the "phlegm and blood") that is "fully open to perception," in order to glean the "principle" of human activity, which is itself "far removed from perception."[27] These very ordinary cases give ample expression of the Silenus factor, so that as a good rule to follow, Erasmus advises, one ought not overlook small and obvious things, as they well may harbor something of great power and hidden value.

All too often, just the opposite is true: what is seen may appear great or splendid, when in fact the reality is small or ordinary. Some such cases are harmless enough, as when someone makes "an elephant out of a fly," for instance, by using "big words about little things" to exaggerate their importance.[28] One might, in another situation, "wear an expression of cheerfulness and good will when one's real feelings are very different," though that dissimulation is innocent enough, even if the appearances have been made to cover over a sour state of mind.[29] More seriously, however, are those times and places where someone manipulates their appearance to embellish the ordinary or to camouflage the sordid quality of their life. Here again, we meet the Sileni turned inside out (*praeposterum silenum*), the same treacherous characters who, as

26. Erasmus, "The Sileni of Alcibiades," CWE 34: 266. Erasmus describes the excellence of measured speech, in a similar manner, as "talk that contains a great concentration of meaning in a few words is like a dry seed, tiny and insignificant to look at; you bury it in the earth, and it sends forth a magnificent tree" (*The Tongue (Lingua)*, trans. Elaine Fantham, CWE 29: 289).

27. Erasmus, "The Sileni of Alcibiades," CWE 34: 266.

28. Erasmus, "You make of a fly an elephant," adage I. ix. 69, CWE 32: 219. See also "Wondrous words about a lentil," adage IV. v. 30, CWE 36: 162.

29. Erasmus, "Put on an appearance," adage V. i. 53, CWE 36: 571. Then again, Erasmus notes, one might legitimately "feign" happiness when actually sad—"making a lie of joy," so to speak—though he insists that this is lying only in an "extended sense." See Erasmus, *The Apology of Desiderius Erasmus against the Patchworks of Calumnious Complaints by Alberto Pio, Former Prince of Carpi*, trans. Daniel Sheerin, *Collected Works of Erasmus: Controversies*, vol. 84 (Toronto: University of Toronto Press, 2005), 352–53.

we saw in the first chapter, turn the world upside down for their own benefit and to the detriment of others.

They manage this, Erasmus repeatedly observes, by "practicing an imposture and deceiving by skillful pretense,"[30] effectively advertising their wisdom with an august exterior and skillfully broadcasting their holiness by means of the trappings of piety.[31] Everything is reversed in these cases, Erasmus complains, though if one were to peel away the facade and peak behind the show, it turns out that what was offered with fanfare "vanishes in no time," as there was nothing there but "false ostentation" and mere "display";[32] or that what seemed like a great achievement, ends up as nothing but "a label, or mere expectation";[33] or again, that the one who "displays kindness in word," never manages to "back them up with deeds";[34] or worse yet, that those who lay the greatest claim to piety are, in fact, "steeped in vices neither to be tolerated nor mentioned."[35]

Erasmus has an especially keen eye for spotting the devious machinations of these Sileni turned inside out, and he warns his readers to beware their false appearances. At the same time, however, he consistently emphasizes the positive revelatory value of those things and persons where wisdom and virtue are manifest through the most ordinary and unassuming appearances. Here, we have the principle of revelation characteristic of authentic Sileni—those signal moments of unconcealment that emerge unexpectedly from beneath quiet, plain, and quite unremarkable sources—and such cases are to be found, Erasmus observes, throughout human life. The unexpected quality finds expression, for example, where someone discovers—"in the midst of their perplexities"—"some unhoped-for person who comes to their rescue

30. Erasmus, "To play a trick," adage I. v. 52, CWE 31: 427.

31. See Erasmus, "Bearded, therefore wise," adage I. ii. 95, CWE 31: 223; "A whited wall," adage III. vi. 23, CWE 35: 136–37. Even in "religious foundations" where "life is lived willingly according to the rule of religion," Erasmus writes, "if you were to open the Silenus and look inside, ... it is amazing how little sincerity you would discover" (Erasmus to Lambertus Grunnius, letter 447, CWE 4: 25). On the "inverted holiness" attributed to the Pharisees, see *Paraphrase on Matthew*, CWE 45: 235.

32. Erasmus, "To sell smoke," adage I. iii. 41, CWE 31: 270–72.

33. Erasmus, "Shadow instead of substance," adage III. ii. 98, CWE 34: 261.

34. Erasmus, "A friend in word," adage III. iii. 57, CWE 34: 300.

35. Erasmus, "What is one's own is beautiful," adage I. ii. 15, CWE 31: 160–61.

and solves the problem for them."[36] Though just another person, the source of "sudden and unlooked-for salvation" might seem to be something of a god, a notion that Erasmus insists is neither "immoral nor unfitting" among Christians, provided it is taken as a figurative manner of speaking.[37]

Then again, Erasmus notes, no one should "despise salutary advice [just] because it comes from a humble source," for as he reminds us, "it sometimes happens that a man of lowly position and of no account, or of very little education, says something that even persons in high places should not despise."[38] In keeping with the Silenus factor, therefore, Erasmus insists once again that one "should not look down on anyone simply because he lacks experience or cannot express himself," since the most common of persons—"though in rustic dress" and though speaking in "an uneducated style"—may in fact "possess the truth."[39] It behooves everyone to pay close attention not just to what is regal or triumphant but to what appears unremarkable or even unappealing, and with that, to carefully peer behind the lowly facade in order to glean the unexpected wisdom that may be on offer.

"Like Those Images of Silenus"

A good way into the *Praise of Folly*, as the goddess Folly is running through all the great achievements of humankind for which a debt is owed to her, she pauses to offer an overview of "human affairs"—one she suspects will be too philosophical for many—that appeals to the "figures of Silenus described by Alcibiades" in Plato's *Symposium*.[40] These small wood carvings of Silenus—we might call them "figurines"—have "two completely opposite faces," as Folly puts it, one

36. Erasmus, "Unexpected appearance of a god," adage I. i. 68, CWE 31: 110–12.

37. Erasmus, "Man is a god to man," adage I. i. 69, CWE 31: 112–15.

38. Erasmus, "Even a gardener oft speaks to the point," adage I. vi. 1, CWE 32: 3–4. "Even a foolish man oft speaks to the point," Erasmus adds, and even a "silly man, either by accident or inadvertently, says something excellent and very much to the point."

39. Erasmus, "Do not despise a country speaker," adage II. vi. 45, CWE 33: 314.

40. Erasmus, *Praise of Folly*, CWE 27: 102. The reference is to Plato's *Symposium*, where Alcibiades compares Socrates to "the Sileni that sit in the statue-makers' shops" (215a–b). See *The Symposium and The Phaedrus: Plato's Erotic Dialogues*, trans. William S. Cobb (Albany: State University of New York Press, 1993), 52.

external and one on the inside, but they are completely opposite in character. So, for instance, "what is death at first sight … is life if you look within," and the same applies, she continues, for "beauty and ugliness, richness and poverty, obscurity and fame, learning and ignorance, strength and weakness, the noble and the baseborn, happy and sad, good and bad fortune, friend and foe, healthy and harmful." With each of these oppositions, in fact, "you'll find everything suddenly reversed if you open the Silenus," rather than relying on the first impression of what appeared on the outside.

In this context, Erasmus allows Folly to proceed in very general terms, such that "the whole life of man" is said to be a "sort of play," where the actors wear masks to portray a certain character, so that, she continues, if some maniac were to leap onto the stage and try to "take the masks off the actors," he would "spoil the whole play and deserve to be stoned."[41] Though Folly makes an interesting point—life is like a play and it requires masks to work—she fails to make any distinction between the different types of Sileni, and that distinction, as we have seen, makes all the difference in the world for Erasmus. It is Erasmus, after all, who plays that maniac when he proceeds satirically, again and again, to expose the twisted reversals of appearance and reality practiced by the Sileni turned inside out.[42] But of equal importance, and central to the concerns of this chapter, it is Erasmus as well who invites and encourages us to look closely at the authentic Silenus figures, those ordinary or even repulsive persons and things that, if opened up, reveal something extraordinary or fine. It is this latter move on the part of Erasmus—the constructive side of his work, in this respect—that proves so essential for his Christology.

Erasmus finds an ample supply of authentic examples in the "succession of Sileni" found in historical persons over time. In this regard, as Bietenholz aptly puts it, Erasmus may be called "the historian of the

---

41. Erasmus, *Praise of Folly*, CWE 27: 102–3.

42. Consider, for instance, the long satirical section of the *Praise of Folly*, in which Erasmus lets Folly deride the treacherous deceit of a host of professional fools. See Erasmus, *Praise of Folly*, CWE 27: 120–141. Interestingly, Erasmus credits Luther with helping to expose these twisted Sileni in the world of religion. It is thanks to Luther, he writes, that "the world has learnt to recognize those Sileni turned inside out, who seemed to be pillars of religion, who were thought to know everything, and were a very long way from both" (Erasmus to Vincentius Theoderici, CWE 8: 194).

Sileni," as he scans classical philosophy, biblical traditions, and a small bit of later history for places where profound ethical wisdom is to be found emerging from behind the most ordinary and undistinguished exteriors.[43] Erasmus begins with the ancient Cynics, hardly one of the more attractive lots among early Greek philosophers, with a quick glance at Antisthenes, who was famous for living with nothing but "his staff, his satchel and his cloak," though, as Erasmus interjects, in his remarkable freedom he "surpassed the wealth of the greatest kings."[44] Then there is Diogenes, the so-called "dog" philosopher, who is admired by Alexander the Great for his "nobility of mind," despite his famously blunt manner and shameless behavior.[45] "A Silenus of this sort was Epictetus," Erasmus adds, "a slave and penniless and lame," it is said, "but at the same time … dear to the heavenly powers in a way that only integrity of life combined with wisdom can secure."[46]

Turning to biblical tradition, Erasmus cites the Hebrew prophets, by no means an impressive cast with their lives "among wild beasts, their food the poorest greenstuff and their garments the skins of sheeps and goats," though the "inside of these Sileni" proves to be of incomparable wealth. "A Silenus of this sort was John the Baptist," Erasmus continues, "who was clothed in camelhair with a leather girdle round his loins, yet far surpassed kings with their purple and their precious stones, and who lived on locusts and yet outdid the luxury of all the princes." "Sileni of this sort were the Apostles," as well—on the outside "poor,

43. Bietenholz, *History and Biography*, 40, 48.

44. Erasmus, "The Sileni of Alcibiades," CWE 34: 263. On Antisthenes and his philosophy, see *Diogenes Laertius: Lives and Opinions of Eminent Philosophers* (London: William Heinemann, 1925), 6.1.1–19. Many of these accounts are collected with brief commentary in Erasmus, *Apophthegmata*, trans. Betty I. Knott and Elaine Fantham, in *Collected Works of Erasmus*, vol. 38 (Toronto: University of Toronto Press, 2014), 775–90.

45. On the encounter between Diogenes and Alexander cited by Erasmus, see *Diogenes Laertius*, 6.2.32. "Being asked what he had done to be called a hound, he said, 'I fawn on those who give me anything, I yelp at those who refuse, and I set my teeth in rascals'" (60). Erasmus recounts the same tale in his collection of the sayings of Diogenes in *Apophthegmata*, CWE 37: 280–81. For the fuller collection on Diogenes, see *Apophthegmata*, 271–334. Horace later advances the canine epithet when referring to himself as the faithful, tough, courageous Molossian (mastif), facing any danger, "whatever wild beast is ahead," in contrast to the "turntail mongrel," who "picks on innocent strangers" and "sniffs at the food that's flung" to it. See *The Odes and Epodes of Horace*, trans. Joseph P. Clancy (Chicago: University of Chicago Press, 1960), epode 6, 211. See Kirk Freudenburg, *The Walking Muse: Horace on the Theory of Satire* (Princeton, NJ: Princeton University Press, 1993), 78–80.

46. Erasmus, "The Sileni of Alcibiades," CWE 34: 264.

unkempt, illiterate, of humble birth, weak and rejected"—but if one were to "open the Silenus," Erasmus suggests, they will be found to have more miraculous powers than any tyrant might enjoy. When it comes to postbiblical Sileni, Erasmus regrettably fails to follow through with his survey, referring only generally to "early bishops" and mentioning only one rather obscure example by name (Saint Martin of Tours),[47] though presumably the Silenus pattern is clear enough for readers to continue with their own historical discernment. Exactly that happens, ironically enough, when the French philologist Guillaume Budé observes in a letter of May 19, 1517, that Erasmus himself is very much a Silenus, quite ordinary in "general appearance and bearing" but "upon closer examination ... a "Mercury in speech, a Genius in intelligence, Venus and the Graces in the charm of his style, carrying the goddess of wisdom herself in his head as Jupiter once carried Pallas."[48] So it would seem that the historian of the Sileni is a bit of a Silenus himself, at least for those able to peer behind the outer persona.

Erasmus, of course, was a man of literature far more than he was an historian. In this regard, firstly, he was rightfully famous for the vast collection of proverbs drawn from the literature of antiquity and presented to readers with comments of varying length and depth.[49] For the purposes of this chapter, it is important to note that these sources prove interesting to Erasmus, not just because they contain examples of Sileni but because they themselves are Sileni in structure and presentation. As Erasmus observes in the introductory essay to the *Adages*, for example, proverbs are nuggets of wisdom, often "useful in the conduct of life," though they are clothed in "some kind of metaphorical disguise." On the outside, they sometimes "give pleasure by their figurative

---

47. Erasmus, "The Sileni of Alcibiades," CWE 34: 265.

48. Guillaume Budé to Cuthbert Tunstall, letter 583, CWE 4: 359–60. Budé attributes the suggestion to an unnamed "man in authority." Also noting that—to some extent—Erasmus himself plays the part of Silenus, see Ernst Benz, "Christus und die Silene des Alcibiades," in *Christliche Wirklichkeitsschau*, Aus der Welt Der Religion, ed. Heinrich Frick (Berlin: Alfred Töpelmann, 1940), 21–22.

49. On the production and development of the Adages, see Grant, "Erasmus' Adages," CWE 30: 1–38; Phillips, *The 'Adages' of Erasmus*, 3–165. The first volume of proverbs (*Adagiorum collectanea*) appeared in 1500 and included roughly eight hundred citations, though the vastly expanded *Adagiorum Chiliades* of 1508 contained about 3,260 proverbs, followed by a series of significant editions in 1515, 1528, and 1533, culminating in a final edition of 1536, in which the tally had grown to 4,151 proverbs.

colouring," though just as often they provoke thought by way of the "novelty of an expression," or they "wake interest" with a "touch of the enigmatic." Puzzling though their phrasing may be, therefore, proverbs invite readers to look "closely and deeply," since beneath the surface— we are assured—are the "sparks of ancient philosophy."[50] Thus, Erasmus says by way of an example, "the whole of human happiness" is to be found beneath the surface of the brief saying of Pythagoras—that "between friends all is common"—which no doubt is why Erasmus places it at the head of all his adages; so too, Erasmus adds as a biblical example, "an ocean of philosophy, or rather of theology," is contained within Christ's simple "precept of love," something ready for discovery for the one who manages to open up "this tiny proverb."[51] "If the adage seems a tiny thing," Erasmus advises with an eye on these proverbial gems, "we must remember that it has to be estimated not by its size but by its value."[52] And that value—as is true of all authentic Sileni—must be sought diligently beneath the surface of the words.

Exactly this, Erasmus continues, is true for scriptures. When addressing the story of how David "changed his face before Abimelech" (1 Sam 21:12–15)," for instance, Erasmus notes that a literal reading remains a "closed Silenus," where we taste "only the husks of the grain." But, he adds, if we "open the Silenus," then our "minds will be delighted with spiritual dainties and fed with health-giving food," and, too, they "will be astonished in the contemplation of divine wisdom."[53] In this textual Silenus, therefore, as with many others of the same kind, readers must peel away the literal surface to glean something of the hidden

50. Erasmus, "Introduction," CWE 31: 3–28. On the *Adages* as a "moral guide to *felicitas*," and thus, as providing an "implied ethic"—at once "fragmentary, indirect, and non-systematic," yet prompting and inviting for those who savor them—see William Barker, "Implied Ethics in the *Adagia* of Erasmus: An Index of *Felicitas*," *Renaissance and Reformation; Renaissance et Réforme* 30: 1 (2006), 87–102. As Barker notes, the "truth function is not dominant" in the adage, though like all good Sileni, the truth they harbor is "plural, shifting, a chameleon figure that suddenly emerges out of obscurity, and then just as suddenly disappears."

51. On the saying of Pythagoras, see Erasmus, "Between friends all is common," adage I. i. 1, CWE 31: 29–30; on the proverb of Christ on love, see Erasmus, "Introduction," CWE 31: 15.

52. Erasmus, "Introduction," CWE 31: 13–14. "In the domain of literature," Erasmus adds, "it is sometimes the smallest things which have the greatest intellectual value."

53. Erasmus, *An Exposition of Psalm 33*, trans. Emily Kearns, CWE 64: 278–79. Compare Erasmus, *Enchiridion*, CWE 66: 32: "If one touches only the surface or the husk, so to speak, of Scripture, what is harder or more unpleasant to the touch?" But "search out the spiritual meaning, and you will find nothing more sweet or succulent."

and richer meaning. Making this interpretive move, one should note, is the first step in allegorical readings of scripture, by which the reader of scriptural Sileni must "search beneath the surface" of the words to glean the "spiritual sense."[54]

Consider, Erasmus suggests, some of the many Sileni of Hebrew scriptures, those passages about "the formation of the figure of Adam from moist clay and the breathing into it of a soul, the creation of Eve from his rib, the prohibition to eat of the tree, the beguiling serpent, God strolling in the breeze, the angel placed at the gate of paradise … to prevent their return into the garden"—"in a word, the whole story of creation." "If in all of this you were not to search beneath the surface," Erasmus asks, then how would such tales be any richer than ancient poetic fables?[55] Recall so many other passages—that of Lot's incest, David's adultery, or Hosea's marriage to a prostitute—surely these are scandalous stories if taken at face value, Erasmus grants, but "under these wrappings, in heaven's name," he exclaims, "how splendid is the wisdom that lies hidden." It is very much the same, he continues, with the parables in the Gospels: if judged by their "outward shell," surely, they would be thought "by everyone to be the work of an ignoramus." But "crack the nutshell," Erasmus counters, "and of course you will find that hidden wisdom which is truly divine."[56] Such texts and many more like them, Erasmus argues, are exactly "like those images of Silenus mentioned by Alcibiades" in Plato's *Symposium*, in that they "enclose unadulterated divinity under a lowly and ludicrous external appearance."[57]

Silenus of old was a joyously dissolute figure, and thus hardly someone the world would find impressive or worthy of respect, but take a closer look, Erasmus advises, or crack the nut, as he likes to say, and

---

54. Erasmus, *Handbook of the Christian Soldier*, CWE 66: 68–69. On the interpretive "drive towards interiority," see Boyle, *Erasmus on Language and Method in Theology*, 116.

55. Erasmus, *Handbook of the Christian Soldier*, CWE 66: 68.

56. Erasmus, "The Sileni of Alcibiades," CWE 34: 267.

57. Erasmus, *An Exposition of Psalm 33*, CWE 64: 67–68. When reading scriptures, Erasmus observes, the person must proceed "soberly," "eagerly," "attentively," and "assiduously," for these books truly are Sileni. Indeed, he writes, readers "will find in that very simple and unpolished writing the unspeakable design of the heavenly wisdom. He will see in that foolishness of God (if one may speak thus), at first glance lowly and contemptible, something that far surpasses all human wisdom, however lofty and wonderful that may be" ("To the Pious Reader," CWE 45: 15–16).

one just might discover a font of uncommon wisdom. This, in sum, is the Silenus factor at work, and, as we have seen, this pattern pervades the thinking of Erasmus. It is, as Erasmus tells us, "the nature of things really worth having"—their excellence is deliberately buried or hidden. In a word, as Erasmus puts it, "they wear what is most contemptible at first glance on the surface, concealing their treasure with a kind of worthless outward shell and not showing it to uninitiated eyes."[58] That their concealment is in some manner intentional is something Erasmus similarly attributes to Christ, as well, "as it seems to have been his policy," Erasmus writes, "to hide his deepest mysteries in the very commonest things of daily life."[59]

Saying this gives an ironic twist to the traditional notion of divine incarnation—to which we will return in later chapters—since embodied revelation winds up being strangely tied together with deliberate concealment. The lowly human life, in other words, is both the vehicle for divine manifestation and a common cover meant to conceal what is excellent and fine. This means that the outer appearance has an important role in three respects: first, as the venue for revelation; second, as a simple and unpretentious cover for what is ultimate and divine; and third, as an invitation and enticement to look beneath and beyond the surface to discern the treasure hidden within. With respect to textual Sileni, for example, the literal sense is "only rubble," Erasmus declares, but more importantly, it is "rubble that carries the august weight of the whole marvellous edifice."[60] This means that the plain words are the carriers of the precious wisdom hidden in the simple adage or the obscure parable, something that is revealed only to the one who manages to "ignore the letter and look to the mystery."[61] That requires a readiness to tend carefully to what is small, ordinary, laughable, ineffectual, repulsive, or even grotesque, as such apparently worthless appearances just may—though this is never assured[62]—reveal something of great

58. Erasmus, "The Sileni of Alcibiades," CWE 34: 264.

59. Erasmus, "Transgress not salt and trencher," adage I. vi. 10, CWE 32: 10.

60. Erasmus, "To the Reader," letter 373, CWE 3: 201–2.

61. Erasmus, *Handbook of the Christian Soldier*, CWE 66: 67.

62. In Erasmus, "A Fish Diet," in *Collected Works of Erasmus: Colloquies*, vol. 40, trans. Craig R. Thompson (Toronto: University of Toronto Press, 1997), 707–8, we find the Butcher (*Lanio*) telling the Fishmonger (*Salsamentarius*) of a drunken group of people he witnessed on Palm Sunday in a nearby village. Some were staggering about and others repeatedly falling, while "one

value to the one who manages to open the Silenus and peer within. Doing this, however, is neither common nor so easy, as it mandates unusual patience and attentive regard for things normally overlooked as worthless or shunned as despicable. Precisely this is the imperative at work in Erasmus's comparison of Christ and Silenus.

"Was Not He Too a Marvellous Silenus?"

It is Plato who has the drunken Alcibiades compare Socrates with "the Sileni that sit in the statue-makers shops, the ones artisans make that hold shepherds pipes or flutes, which when pulled apart are found to have statues of gods inside" (215b). What a "humorous surprise" it is, Erasmus comments, when what looked to be "a caricature of a hideous flute-player" suddenly is shown to be a god when opened to view. The pattern for these carvings, he rightly notes, draws from "the well-known comic figure of Silenus, Bacchus' tutor and court buffoon of the gods of poetry." The comparison, then, is complete—for Plato and for Erasmus—in that the figure of Socrates is very much like "Sileni of this kind," and hence also like Silenus himself, "because like them he was very different on close inspection from what he seemed in his outward bearing and appearance."[63]

The classical sources do not paint a pretty picture of Socrates's persona. Alcibiades, for one, compares his "outer form" to the satyr Marsyas, signaling thereby not only his ability to "bewitch human beings" but also his bestial visage.[64] As Erasmus notes, other classical sources are

---

old fellow, playing the part of Silenus, was carried aloft on their shoulders, in the position corpses are sometimes borne—feet first—except that he was carried head down to prevent his choking with vomit, as would have happened had he had his head up. He was vomiting wretchedly on the legs and heals of the hindmost carriers. There wasn't a sober man among the bearers." An all too vivid depiction, something akin to the "Bacchanal with Silenus"—first of Andrea Mantegna, then by Albrecht Dürer—there is no indication that Erasmus thought that this drunken character was anything but a repulsive old lush. For an almost identical account, see Erasmus to Udalricus Zazius, letter 1353, CWE 9: 446–47. See also www.albrechtdurer.org/bacchanal-with-silenus.

63. Erasmus, "The Sileni of Alcibiades," CWE 34: 262. On Socrates as a philosophical Silenus in Plato and Erasmus, see Benz, "Christus und die Silene des Alcibiades," 2–8, 14–15.

64. *The Symposium and The Phaedrus: Plato's Erotic Dialogues*, 215b. See also *Symposium*, 216d. As Philostratus puts it, the satyrs are pictured as "hardy, hot-blooded beings, with prominent ears, lean about the loins, altogether mischievous, and having the tail of horses." See Philostratus (the Elder), *Imagines*, 1.22.326. One should add that they usually have stubby and upturned noses; they are often naked with erect phalluses; and they regularly are on the hunt for

more pointed in their depiction—Athenaeus, for instance, records that the young Critobulus mocked Socrates as "old and ugly," while also calling him "far more hideous than the Sileni."[65] "With his peasant face, glaring like a bull, and his snub nose always sniffling," Erasmus adds, "he might have been taken for some blockheaded country bumpkin."[66] His manner of speaking was also plain and homely—nothing with which to be impressed—"for his talk was all of carters and cobblers, of fullers and smiths, and it was from them, as a rule, that he derived the analogies which he used to press home his point."[67] No wonder he was "laughed out of court," Erasmus adds, as he was "clearly unfitted" for the "duties of public life." What is more, his "unbroken flow of humour gave him the air of a buffoon," so it is understandable that he would not be taken seriously. All in all, therefore, the world could hardly be expected to celebrate such a man, though what makes Socrates so unusual, is that, unlike renowned sophists like Gorgias, he also did not celebrate himself but freely and frankly acknowledged his own ignorance.[68]

---

sexual pleasure. As Nonnus comments, moreover, they are "hares in the battlefield, lions outside, [and] clever dancers who know better than all the world how to ladle strong drink from the mixing bowl." See Nonnus, *Dionysiaca*, 14.105ff.

65. Erasmus, "The Sileni of Alcibiades," CWE 34: 262. For the comments of Critobulus, a young follower of Socrates and reportedly one of those offering to pay the fine for the offence of Socrates, see *The Deipnosophists. Or Banquet of the Learned Athenaeus*, trans. C.D. Yonge (London: Henry G. Bohn, 1854), 5, 300. See also Xenophon, "Symposium," in *Xenophon: Anabasis, Books IV-VII and Symposium and Apology*, trans. O.J. Todd (London: William Heinemann, 1932), 4.19.421. On the traditions regarding the physical portrayal of Socrates, see Allessandro Stavru, "Socrates' Physiognomy: Plato and Xenophon in Comparison," in *Plato and Xenophon: Comparative Studies*, ed. Gabriel Danzig, David Johnson, and Donald Morrison (Leiden: Brill, 2018), 208–51.

66. Erasmus, "The Sileni of Alcibiades," CWE 34: 262–63.

67. Erasmus, "The Sileni of Alcibiades," CWE 34: 262. Alcibiades makes the same points in Plato's *Symposium* (221d 221c) when he says that the "arguments" of Socrates are "most like those Sileni that can be opened up." At first glance, they appear "quite ridiculous," as they are "covered over on the outside with words and phrases that are like the hide of an outrageous Satyr, for he talks about donkeys and pack-asses, about black-smiths, cobblers, and tanners"—always in the most common and coarse terms—"so that an inexperienced and ignorant person would take everything he says as a joke."

68. Erasmus, "The Sileni of Alcibiades," CWE 34: 263. With the reference to Gorgias's claim to be able to answer any question, Erasmus draws on Plato's *Gorgias* 447d–48a. See *The Collected Dialogues of Plato*, ed. Edith Hamilton and Huntington Cairns (Princeton, NJ: Princeton University Press, 1961), 231. For Socrates's famous acknowledgment of his own ignorance, see Plato's *Apology* 21d, *The Collected Dialogues of Plato*, 8. It should be noted, however, that Plato's Alcibiades also adds many "astonishing things" to his description of Socrates, and these serve not so much to accent the plain or worthless appearance of Socrates but to strongly hint at something

And yet, Erasmus says with a quick turn of course, "had you opened this absurd (*ridiculum*) Silenus," then you would have discovered "a divine being rather than a man, a great and lofty spirit worthy of a true philosopher; and, in fact, one who despised all the things" most people spend their whole lives seeking. Unlike other people, moreover, here was "a man above resenting any injury" inflicted on him, and here, too, was someone over whose judgments "fortune had no power."[69] What a remarkable man this was, Erasmus insists in chorus with Alcibiades. Indeed, the latter says, when Socrates is "serious and opens up," what "glorious figures" appear within, at once "divine, golden, splendid, and amazing."[70] So remarkable and so unique, Erasmus continues the panegyric, Socrates "despised even death, of which all men are afraid," though if one only glanced at his public appearance, one would think there was nothing at all special about him.

How wrong that would be, however, as this astonishing man stands the world's judgments on their head, we are told. Compared with those "professional wits," after all, who think they know everything and are paid well accordingly, the one "who knew nothing" and knew that he knew nothing, was "judged [by the oracle] to know more than those who boasted there was nothing they did not know."[71] So this man who looked for all the world to be so plain, in fact unappealing, and frankly irritating, turns out to be—if seen within, for who he truly was—an utterly unique individual, amazingly free from the common avocations and passions of humanity; the wisest of the wise, because he was resolutely modest in what he claimed to know; and perhaps even divine, both in his personal transcendence and in the often unsettling lessons he was capable of revealing. Indeed, as Alcibiades plainly discovered,

____

exceptional about him—for instance, that he was immune from sexual seduction; that he outlasts everyone in drink, though "nobody has ever seen Socrates drunk"; that during a "terrible frost," he "walked around barefoot on the snow and ice"; that he was fearless in battle, having "actually saved" Alcibiades; and, finally, that he stood motionless while "thinking about something" for an entire day and night. See *The Symposium and The Phaedrus: Plato's Erotic Dialogues*, 217e–21d. With these accounts of such unusual traits, Plato entices readers to look beneath the common and hapless persona of the public Socrates, though, of these, Erasmus mentions only the first, that he was far "removed from [amorous] emotions" (Erasmus, "The Sileni of Alcibiades," CWE 34: 263).

69. Erasmus, "The Sileni of Alcibiades," CWE 34: 263.

70. *The Symposium and The Phaedrus: Plato's Erotic Dialogues*, 217a.

71. Erasmus, "The Sileni of Alcibiades," CWE 34: 263.

this strange man possessed the disquieting power to make people question the very way they have been living.[72] What we have in Socrates, therefore, is the paradigmatic example of the Silenus factor in classical philosophy; in this regard, as we now will see, he represents a stepping stone for Erasmus to think about Christ in much the same dialectical and ironic terms.[73]

"And what of Christ," Erasmus asks? "Was not he too a marvelous Silenus?"[74] The response of Erasmus, of course, is that Christ is very much a Silenus, so much so, in fact, that he insists that anyone who is proud to call themselves a Christian must certainly strive to imitate this Silenus "to the utmost of their power." To speak of Christ as Silenus, consequently, is not only "allowed" but is important, helpful, and even necessary for gleaning something of the ironic pattern of divine revelation in Christ, and with that, as well, it is required for reproducing his wisdom and virtue in the manner in which life is lived.[75] In "The Sileni of Alcibiades," Erasmus does not go into detail on this point, though it is not so difficult to surmise what he has in mind, based on other things he regularly says. The key is to be found in the rhetorical principle of accommodation, whereby a good and effective speaker will adjust and vary the language and delivery to fit the circumstances and the audience, ideally such that the message is conveyed by media that condescend to the specific capacities of listeners and thus allow the message to be compelling and fruitful.[76]

72. Consider, for instance, the sense of shame Alcibiades felt when confronted with Socrates's questions. Though Alcibiades had relied on his power and good looks to define the value of his life, the words of Socrates made it seem that he ought not to live as he had, so much so, in fact, that Alcibiades would "forcibly stop up" his ear and "run away" when spotting Socrates. See *The Symposium and The Phaedrus: Plato's Erotic Dialogues*, 215d–16c.

73. See Lynda Gregorian Christian, "The Figure of Socrates in Erasmus' Work," *Sixteenth Century Journal* 3, no. 2 (October 1972): 1–10.

74. Erasmus, "The Sileni of Alcibiades," CWE 34: 264.

75. On Christ as Silenus, see Benz, "Christus und die Silene des Alcibiades," 16–18; Van Herwaarden, *Between Saint James and Erasmus*, 584.

76. Thus, Quintilian writes, "the all-important gift for an orator is a wise adjustability since he is called upon to meet the most varied emergencies." "In speaking," in other words, "there are certain things which have to be concealed, either because they ought not to be disclosed or because they cannot be expressed as they deserve." See Quintilian, *Institutio oratoria*, trans. H. E. Butler (Cambridge, MA: Harvard University Press, 1933), 2.13.2–14. Erasmus similarly accents the importance of variation and adaptability in the writing of letters. See Erasmus, *On the Writing of Letters* (*De conscribendis epistolis*), trans. Charles Fantazzi, *Collected Works of Erasmus: Literary and Educational Writings*, vol. 25, ed. J. K. Sowards (Toronto: University of Toronto Press, 1985), 19.

Exactly this principle is at work throughout the theology of Erasmus, and it serves to explain how Christ and his message are truly Sileni. In God's accommodating revelation in Christ, Erasmus tells us, "divine wisdom speaks to us in baby-talk and like a loving mother accommodates its words to our state of infancy."[77] So, too, Erasmus continues, Christ "adapted himself to those he was eager to attract: he became a human being to save human beings; he associated on familiar terms with sinners to restore sinners to health; [and] to entice the Jews he was circumcised, was purified, he observed the sabbath, was baptized, [and] fasted."[78] Then again, Erasmus tells us, "Christ would frequently accommodate himself to the frailties of the disciples ... with the hope nevertheless that they would progress."[79] And, in fact, he adds, Christ's very message—the philosophy of Christ conveyed in Scripture and ideally brought to life in effective preaching—"accommodates itself equally to all," variously adjusting itself to the needs of different people.[80]

The principle of accommodation, therefore, rests at the heart of the Christology of Erasmus. As we saw in the first chapter, this principle underscores that Christ as the *scopus* of life is available for everyone, no matter how simple or lacking in education, while in the present context, it shows how every feature of Erasmus's thinking about Christ involves a certain concealment, whether that be a shift in appearance or an adjustment in wording, meant as a concession to people's needs and limitations. As with other Sileni, however, what conceals also invites and entices, precisely because, like a proverb or a parable, the way that Christ appears and the medium of his message are both simple and familiar, and yet puzzling and intriguing.

Look first, Erasmus invites us, at "the outside surface of this Silenus." Judging by "ordinary standards," he continues, "what could be humbler or more worthy of disdain?" Much like Silenus himself,

---

So, too, Erasmus observes that "it is the mark of a good teacher to lower himself to the capacity of those whom he is instructing" (*Paraphrase on Matthew*, CWE 45: 77).

77. Erasmus, *Handbook of the Christian Soldier*, CWE 66: 35.

78. Erasmus, *System of True Theology*, CWE 41: 570. That "Christ himself conducted himself in different ways toward different people," see Erasmus, *System of True Theology*, CWE 41: 595.

79. Erasmus, *System of True Theology*, CWE 41: 535, 623.

80. Erasmus, *System of True Theology*, CWE 41: 409. See Boyle, *Erasmus on Language and Method in Theology*, 122.

therefore, there is nothing in Christ that is grand or regal; in fact, there is much that might be disparaged or shunned. Who would ever think—we must ask, as we did for Silenus and many did with Socrates—that someone like this would be the bearer of divine gifts? Described in the words of Erasmus, he had

> parents of modest means and lowly station, and a humble home; poor Himself and with few and poor disciples, recruited not from nobleman's palaces or the chief sects of the Pharisees or the lecture-rooms of philosophers, but from the publican's office and the nets of fisherman. And then His way of life: what a stranger He was to all physical comforts as He pursued through hunger and weariness, through insults and mockery the way that led to the cross![81]

What an unlikely candidate for divine revelation, or so one would think, if one thought as most people do—those called "the worldly man" by Erasmus—by chiefly adhering to what is "immediately presented to the eye."[82]

And who, for that matter, would ever dream of turning to such a figure as a source of wisdom? Who would take his life as a goal (*scopus*) to be pursued? He seems, in fact, to be a failure from start to finish. While it is true that he is not depicted as being ugly like a satyr (as Socrates was), and though he also is not described as a lascivious drunk (as apparently fit Silenus), Christ is portrayed in terms that are lowly and weak. As the passage just quoted makes clear, his origins were modest rather than privileged; his adherents were drawn from among those generally shunned by proper society, and his life was anything but comfortable or regal. Like Socrates, moreover, his teachings were couched in terms that were frankly pedestrian and often puzzling. As with any Silenus, therefore, what appeared on the surface did not portend anything remarkable.

At this point, Erasmus would normally call attention to the pivot from the exterior to the interior, and he would do so by way of an exhortation to open the Silenus or crack the nutshell. In this case, however, he hesitates a bit and backs into the main point, since it is for Christ and not for us to reveal what lies within him. "If one has the good fortune

81. Erasmus, "The Sileni of Alcibiades," CWE 34: 264.
82. Erasmus, "The Sileni of Alcibiades," CWE 34: 268–69.

to have a nearer view of this Silenus," Erasmus writes, if one were to have the opportunity to see him "open"—which means, in short, if "He shows Himself in His mercy to anyone," having "washed clean" the eyes of someone's soul—then, we are told, "in heaven's name what a treasure you will find."

> In that cheap setting what a pearl, in that lowliness what grandeur, in that poverty what riches, in that weakness what unimaginable valour, in that disgrace what glory, in all those labours what perfect refreshment, and in that bitter death, in short, a never-failing spring of immortality![83]

The Silenus factor, therefore, persists in Christ, though admittedly there is no need to ply him with wine or take him captive in order to hear his wisdom. It is Christ, we are told, who "shows Himself in His mercy to anyone," and what marvelous treasures are to be found therein.

What life and what wisdom are at hand when he allows himself to be seen and heard, by which, Erasmus means, the philosophy of Christ discussed in the previous chapter. For "this above all was the philosophy of His choice," that "one and only way to achieve the end," which is "true felicity," the very goal (*scopus*), Erasmus notes, that everyone seeks in one way or another.[84] At once unique in its difference from the "reasoning of the world," and yet also universal in its range of invitation, the philosophy of Christ—that integral ethic of godly and virtuous life—turns out to be a perfect and exemplary Silenus.[85] Indeed, Erasmus writes in his paraphrase of *Matthew*, what was at first "contemptible in appearance and lowly … would gradually grow strong by the force of truth until it occupied the whole earth and occupied every class of people."[86]

In comparing Christ with Silenus, Erasmus knows full well that he is saying something that at first glance may seem disturbing to pious

83. Erasmus, "The Sileni of Alcibiades," CWE 34: 264.

84. Erasmus, "The Sileni of Alcibiades," CWE 34: 265. On the philosophy of Christ in "The Sileni of Alcibiades," see Margaret Mann Phillips, "La 'Philosophia Christi' reflétée dan les 'Adages' d'Érasme," in *Courants religieux et humanisme à la fin du XVe et au début du XVIe siècle* (Paris: Universitaires de France, 1959), 53–71.

85. Erasmus, *System of True Theology*, CWE 41: 417.

86. Erasmus, *Paraphrase on Matthew*, CWE 45: 213. See also "The Sileni of Alcibiades," CWE 34: 265.

ears, and yet, as we have seen, he knows equally well that a fair-minded reader, or at least one with the patience and persistence to look beneath the lowly and disconcerting appearances, will discover a surprising and ultimately transforming message. Such is Erasmus's contribution to the traditional doctrine of incarnation in Christ, though now rendered with a deeply ironic twist that seeks to amplify the revelatory power embodied in Christ. Divine revelation, in short, occurs through the concealing veil of surprisingly lowly or off-putting appearances, though for the one who responds to the intriguing invitation to look more closely, the full revelation of Christ and his teaching transpires finally in a moment of unconcealment, where what was hidden unexpectedly comes marvelously to the fore.[87] This, in a word, is what it means to call Christ an extraordinary Silenus. Indeed, as P.-B. Pineau wrote almost a century ago, this "humanist paradox" of linking Christ and Silenus is perfectly designed to unsettle theologians while arousing the curiosity of simple readers, or for that matter, to spark the surprised delight of the one who is attentive and open to the happy discovery arising from this jarring combination.[88]

It is true, Erasmus concedes, that there are Christians who will be "revolted by this picture of Him" as lowly, weak, and disgraced. In response, somewhat surprisingly, Erasmus claims that it would have been "easy for Christ to have taken over the monarchy of the whole world," and indeed to outpace anyone in the number of adherents, to outdo everyone in wealth, and to "silence all the philosophers and strip them of their pointless plaudits."[89] Such a reply to those who cringe at anything but an all-mighty Christ, would seem to suggest that the external appearance of Christ was a mere shell, with the real Christ standing behind the appearances and resting immune from weakness or poverty. In fact, however, as we will see in chapters six and seven, the Christology of Erasmus is anything but "docetic," where the humanity of Jesus would be regarded as an illusory or insignificant appearance. To speak

---

87. On the comparison of Christ and Silenus as a theological principle for understanding divine revelation, see Benz, "Christus und die Silene des Alcibiades," 19.

88. Pineau, *Érasme: Sa pensée religieuse*, 152.

89. Erasmus, "The Sileni of Alcibiades," CWE 34: 264. Erasmus often makes these kinds of statements in the *Paraphrases*. See, for instance, *Paraphrase on Matthew*, CWE 45: 196 (commenting on Matt 12:14–17) and 357 (concerning Matt 26:51–56).

of Christ as a Silenus, however, is not meant as a doctrinal statement about the humanity of Christ but rather as a metaphorical way of high-lighting the paradoxical and ironic mystery of divine revelation; thus, too, it is an invitation to approach this Silenus with patient and yet penetrating interest.

"Christ is Quite the Opposite"

"I, a child among children, shall now speak to you of the child Jesus, who cannot be expressed in words."[90] So begins the little homily composed by Erasmus to offer some "honorific publicity" for the new school founded by his friend and Pauline scholar John Colet in 1510. Ostensibly a sermon to be delivered by one of the school boys—a child speaking to children about the child Jesus—it is, in fact, a display piece for the kind of "spirit of devout learning" at the center of school's mission.[91] While the text at times reflects its original context and purpose—where the speaker pauses to exhort his young audience to listen to their teachers and respect their parents, for instance—it also bursts the bounds of this literary pretext. Much like a Silenus, in fact, the *Homily on the Child Jesus* reveals much more than what appears at first glance.

Right from the start, we can discern the playful sense of paradox typical of Erasmus, when the speaker says in the opening words quoted above, that he will now speak of what is fundamentally unspeakable. So, too, the remarkable eloquence of Erasmus shines through, when the young speaker grants that he will not try to speak with the "eloquence of Cicero" but then prays for divine help to speak eloquently of Jesus, in what surely is a most eloquently crafted prayer. There and throughout the *Homily on the Child Jesus*, the pretext of a young child speaking collapses from the sheer weight of Erasmus's rhetorical and theological agenda. One cannot help but discern, for example, as Emily Kearns puts it, "the evangelical nature of Erasmian humanism" at work,

---

90. Erasmus, *Homily on the Child Jesus*, CWE 29: 56.

91. Emily Kearns, introductory note, CWE 29: 52. See also James Henry Rieger, "Erasmus, Colet, and the Schoolboy Jesus," *Studies in the Renaissance* 9 (1962): 187–94; Richard DeMolen, "*Puero Christi Imitatio*: The Festival of the Boy-Bishop in Tutor England," *Moreana* 12, no. 1 (1975): 17–28; and John B. Gleason, *John Colet* (Berkeley: University of California Press, 1989), 217–34.

in which Erasmus treats the mystery of divine incarnation and its ethical application to life. Then again, in a manner that directly pertains to the concerns of this chapter, the *Homily on the Child Jesus* proves to be a provocative exercise in the kind of ironic Christology evident in Erasmus's comparison of Christ and Silenus.

It is truly worthy of wonder and thanks, Erasmus says through the child speaker, that "our teacher and commander Jesus," who is "continually being born beyond time, God from God, in all things equal to the highest and eternal Father," graciously "reduced" himself by giving himself "over to us entirely, so that by [his] loss—were such a thing possible—[he] might save us, who were lost."[92] "What humble sublimity and sublime humility," the young speaker declares in a perfectly crafted Erasmian phrase, when the incomparably great, infinitely powerful, and unimaginatively majestic "splendour of the Father's glory" "became a wailing infant, and was bound in rags and laid down in a feeding trough." What a remarkable act of divine self-giving, that is, but also, what an obscure and unlikely venue in which to dwell. Yet there he was, a mere child, and yet "how great he was," for those able to peer beneath the surface, as with any authentic Silenus. "To wish to contain his greatness in speech," however, "is much more senseless than to try to drain the huge ocean using a tiny cup."[93] And "how vast is the pile of benefits" he bestows upon us, Erasmus observes.

"But although his love extends to all people," the child speaker notes, throughout his life Jesus especially proved to be a "loving and concerned champion of children."[94] Indeed, he declared to the apostles, who with envy and ambition were wondering who would be the greatest in the kingdom of heaven, that "unless you are changed, and become like this child, you will not enter the kingdom of heaven."[95] In

---

92. Erasmus, *Homily on the Child Jesus*, CWE 29: 56–58. Indeed, Erasmus writes with an echo of Athanasius, "you assumed our humanity so that you might win for us a share in your divinity." For his part, Athanasius wrote, "for he was made man that we might be made God," thereby signaling the work of divinization in the incarnation. See Athanasius, "On the Incarnation of the Word," in *Christology of the Later Fathers*, ed. Edward Rochie Hardy (Philadelphia: Westminster Press, 1954), sect. 54, 107.

93. Erasmus, *Homily on the Child Jesus*, CWE 29: 57–59.

94. Erasmus, *Homily on the Child Jesus*, CWE 29: 61.

95. Erasmus, *Homily on the Child Jesus*, CWE 29: 62. See also Erasmus, *Paraphrase on Matthew*, CWE 45: 258–59 (paraphrasing Matt 18:1–5).

this and many similar statements, the child preacher continues, Jesus introduced into the world the ideal of a "new kind of childhood," one measured not by one's "date of birth" but by the "simplicity and purity" of one's life.[96] What Erasmus has in mind, at this juncture, is not a childish and silly life but a "sort of aged childhood,"[97] as he puts it paradoxically, and that would be an adult life, in other words, that exudes a "natural sort of goodness" and "innocence" often associated—rightly or wrongly—with children. Indeed, Erasmus has the boy declare in a manner far beyond his years, "Christianity is nothing other than a rebirth and a sort of renewed infancy."[98]

In pinpointing rebirth and renewal as the centerpiece of Christian life, Erasmus returns once again to the idea of Christ as goal (*scopus*) and model we encountered in the first chapter, where the task of Christian life is—as he now puts it—"to the best of our ability to express Jesus, or rather to be transformed into him," though Erasmus stresses that this is not something won by nature but accomplished by the "action of grace." The "child Jesus" is a "perfect model," we are told, so that "there is nothing that we need to seek elsewhere."[99] And what a startling ideal this turns out to be—this "new kind of childhood," and hence a new way of being human—something vividly evident in the story of the young Jesus conversing with the learned men of the temple (Luke 2: 41–55). There, Jesus was found by his parents, "in the midst of the doctors, listening and answering them by turns, and by his answers causing them all to marvel at this wisdom."[100] Here was a mere child, after all, but a "child not merely wise, but [one] filled with wisdom." It is little

96. In this sense, DeMolen argues, festivals in this child's honor could truly function as a "religious ceremony," one "which acknowledges the innocence of children and promoted such virtues as were commonly associated with the Child Jesus." See DeMolen, "*Pueri Christi Imitatio*," 17.

97. Kearns observes that this is a "common medieval and Renaissance topos" (CWE 29: 440, n. 52). Following her reference, see E. R. Curtius, *European Literature and the Latin Middle Ages*, trans. W. R. Trask (Princeton, NJ: Princeton University Press, 2013), 98–101, for examples from late Antiquity and biblical tradition. Erasmus's use of this phrase reflects his fondness for the paradoxical juxtaposition of opposites, much like the ironic equipoise of virginity and marriage in Erasmus, "Courtship," CWE 39: 265–68. See also Thompson's comments on this "deliberate conjuncture of terms ordinarily unidentical or even incompatible" (CWE 39: 272–74, n. 53); Martin, *Truth and Irony*, 201–9.

98. Erasmus, *Homily on the Child Jesus*, CWE 29: 62.

99. Erasmus, *Homily on the Child Jesus*, CWE 29: 63–64.

100. Erasmus, *Homily on the Child Jesus*, CWE 29: 64–65.

wonder, therefore, that the doctors and those "observing the exchange were very much astonished," Erasmus notes in his *Paraphrase on Luke*, "not just because of the boy's unusual wisdom" but also "because of the rare modesty of expression and gesture, and of language, all of which added grace to his intelligence."

A great deal in this scene is unexpected, clearly enough, so that those who were "apparently masters of the height of wisdom were not embarrassed to learn" from a mere child, though a child who did not behave with the "faults usually present in boys of precocious intellect."[101] Here, the boy preacher declares, was one "compared with whom all worldly wisdom is foolish." "You see," Erasmus has the child declare, "how this child turns the whole order of things upside down."[102] And with that dramatic comment, we get a sense of the redemptive capacity of the Christ child, for the rebirth and renewal held out before human life signals the reversal of all those preposterous inversions of life common among the Sileni turned inside out. As Erasmus puts it in the deeply ironic language that was also deployed in *Praise of Folly*, "he is truly wise who is foolish to the world and whose wisdom is in nothing but Christ."[103]

"Christ and the world are entirely different in nature," Erasmus declares through the increasingly profound voice of the youthful preacher. "The world," he says, "is like a painted whore; its first outward appearance strikes us as charming and all gold, but later, the deeper you tread and the closer you look in, the more bitter, foul, and disgusting in every aspect." But, in contrast, "Christ is quite the opposite: when you see him from far off, the prospect seems somewhat dour, as we look at the cross and the contempt for pleasures and for life." Yet, he continues, "anyone who in trust throws himself completely on Christ"—that is, anyone who opens the Silenus—will find that nothing is more pleasant, more beneficial, or more delightful."[104] Here, once again, we find the ironic

---

101. Erasmus, *Paraphrase on Luke*, CWE 47: 94.

102. Erasmus, *Homily on the Child Jesus*, CWE 29: 64–65. On the "Saturnalian inversion" at play in this work, see Gordon, *Humanist Play and Belief*, 95–98.

103. Erasmus, *Homily on the Child Jesus*, CWE 29: 65. On the paradoxical contrast of "human wisdom and divine folly" in the *Homily on the Child Jesus*, see Kirk Essary, *Erasmus and Calvin on the Foolishness of God: Reason and Emotion in the Christian Philosophy* (Toronto: University of Toronto Press, 2017), 49–51.

104. Erasmus, *Homily on the Child Jesus*, CWE 29: 67.

contrast between a world dominated by Sileni turned inside out and the authentic Silenus figure of Christ. Neither is what they appear to be, yet how different are the "harvests" they promise. Again, reflecting the pattern of inversion typical of Sileni inside out, "the world entices … with its painted imitations of good things," but what they yield turns out to be "nothing but poison glozed with honey." But when such attractions have "won them over," he continues, "dear God! what cares, what anxieties, what turmoil, what losses what dishonour! What tortures of a guilty conscience, what a miserable end it brings the unfortunates!"[105]

Misery, worry, and guilt, then, are the unexpected payoff from those things that promised pleasure, power, and wealth. But it is just the opposite with Christ, we are told, as the onerous burdens associated with Christ's "path of virtue" give way to "the hidden but real riches of Christ," that "heavenly and unceasing life which is to reign forever with Christ."[106] Everything is flipped, Erasmus writes, when the inversions of worldly life are turned round upon themselves, such that "what was beautiful is ugly; what was noble is base; what was rich is poor; what was lofty is humble; what was gain is loss; what was wise is foolish; what was life is death, and what was sought is shunned, and vice versa."[107] From Christ as Silenus, therefore, arises a life-transforming reversal of consciousness, in that suddenly and ironically, "the appearance of things changes," so that true and complete happiness is found not among the "vain and empty shadows" of the world's display but through Christ, in whom one "will find gathered together all truly good things." That felicity—truly a taste of the redeemed life, as Erasmus conceives it—is marked by a "freedom from error" and a tranquility of conscience, just the reverse of the "tortures of a guilty conscience" arising from the world's apparent goods.[108] This very sense of tranquility, as we will see in chapter eight, constitutes the personal life of peace in Christ, as Erasmus understands it, and thus, it serves as the bedrock for the ethic of peacemaking, which serves as the ultimate fruit of the Christology of Erasmus.

---

105. Erasmus, *Homily on the Child Jesus*, CWE 29: 68.
106. Erasmus, *Homily on the Child Jesus*, CWE 29: 67–68.
107. Erasmus, *Homily on the Child Jesus*, CWE 29: 69.
108. Erasmus, *Homily on the Child Jesus*, CWE 29: 69.

The Christology of Erasmus, as we have seen in these first two chapters, begins with his take on the condition of the world in which we live, since it is that sorry and sinful condition to which he offers Christ as the remedy. Though Erasmus often speaks quite harshly about the "world," thereby reflecting the kind of entrenched duality he inherits from the Christian tradition, it would be a mistake to think that Erasmus is actually contemptuous of everyday life. While it is true, similarly, that Erasmus sometimes speaks of worldly life as "fleeting" and even wretched, as we will see again in chapter three, he also speaks with striking relish about the various goods of natural existence. To those who are weary of life—the ones, in fact, who sound like the Silenus of Aristotle's *Eudemus*, who declares that it would have been best for people "not to be born," and once born, "to die as quickly as possible"[109]—Erasmus offers a classical counterpoint from Metrodorus of Lampsacus, a close friend and avid disciple of Epicurus, who after recounting the many pleasures life offers, concludes by saying that "life is good every way."[110] This very sentiment, in fact, is on display in many of the Erasmian characters from the *Colloquies* who approach life in what Erasmus calls an Epicurean manner, those who are not afraid of life and do not tremble at death, who embrace the goods of natural and social existence with a steady resolve and a good conscience, and who are keen on living well and eventually dying well.[111] So while Erasmus frequently speaks of the world in the negative terms of Christian tradition, this never nullifies his affirmation of the goodness and value of created life.

What *is* negative about the world, for Erasmus, and the reason he persists in using the standard dualities from tradition, is that so much about human life is twisted, inverted, and corrupted. Christ as *scopus*, as was evident in the first chapter, offers a unifying and universal target and measure that cuts through and reverses the world's inversions,

---

109. Plutarch, "A Letter to Apollonius," *Plutarch's Moralia*, 115 D-E.

110. See Erasmus, "Not to be born is best," adage II. iii. 49, CWE 33: 160–62. See *The Greek Anthology*, 3.9, epigram 359, ed. E. Capps, T. E. Page, and W. H. D. Rouse (London: William Heinemann, 1915), 193–95.

111. See, especially, Erasmus, "The Old Men's Chat," CWE 39: 451–54; "Courtship," CWE 39: 256–78; "The Funeral," CWE 40: 776–79; the banquet colloquies, including "The Sober Feast," CWE 40: 925–30; and "The Godly Feast," CWE 39: 171–243. For a discussion of the "Christian Epicurean" in these and other works of Erasmus, see Martin, *Truth and Irony*, 197–222.

thereby opening the way for a life transformed in imitation of the wisdom and virtue of Christ. Christ as Silenus, this chapter has shown, embodies the ironic dialectics of divinely accommodating revelation, thereby turning the twisted standards of the world upside down by encouraging everyone to tend critically to the world's seductive appearances, while also inviting us to peer beneath the ordinary surfaces of authentic Sileni. But Christ as *scopus*, as we have seen, is buried in the scriptures, which are themselves Sileni, Erasmus reminds us; thus, they require forms of interpretation that probe deeply behind the literal meaning of the text in search of a deeper and more profound wisdom. Taking this approach, we will see in the next chapter, leads by way of allegory to some truly dazzling features of the Christology of Erasmus.

CHAPTER 3

Christ as the "Greatest of Leapers"

As the "supreme authority" for Christian life, Erasmus writes in the *Paraclesis*, the "Gospels and Epistles" engage readers with the "living and breathing image" of Christ. Indeed, he adds, the wisdom of Christ—that "new and wonderful kind of philosophy"—is so "simple and available" that it can be "drunk from these few books as from the clearest streams, [and] with far less trouble" and with "greater profit" than "the teaching of Aristotle."[1] But though the truth in scripture may be "clear as crystal,"[2] as Erasmus puts it elsewhere, he is keenly aware that biblical books can be exceedingly difficult to understand, which is why he writes at great length to lay out the requirements for good interpretation of biblical literature. Sound and fruitful reading of these books, as he describes it, demands a "pious and ready mind" that is "willing to learn," but it also requires, as mentioned in chapter one, an interpreter who is proficient in biblical languages, trained in the "more liberal disciplines," familiar with both the "objects of nature" and

1. Erasmus, *Paraclesis*, CWE 41: 409, 419.
2. Erasmus, *Warrior Shielding a Discussion 1*, CWE 76: 220.

"historical literature," "carefully practiced in the figures and tropes of the grammarians and rhetoricians," and adept with "allegorical explanation of stories, especially those that look towards good conduct."[3] So a great deal of effort and expertise is demanded from the good interpreter of biblical texts, as the sense and significance of these books are, in fact, not always so clear and so available.

Facility in handling metaphors and allegories is especially important, Erasmus insists, because "almost all Divine Scripture, through which the eternal wisdom speaks with us in a stammering tongue ... rests upon allegories."[4] This is true, he boldly avers, because "God wanted there to be some obscurity" in these books, so their truth was wrapped in "figures and enigmas"—partly "to arouse us from dullness and also to set us to work"; partly because "truth is more pleasant and affects us more deeply when it has been dug out and shines through the cover of darkness"; and finally, "because he did not want that treasure of wisdom to be prostituted to anyone no matter who."[5] Whatever one makes of this claim to know what God was thinking in revealing truth through "figures and enigmas," it surely is the case that readers regularly encounter odd and puzzling expressions when approaching biblical texts.

Think, for instance, of the parables of Jesus, Erasmus suggests, which with their "allurement of similitude" often prove delightful for readers, even though their familiar cover must be carefully peeled away to reveal the underlying lesson.[6] Recall, as well, the many stories from

3. Erasmus, *Paraclesis*, 409. See also *System of True Theology*, CWE 41: 491–93, where Erasmus underscores the necessity of an unsullied mind and a "pure heart" for entering into "conversation" with God in scriptures. On the knowledge required for good interpretation of biblical books, see *System of True Theology*, CWE 41: 496–507. Erasmus is well aware of his debt to Augustine regarding the extensive knowledge of things and signs required to interpret biblical texts. See Augustine, *On Christian Doctrine*, especially bks. 2 and 3. On the prerequisites of purity and knowledge for biblical interpretation in Erasmus, see Hoffmann, *Rhetoric and Theology*, 89–93, 109–10.

4. Erasmus, *System of True Theology*, CWE 41: 661.

5. Erasmus, *Warrior Shielding a Discussion 1*, CWE 68: 220. These reasons are taken from a section in which Erasmus debates with Luther over the clarity and obscurity of scriptures. See Erasmus, *Warrior Shielding a Discussion 1*, CWE 68: 214–35. For a similar set of explanations why "God wanted Scripture to be covered and encased in such wrappings and obscurities," see Erasmus, *Evangelical Preacher*, CWE 68: 968. See also *System of True Theology*, CWE 41: 662.

6. Erasmus, *System of True Theology*, 633–40. See also *Paraphrase on Matthew*, CWE 45: 214, where Erasmus suggests that Jesus taught "under the veil of parables" so that "by the obscurity of his speech he might at one and the same time arouse their minds to a desire of learning, and still not give an opening to those who were hunting for a chance to bring false charges." See the

Hebrew scriptures—from the fanciful accounts of creation and paradise to the saucy and indecent stories of David's "adultery bought at the price of murder, Samson madly in love, the secret intercourse of Lot's daughters with their father, and a thousand other such stories"—all of which require considerable interpretive agility to "ferret out the spiritual sense" from the literal account.[7] Then again, there are the Psalms, all of which pose significant challenges in interpretation, but many of which have long been appropriated by Christian theologians looking for poetic hints of Christ.[8] Good reading of these sources, Erasmus insists, demands informed and respectful handling of the text in a manner that serves the interests of piety with inquiry that is both agile and imaginative.

Consider, once again, the strange title of Psalm 33 (34): "Of David, when he feigned madness before Ambilech." On the level of history, this may refer to the story in 1 Samuel 21: 10–15, when David concealed his identity from Achis by acting like a crazed man.[9] But a literal reading like this remains a "closed Silenus," Erasmus observes, where readers taste "only the husks of the grain." If, on the other hand, we "open the Silenus," he tells us, then "your minds will be delighted with spiritual dainties and fed with health-giving food, and will be astonished in the contemplation of divine wisdom."[10] Here we find Erasmus once again

---

similar explanation about why Jesus spoke to the crowd "through the veiled references of similitude" (*Paraphrase on Matthew*, CWE 45: 208).

7. Erasmus, *Handbook of the Christian Soldier*, CWE 66: 68–69.

8. On the appropriation of the Psalms for Christological use, where Hebrew scriptures become a "repertory of types … which find their true, spiritual meaning in the antitype, Christ," see Dominic Baker-Smith, "Introduction," in *Collected Works of Erasmus: Expositions of the Psalms*, vol. 63, ed. Dominic Baker-Smith (Toronto: University of Toronto Press, 1997), xix–xx, xlviii–xlix.

9. For the literal account from Erasmus, see *An Exposition of Psalm 33*, CWE 64: 278. The confusion of names may be misleading, as Ambilech ("father-king") could refer to Achis (the king of Gath). Erasmus treats the names figuratively, with Ambilech representing "one who boasts of his noble birth," and Achis as one "moved by surprise and lack of trust" (297).

10. Erasmus, *An Exposition of Psalm 33*, CWE 64: 278–79. As Erasmus puts it, now using the contrast between authentic Sileni and Sileni turned inside out, "divine books" "conceal wisdom beneath the contemptible appearance, so that the more deeply you delve, the more and more you are astonished." Human books, by contrast, have an "outstanding appearance at first sight, but if you look more closely, it often happens that a clever reader exclaims that he has found coals instead of treasure" (*Evangelical Preacher*, CWE 68: 258). On Erasmus's treatment of "David's feigned madness" as a Silenus both hiding and revealing the "glory of Christ," see M. A. Screech, *Laughter at the Foot of the Cross* (Boulder, Colo.: Westview Press, 1977), 90–91; Bietenholz, *History and Biography*, 13, 24–25. On food and feeding as imagery of the assimilation of God's word,

applying the pattern of the Silenus, in which readers must peer beneath the surface of the words to discern their concealed though surprising meaning. In this case, however, something more is afoot, as readers are invited not only to follow the ironic reversal from the apparent to the actual meaning—discerning the extraordinary reality beneath the ordinary appearance, for instance—but now also to be uplifted and amazed by the divine reality hidden in the strangely worded title. In this regard, irony and allegory are roughly synonymous, since with both, "one thing is said, another understood," and in both, readers must jump to a level of meaning that is hidden or "spiritual," though with scriptural allegories, Erasmus seems to suggest, the transference of meaning yields a more amazing taste of divine transcendence.[11]

When it comes to biblical interpretation, however, Erasmus prefers a measured approach, one where the reader allows the text to speak for itself, which often means sticking with the historical sense rather than foisting some contrived meaning onto the author's words.[12] At the same time, Erasmus clearly relishes a variety of exegetical forms, and that very much includes the turn to allegory for Christological purposes.[13]

---

see Baker-Smith, "Introduction," CWE 63: xxxi–xxxvi; with that imagery in mind, consider the figure of scripture as "manna," with the "tiny particles" signifying "the lowliness of speech that conceals the immense mysteries in almost crude language" (Erasmus, *Handbook of the Christian Soldier*, CWE 66: 32).

11. On irony and allegory, see Erasmus, *Evangelical Preacher*, CWE 68: 933–34. Screech suggests that "the truth revealed" in "prophetic exegesis" of this psalm "may lead to an ecstasy of amazement." See M. A. Screech, *Erasmus: Ecstasy and The Praise of Folly* (London: Penguin Books, 1980), 225. While he insists that Erasmus is "not indulging in overstatement simply for the sake of literary effect," Screech tends to overplay the association of exegetical amazement from reading allegory with the rapturous ecstasy suffered by the mystical fools at the end of the *Praise of Folly*. See Screech, *Erasmus*, 62.

12. Erasmus consistently proposes a "straightforward" interpretation of scripture, one that is "the least complicated and most suited to the tone and the logic of the psalm as a whole." While a "certain license" is allowed to those "who use allegory in their interpretation," largely because "allegory—even when it is misleading—has a charm and piety of its own as long as it is handled carefully," it is best not "to depart from the true sense of Scripture," he advises, but to concentrate on "those things which seem closest to the truth when compared with other scriptural passages and accommodated to the continuity of sense in the argument as a whole" (*An Exposition of Psalm 38*, CWE 65: 123). Above all, Erasmus suggests, readers must avoid twisting the words of scripture to fit "their own doctrinal formulations," something he pins on "certain men" of the Sorbonne of his day, but also on the ancient fathers when in the heat of controversy. See *System of True Theology*, CWE 41: 678–90. "The best reader of the divine books," he adds with a citation from Hilary of Poitiers, "is one who looks for the understanding of the words from the words, rather than imposes it on them, and who has carried away more than he brought" (679).

13. The embrace of diverse forms of interpretation is nicely on display in the conversation

Indeed, he says once again, the "divine Spirit combines things that are ridiculous and do not cohere literally, in order to drive our intellect from the literal sense and compel it to seek something more recondite in those words."[14] Faced with absurd narratives and incongruous expressions, Erasmus advises, it is necessary, useful, and legitimate for readers to "apply the remedy" of allegory by searching for a "spiritual meaning," though he quickly and consistently warns against excessive use of allegory.[15] When it comes to the opening of Psalm 33, Erasmus suggests, David's righteous deceit prefigures the mystery of Christ, who without pretense "changed his face—not in front of the Father, for the Word remained God with God," but rather, "he hid that face which is the splendour of his glory, and took on a human body and came as though masked in a play."[16] What a remarkable change of face that was, Erasmus declares with a bit of flair, for the "creator, preserver, and

---

over lunch among friends in Erasmus, "The Godly Feast," CWE 39: 183–92. Erasmus also is well aware of the "four senses" of scripture suggested by what he calls the "modern schools of writers," though he follows the "early Doctors" who "recognize only two interpretations, the grammatical (or literal or, if you prefer, the historical) and the spiritual," with the latter variously called "allegory," "tropology," or "anagogy" (*Evangelical Preacher*, CWE 68: 932–33; *System of True Theology*, CWE 41: 677). On the shift from four to two senses, see Baker-Smith, "Introduction," CWE 63: xxix; Hoffmann, *Rhetoric and Theology*, 101–6.

14. Erasmus, *Evangelical Preacher*, CWE 68: 528, 954.

15. Erasmus, *System of True Theology*, CWE 41: 662–67. Erasmus points especially to the eloquent and learned handling of "theological allegories" in the commentaries of the fathers, in stark contrast to "theologians of the present day" whose work is not "seasoned with the powers of eloquence and a certain gracefulness of style" (*Handbook of the Christian Soldier*, CWE 66: 69). As much as he respects the ancient fathers, however, he frequently criticizes the excessive and extravagant use of allegory in Origen, Ambrose, Hilary, and Augustine. See, for instance, *System of True Theology*, CWE 41: 667–73. In general, Erasmus faults those who are too quick to turn to allegorical interpretation, as well as those who reject allegory altogether. See *Evangelical Preacher*, CWE 68: 943–54. Those who too readily opt for a spiritual reading, he notes, underestimate the value of the literal sense, as generally "both senses stand together" (*System of True Theology*, CWE 41: 662). Those who "disdain all allegories as arbitrary and dreamlike," conversely, miss out on the richness of the spiritual meaning (673); see also Erasmus, *Handbook of the Christian Soldier*, CWE 66: 34–35. Many things can be interpreted without "allegorical significance, Erasmus concedes to the latter, but one should still make room for those engaged in the "fruitful contemplation" of scriptural allegories (*Exposition of Psalm 33*, CWE 64: 301). On the enduring value of allegory for Erasmus, see Sider, "New Testament Scholarship of Erasmus," CWE 41: 17.

16. Erasmus, *An Exposition of Psalm 33*, CWE 64: 299–300. Speaking of Christ as masked in a play raises interesting questions regarding his humanity, an issue that will be addressed in chapters 6 and 7. In the present context, Erasmus writes more precisely that "David pretended to be mad," though "in Christ there was no pretense. He hid for a while his divine nature, he did not abandon it; he put on human nature, he did not feign it." On the dissemblance of Christ in the incarnation and in teaching with parables, see *Evangelical Preacher*, CWE 628: 528.

controller of all things, to become an infant crying in the bosom of his mother."[17]

A similar approach, both straightforward and yet richly allegorical, appears when Erasmus offers a reading of Psalm 38 (39), again, oddly titled "For the end, to Idythun, a song of David," which, as we will see in this chapter, offers great Christological potential when read allegorically.[18] The psalm is a song said to be composed by David (often a type fulfilled in Christ, as Erasmus notes) that is performed by Idythun (Jeduthun in modern Bibles), a musician and prophet in the court of David (1 Chron 25:1) whose name—wonderfully enough, Erasmus points out—means "leaping over them."[19] As the central figure of the song, Erasmus writes, Idythun represents someone "who, as a result of the most grievous sufferings and despair, rejects all forms of assistance by the world and turns with his whole heart to Christ alone." It is his situation and his struggles that provide the focus of the psalm, and, as we will see in the first section of this chapter, Idythun produces "a song most pleasing to God's ears," precisely because it expresses both "weariness of this earthly life" and a "longing for the heavenly life."[20] And yet, we are told, what Idythun accomplishes is unfinished, as this is a man still "struggling with overwhelming temptation."[21] In fact, Erasmus declares, the "most excellent of all lyre players" is Christ, and, too, we are told, "even among those who are renowned as great leapers [Christ] holds by far the highest position."[22] So what is anticipated in Idythun is realized in Christ, the "supreme Idythun," as it were, and the ultimate end for which Idythun's prophetic music is performed, and toward which his "great leaps" aspire.[23] This richly allegorical material will provide the focus for the second and third sections below.

17. Erasmus, *An Exposition of Psalm 33*, CWE 64: 299.

18. Here again, Erasmus calls attention to the utility of the obscure title—it is "like some exceptionally bright star, forcing us to open the eyes of our minds" to receive "what is brought forth from the mystical sanctuary of the divine spirit" (Erasmus, *Exposition of Psalm 38*, CWE 65: 11).

19. As Gordon notes, Erasmus owes a debt to Augustine's *Exposition on Psalm 38*, who "in explaining the term 'Idythun,' yokes the notion of leaping beyond to the motif of spiritual music" (Gordon, *Humanist Play and Belief*, 172). See Augustine, *Expositions on the Psalms*, in *Nicene and Post-Nicene Fathers*, series 1, vol. 8, trans. Philip Schaff (Grand Rapids, MI: Eerdmans), 236.

20. Erasmus, *Exposition of Psalm 38*, CWE 65: 12.

21. Erasmus, *Exposition of Psalm 38*, CWE 65: 68. See also 37 and 119, where Erasmus notes Idythun's ongoing "struggle with temptation."

22. Erasmus, *Exposition of Psalm 38*, CWE 65: 17.

23. Erasmus, *Exposition of Psalm 38*, CWE 65: 71. As Gordon puts it, "the music coincides

In all of this, the imaginative key of allegory yields language that is fresh and lively for conceiving the exceptional activity of Christ, but it also issues in pointed exhortations to "imitate that most perfect model" in individual and collective life. Pastors and bishops, in particular, but, in fact, "all who profess the name of Christ," Erasmus insists, should muster the courage to leap over themselves and the world's many hills with harmonious and joyful songs. As we will see in the final section of this chapter, therefore, Idythun's severe statements about life in the world do not lead to a life-denying mysticism, but rather—in the hands of Erasmus—culminate in advice for gaining the perspective on life required for effective pastoral care, matched with the spiritual vision and ethical purpose required for individuals to deal virtuously with the empty, fleeting, and treacherous quality of human existence by leaping over it as Idythun did.

"Amazed by Men's Madness"

Idythun is someone who has been worn down by the stress and strain of heated controversy. It would seem, in fact, that he has erred in speaking harshly of others, and now he finds himself "wounded by men's tongues" in turn. Unable to escape their derision, the psalm opens with Idythun simply exhausted by the "false accusations, reproaches, and insults" of his "wicked" antagonists.[24] Erasmus acknowledges that this may refer to "the story of how Shimei insulted David," though he dismisses this historical reading as mere "conjecture."[25] It is far better, he suggests, to interpret Idythun's situation as a depiction of an all-too-common predicament, for "not even the most distinguished men have been able to avoid committing occasional errors," Erasmus notes, and thus "no amount of circumspection has enabled them to escape the backbiting of their critics."[26] Think, for instance, of those illustrious fa-

---

with a leap to its rhythms, a sublime ascent towards the things of heaven" (Gordon, *Humanist Play and Belief*, 169).

24. Erasmus, *Exposition of Psalm 38*, CWE 65: 11.

25. Erasmus, *Exposition of Psalm 38*, CWE 65: 36. For the story of Shimei and David, see 2 Samuel 16:7–13; for the sequel involving Solomon, see 1 Kings 2:8–9, 36–46.

26. Erasmus, *Exposition of Psalm 38*, CWE 65: 53. The church fathers, Erasmus notes, "were very great men, but men after all," and hence they must be read carefully and with a certain "indulgence," as they can err. See Erasmus to Henry Bullock, letter 456, CWE 4: 48; Erasmus to Jean

thers of the church, many of whom frequently complain of the "carping critics" with whom they must contend; or recall as well how "many of the things stated in the papal decrees and decretals" later come to be "regarded as heretical."[27]

Indeed, Erasmus adds with a decidedly autobiographical sound, even things expressed with great caution and in "a spirit of devotion" fall prey to "some trap set by the critics." And should an error or two slip into an author's work, then "the poor man is rewarded with furious abuse for his dedication and hard work, stabbed by tongues dipped in poison, stoned by the most impudent pamphlets, and beaten by the voices of people disputing and reviling on every side."[28] The situation of Idythun is something like this, we are told, as he is "a devout and right-thinking man who, in accordance with God's will, has been persecuted by ungrateful and wicked people to such an extent that life has become hateful to him." Looking everywhere for a means to escape, Idythun resolves to take "refuge in silence." He simply will not respond to his adversaries. Instead, he will "put a hold on [his] mouth" and rest safely in "obstinate silence"—or so he thinks.[29] Idythun's resolve to keep silent, therefore, represents a huge leap over the common urge to strike back, though as sensible as this strategy is, Erasmus makes clear, it is a solution in vain, since the "mental agony" will only grow "increasingly violent and painful."[30]

---

de Carondelet, letter 1334, CWE 9: 248. See also "A Response by Desiderius Erasmus," CWE 73: 143–44. Erasmus says much the same thing of Seneca but then asks more generally, "what author was ever so perfect that no fault could be found in him at all?" (Erasmus to Thomas Ruthall, letter 325, CWE 3: 67). Indeed, he insists, "no one who has ever written, down to the present day, is free from error, the canonical Scriptures alone excepted" (Erasmus to Lorenzo Campeggi, letter 1167, CWE 8: 116). See, for instance, the lengthy and detailed review of errors in the church fathers in *Exposition of Psalm 38*, CWE 65: 43–51. On the lethal results of the "slanderous tongue," especially under the cover of religious garb, see *The Tongue*, CWE 29: 340–64.

27. Erasmus, *Exposition of Psalm 38*, CWE 65: 44–51.

28. Erasmus, *Exposition of Psalm 38*, CWE 65: 53–54. That Erasmus's own experience is reflected in these words, see Carolinne White, introductory note, CWE 65: 2–3, 6. On the vicious tongue of the slanderer, see Erasmus, *Exposition of Psalm 38*, CWE 65: 54–58; on the ignorant rage that drives these critics to attack others with "dreadful slander," see 60. On the venoms of the tongue more generally, see *The Tongue*, CWE 29: 317–23.

29. Erasmus, *Exposition of Psalm 38*, CWE 65: 60–64. As Erasmus puts it elsewhere, "while silence may not always be the outcome of good sense, it is still an indication of seriousness and good judgment" (*The Tongue*, CWE 29: 287). On the benefits of self-restraint for the "disease of a loose tongue," see 376–94.

30. Erasmus, *Exposition of Psalm 38*, CWE 65: 72. Though silence may be the "most sensible

Resolute in his "stubborn silence," therefore, Idythun continues to seethe—his "heart grew hot" and "a fire burned" in his thoughts—and thus he finds "no effective relief."[31] Finding himself "hemmed in on all sides," therefore, he finally turns to God, asking that he may know his "end," by which Idythun means, among the many things considered by Erasmus, both "the end of misfortune" and the end of his days.[32] In turning to God, however, Idythun leaps over his self-reliance—as neither "noose or poison" are fitting solutions for the "just man"—and he comes to see clearly that human life is "not only short but also wretched and full of hardship."[33] Our lives are but "an instant compared with eternity," Erasmus writes in sympathy with Idythun, and yet—"attached to the earth as we are"—"we divide up the instant as if it amounted to something."[34] With respect to this condition, Idythun has "made an exceptional leap." Indeed, Erasmus writes, "he has leaped over all earthly things, all the heavens and, in addition, the angels, and all things affected by time and change, and has reached the very summit of eternity."[35]

---

reaction," Erasmus grants, "the mark of perfect gentleness" would be to "bestow kind words on the person cursing us" (68). Erasmus's ambivalent response to the strategy of silence is clearly evident in his consternation with the sudden turn to silence by two French humanists—the first, Jacques Lefèvre d'Étaples, who broke off his controversy with Erasmus without further communication, even as Erasmus continued to correspond with pleas for reconciliation, and the second, Guillaume Budé, who went silent in the midst of the furor created by his supporters over an apparent slight to Budé in the *Ciceronian* of Erasmus. Concerning Lefèvre, see chapter 6 of this book; on the life of Budé and his correspondence with Erasmus, see Marie-Madeleine de la Garanderie, "Qui était Guillaume Budé?" *Bulletin de l'Association Guillaume Budé*, no. 2 (June 1967): 192–211; David O. McNeil, *Guillaume Budé and Humanism in the Reign of Francis I* (Travaux d'humanisme et renaissance, no. 142) (Geneva: Droz, 1975); and Louis Delaruelle, "Une amitié d'humanistes, Etude sur les relations de Budé et d'Erasme d'après leur correspondance," *Musée Belge*, 1905, 321–51.

31. Erasmus, *Exposition of Psalm 38*, CWE 65: 72.

32. Erasmus, *Exposition of Psalm 38*, CWE 65: 75–77.

33. Erasmus, *Exposition of Psalm 38*, CWE 65: 76, 79–80. As Erasmus notes, Idythun "is not permitted to seek an end to his troubles by means of suicide" (93). Erasmus attributes the hardship of human life to the "sin of Adam," and he blames the brevity of life on "the excessive wickedness of mankind." Very few people are found, he continues, who live more than eighty years, though he is convinced that "life beyond the age of eighty cannot be called life." Indeed, he asks all too vividly, "who would call it life when the whole body trembles, the eyes cloud over, the ears go deaf, the tongue stammers, the voice fades, the teeth have fallen out, the feet falter and no part of the body can perform its proper function; even the mental powers are failing and the intellect becomes less acute, the rational faculties become paralyzed, [and] the memory retains nothing" (80).

34. Erasmus, *Exposition of Psalm 38*, CWE 65: 81.

35. Erasmus, *Exposition of Psalm 38*, CWE 65: 84, 86.

True to his name, therefore, he achieves a rare perspective on life: compared with "the creator of all things in whom alone all things are true, pure, and everlasting," he comes to see that "man is a bubble" chasing after "bubbles and shadows" as if they were real and lasting. All the "wealth, beauty, strength, honours, and pleasures" that people value so highly, therefore, are but "a shadow, a wisp of smoke floating past and soon to vanish."[36] Continuing with a tone reminiscent of Ecclesiastes, Erasmus baldly declares for Idythun, "all together is vanity." Indeed, he continues, "trivial and empty are all those things which men do in their world, relying on their own resources, [and] fighting among themselves" over things—like honor, wealth, pleasure, comfort, position, authority, and inheritance—that, in the end, are simply worth nothing.[37] So much "bitterness is mixed in with those very things which attract men because they appear to bring happiness and in which they hope to find comfort," he concludes, but those things are simply lies, empty promises, and "equally futile."[38] It is exactly this that Idythun has come to see, as "he has leapt over the earth, the moon, the sun, and finally all the heavens" to discover that "lasting happiness" rests in the "pure and everlasting" life with God, and not in the "deceptiveness of human existence" as normally lived.[39]

So much of human life is lived "among empty and shadowy things," Erasmus writes, and the "common run of men" cling to these things as if they were "permanent and real," and thus, they are "carried away by them." For his part, however, Idythun has "raised himself above man," having "leaped out of the cave in which, according to Plato, the people

36. Erasmus, *Exposition of Psalm 38*, CWE 65: 82. See also "Man is but a bubble," adage II. iii. 48, CWE 33: 156–60. "The lesson of this proverb," Erasmus says, "is that there is nothing so fragile, so fleeting and so empty as the life of man." What a perfect image, he muses rather negatively, of "the utter nothingness of this life of ours" (156). The adage ends with a eulogy for the recently deceased Prince Philip (September 25, 1506), an event that Erasmus describes as a "needlessly cruel demonstration of the truth that no mortal man, however close he may come to the heavenly powers, is other than a bubble" (*Exposition of Psalm 38*, CWE 65: 160).

37. Erasmus, *Exposition of Psalm 38*, CWE 65: 84–85. Earlier, Erasmus observes that the "more bitter complaints" of Idythun are "borrowed from Job," while "the lament about the vanity of human affairs is taken from Ecclesiastes" (37). At this point, it should be noted, Erasmus goes out of his way to emphasize that he is not only "speaking about vices" but also "legitimate" honors and duties, all of which include so much "bitterness" that it proves "impossible for anyone to find lasting happiness" in the world of these goods (88–89).

38. Erasmus, *Exposition of Psalm 38*, CWE 65: 89.

39. Erasmus, *Exposition of Psalm 38*, CWE 65: 85–89.

who are held fast there are aware only of the shadow of things."[40] What remarkable courage and what singular audacity that was to break free from the chains of custom and convention with what surely must have seemed like an insane claim about the illusions suffered by everyone else. "They would kill him," Socrates says to Glaucon in Plato's *Republic*, or at least they would "laugh at him as if he were crazy and turn him out," Erasmus has Folly tell his readers in *Praise of Folly*.[41] But Idythun assumes a similar position by leaping "above the world," "over all the heights of human happiness," Erasmus writes, "right up to this mountain," from which lofty perch he "surveys the whole of creation," much as Menippus once did (in a dialogue of Lucian) when observing human life from the vantage point of the moon. And exactly as Erasmus does throughout the *Praise of Folly*, as he allows Folly to join the gods on high in watching the crazy "goings-on of mankind" below."[42]

When Idythun observes human life, indeed, he, too, is utterly "amazed by men's madness" (*dementiam*), for "they neglect the good things which are real and cling to the insubstantial reflection of good things," and all the while, they rush about with frenzy, "endlessly fighting for things which are transitory and illusory."[43] What an empty and fretful existence is led by the "common lot of mankind," Erasmus sadly concludes.[44] For his part, conversely, Idythun has placed his life and his hope in God, "giving him thanks for sadness and joy alike."[45] For what "spiritual comfort" he receives, he is grateful, but he also has surmounted the temptation to despair over the distress suffered at the hands of others, for he now understands that he has been "made weak by the strength of God's hand," precisely so that he would abandon all

40. Erasmus, *Exposition of Psalm 38*, CWE 65: 90. For the myth of cave, see *The Republic of Plato*, trans. Francis MacDonald Cornford (New York: Oxford University Press, 1945), 227–31, VII. 514a–517a. For a similar use of the image of the cave and its deluded residents, see Erasmus, *Praise of Folly*, CWE 27: 119, 150–51; Erasmus, *Handbook of the Christian Soldier*, CWE 66: 86.

41. *Republic of Plato*, 231, VII. 517; Erasmus, *Praise of Folly*, CWE 27: 150.

42. Erasmus, *Exposition of Psalm 38*, CWE 65: 90, 97. See Lucian, "Icaromenippus, or the Sky-Man, in *Lucian*, vol. 2, trans. A. M. Harmon (Cambridge, MA: Harvard University Press, 1988), 267–323. Erasmus appeals to the image from Lucian in *Praise of Folly*, CWE 27: 121.

43. Erasmus, *Exposition of Psalm 38*, CWE 65: 90–1. In *Praise of Folly*, CWE 27: 122, Erasmus has Folly say that "if you look down from the moon, as Menippus once did, on the countless hordes of mortals, you'd think you saw a swarm of flies or gnats quarrelling amongst themselves, fighting, plotting, stealing, playing, making love, being born, growing old, and dying."

44. Erasmus, *Exposition of Psalm 38*, CWE 65: 111–12.

45. Erasmus, *Exposition of Psalm 38*, CWE 65: 95 and 116–17.

"self-confident attitudes."[46] Idythun now regards himself as a "sojourner," as the psalm puts it, for though he despises the "transient things" of life, he hastens forward with hopeful anticipation "towards the things of eternity," which he sees with the "eyes of faith." Though very much a human being—and thus still "wrestling with the flesh," as Erasmus puts it—he nonetheless "leaps forth joyful," for he is "returning home from exile."[47] And with that upbeat note, the song of Idythun turns from a somber "weariness of this earthly life" to a jubilant "longing for the heavenly life."[48]

"Most Excellent of all Lyre Players"

In his line-by-line exposition of Psalm 38 (39), Erasmus takes care to point out that, while Idythun has made remarkable progress toward "things of eternity," he has by no means reached his destination. "For the end," therefore, that richly ambiguous phrase in the title of this psalm, should be taken to mean not simply the conclusion of Idythun's life but his "fulfilment," his true and proper goal of which he sings and toward which he leaps, but that "end" (*finum*), Erasmus adds, is "nothing trivial" or "commonplace" but rather eternal life in peace with God.[49] To unpack this richer meaning, Erasmus notes, some "ancient writers" have "indulged in allegorical explanations"—"following Origen's example," as he puts it—even though that led to what Erasmus deems some "rather far-fetched interpretation" in "certain parts."[50] But the risk apparently is worth the discovery, for Erasmus is not adverse to offering his own allegorical readings. And besides, he observes, there are some interesting similarities between Idythun and Jesus, and these

46. Erasmus, *Exposition of Psalm 38*, CWE 65: 106. Thus, Erasmus writes, "he whose substance is in the Lord's hands does not despair, realizing that it is the Lord who has made him an object of scorn to the fool" (99).

47. Erasmus, *Exposition of Psalm 38*, CWE 65: 115.

48. Erasmus, *Exposition of Psalm 38*, CWE 65: 12.

49. Erasmus, *Exposition of Psalm 38*, CWE 65: 11, 35.

50. Erasmus, *Exposition of Psalm 38*, CWE 65: 121. In a letter to Archduke Ferdinand that served as the preface to the *Paraphrase on John*, Erasmus observes that "some of the ancients devoted so much space" to allegorical interpretations "that it became a superstition" (Erasmus to Archduke Ferdinand, letter 1333, CWE 11: 243). See also Erasmus to Jean de Carondelet, letter 1334, CWE 11: 265, in which Erasmus complains that Hilary lost the "historical sense" due to his "excessive preoccupation with allegorizing."

comparisons give warrant for some more creative and imaginative association of the two. Like Idythun, after all, Jesus was assailed by slanderous critics, and yet, within certain limits, he held his tongue and remained silent when questioned by Jewish and Roman authorities.[51]

Far richer links between Idythun and Christ, however, are to be found in their "songs" (a term Erasmus reserves for someone's fundamental resolve expressed with "strong inner emotion") and their "leaps" (a word signifying their agility in overcoming the obstacles and limits of life).[52] In this regard, Erasmus argues, Christ is the true end and fulfilment of Idythun, who prefigures him as a type in both singing and leaping. In this sense, we are told, Christ is the "true Idythun"—as a "spiritual being," he has "leaped over all human passions" and sings "nothing but prophecies," where the title of "prophet" signifies one who uncovers the "hidden meaning" of scripture's lessons.[53] In this regard, Erasmus writes, David and Idythun excelled in producing a kind of "spiritual music," where the lyre is played "in harmony with the will of God," though, as he reminds us yet again, the mind of Idythun is "still in a turmoil," and thus the harmony of his music is spoiled by discordant notes stemming from one or another emotion.[54] Christ, in contrast, is the "most distinguished of all cithara players and prophets," we are told, precisely because his song, that living expression of his very being, is tuned in perfect harmony with the divine will.

Among all those who have sung heavenly songs, Erasmus declares, Christ is "the most excellent of all lyre players."[55] And, interestingly enough, now showing the elastic quality of meaning in allegory, Christ's "body" is said to have been the "chosen lyre," that is, the instrument through which his fundamental sentiment is sung with perfect

---

51. Erasmus, *Exposition of Psalm 38*, CWE 65: 54, in which Erasmus recalls the stories where the Scribes and Pharisees sought to attack the "reputation" of Christ in order to stir up the people against him. "And yet," Erasmus writes using the words of Psalm 38 (39), "Christ alone could honestly say, 'I shall guard my ways that I may not sin with my tongue.'" He similarly "maintained a complete silence before Herod," Erasmus observes, and "while in the presence of Caiaphas and also of Pilate he spoke but a few words." In other situations, however, he did not remain silent, as "he often responded sharply to the Pharisees when they put him to the test" (65).

52. On the meaning of "song," see Erasmus, *Exposition of Psalm 38*, CWE 65: 11–12.

53. Erasmus, *Exposition of Psalm 38*, CWE 65: 13.

54. Erasmus, *Exposition of Psalm 38*, CWE 65: 28, 68.

55. Erasmus, *Exposition of Psalm 38*, CWE 65: 17.

harmony by never ceasing "to celebrate the glory of the Father."[56] Everything he did and said while "present on earth and living on earth," in fact—miraculous healings, subduing powerful winds, bringing the dead back to life, and even his "obedience unto death"—in all of these deeds, Erasmus observes, Christ "assigned the praise and the glory" to "the Father as their principal cause."[57] What is more, Erasmus adds, "with his lyre," that is, with the physical life he assumed, replete with need and weakness, he "fulfilled every kind of prophecy" with respect to his "death, burial, and resurrection," even as he promised his followers "that they would rise again from the dead and have eternal life."[58]

His "greatest performance," however, the ultimate crescendo reserved for the "final act," came "when his whole body was stretched out on the cross," for never had he "played his lyre more melodiously," in a manner "so pleasing to his Father's ears and so beneficial to us."[59]

> What [was] more wonderful than that voice with which he intercedes with the Father on behalf of those who were not only responsible for his death but assailed him as he hung upon the cross with insults more painful than death itself: "Father," he said, "forgive them, for they know not what they do." (Luke 23:34) This was undoubtedly the voice of perfect love and it did not speak in vain, for the lyre player's plea was granted because of the reverence due to him.

"The strings of love could hardly be more perfectly tuned," Erasmus comments, now rendering the self-sacrificing love of Christ on the cross through the figure of the lyre. Thus, we are told, the "final utterances" of Christ, in which he "commended his spirit with a loud cry into his Father's hands," was "produced with the strings of faith stretched to utmost." The "chord" that sounded at that point, Erasmus notes by drawing on Matthew 27:50–54, produced the most astounding

---

56. Erasmus, *Exposition of Psalm 38*, CWE 65: 14. Emphasizing the "elasticity" of allegorical wording, Erasmus notes that in "allegorical interpretation" it is "not absurd for the same man to be both cithara and cithara player, or the same person to be David the king as well as Idythun who plucked the strings" (12). For that matter, singer and cithara player are frequently interchanged, as well.

57. Erasmus, *Exposition of Psalm 38*, CWE 65: 14, 71.

58. Erasmus, *Exposition of Psalm 38*, CWE 65: 14.

59. Erasmus, *Exposition of Psalm 38*, CWE 65: 14–15.

effects, as the temple veil was torn, the earth shook, the attendants were terrified, tombs were opened, and the sun was covered in darkness.[60]

It is true, of course, that nowhere in Christian scriptures is Jesus explicitly portrayed singing; neither is he depicted playing the lyre.[61] Nor is his execution cast as a melodious song, for speaking of the agony of such a death in terms of musical harmony completely conceals the horrific brutality of the event. Perhaps here Erasmus's turn to allegorical figures has led to his own rather far-fetched reading, or so it might seem. On his behalf, however, it must be recalled that Erasmus never suggests that a "spiritual" reading of biblical materials replaces the literal reading, as the two necessarily stand together, so the musical account of Christ's death by no means replaces a reading that records the gruesome details in a seriously graphic manner.[62] Nor, for that matter, does Erasmus intend for his reading of Psalm 38 (39) to exclude other allegorical readings, as he clearly allows that "pious and learned men" among the "ancient writers" of the church produced interpretations of value that differed from his own and from each other's.[63]

What Erasmus's rendering of the life and death of Jesus through the figures of song and harmony accomplishes is to highlight the "voice of perfect love" at play in the cross of Christ, and he manages this, significantly enough, with the help of imagery borrowed from a psalm in Hebrew scriptures. What is more, this approach to Christology allows Erasmus to underscore the incomparably powerful effects of Christ's love. It is true, Erasmus observes in a short interlude, that "there is no person of any age or of either sex who is not sensitive to the power

60. Erasmus, *Exposition of Psalm 38*, CWE 65: 15. Compare with Erasmus to Adrian VI, letter 1304, CWE 9: 157.

61. It is noted in two canonical Gospels that Jesus joined his disciples in singing the customary hymns following the Passover meal before going out to Gethsemane (Mk 14:26 and Mt 26:30). Placed in the same context, the second century Acts of John describes Jesus singing while the disciples respond "Amen" in the circle they form around him. See "Acts of John," in *The Apocryphal New Testament*, trans. M. R. James (Oxford: Clarendon Press, 1924). For possible origins of this reference, see W. C. Van Unnik, "A Note on the Dance of Jesus in the 'Acts of John,'" *Vigiliae Christianae* 18 (1964): 1–5.

62. Erasmus scolds Origen, whose interpretive playing "at times" is "devoid of harmony when he produces the sounds of allegory but scorns the literal meaning" (Erasmus, *Exposition of Psalm 38*, CWE 65: 32).

63. Erasmus, *Exposition of Psalm 38*, CWE 65: 121–23. Bietenholz calls attention to the "'relaxed' adogmatic form" of Erasmus's use of allegory (Bietenholz, *History and Biography*, 40).

of music, even if they cannot appreciate the artistic skill." Some music can "rouse people to fury," for instance, while other kinds can calm an angry man, as David reportedly did with his lyre "to control Saul's madness" (1 Sam 16:23). Similarly, Erasmus continues, "ancient literature" reports that "certain melodies" relieve "severe pain," while in his own day, he reports, songs served to revive people from "an epileptic fit," even as music was well-known to "bring sleep to those who suffer from insomnia." None of these effects of music, however, can match "the all-powerful lyre of Christ," Erasmus counters, which alone can "drive out demons and transform the anger of God into pity."[64] Consistent with his emphasis on the living presence of Christ's words in scripture, moreover, Erasmus emphasizes here again that this "same lyre player performs for us even today in the sacred writings," as long as "we listen to his music with ears unblocked."[65]

"The Foremost and Greatest of Leapers"

Then again, Erasmus observes, "even among those who are renowned as great leapers," Christ "holds by far the highest position." It is Christ, he suggests with another turn to allegory, whom the bride in the Song of Songs sees with "prophetic eyes" when she exclaims, "The voice of my beloved, Behold, he comes leaping upon the mountains, bounding over the hills" (Song of Sol 2:8). What a vivid picture, and how kinetic is the language of Erasmus, as he stresses that this is "no ordinary step," for the beloved is "transported by a violent emotion" and thus "leaps forward" with enormous energy. Indeed, Erasmus continues, "he leaps from mountain to mountain, bounding over the hills in his eagerness to hurry on."[66] Just so, Erasmus points out, Christ, that wonderful

---

64. Erasmus, *Exposition of Psalm 38*, CWE 65: 15–16. On the various "wonders music can perform" as reported in classical literature, see Erasmus to Adrian VI, letter 1304, CWE 9: 155–56. "If then man-made music has such power to change the affections of both body and soul," Erasmus continues, "how much more effective we must suppose this heavenly and divine music [the Psalms] to be in purging our hearts of spiritual diseases and the evil spirits of this present world." Superior to that, he writes, "Christ's music has words and spells with which we can charm out of our hearts the love of things transient and charm into its place the love of heavenly things" (156).

65. Erasmus, *Exposition of Psalm 38*, CWE 65: 17.

66. Erasmus, *Exposition of Psalm 38*, CWE 65: 17. On the use of imagery from the Song of Songs in Erasmus, see Screech, *Erasmus*, 190, 238.

Idythun, leaped over the heavenly "mountains" without pause, and, too, when faced with "the mountains of exceptional prominence" in Hebrew tradition—Job, Melchizedek, Abraham, Isaac, Jacob, Moses, and the prophets—he did not rest, but "step by step, as it were, he leaped towards his bride the church with the impatience of love, bounding over all the wise men of this world as if they were little hills." This greatest of leapers, after all, is not daunted by obstacles, nor is he distracted by other pursuits, nor again does he rest at one or another point; rather, steadfast with love, driven by desire, animated with energy, and focused with resolve, he hurries onward while overcoming one rise after another as if they were nothing.

Erasmus suggests somewhat tentatively that the hills over which Christ leaps are the "ceremonies and precepts of the Old Law," though this example does little to capture what the energy and agility of such a powerful leaper surmounts.[67] For that, one needs something that will express the powerful but graceful agility and speed of a champion hurdler, or, since Erasmus also speaks of the superb rhythms and harmonies of Christ's lyre playing, the leaping of Christ should convey the energy and beauty of an accomplished dancer, perhaps performing a magnificent grand jeté, or at least one of the leaps common to Renaissance dances like the "galliard." No doubt these suggestions must seem rather peculiar, if not irreverent, or at least irrelevant, for anyone accustomed to the staid and proper images for Jesus in conventional catechesis. Where, after all, is Jesus found leaping and bounding with grace and speed? It is precisely that, however, that the allegorical exercise of Erasmus brings to the surface from the otherwise rather ordinary language of everyday piety and doctrine—descent, incarnation, and ascension, for instance—thereby refreshing traditional language with the expressive freedom and sprightly imagery only possible through figurative expression. The work of Christ is no "ordinary step," Erasmus surely would say, as he did for the beloved in the Song of Songs, so what could be more fitting, or for that matter, more necessary, than language that conveys the athleticism of great leapers and the beauty of marvelous dancers?[68]

67. Erasmus, *Exposition of Psalm 38*, CWE 65: 17.
68. Thus, Gordon writes along the same lines, that "with the striking of the harp, the soul

So it is to the grand saga of the works of Christ—from the incarnation to the ascension—that Erasmus applies the figures of leaping and bounding. Initially, of course, Erasmus reminds us that the "Son of God" "always existed with the Father," from eternity "dwelling in light inaccessible." But then Erasmus urges his readers to consider "the extraordinary leaps" that Christ makes "in every direction." From "these ineffable heights," Erasmus says, "that mighty Man of strength came down with great eagerness into the Virgin's womb, not dragged by force but drawn by love." What "an amazing leap" that was—the descent from the heavens to the human world—when "the Son leaped out of the Father's bosom into the Virgin's womb." It was just as dazzling, "when he leaped up from the earth to the heights of the cross whence he was to draw everything to himself," as the Gospel of John puts it (12:32). So, to human life Christ leaped, but then he leaped again to his own human death, and in both cases, significantly enough, it is his own decision and agency that propels the leap. Following that, "he leaped [bodily] down from the cross into the tomb, while in spirit he leaped down to the uttermost corners of hell."[69] From there, finally, in an astounding double leap, he "leaped up again onto the earth," and from there "he leaped up again" to "the throne of God," thereby returning "to that same brilliant light in which he had existed before the creation of the world."[70]

We have, in sum, then, a full loop of leaping from Christ the supreme Idythun. "He emanated from the Father," as Erasmus puts it, "and he returned to the Father."[71] And yet, once again, there is more to be said than is conveyed in simply saying that Christ "emanated" from God and "returned" to him, and it is precisely that energy, love, resolve,

---

moves, or rather leaps, in ballet fashion. Because he is the player of mystical, soul-transforming music, Christ is also the great leaper in a dance that transcends the tyranny of manner and selfish desire" (Gordon, *Humanist Play and Belief*, 179).

69. Erasmus, *Exposition of Psalm 38*, CWE 65: 18. In the first rendering of this leap, Erasmus notes that Christ "leaped down to the underworld with great force." In the similar circuit of leapings taken from an Ascension Day hymn, the text describes how "he leaped into the loathsome darkness of Phlegethon, and after destroying the dominion of its prince and rescuing large numbers of those who fought for him, he shone his light on the world" and "presented himself, restored to life, to those who were his disciples, servants, and friends" (19).

70. Erasmus, *Exposition of Psalm 38*, CWE 65: 18–19. The Ascension Day hymn quoted by Erasmus reads, "Finally, he made what is to this day the greatest leap of all, leaping up through the clouds and the heavens in one sweep."

71. Erasmus, *Exposition of Psalm 38*, CWE 65: 18.

agility, and gracefulness that is captured in the imagery of dance-like leaping that Erasmus derives from the simple name of Idythum. Such in a nutshell is what allegory contributes to Christology in the hands of Erasmus, and it yields, interestingly enough, a Christology in animation, where a powerfully kinetic character is given to every aspect of his mission.

The image of Christ as the consummate leaper is startling, to say the least, but it is precisely that quality that prompts readers to wonder and explore beneath the surface of the standard wording of creedal formulas. What one discovers with the help of Erasmus's allegorical reflections is a vivid manner of conveying something of the divine power and love at play in the earthly ministry of Christ. His rapid motion punctuated with rises and descents, after all, requires strength and agility, but also purpose and resolve, and in this case certainly, an amazing love that "gave his feet wings," as Erasmus puts it.[72] What a novel way this is to speak of the power and love of Christ, but in so speaking, we also are shown something new about this very power: it is energetic and agile, for instance, and we find something more about this love, in particular, its urgency and passion. With those qualities in mind, of course, one must remember that the kinds of leaping described by Erasmus entail an overcoming of one or another significant obstacle, as when the beloved in the Song of Songs leaps over hills, or where Idythun is said to have leaped over the natural urge to retaliate against his critics. Where Erasmus describes the series of leapings by Christ, however, there is a more profound surmounting of difference at play, as the gulf between divinity and humanity is overcome twice: first, when Christ jumps into humanity, and second, when he leaps back to the heavens. What agility Christ shows in maneuvering between the realms, leaping from great heights to the earth and then later back again, bounding from human life to his own death, and then rushing down to the realm of the dead and back again to earth, from whence he leaped once more to the heavens.

It is true, as Erasmus readily concedes, that other biblical metaphors can express something of the same power and love in motion, so leaping might be thought of as "running," he tells us, as such movement

---

72. Erasmus, *Exposition of Psalm 38*, CWE 65: 18.

involves "no compulsion" but "only love, rushing on its accord, filled
with desire"; leaping can also be rendered as "flights," mainly to convey a "longing for the heavenly country" and the soaring movement
required to reach that destination.[73] All of these suggestions, of course,
are not meant as some kind of doctrinal innovation but as figurative
amplifications that bring long-buried features of Christological thinking to the light of day, and since Christ is the perfect model for human
life, as we have heard earlier from Erasmus, it is not surprising that
harmony and leaping will feature among the virtues of a Christ-like life.

"Leap Over this Swamp"

Looking at the world of his own day, Erasmus observes that many play
the cithara, but "there are few who prophesy," which is to say that few
people reflect in their lives the "hidden meanings of Scripture's mysteries."[74] This is a familiar sentiment in the works of Erasmus, for as
we have seen in the first two chapters, he never passes up a chance to
expose and criticize those who lead twisted and corrupted lives, even as
they continue to sport the familiar facade of Christian faith. Their lives,
however, have "nothing to do with the lyre," as Erasmus says elsewhere,
since their "behaviour is different from their words."[75] Only true lyre
players "can produce a pure and clear sound" in their prophecy, Erasmus now says more positively, "whose lyre has been granted to him by
David" (again, one who anticipates Christ) and "whose sonorous instrument has been skilfully tuned to the spirit of Christ."[76] The apostles
and early martyrs were "outstanding in these fields," Erasmus observes,

73. Erasmus, *Exposition of Psalm 38*, CWE 65: 19–20. It is true, of course, as Erasmus duly
notes, that other expressions, such as "runnings" or "flights," carry roughly the same sense, the
former suggesting "rushing on its own accord" and the second pointing at hurried movement
"to and fro," but also elevation.

74. Erasmus, *Exposition of Psalm 38*, CWE 65: 13. Compare with "Many bear the wand, few
feel the god," adage I. vii. 6, CWE 32: 69–70, in which Erasmus addresses the sad fact that "many
mortals enjoy the outward signs and even the reputation of virtue, who lack virtue itself." Along
the same lines, see the five adages that follow (I. vii. 7–11), in which Erasmus sharpens the focus
on pretense and hypocrisy (CWE 32: 70–72).

75. Erasmus, "Nothing to do with the lyre," adage I. v. 46, CWE 31: 424. See also "An ass to
the lyre," adage I. iv. 35, CWE 31: 344–45, in which Erasmus takes a swipe at people whose ignorance and dullness causes them to listen to the lyre like a donkey, who at most will "twitch its ears
as if to convey that it has understood, when it has not even heard."

76. Erasmus, *Exposition of Psalm 38*, CWE 65: 13–14.

as was Paul, who with renowned versatility and perfect sincerity was "as distinguished as a lyre player as he excelled in the art of leaping."[77]

And yet, Erasmus writes with lament, it is now very difficult to find "a lyre player of this calibre among Christians."[78] So much of actual Christian life, in fact, is simply discordant with the wisdom of Christ and precisely for this reason, Erasmus continues, it is incumbent on the bishop to "leap over himself " and his own interests, thereby flying "up to the heights of the gospel," where his lyre playing will not "distort the meaning of Scripture" but proclaim its true meaning with power and skill.[79] Christian teachers, we are told, share the same "pastoral duties" of "expounding faithfully" the transcendence of Christ's leaping and the "edifying" harmonies of his song.[80] On both counts, it should be noted, Erasmus emphasizes the pastoral responsibilities of the ones charged with the practical task of disseminating the songs of Christ among the faithful.

In fact, Erasmus makes perfectly clear, it should be the goal of "all who profess the name of Christ"—"to the best of their ability"—to hasten toward Christ by emulating the leaping of Idythun, while singing songs in harmony with the divine will. Here, we have the ethical upshot of the allegorical section of the Christology of Erasmus, and it should be understood, once again, that "ethics" here does not merely refer to a set of moral prescriptions but to a profoundly ideal way of being in the world. In this case, of course, the ethical virtues and vices in question involve moral challenges of dealing with the world around us, exhortations to live in harmony with others, as well as the religious injunction

77. Erasmus, *Exposition of Psalm 38*, CWE 65: 24.

78. Erasmus, *Exposition of Psalm 38*, CWE 65: 21. As Erasmus observes, "those things which are most beautiful are also the most difficult and the hardest to find." See "Good things are difficult," adage II. i. 12, CWE 33: 22–24, which, as Erasmus illustrates, applies both to things requiring "skill and excellence," but especially to the challenge of being a good person.

79. Erasmus, *Exposition of Psalm 38*, CWE 65: 21–22. Thus, Erasmus writes with serial musical metaphors, "a bishop must be above all a good lyre player, a skilled harpist, and an expert with the tambourine and the cymbals, always singing and playing something, producing a powerful noise and making the ears of Christ's flock ring with his sound." See also Erasmus to Adrian VI, letter 1304, CWE 9: 157, on the "special duty of bishops and priests."

80. Erasmus, *Exposition of Psalm 38*, CWE 65: 23. Erasmus speaks of "teachers of the church" as "instruments of the Spirit, using the human tongue to convey its sounds to men" (12). On the pastoral theology at work Erasmus's reading of this psalm, see Bruce K. Waltke, James M. Houston, and Erika Moore, "Psalm 39: The Lament of Silence in the Theology of Erasmus," in *The Psalms as Christian Lament: A Historical Commentary* (Grand Rapids, MI: Eerdmans, 2014), 149–55.

to orient our lives toward the ultimate and divine end of human aspirations. The physical and social worlds in which we dwell, after all, "contain many hills" that block the way for someone "who is hastening towards Christ." Some of these hills are legitimate goods ("love for his family"), others are lures and traps ("the attraction of pleasure" and "the weakness of the flesh"), and still others are social seductions ("the glitter of wealth, the respect gained by holding high office" and "the distinction of being famous"), though Erasmus adds, importantly enough, there also are "the opposite kind of obstacles presented by things like wretched loneliness, poverty … or humble position, subject to every kind of injustice."[81] Then again, there are the treacherous "mountains of pride," which Erasmus observes, "even today cause the death of many who appeared to have reached the summit of piety."[82]

"To become like Idythun," therefore, we must be "ready to leap," but to accomplish that, Erasmus tells us, we must "rid ourselves of all the burdens weighing down our mind which churn over many matters." How, after all, "can we fly up when we are entangled by pleasure, trapped by the thorns of wealth, enveloped by luxury, intoxicated by the sweetness of worldly fame, and stuck deep in the mud of earthly care?" All these things make it impossible to leap, as their weight keeps us earthbound, even as their allure softens our resolve to leave these things behind. Erasmus follows, therefore, with a series of pointed exhortations designed to prod his readers to overcome their fear of leaping. Should someone fear a financial penalty for making an important piece of news public, then Erasmus prompts this person to drop what he is doing and simply "leap over this swamp." Then again, if someone fears the consequences of telling the truth frankly, then he should take the risk and "leap over this rock" that blocks the way for honesty. Or again, finally, if someone dreads the loss of life, then Erasmus dramatically challenges them to go ahead and "leap over this cliff."[83] The first and fundamental step on the way to Christ, then, as Erasmus tells it, is

---

81. Erasmus, *Exposition of Psalm 38*, CWE 65: 24.

82. Erasmus, *Exposition of Psalm 38*, CWE 65: 25. As Erasmus observes with his characteristic sense of ironic reversal, "to climb up here"—atop the mountain of pride—"involves a fall from a great height, just as the true ascent means abasing oneself."

83. Erasmus, *Exposition of Psalm 38*, CWE 65: 26.

the simple but monumental leap beyond ourselves and our customary worlds.

What Erasmus puts forward in the *Exposition of Psalm 38*, however, is more than an ethic of personal resolve, as he consistently underscores the divine agency involved: first, in prompting and inviting the self-transcending leap in imitation of Christ, "that most perfect model,"[84] and second, by enabling and supporting the living of life that is filled with harmony and peace, for as Erasmus puts it, Christ "flows to all so that they may be worthy to be called cithara players or Idythuns."[85] This amounts, in short, to a thorough-going religious ethic of transcendence and harmony, where Erasmus blends—suggestively, but somewhat awkwardly—the ideals of transcendence (by means of leaping) and harmony (by playing the lyre). The question, of course, is how the two images are connected, since now the question is not theoretical (referring to Christ's dancing leaps in perfect harmony with the divine lyre) but redemptive and ethical, where the focus shifts to how, as Gordon puts it, the lyre of Christ initiates in us an emotional shift "from the carnal to the spiritual," while "the leap to this music" represents a corresponding transcendence of "what is earthly to what is heavenly."[86] For those who would truly imitate Christ, we are told, there is an interior transformation of affections, which in turn engenders a fully existential transference of our loves and our lives.

As Erasmus tells it, the human person is said to be capable of acting on its deepest aspirations, whereby one leaps toward a goal spotted with its interior "eyes" and upon which it lands with the "feet of the soul."[87] What this means, it would seem, is that what we leap toward in life is a function of what we regard and feel emotionally to be objects worthy of pursuit. The goods perceived move us to act, prompting us to leap toward them, but, Erasmus observes with the curious freedom of expression typical of allegorical thinking, the human person has "as many spiritual feet and as many strings to his lyre as he has emotions," and these emotions are variously wicked, natural, or spiritual, depending on

---

84. Erasmus, *Exposition of Psalm 38*, CWE 65: 14.
85. Erasmus, *Exposition of Psalm 38*, CWE 65: 13.
86. Gordon, *Humanist Play and Belief*, 180.
87. Erasmus, *Exposition of Psalm 38*, CWE 65: 26.

how they are tuned.[88] While both the external and the internal senses can hold a person's attention in their grip, he observes, the human soul is often tyrannized by four key emotions—hope, fear, joy, and sorrow. "Different strings" (that is, different emotions), after all, produce "difference sounds" in response to the different things that are pursued. Some of these strings "spoil the harmony" of life, Erasmus declares, so they must either be suppressed or "one must leap over them."[89] Discordant music results, in short, when producing "only sounds which accord with this world," which Erasmus roughly translates as "making money, flattery, and public acclaim."[90]

Those who would emulate Idythun in hurrying toward Christ, however, are called to play a "spiritual kind of music," and the "most important things in this type of music is for every man to be in harmony with the divine will which," Erasmus emphasizes, "is the most reliable guide to what is right."[91] Harmony in life, therefore, that optimal attunement of the emotions toward things that are good, can be personal—where there is concord between what one says and one's "real feelings";[92] it

88. Erasmus, *Exposition of Psalm 38*, CWE 65: 26–27.

89. Erasmus, *Exposition of Psalm 38*, CWE 65: 27. Erasmus tells the story of a man giving a sermon where "two strings—of a desire for profit [in commending papal indulgences] and for adulation [by means of physical showmanship] vitiated a melody which was otherwise in tune" (30–31).

90. Erasmus, *Exposition of Psalm 38*, CWE 65: 30. Some people, Erasmus observes, "destroy the divine harmony" by "using the wrong instruments," as when "they mix heretical errors with true doctrine," something he attributes to Origen, Tertullian, and Arius, "who ruined their whole song because a single string was badly out tune." Others spoil "the simplicity of the music by trying to be oversubtle," or alternatively, by corrupting "the divine teaching with unnecessary subtleties and affectations and complexities." Then again, Erasmus echoes the church fathers' "complaints about churchmen who use the charm of their delivery and frequent exclamations to try to win the applause of the ignorant congregation" (31). See also Erasmus to Adrian VI, letter 1304, CWE 9: 157, on the "unlovely sound" and brutal effects of the world's music.

91. Erasmus, *Exposition of Psalm 38*, CWE 65: 28. Thus, Erasmus says, if these strings are tuned to "worldly matters the harmony is spoiled," but "if you set your hope in God, "the strings produce the sweetest sounds" (27). Erasmus has in mind the kind of "inner, spiritual song" eulogized by "Paul" in Colossians 3:16 and Ephesians 5:18–20. For the emphasis of Erasmus on the inner songs of joy and gratitude to God expressed in these Pauline texts, see Erasmus, *Paraphrase on the Epistle to the Ephesians* and *Paraphrase on the Epistle to the Colossians*, CWE 43: 344–45, 423.

92. Conversely, individual life is discordant, Erasmus observes, where "the whole man is [not] in harmony with himself"—if, for instance, "the tongue sings God's praises while the heart is plotting revenge against one's neighbors" (Erasmus, *Exposition of Psalm 38*, CWE 65: 32). Disharmony also prevails for individuals when their desires are "at variance with one another"—if, for example, "the string of greed tries to drown the sound produced by the string of lust" (33).

may be social—where all "perform their proper function";[93] or, finally, it may be religious—"where the peace of God exists," in which "one can hear the symphony and chorus of the gospels in the house of the Lord."[94] "To please a divine audience," Erasmus concludes, "we must adjust our heart, that is our thoughts, and must tune its strings, in other words our feelings, correctly," and "this is done if we strive for the glory of Christ and our neighbour's benefit."[95]

The point of Christology, for Erasmus, is to persuasively describe the works of Christ in a manner that moves and ultimately transforms those who opt to emulate his actions. As we have seen in this chapter, Erasmus's allegorical rendering of the figure of Christ yields a portrait of the ultimate leaper—the one who uniquely transits between heaven, earth, and hell, and the superior lyre player—the one who optimally lives in complete harmony with the divine will. Consistent with what we saw in chapter one, Christ thereby is the "most perfect model," first, for our own leaping—determining where we plant our feet, so to speak, and empowering us in our highest efforts to transcend discordant emotions—and, second, for our own singing—pointing the way to harmony in life with ourselves, with others, and with God. As the supreme model for our lives, therefore, Christ is the agent of human transformation, prompting and enabling transcendent leaping and harmonious living.[96] In this regard, we once again see the Erasmian emphasis on the transformation of human life and thus the genesis of a new character of being.

93. The music of social life is discordant, Erasmus observes, if the social order itself is disrupted, something that can result, Erasmus notes with an eye on the Reformation debates of his day, from disputes about which books belong in the New Testament canon, or from conflicts between "those who value faith so highly that they scorn works, and vice versa, or from differences between those who are overly bound to religious regulations and those who "scorn all regulations" (Erasmus, *Exposition of Psalm 38*, CWE 65: 32–33). More broadly construed, he observes, the discordant music of the world too often "intoxicates and maddens us, and so we fight wars, we raise rebellion, we are ambitious, greedy, wrathful, and vindictive; we bite each other and we are bitten in turn" (Erasmus to Adrian VI, CWE 9: 157).

94. Erasmus, *Exposition of Psalm 38*, CWE 65: 34. Sadly, Erasmus notes, in his day "even people who are reckoned to be Christian do not produce a harmonious song."

95. Erasmus, *Exposition of Psalm 38*, CWE 65: 30.

96. As Boyle observes, the allegorical rendering of Christ "stirs" us to a "new comprehension of things, which may eventually flower in the transformation of life" (Boyle, *Erasmus on Language and Method in Theology*, 120). See also Hoffmann, *Rhetoric and Theology*, 112; Gordon, *Humanist Play and Belief*, 177–78, 180.

We are challenged, in a word, to become a different kind of person, leaping up from what Erasmus aptly calls a "monster," to become a human being, and then leaping up again until "you have begun to approach the heights where the angels dwell." Being a monster, as Erasmus describes it, entails the practice of life determined by "wicked emotions." There, presumably, one would find thoroughly discordant individuals, fractured social relations, and a completely severed relation with God. To be a human being, on the other hand, is a noble though precarious achievement, since it is shaped by "natural emotions" that yield both virtues and vices. But, Erasmus concludes, "if you have leaped over what is natural and flown up to what is spiritual, you are now something greater than man," having become a spiritual creature.[97] The challenge to make these leaps is fully ethical, in the richest sense of the word, and with that, it is also entirely religious, as it involves the transformation of the very character of personal life with others and with God.

The pending question, however, is what kind of life would this be? When Idythun describes his own life, the portrait is extraordinarily grim, as life is found to be wretched, fleeting, empty, and vain. Indeed, Erasmus says for Idythun, "anyone who wishes to escape from the deceptiveness of human existence ought to depart from this life."[98] But since suicide is not an option, he concludes, the only recourse is to place "all [our] hopes of happiness in God alone."[99] The sentiments of Erasmus run in parallel with those of Idythun, naturally enough, though as we have just heard, there is plenty of language from Erasmus urging a transcendence of human life itself. So, once again, exactly what kind of life would that be? What would our lives be like if we were to leap over the earth and human existence, while beginning to "approach the heights where the angels dwell?"

One answer is proposed by M. A. Screech, who construes the leaping transcendence extolled in the *Exposition on Psalm 38* as a mystical form of ecstasy which, as he puts it, would seem to involve a "departure of the mind from the body" for the sake of a "soaring of the soul aloft

---

97. Erasmus, *Exposition of Psalm 38*, CWE 65: 27.
98. Erasmus, *Exposition of Psalm 38*, CWE 65: 85.
99. Erasmus, *Exposition of Psalm 38*, CWE 65: 97.

toward union with God."[100] As mentioned earlier, Screech concentrates on Folly's praise of rapture at the end of the *Praise of Folly*, though he rightly hedges his wording when it comes to the question whether Erasmus believes it to be possible or desirable for someone to shun their body altogether. Thus, for example, Screech speaks positively, though with two qualifications, of a mind "caught up into God through divine erotic insanity when it leaves, *as it were*, the corruptible body, a body purged and purified, *as far as may be* in this world."[101] Then again, however, as he puts it more directly and now more definitively, "Erasmus' concept of ecstasy has no room for a litter of dead bodies temporarily abandoned by their souls."[102] Such a statement makes it perfectly clear—certainly for Screech but also for the rest of us—that Erasmus is not thinking of a mystical rapture that would shun bodily life when he extolls transcendent leaping in the *Exposition of Psalm 38*.

Given this conclusion, there must be an alternative Erasmian model for understanding what human life would be like if someone were to embrace the ethic of transcendence and harmony advanced in the *Exposition of Psalm 38*. Admittedly, this model is not well developed in this text, though there are enough hints in what Erasmus says to warrant some conclusions based on other writings. To begin with, when he describes those who have joined Idythun in his "leap over all the heights of human happiness and who have contemplated with the eyes of faith the Ideas of things which are truly good," Erasmus employs a distinction from Augustine that allows for a measured yet viable life in the world. Such people, Erasmus says, "do not *enjoy* this world capriciously and in passing," though they do "make *use* of it as if they were not using it."[103] True leapers do not rest their hearts in ordinary things, for such things are not their dearest treasures, as Erasmus goes on to say, though they also do not shun the many good things of ordinary

100. Screech, *Erasmus*, 58. "A commonplace of medieval mysticism," Screech argues, the discussion of Erasmus is said to culminate in a "praise of ecstasy" centered on "ecstatic joy," which become a "corner-stone" of the spirituality of Erasmus (58, 62).

101. Screech, *Erasmus*, 173, my italics.

102. Screech, *Erasmus*, 198.

103. Erasmus, *Exposition of Psalm 38*, CWE 65: 91. For the distinction between using (*uti*) and enjoying (*frui*), see Augustine, *The City of God against the Pagans*, bk. 19, chap. 10, 930; chap. 13, 938; chap. 14, 938; and chap. 17, 943–45. Interestingly, Screech acknowledges the importance of this distinction for actual religious life—among the living, that is. See Screech, *Erasmus*, 173.

life, for such things are very useful, often in truly life-enhancing ways, and very possibly as practical means for further leaping.

Those who follow Christ by embracing the ethic of transcendence and harmony—what Erasmus calls the "pious man"—may be "a stranger to the body *as far as possible*,"[104] since physical charms and pleasures are not the final good to which they aspire, though these things surely have their place in life. And this same person may "no longer weep when death is at hand," as his heart is set on something beyond his own life, and hence he "leaps forth joyful," for he is "returning home from exile."[105] What Erasmus has in mind, therefore, is not a dour mystic bent on fleeing from earthly life but a living person filled with peace and happiness who—with a "clear conscience and a joyful spirit"—takes a leap over the glamorous though empty seductions of the world in order to "commit himself with all confidence to the hand of God."[106] It is exactly this kind of life that Erasmus has in mind in several *Colloquies*, when he describes the characters of those who have lived and died so well, with joy rather than fear, among friends and family, at peace with their past and hopeful for the future.[107] Little wonder, therefore, that Erasmus carefully tends to the importance of pastoral work and ethical challenge in the *Exposition of Psalm 38*, as his purpose is not to leave a litter of dead bodies abandoned by crazed mystics but rather to propagate rich and vibrant lives filled with transcendence and harmony.

104. Erasmus, *Exposition of Psalm 38*, CWE 65: 115, my italics.

105. Erasmus, *Exposition of Psalm 38*, CWE 65: 119, 115.

106. Erasmus, *Exposition of Psalm 38*, CWE 65: 111.

107. Think, for instance, of the long, full, and pious life of Glycion in "The Old Men's Chat; or The Carriage," CWE 39: 448–67, and recall also the calm, warm, and pious death of Cornelius in "The Funeral," CWE 40: 763–95. As we will see in some detail in chapter eight, when discussing the personal life of peace in Christ, such cases fill out what Erasmus has in mind for those who would embrace the ethic of transcendence and harmony in a life well-lived.

CHAPTER 4

The Dignity and Divinity of Christ

When Erasmus's Greek and Latin translation of the New Testament emerged from the presses of Johann Froben in March of 1516—accompanied by extensive annotations explaining his philological decisions, offering observations on textual variants and corruptions, citing assorted lines of interpretation from patristic and medieval authors, and proffering some fresh and sometimes pungent takes on ecclesial culture and practice—criticisms were quickly launched and were lasting in their challenge.[1] Erasmus knew they were coming,[2] of course, which no doubt is why he prefaced the work with the *Paraclesis* (a spirited

---

1. On the *Annotations* to the first edition of Erasmus's New Testament, see Sider, "The New Testament Scholarship of Erasmus: An Introduction," CWE 41: 49–85. On the genesis and audience of the *Annotations*, see Erika Rummel, *Erasmus' Annotations on the New Testament*, 3–34. On the aims, methods, and accomplishments of Erasmus's project on the New Testament, see Jan Bloemendal, "Erasmus and Biblical Scholarship," in *A Companion to Erasmus*, ed. Eric MacPhail (Leiden: Brill, 2023), 68–89.

2. "I knew there was going to be trouble," Erasmus writes, "for there was no lack of protests before the work was even published." See Erasmus, "Apology against the Dialogue of Latomus," trans. Martin Lowry, in *Collected Works of Erasmus: Controversies*, vol. 71, ed. J. K. Sowards (Toronto: University of Toronto Press, 1993), 58.

invitation to read and absorb the philosophy of Christ embedded in Scripture); the *Methodus* (the practical outline for undertaking sound theological interpretation of biblical texts); and the *Apologia* (a carefully crafted defense of the critical revision of the New Testament from Greek manuscripts).[3] As Erika Rummel puts it, this prefatory material served as "pre-emptive strikes" against the criticisms that would soon arrive with force.[4]

In fact, Erasmus had already heard some of these challenges in the two letters of amiable criticism from Maarten van Dorp, the young theologian of Louvain with a taste for classical literature, who was—as he himself put it—"playing a role" as the mouthpiece for those in the faculty of theology at Louvain who resented their satirical maltreatment in *Praise of Folly*, while also objecting to Erasmus's efforts "to correct the Scriptures, and in particular to correct the Latin copies by means of the Greek."[5] With the New Testament and *Annotations* published in 1516, Erasmus immediately began working on revisions for a second edition, and it is in this period, from roughly 1517 to 1520, that another controversy arose, this one with Edward Lee, the English student and scholar resident at Louvain, later archbishop of York, and a diplomat for Henry VIII at the imperial court in Spain.[6]

Open for constructive input from other scholars, at least in principle, Erasmus writes to Lee in January of 1518 that he had not been able to profit from the notes Lee was then writing on Erasmus's work, as he could not extract them "from the hands of the copyist," though

3. See Erasmus, *Paraclesis*, CWE 41: 393–422; "The *Methodus* of Erasmus of Rotterdam," trans. Robert D. Sider, CWE 41: 424–54; and "The *Apologia* of Desiderius Erasmus of Rotterdam," trans. John M. Ross, CWE 41: 456–77. The dedicatory letter to Pope Leo X (letter 384) also was intended to bolster the legitimacy of his work, an appeal that earned a letter of "commendation" from Leo in 1518, a document "printed prominently" in the editions of 1519 and following. See "Prefaces and Letters Printed in the New Testament," trans. Alexander Dalzell, CWE 41: 764–73.

4. See Rummel, *Erasmus and His Catholic Critics*, vol. 1, 15–26.

5. See Maarten van Dorp to Erasmus, letters 304 and 347, CWE 3: 17–23, 155–67. Erasmus published Dorp's first letter along with his reply (letter 337, CWE 3: 111–39) in October 1515, thereby giving Erasmus the opportunity to publicly defend his work. Dorp later regretted his role in the dispute, telling Erasmus that "whatever has passed between us, [he] should like to wipe off the slate, and be friends without reserve" (Maarten van Dorp to Erasmus, letter 496, CWE 4: 159). Erasmus accepts Dorp's change of heart in Erasmus to Maarten van Dorp, letter 536, CWE 4: 253. On the brief controversy with Dorp, see especially Rummel, *Erasmus and His Catholic Critics*, vol. 1, 1–13.

6. On Edward Lee, see Marjorie O'Rourke Boyle, "Edward Lee," COE, vol. 2, 311–14.

by October of the same year, he reports that his relations with Lee had soured, having learned that Lee was "planning some move against me," apparently focused on "risky" statements Erasmus had made of Christ.[7] Lee's challenge, as we will see in this chapter, is decidedly polemical, just as the response from Erasmus is often indignant and defiant, first in their rival accounts of their feud, and then second, in their dueling annotations, where philological questions give rise to discussions of theological substance by way of controversy. Though much of what Erasmus provides in this exchange lacks his familiar eloquence, it is here—in the choppy and often fragmented controversy with Lee—that we first encounter his reflections on the dignity and divinity of Christ.[8]

The sad and sordid details of this controversy are meticulously chronicled by both Lee and Erasmus, though as one might expect in such a quarrel, their accounts share little in common, save for the suspicion and hostility each expresses for the other.[9] Apparently, Lee shared some early notes with Erasmus, which, at least as Lee tells it, were not met with the respect they deserved, though, in the telling of Erasmus, he found them "for the most part minutiae and about minor points."[10] With relations broken off, Lee continued to build his collection of notes,

7. For Erasmus's letter to "his friend Lee," see Erasmus to Edward Lee, letter 765, CWE 5: 282; on the report that Lee was beginning to mix into his notes "little spurts of indignation" on Christological questions, see Erasmus to Cuthbert Tunstall, letter 886, CWE 6: 162.

8. Many of the same issues will appear again in the controversy with Diego López Zúñiga (Stunica), the relentless and aggressive critic of Erasmus from 1521 to 1529, and then again in the Valladolid Articles issued at the inquisitorial meeting of Spanish monks and scholars in 1527. On the former, see H. J. de Jonge, "Introduction," in *Opera omnia Desidirii Erasmi Roterodami*, IX - 2 (Amsterdam: North Holland Publishing,1983), 3–49; Charles Fantazzi, "Introduction," in *Collected Works of Erasmus: Controversies*, ed. Jan Bloemendal, vol. 74 (Toronto: University of Toronto Press, 2022), ix–xviii; and Richard Homer Graham, "Erasmus and Stunica," *Erasmus of Rotterdam Society Yearbook* 10, no. 1 (1990): 9–60. On the latter, see Rummel, *Erasmus and His Catholic Critics*, vol. 2, 81–105; Lu Ann Homza, "Erasmus as Hero, or Heretic? Spanish Humanism and the Valladolid Assembly of 1527," *Renaissance Quarterly* 50, no. 1 (Spring 1997): 78–118.

9. Erasmus narrates the course of their controversy in *Apologia in Response to the Two Invectives of Edward Lee*, CWE 72: 3–65, while Lee's account appears—among other places—toward the end of From Edward Lee, letter 1061, CWE 7: 185–95. For an overview of the controversy between Lee and Erasmus, see Cecilia Asso, "Martin Dorp and Edward Lee," trans. Denis Robichaud, in *Biblical Humanism and Scholasticism in the Age of Erasmus*, ed. Erika Rummel (Leiden: Brill, 2008), 174–95.

10. See Erasmus, *Apologia*, CWE 72: 10. On the genesis of their dispute, see especially Erika Rummel, "Introduction," CWE 72: xv–xvi; Rummel, *Erasmus and His Catholic Critics*, vol. 1, 95–97.

distributing them, or so Erasmus thought, in circles hostile to Erasmus.[11] From that point forward, therefore, Erasmus is keen to get his hands on Lee's growing collection of annotations, as he clearly fears the circulation of charges of impiety without the ability to respond. A series of letters are sent to common friends seeking help in securing a copy of these documents,[12] and Erasmus writes to Richard Foxe requesting help in advising Lee "to desist entirely from these false accusations," or "at least to meet me fairly in argument."[13] Behind the scenes, Erasmus maneuvers surreptitiously—"leaving no trick untried," as he later puts it—to secure a copy of Lee's work, though without success.[14] In July 1519, after the publication of the second edition of the New Testament, Erasmus writes directly to Lee, questioning with considerable condescension and sarcasm why Lee has not published his book, warning, rather ominously, that he may not be able to restrain his friends in Germany from attacking Lee with pamphlets or even "more violent measures."[15]

11. See Erasmus to Edward Lee, letter 998, CWE 7: 13; Erasmus, *Apologia*, CWE 72: 13, 26. Erasmus later claimed that Lee prepared "twenty copies for private distribution among his friends." See Erasmus to Noël Béda, letter 1581, CWE 11: 137. For Lee's denial, see From Edward Lee, letter 1061, CWE 7: 176.

12. Consider, for instance, Erasmus to Maarten Lips, letters 897–99 and 901, which reveal obliquely that Lips was passing individual notes to Erasmus (CWE 6: 180–87). Erasmus writes to Thomas Lupset in October of 1519 to request that he "contrive somehow to get me a sight of that book" (Erasmus to Thomas Lupset, letter 1026, CWE 7: 99). In Erasmus to Cuthbert Tunstall, letter 1029, CWE 7: 102, Erasmus similarly asks for "a copy of Lee's annotations." Then again, in the same series of letters, Erasmus pleads with John Fisher to lend him "the whole book," or at least to send "a note of the points which you think of some importance." Should Fisher be too busy, Erasmus requests that Thomas More "be asked to undertake it, if you think fit, even if you have to urge him" (Erasmus to John Fisher, letter 1030, CWE 7: 103).

13. Erasmus to Richard Foxe, letter 973, CWE 6: 384.

14. Erasmus admits—comically enough—that he "tried to bribe the third copyist" working in the house of Jan Briart of Ath but only "intercepted two short pages" before Ath discovered what was happening (Erasmus, *Apologia*, CWE 72: 13–14).

15. Erasmus to Edward Lee, letter 998, CWE 7: 13–14. This letter apparently was for sale in the bookshops before it reached Lee, telling us something of Erasmus's public designs for the letter. In August 1520, Erasmus expresses regret over the "outburst of pamphlets" against Lee, as this is a "devotion to me which does so much harm." See Erasmus to John Fisher, letter 1129, CWE 8: 25; see, similarly, Erasmus to Sebastian von Rotenhan, letter 1134, CWE 8: 32. In the spring of the same year, however, we find Erasmus encouraging his friends "to write letters highly critical of Lee," which were later revised and published by Erasmus (Erasmus to Justus Jonas, letter 1088, CWE 7: 255). Should this letter be authentic, and there is some debate on that question (see the introductory note, CWE 7: 254–55), the efforts to mobilize supporters against Lee were taking place—oddly enough—at the same time that Erasmus was counseling Thomas More to rise above his "squabble" with Germain de Brie. See Erasmus to Thomas More, letter 1093, CWE 7: 262. In any case, Erasmus reports that he received "some bundles, or more truly volumes, of

Erasmus follows up toward the end of the year with a letter to Thomas Lupset in which he denies that he and his friends had blocked the publication of Lee's book, when in fact, or so Erasmus claims, he had offered to have the book printed at his own expense, wryly insisting that his mention of threats to Lee was meant as a friendly warning.[16] Lee responds in February 1520 with a dialogue composed of Erasmus's words and his own rejoinders, after which he highlights his own role of liberating "the Scriptures and the doctrines of the church from foul aspersions," while casting Erasmus as one who seems "more than once to take up the cause of heretics" so that "the true and genuine reading" of scripture "may sometimes be corrupted."[17]

With the publication of Lee's book, the rhetoric of Erasmus becomes more cutting in his letters—he now describes Lee as ignorant, mad, and malevolent[18]—even while Erasmus claims in the *Apologia* that he "behaved with far greater moderation than was demanded by the matter, indeed with greater moderation than Lee himself."[19] In fact, as Rummel rightly observes, "neither man emerges unblemished from the controversy." As she puts it, "Lee appears peevish and self-righteous, Erasmus manipulative and less than forthright in his dealing with Lee."[20] What an odd and unexpected context this is, consequently, for discovering something of significance in the Christology of Erasmus, but it is precisely here—in this messy and often testy crossfire of controversy—that Erasmus is drawn out to address the most transcendent and mysterious dimensions of Christology.

The fundamental charge leveled by Lee against Erasmus, as will be the case so often for those taking issue with Erasmus's work on biblical literature, is that he abuses scripture by daring to revise its words, and

letters, in which they cut Lee up into little pieces," though he claims to have allowed no one to read them. See Erasmus to Willibald Pirckheimer, letter 1139, CWE 8: 41; see also Erasmus to Justus Jonas, letter 1157, CWE 8: 83.

16. Erasmus to Thomas Lupset, letter 1053, CWE 7: 149–53.

17. From Edward Lee, letter 1061, CWE 7: 192–93.

18. See, for instance, Erasmus to Hermann von Neuenahr, letter 1082, CWE 7: 228. Indeed, Erasmus writes of Lee, "on facts he is frigid and foolish, in scurrilities he is hot enough—raving mad, indeed—and yet his petty mad-dog spirit is never satisfied" (Erasmus to Wolfgang Faber Capito, letter 1074, CWE 7: 219).

19. Erasmus, *Apologia*, CWE 72: 27. Lee, in turn, mocks the "famous humility" and "famous modesty" of Erasmus. See From Edward Lee, letter 1061, CWE 7: 181–82.

20. Rummel, "Introduction," CWE 72: xvii.

by so doing—here is Lee's great doctrinal fear—Erasmus increases "the risk of the Arian heresy once more rearing its head."[21] With regard to changes made to scripture, Erasmus is quick to assure his readers that he is "not editing the text in order to displace the received translation" used in the church. Whenever this question arises, in fact, Erasmus insists that what he has written "can be read without any danger in one's study," and thus without any detriment to "the authority of Scripture."[22] Be that as it may, Erasmus is resolute in facing the fact that the traditionally accepted texts of scripture (the Vulgate) had been corrupted by the "ignorance, carelessness, and indiscretion" of errant translators and sleepy copyists, and that corruptions were also inserted by various parties to combat one heresy or another.[23] What we find in these remarks, importantly enough, is the keen sense of history that Erasmus brings to the study of biblical literature, something that for him renders critical revision of these texts both necessary and legitimate, even while, for Edward Lee and others like him, this same historical posture represents a brazen assault on the inviolable sanctity of scriptural authority.[24]

In fact, Lee warns dramatically, the work of Erasmus makes it possible that "we will fall once again on Arian times," as key proof-texts used to defeat the Arian view of Christ are undermined by Erasmus's critical exegesis, or so he claims.[25] Erasmus mocks this fear—hoping in jest

21. On Lee's fear of a revival of Arianism, see Erasmus, *Responding to the Annotations of Edward Lee*, CWE 72: 408.

22. Erasmus, *Apologia*, CWE 72: 33–35. See also Erasmus, *Responding to the Annotations of Edward Lee*, CWE 72: 225. In response to Lee's claim that Erasmus "slanders" scripture, Erasmus replies, "I use Greek sources, old and trustworthy manuscripts, and the quotations and commentaries of orthodox exegetes in an attempt to make our codices less vulnerable to corruption and to effect a better understanding of them. At the same time I leave intact the Vulgate text as it is, and everywhere subject myself to the judgment of the church" (39). See, similarly, Erasmus, *The Apologia of Erasmus of Rotterdam against Several Articles Presented by Certain Monks in Spain*, in *Collected Works of Erasmus: Controversies*, vol. 75, ed. and trans. Charles Fantazzi (Toronto: University of Toronto Press, 2019), 35–36. Nor would the church be in danger, Erasmus suggests in the manner of a good scholar, if he had "discovered the books of Arius and published them" (*Apologia*, CWE 72: 40).

23. Erasmus, "The *Apologia* of Desiderius Erasmus of Rotterdam," CWE 41: 462. For anyone who fears that changes made to correct the Bible will undermine the "authority of sacred literature," Erasmus offers the unconsoling but perfectly honest reply, that there have been change and variation in manuscripts already for a millennium, though he piously adds that such changes have not meant the demise of the Christian religion (462–63). On corruption and change in scriptural texts, see Erasmus, *Responding to the Annotations of Edward Lee*, CWE 72: 76–82.

24. On the historical consciousness of Erasmus, see Christ-von Wedel, *Erasmus of Rotterdam*, 104–5.

25. Erasmus, *Responding to the Annotations of Edward Lee*, CWE 72: 412.

that Lee can find a "good physician"—and he bluntly observes that "no heresy is as dead as that of the Arians."[26] What Erasmus means by this is that the theological teachings of Arius (256–336 CE)—the Christian presbyter in Alexandria (Egypt) who insisted above all on the oneness and transcendence of God, while fully respecting (as worthy of worship) the Son as a divine but created agent of God, active in both the creation and the salvation of the world—were condemned at the council held at Nicaea (325 CE) and then again following the deaths of both Arius and Emperor Constantine at the first council of Constantinople (381 CE).[27] As an obedient man of the church, which Erasmus most certainly was, he often sounds pleased that this heresy was vanquished, though, as a critically minded scholar who looks at the issues in these debates with a remarkable degree of impartiality, he also appears genuinely impressed with the Arian manner of thinking.[28]

26. Erasmus, *Responding to the Annotations of Edward Lee*, CWE 72: 412, 408. So "who are the heretics Lee is telling us about?" Erasmus asks. "Those of whom nothing is left but the name! So afraid of ghosts is our fearful fellow, where there is no need" (412). There is historical irony in the fact that anti-Trinitarian thought—reminiscent of, though by no means identical with, Arian theology—flourished in the sixteenth and seventeenth centuries, often with an explicit debt to Erasmus's *Annotations* on the New Testament, even though Erasmus would not have shared their conclusions. See Peter G. Bietenholz, *Encounters with a Radical Erasmus: Erasmus' Work as a Source of Radical Thought in Early Modern Europe* (Toronto: University of Toronto Press, 2009), 33–68. In a sharply polemical tone, Robert Coogan contends that the *Annotations* of Erasmus are responsible for "a revival of Arian-like Christologies which had been absent from theology for almost a millennium." See Robert Coogan, *Erasmus, Lee and the Correction of Vulgate: The Shaking of the Foundations* (Genève: Librairie Droz, 1992), 13–14. Coogan uses the existence of anti-Trinitarian thinking in the "Radical Reformation" as evidence against Erasmus, all of which, strangely enough, he regards as confirming Lee's "prophecy" that Erasmus' changes to the Vulgate will "shake the foundations" of the "ecumenical authority of the Catholic Church," a judgment against Erasmus that is, according to Coogan, later confirmed by Cardinal "Bellarmine and others at [the Council of] Trent." While Bietenholz wisely leaves the questions of intent and responsibility open and fluid, Coogan, writing more like an inquisitor than a historian, has no doubts whatsoever about the guilt and culpability of Erasmus.

27. Erasmus is relatively well-informed about Arian theology and the controversies it aroused. For two surviving documents expressing Arius's thinking, see "The Letter of Arius to Eusebius of Nicomedia" and "The Confession of the Arians, Addressed to Alexander of Alexandria," in *Christology of the Later Fathers*, 329–34. On Arian theology in the context of the historical development of Trinitarian doctrine, see Jaroslav Pelikan, *The Christian Tradition: A History of the Development of Doctrine*, vol. 1, *The Emergence of the Catholic Tradition (100–600)* (Chicago: University of Chicago Press, 1971), 172–225. On Arius and Arian theology up to the Council of Nicaea, see R. P. C. Hanson, *The Search for The Christian Doctrine of God: The Arian Controversy, 318–381* (Grand Rapids, MI: Baker Academic, 1988), 3–178.

28. "Though I am pleased that their faction has been vanquished," he says to Lee as churchman, "still, because of their learning, I wish their books had survived," he adds as scholar. See

Thus, he acknowledges elsewhere, the Arian view of Christ was "strongly defended in their writings," as it relied on "what seemed impregnable support from Holy Scripture," even as they enjoyed the "backing both political and financial of emperors and whole peoples."[29] So when Erasmus says—as any good historian might say today—that it was "long in doubt which way the uncommitted church would turn," one can discern his broad-minded regard for the historical currents of Christian thinking, matched with an intellectual modesty that demands that disputed biblical texts be treated with critical honesty, even if that means relinquishing their long-standing use on behalf of what has come to be considered orthodox thinking.[30] Taking this approach, however, is already excessive and hence dangerous for Lee, which is why he contends that Erasmus supports the "ravings of heretics."[31]

Any reading of the Christology of Erasmus must acknowledge his affirmation of the orthodox account of the doctrine of the Trinity, and hence one that speaks of the Son as one in being with the Father and the Spirit.[32] This point is repeated so often and with such insistence that it must be considered sincere, though—as always with Erasmus—not without some qualification, as he rightly claims the freedom to explore the nuances (and the limits) of Trinitarian language, to debate

---

Erasmus, *Responding to the Annotations of Edward Lee*, CWE 72: 409; see also 401, where Erasmus expresses admiration for their "learning," even while he "detest[s] their impiety."

29. Erasmus to William Warham, letter 1451, CWE 10: 271–72. See also Erasmus to Jean de Carondelet, letter 1334, CWE 9: 261. Like "their teacher Origen," Erasmus says to Lee, "no faction was more knowledgeable in sacred letters than the Arians" (*Responding to the Annotations of Edward Lee*, CWE 72: 409).

30. Erasmus to William Warham, letter 1451, CWE 10: 272. Erasmus later defends his appraisal of the Arians, noting that while they may have been a "heresy before God, ... among men there was uncertainty, for the pubic declaration of the church had not yet been heard." See Erasmus, *Apology against the Patchworks of Alberto Pio*, CWE 84: 276.

31. See Edward Lee to Erasmus, letter 1061, CWE 7: 178, among other places. As Erasmus sees it, "one is not necessarily a heretic if one disagrees with the decision of some theologians," though he hastens to add, that Lee is "hardly qualified to present himself as a candidate in theology" (*Responding to the Annotations of Edward Lee*, CWE 72: 330–31).

32. Erasmus wrote to Lee that he has "never knowingly written anything that goes against piety or Christ's glory" (*Responding to the Annotations of Edward Lee*, CWE 72: 241); see also CWE 72: 175–76. In response to the Valladolid articles, Erasmus asserts that he professes "openly, clearly, and expressly that the three Persons are distinct in their particular properties, not in their essence." See Erasmus, *Apology against Certain Spanish Monks*, CWE 75: 41; see also 50. Erasmus began his response to the Spanish monks with eighty quotations from his work that show that he holds the orthodox view of the Trinity (17–33).

the meaning and strength of support in various biblical passages, and to consider the larger implications of this doctrine for life, all of which his exchanges with Lee and other critics richly illustrate. When, for instance, Erasmus defends his choice of terms to convey the relation of the Father and the Son, he is well aware how weak and misleading language can be for talking of such matters, which is why he takes exception to Lee's suggestion that he is giving a "handle to the Arians," as all language, even the formulas decreed in councils and certainly anything Lee might have to say, is finally inadequate to the task.

It is in this context, as we will see in the first section of this chapter, that Erasmus insists—as he often and habitually does—that the limits of language for speaking about what is ultimately ineffable must be respected by everyone with all due modesty. Moreover, much of Trinitarian theology looks for support in one or another biblical passage, but as will be evident in the second section, many texts used by the orthodox to prove their point also can be read—sometimes with greater warrant—to support the Arian view. It is here, then, that we witness the critically honest appreciation for the variety of interpretations that Erasmus brings to bear over disputed passages, much to the dismay of someone like Lee, but ultimately for the benefit of sound Christological reflection. Too often in the early development of Christology, however, biblical texts were willfully corrupted to bolster orthodox thinking. In response, as we will see in the third section, Erasmus firmly rejects the manipulation of scripture to combat heretical thinking, even if that unmoors Trinitarian orthodoxy from helpful proof-texts, though the outcry from self-styled defenders of orthodoxy sometimes proves too difficult to bear. In the end, however, full-fledged Trinitarian thinking rests upon the grammatical novelties of the council of Nicaea—specifically, where the Son is deemed "one in being" (*homoousios*) with the Father—and such language, Erasmus contends, can only be demonstrated by means of "speculative reasoning."[33] However, because such questions surpass the capacity of human understanding, we will see in the final section of this chapter, Erasmus encourages agreement on the substance of what is meant, if not the exact wording, in order to achieve

---

33. Erasmus, *Apology against Certain Spanish monks*, CWE 75: 44.

concord between disputants, while shifting emphasis to what will be "conducive to a pious life."[34]

"The Dignity of the Son"

In commenting on Erasmus's annotation to the opening verse of the Gospel of John, Lee takes exception to the use of "the little word *particeps* (partaking)" to explain the manner in which the Son can be said to share in (or "partake" of) the divine nature. Lee's objection is not unwarranted, of course, since such terminology begs unwanted questions with doctrinally awkward answers, mostly implying some sort of unwanted division (each Person takes a part, for instance) or positing an inexplicable fourth (the divine essence or "Godhead" over and above the three Persons). The response of Erasmus is instructive, both in what he says directly to the objection and for what it shows more broadly about the limits of language for speaking of these matters. When directly addressing Lee's objection, Erasmus must first explain what he does not mean, in short, that "the Son does not 'partake' of the divine essence in the sense that he is just a part of the divine essence" (implying, it would seem, that each Person might take a distinct part),[35] or that "he does not 'partake' of divinity as we partake of it" (as something general, or even common).[36]

What Erasmus wants to say, in contrast, is that "the Son 'partakes' of the divine nature because he has it from the Father yet in such a way that the Father nevertheless has the very thing that he gives to the Son."[37] In this sense, he continues, the Son "'partake[s]' of it with the Father, from whom he has the quality that makes him God."[38] In mak-

---

34. Erasmus, *Responding to the Annotations of Edward Lee*, CWE 72: 397.

35. Erasmus, *Responding to the Annotations of Edward Lee*, CWE 72: 176, 178.

36. Erasmus, *Responding to the Annotations of Edward Lee*, CWE 72: 176.

37. Erasmus, *Responding to the Annotations of Edward Lee*, CWE 72: 176–77. See, similarly, Erasmus, *Apology against Certain Spanish Monks*, CWE 75: 55.

38. Erasmus, *Responding to the Annotations of Edward Lee*, CWE 72: 177. The emphasis on the Son's "participation" in a unified divine essence by way of the Father's preeminent causality echoes the Trinitarian theology of the Cappadocian fathers. See Pelikan, *Emergence of the Catholic Tradition*, 220–25. See, for instance, Gregory of Nyssa, "An Answer to Ablabius: That We Should Not Think of Saying There Are Three Gods," in *Christology of the Later Fathers*, 256–67, especially 260–63.

ing this effort to clarify his meaning, of course, Erasmus is well aware that he is treading through a thicket of words overgrown with multiple and misleading connotations. What that ultimately means is that "there are no human words through which we could express the ineffable and incomprehensible nature of the Trinity," and thus, Erasmus adds with emphasis, "like it or not, we must speak inadequately about them, using what words we have."[39] If Lee insists on using only the "proper meaning of words"—presumably meaning the terms of conciliar orthodoxy said in a clear and distinct manner—then, Erasmus boldly and correctly observes, Lee eventually will have to face the fact that "of the same essence" (*homoousios*) also "does not describe the relationship of the Son to the Father." In fact, anyone who insists on speaking of divine matters in "terms that are suited in every respect," Erasmus concludes, will simply "have to remain silent," as experience teaches nothing useful in this regard and language is woefully ill-equipped to speak "properly" of the divine.[40]

With that said, it is interesting to watch Erasmus working to explain how his annotation on the early verses of the Gospel of John does not diminish the "dignity of the Son," as Lee suggests it does. Erasmus had said in his annotation, as he recalls and as he will say again in his defense, that "the principle of first-beginning [*principium*] applies to the Father in the fullest and absolute sense, whereas the preposition 'through' suits the Son better than the Father."[41] Different things are attributable to each Person, in accord with what is said in the Gospel, so that, Erasmus observes, "everything has been created by the Father through the Word," while it does not hold that everything has "been created by the Word through the Father."[42] The relation is not reversible, and hence, these characteristics are not shared. So, once again, Father and Son are not "both God from God," as Hilary also observes,

---

39. Erasmus, *Responding to the Annotations of Edward Lee*, CWE 72: 176. Similar difficulties arise, Erasmus notes, with respect to "that ineffable union of human and divine nature" in Christ. Whatever terms are used to convey this "union," he continues, "we are merely stammering when we speak of God in his way."

40. Erasmus, *Responding to the Annotations of Edward Lee*, CWE 72: 177–78.

41. Erasmus, *Responding to the Annotations of Edward Lee*, CWE 72: 179.

42. Erasmus, *Responding to the Annotations of Edward Lee*, CWE 72: 185. Put differently, "the Son is not said to work through the Father as the Father works through the Son," so one is correct to insist on different attributions.

because "first-beginning" is something "specifically associated with the Father."[43]

At the same time, Erasmus insists with an added layer of complexity, "it does not follow that the Son is not *in some sense* the first-beginning," as the Son gets this "very quality" from the Father.[44] Thus, Erasmus acknowledges, while "'through' suits the Son better than the Father," this does not mean that he is "a created instrument of the Father through which all the rest was created, as some heretics [the Arians] have imagined." Having said that, however, he immediately recalls that "mystic Scripture nevertheless speaks of the Son in terms that make him appear to function as a sort of instrument of the Father (*if I may be allowed to use these terms for the moment*), since he created the world through the Son, redeemed humanity through him, and reconciled us to himself through him."[45]

With this heavily qualified statement, of course, Erasmus is knee-deep in the grammatical morass so common in Trinitarian discussions, and he is well aware of that. Little wonder that he insists, therefore, that a "fair interpreter" will allow that these kind of statements are "not so much concerned ... with the nature of God as with the linguistic usage of human beings."[46] In keeping with John 1:1–3, consequently, one will say first, that the Word was "with the Father in the beginning" and thus was "not at all one of things created in time," but also second, that the Father "created through him all things," though this does not mean, Erasmus quickly adds again, "that the Son is an instrument of the Father," even though—based on our experience of such things in "human matters"—"there is *a kind of notion of instrumentality*," through which "we speak of God imperfectly."[47] Nothing can be simple and univocal, clearly enough, when speaking of the divine life described at the beginning of the Gospel of John, and that is why Erasmus expects a

---

43. Erasmus, *Responding to the Annotations of Edward Lee*, CWE 72: 183.

44. Erasmus, *Responding to the Annotations of Edward Lee*, CWE 72: 185, my italics.

45. Erasmus, *Responding to the Annotations of Edward Lee*, CWE 72: 180, my italics. Erasmus understandably qualifies speaking of the Son's instrumentality, for as Pelikan observes, "the particular office of the Logos in Arian cosmology" is "to be the instrument through which the Creator fashioned the universe and all that is therein" (Pelikan, *Emergence of the Catholic Tradition*, 197).

46. Erasmus, *Responding to the Annotations of Edward Lee*, CWE 72: 180.

47. Erasmus, *Responding to the Annotations of Edward Lee*, CWE 72: 182–84, my italics.

fair reader (even if not Lee himself) to understand and appreciate that speaking of the Son as a "sort of instrument of the Father"—when given all due grammatical qualification—does not diminish the "dignity of the Son."[48]

Some of the same issues return in a discussion focused on Erasmus's annotation to John 8: 25, where Lee objects to Erasmus saying (among "several conjectures" offered) that "the term *principium* in the absolute sense did not apply to Christ, for a quality proper to the Son is to be from another."[49] Lee's aim is to push the language of Erasmus to what he takes to be its logical conclusion, at which point, he contends, Erasmus is "not very far from the Arian heresy." Thus, for example, if Erasmus says "that the Word is not the beginning without qualification," which he does by granting that the Word is "God from God," then, as Lee translates it, "the Word is not God without qualification."[50] This is not a conclusion that Erasmus would accept, though he does wonder whether Lee has somehow stumbled into his own heresy by seeming to deny that the Son has a beginning.[51]

The crucial question, of course, is what kind of beginning should be attributed to the Son? In response to this, Erasmus proceeds from an orthodox distinction of the divine Persons, where there are two senses of "beginning"—one absolutely, which is attributed to the Father, as "the beginning absolutely speaking," and another "when one Person

48. Erasmus, *Responding to the Annotations of Edward Lee*, CWE 72: 180, 182.

49. Erasmus, *Responding to the Annotations of Edward Lee*, CWE 72: 201–2. Following tradition, Lee infuses doctrine into his translation in order to protect a useful proof-text, thus rendering John 8:25 in a manner that accents the primordiality of Christ ("The *principium*, I speak to you"). For his part, and quite close to modern translations, Erasmus translates the passage to say, "what I have told you from the beginning."

50. Erasmus, *Responding to the Annotations of Edward Lee*, CWE 72: 203. Lee worries that it is giving "a handle to the Arians" to say with Augustine that "the Father is the beginning of the godhead." What handle can that be, Erasmus wonders? "Will [Augustine's statement] allow them to say that the Son is lower than the Father because he originates from him? [But] that the Son originates from the Father will not be denied by any orthodox writer" (208). On the metaphor of giving a handle, see Erasmus, "To look for a handle, and similar metaphors," adage I. iv. 4, CWE 31: 321–22.

51. Erasmus, *Responding to the Annotations of Edward Lee*, CWE 72: 205. That the Son is "God from God," after all, is well-established orthodox teaching from the Councils of Nicaea and Constantinople. Thus, Erasmus quips, "if it is heretical to deny that the Son originates from the Father, God from God, it must be heretical to say that he is the beginning without beginning," as Lee apparently wished to do by ascribing *principium* to the Son without qualification.

proceeds from another Person," which is said of the Son and the Spirit.[52] But while this distinction underscores the difference of Father and Son, it does not go far enough, as Arius himself says that "the Son is not unbegotten" (since only "God is without beginning") but "was constituted … before times and before ages … divine, unique, unchangeable."[53] So Erasmus adds another distinction, this time between "two kinds of originating, first when one Person proceeds from another Person, [and] second when creature proceeds from Creator."[54] When, therefore, Erasmus cites Colossians 1:15 in saying that the Son is "first-born of all creation," he follows the orthodox Ambrose in saying that "before creation the Son was born, not created, so that his nativity might be distinguished from the making of creation." This is necessary, Erasmus emphasizes, "lest anyone follow Arius in making the Son of God a creature."[55] Then again, of course, any good Arian would not have a problem with the language of Colossians, and while it is true, as Erasmus notes, that the Arians "believed the Son of God was a creature in his divine nature," making him subordinate to the Father (as he was born from him), this was for them an extraordinary creature, superior to anything in the created world, as he was divinely made or begotten uniquely before the created world came to be.[56] So, quite unexpectedly, if granted a fair and accommodating reading, perhaps the Arian view is not so very far from the orthodox view after all, though this is not a possibility that Erasmus pursues in this context.

How strained, how complex, and how slippery language proves to be for speaking about the relation of God and world in Trinitarian terms. Terms drawn from experience prove ill-suited for speaking of the divine

52. Erasmus, *Responding to the Annotations of Edward Lee*, CWE 72: 209, 211. Compare this with Erasmus's discussion of the various senses of "beginning" (204–205, 206).

53. "The Letter of Arius to Eusebius of Nicomedia," *Christology of the Later Fathers*, 330.

54. Erasmus, *Responding to the Annotations of Edward Lee*, CWE 72: 211.

55. Erasmus, *Responding to the Annotations of Edward Lee*, CWE 72: 304. See Erasmus, *Paraphrase on Colossians*, CWE 43: 401–2, where Erasmus writes, "before anything was created, he was, from eternity, the image of the eternal Father, not created, but born of him from whom all things exist and which alone has no beginning." Erasmus proceeds, interestingly to quote the principle that the Arians use to justify the subordinate status of the Son—"for what has been created must necessarily be inferior to its own creator"—in order to demarcate the inferiority of angels and the "eminent ones" from the Father and the Son.

56. Erasmus, *Responding to the Annotations of Edward Lee*, CWE 72: 305. Arius adds, "and before he was begotten or created or ordained or founded, he was not." See "Letter of Arius to Eusebius of Nicomedia," *Christology of the Later Fathers*, 330.

life, as Erasmus makes clear, and trying to say something intelligible about the relation of divine Persons requires so many qualifications as to completely contort the original sense. When Lee suggests, moreover, that Erasmus is "not very far from the Arian heresy" for saying that the Son is "from another," this proposal (strangely enough) would apply equally well for any orthodox account, where the Son is said to be "God from God." One could similarly suggest, once again—far-fetched though it may seem—that the Arian language of "begotten" and "unique" is "not very far" from the orthodox view, should an Arian Lee push Arian theology in the way that Lee himself presses Erasmus, or, better yet, as Erasmus says later, if someone intent on concord would offer a "more accommodating interpretation" of such terms. What if, Erasmus graciously wonders, the Arians "meant that being born from another, and being of another, was somehow the same as being created?" Might it then have been possible to abandon "conflict over words" as long as "they could agree on the substance of faith?"[57] Or on the orthodox side, Erasmus writes, similarly, "when Hilary says that the Father has more authority than the Son, but in such a manner that the Son is not inferior, since the Father has imparted equality to him—I ask you, if I may speak the truth, does this not differ very little from the Arians?"[58]

Maneuvering around Trinitarian topics requires grammatical dexterity, as we have seen from Erasmus, but it also demands a "fair" interlocutor, one who wields theological language with modesty, without "making everything an article of faith," as Erasmus puts it, while listening fairly and with empathy to someone else's views. When Trinitarian theology is played out on the terrain of controversy, after all, the value of a position is determined by reference to its doctrinal boundaries, that is, by which views it manages to exclude or avoid as heterodox or heretical.[59] For Erasmus, however, the ultimate boundary for such

57. Erasmus, *Responding to the Annotations of Edward Lee*, CWE 72: 397–98.
58. Erasmus, *Responding to the Annotations of Edward Lee*, CWE 72: 398. As Erasmus puts it, still paraphrasing Hilary, "If the Father is greater than the Son by the authority of origin, he is greater according to the concept of divine nature. But he does not impart to the Son that by which he is greater, for the Son [as a Son] appears inferior to him in that part [since he is not a Father]." Would not a wise Arian rightly ask how much this differs from their view?
59. Much of the history of Christology is framed as a controversy between orthodoxy and heresy, even where, as a historical discipline, it is no longer a question of promoting orthodoxy against heretical threats, and this unfortunate scholarly habit reappears when interpreters of

discourse is not the heretical but the ineffable, before which "no human words are proper for divine things."[60]

"Handle to the Arians"

Given the "ineffable and incomprehensible nature of the Trinity," Erasmus says, "we must speak inadequately, … using what words we have."[61] And that means not only words drawn from experience, as we have seen thus far, but also and especially language drawn from scripture. With the latter in mind, Erasmus quotes from his "On Praying to God"—in a passage later contested by the Spanish monks meeting in Valladolid—to say that "it is a good principle of Christian doctrine to revere everything pertaining to divinity, but not to affirm anything except what is explicitly stated in the Sacred Scriptures."[62] Rigorous as this statement sounds, Erasmus immediately adds that "expressly stated" includes "that which necessarily follows from the Sacred Writings," a qualification that warrants certain elements of Trinitarian theology, "that the Holy Spirit is not the Son," for instance, not actually found in scripture.

As Erasmus proceeds in his debate with critics, Christian scriptures are the primary resource for language with which to speak of the dignity and divinity of the Son, and hence also the fundamental norm both

---

Erasmus persist in assessing his Christology by how close or how far he stands from Arianism. Though John B. Payne exonerates Erasmus from the charge of Arianism, he continues to use the heterodox label of "Origenistic" for what he calls "a definite strand of subordinationism in his Christology." Payne illustrates this charge by noting the repeated manner in which Erasmus describes how the Son "derives" or "receives" his being "from the Father," language that is hardly heterodox. See Payne, *Erasmus: His Theology of the Sacraments*, 58–59. James D. Tracy cites Payne's work to say that the Christology of Erasmus was "mildly subordinationist, though definitely not Arian." See Tracy, "Erasmus and the Arians: Remarks on the *Consensus Ecclesiae*," *The Catholic Historical Review* 67 (Jan. 1981): 4. Unlike Payne and Tracy, Coogan explicitly indicts Erasmus—leveling his assertions not as a historian, but as a Catholic inquisitor—on charges of Arian thinking, since Erasmus "dares to say that even *homoousios* fails to express the trinitarian unity." Worse yet, Coogan proclaims with unmitigated self-confidence that Erasmus is responsible for the "birth of sects and the renaissance of Arianism." See Coogan, *Erasmus, Lee and the Correction of the Vulgate*, 90, 81.

60. Erasmus, *Apology against Certain Spanish Monks*, CWE 75: 54–55. See also Erasmus, *Paraphrase on John*, trans. Jane E. Phillips, in *Collected Works of Erasmus: New Testament Scholarship*, vol. 46 (Toronto: University of Toronto Press, 1991), 13.

61. Erasmus, *Responding to the Annotations of Edward Lee*, CWE 72: 176.

62. Erasmus, *Apology against Certain Spanish Monks*, CWE 75: 52; Erasmus "On Praying to God," trans. John N. Grant, CWE 70: 186. See also Erasmus to Jean de Carondelet, letter 1334, CWE 9: 253, 260.

for admitting what is said appropriately and for challenging the false "pronouncements" born of the rash "curiosity" of some theologians.[63] With that said, however, the critical care Erasmus takes in handling biblical texts brings readers face to face with the fact that individual passages taken as support by the orthodox often can be read equally well, and sometimes better, from an Arian perspective. In commenting on disputed texts on the divinity of the Son, consequently, Erasmus demonstrates not only his critical sense for biblical wording and context, broadly setting his judgments in conversation with a variety of readings from various church fathers, but also his interpretive empathy, a posture that allows him to appreciate the reasonableness of Arian readings, or at least to concede that either of the rival interpretations possess merit. Consider, for instance, the disputes surrounding the following numbered passages, two from John and two from Pauline sources.

(1) "And this is eternal life, that they may know you, the only true God, and Jesus Christ whom you have sent" (Jn 17:3). "This more than any other passage," Erasmus observes, "gave the Arians occasion to err and say that only the Father was truly and properly God." For good reason, it might be added, since this pericope identifies the source of "eternal life" with the one addressed as "the only true God," from which "Jesus Christ" is distinguished as the one who was "sent" to facilitate this salvific knowledge. And yet, interestingly enough, Erasmus concludes this very remark with the generous suggestion that "perhaps they meant that he [the Father] alone was the source of divinity, which our theologians do not deny."[64] Before explaining this point, Erasmus pauses to correct Lee's account of what the Arians said of the Son— quoting Augustine in his disputation with Maximinus, as well as Hilary, Chrysostom, and Jerome—to show that the Arians held the Son to be true Son but not "truly God," at least in the sense that the Son was not without origin.[65]

---

63. Erasmus, *Apology against Certain Spanish Monks*, CWE 75: 52.

64. Erasmus, *Responding to the Annotations of Edward Lee*, CWE 72: 357. In the annotation, Erasmus wrote, "I do not know whether they meant that he is the only beginning of deity (something our theologians do not deny)" (359, n. 63). As the note indicates, this statement was removed in 1527.

65. Erasmus, *Responding to the Annotations of Edward Lee*, CWE 72: 357–59.

In the following note, Lee quotes Erasmus, and Erasmus cites his own words to say that he does "not consider it impious if anyone says that Father is the only true God, that is, the only source of the whole godhead." It is proper, Erasmus observes with help from Hilary and Augustine, to attribute "to each Person its proper quality," such that "the Father can be understood to be eternal in a particular and proper sense in which the Son is not," if "for no other reason," and a good one at that, which Erasmus draws from Augustine, "that the Father does not have a father from whom he originates, whereas the Son derives from the Father his existence and the fact that he shares eternity with him."[66] With that said, therefore, Erasmus rightly wonders "what would prevent us from calling the Father the only true God as well"—thereby joining with the Arians in reading John 17:3—"because the term 'God' applies to him in a particular sense in which it does not apply to the Son or the Holy Spirit, for he is God in the sense that he is the source and author of all divinity."[67]

(2) "While we wait for the blessed hope and the manifestation of the glory of our great God and Savior, Jesus Christ" (Titus 2:13).[68] Erasmus here observes, to begin with, that Jerome, Chrysostom, and Theophylact read this pericope by "combining" both terms (greatness and savior) as referring to Christ. With this reading, Erasmus continues, they "rejoice, as it were, and celebrate a victory over the Arians." But—he adds with caution—though he, too, "rejoice[s] in our victory," it would be better to "have considered what objections the opponent could immediately raise," as "the passage is plainly ambiguous, and in fact supports the Arians more than us." Indeed, he notes with a keen sense for the nuance of the wording, this passage also can be read "by dividing," whereby "greatness" refers only to the Father, while "savior" is attributed to the Son. "There is nothing in the expression itself," he continues," that prevents it from being understood as two separate phrases, with

---

66. Erasmus, *Responding to the Annotations of Edward Lee*, CWE 72: 360. Erasmus quotes from Augustine, "On the Holy Trinity," in *Nicene and Post-Nicene Fathers of the Christian Church*, ed. Philip Schaff (New York: Charles Scribner's Sons, 1900), bk. 6, chap. 10, 103.

67. Erasmus, *Responding to the Annotations of Edward Lee*, CWE 72: 360.

68. I quote the passage from *The New Oxford Annotated Bible: New Revised Standard Version*, 4th ed., ed. Michael D. Coogan (Oxford: Oxford University Press, 2010). The annotation of Erasmus reads as "of God in his greatness and our Saviour Jesus Christ" (Erasmus, *Responding to the Annotations of Edward Lee*, CWE 72: 400).

the first part referring [solely] to the Father." It is this interpretation that is found in Ambrose, Erasmus notes, though he acknowledges that Jerome and other Fathers read this passage by combining the terms as attributes of the Son.

For his part, however, Erasmus declares himself "satisfied that this passage can be expounded differently," though he personally thinks that "Paul did not mean anything other than what Ambrose interprets." In that case, therefore, the passage should be read by dividing the terms, in which case it could not be used as a proof-text against the Arians. Indeed, Erasmus adds, "the Arians would more quickly take from it the opportunity to say that Christ is inferior to the Father, because Paul calls the Father 'great' but calls the Son neither 'God' nor 'great God.'" Even if there were no ambiguity in this passage, however, it will not be very useful against the Arians, Erasmus concludes, as they "do not deny that the Son is God, and God cannot but be great," and there is no reason for them not to think that the Father is "greater," and in fact, "so great that nothing is greater than he."[69]

(3) "To them belong the patriarchs, and from them, according to the flesh, comes the Messiah, who is over all, God blessed forever" (Rom 9:5). The objection from the Valladolid articles against Erasmus complains that he muddies the "plain, simple, and manifest meaning" of this passage—to wit, that here Christ is called God—by introducing a "shameless equivocation," wherein he suggests that the final clause was added by Paul as a doxology and thus does not refer to the Son.[70] In response, Erasmus reminds his readers both that he often "professes so clearly the divine nature of the Son" and that in his *Paraphrases on Romans*, he renders this passage in a way that expressly identifies Christ as God.[71] At the same time, Erasmus notes—as is characteristic

<hr>

69. Erasmus, *Responding to the Annotations of Edward Lee*, CWE 72: 400–401. See also Erasmus, *An Apologia by Desiderius Erasmus of Rotterdam Replying to Diego López Zúñiga's Criticism of the First Edition of the New Testament*, trans. Erika Rummel, CWE 74: 59; Erasmus, *An Apologia Concerning Three Passages Which the Theologian Sancho Carranza Had Defended as Right Criticized by Zúñiga*, CWE 74: 189–91.

70. Erasmus, *Apology against Certain Spanish Monks*, CWE 75: 64–65.

71. Erasmus, *Apology against Certain Spanish Monks*, CWE 75: 65. See Erasmus, *Paraphrases on Romans*, trans. John B. Payne, Albert Rabil Jr., and Warren S. Smith, Jr., in *Collected Works of Erasmus: New Testament Scholarship*, vol. 42, ed. Robert D. Sider (Toronto: University of Toronto Press, 1984), 53. In his annotation on this passage, Erasmus says that "Paul has clearly pronounced Christ God." See Erasmus, *Annotations on Romans*, trans. John B. Payne, Albert

of his manner of interpretation—there were a variety of readings of this passage among the classics of Christian tradition, and that fact at least shows that Paul's words were not so clear that alternative readings were not possible.[72]

More important, however, are the critical comments Erasmus brings to bear on the punctuation of this passage, allowing for two different readings. On the one hand, Erasmus argues, for someone "learned in the Greek language," the passage reads, "God, who is above all things, be blessed for all ages." In this case, "the meaning is devotional," as it ends with an exclamation of thanks "inspired by divine goodness towards the human race."[73] On the other hand, he grants, this passage can be punctuated with two commas in the second half of the sentence (as is the case in the quotation given above), in which case "the meaning will be that Christ is above all things." For that reading, one may conclude that "Christ is God," though as Erasmus notes, even then "he is not called God simply and openly."[74] For his part, Erasmus prefers the first interpretation, such that this phrase applies "either to the Father

---

Rabil Jr., Robert D. Sider, and Warren S. Smith, Jr., in *Collected Works of Erasmus: New Testament Scholarship*, vol. 56, ed. Robert D. Sider (Toronto: University of Toronto Press, 1994), 249.

72. Erasmus, *Apology against Certain Spanish Monks*, CWE 75: 66. In later editions of the *Annotations*, especially the 1535 edition, Erasmus underscores the plurality of interpretations given to this passage. See Erasmus, *Annotations on Romans*, CWE 56: 242–44, 249–51.

73. Erasmus, *Apology against Certain Spanish Monks*, CWE 75: 66. Erasmus cites other biblical examples (including from Paul) of such doxologies; see 67. For similar comments, see the additions added in 1522 and 1535 in Erasmus, *Annotations on Romans*, CWE 56: 245, 251.

74. Erasmus, *Apology against Certain Spanish Monks*, CWE 75: 66. Erasmus raised a stir with critics, including Lee and the Spanish monks, by noting how seldom Jesus is called "God" in Christian scriptures. See also Erasmus to Jean de Carondelet, letter 1334, CWE 9: 250. Thus, for example, he observes Paul's "usual fashion" of calling the Father "God," while "in very few places is the Son called God," though Erasmus quickly adds that he does not deny "that it may be sufficiently inferred from his words that the Son is also God" (*Responding to the Annotations of Edward Lee*, CWE 72: 283). In the annotation to 1 Timothy 1:17, he similarly observes how rare it is "in the letters of the apostles for the name God to be attributed to Christ or the Holy Spirit, whether to avoid giving offence to some or because they were keeping it for its own time—for the apostles did not immediately preach Christ as God or as the Son of God" (*Apology against Certain Spanish Monks*, CWE 75: 70, n. 291). Erasmus adds, however, that they "were not proclaiming that he was mere man if they did not openly call him God, but Lord" (71). Shortly after that, Erasmus notes "how many times … orthodox writers such as Chrysostom and Jerome remind us that the apostles did not immediately call Jesus God in the presence of unlearned. And of the evangelists only John openly calls him God" (73). Erasmus's sense for the historical development of this practice is regularly explained with a developmental view of revelation. Erasmus returns to these debates in *An Apologia to Diego López Zúñiga*, CWE 74: 59, and *An Apologia to Sancho Carranza*, CWE 74: 180–81.

or to the whole Trinity" but "not peculiarly to Christ." With that said, however, he insists that his comments are meant purely as "things for the reader's consideration," so that "each person [may] have their own uncompromised opinion."[75] Regardless of which reading is given to this passage, Erasmus adds, it will be of little rhetorical value against the Arians.[76]

(4) "I and the Father are one" (Jn 10:30). Here Erasmus acknowledges to Lee that many orthodox readers will instantly assume that this brief passage will force the Arians "to admit that the Son is *homoousios*, 'of one substance with' the Father."[77] But they will be wrong to think that the Arians will be so easily moved by this passage, Erasmus counters, as they can escape easily by saying that the words from John refer to the "mutual agreement" of Father and Son but not to "their being one of substance."[78] Along the same lines, Erasmus cautions, no one should jump thoughtlessly to the conclusion that Jesus' request of the Father that those who follow him may "be one as we also are" (Jn 17:11) in any way vindicates the orthodox belief in the unity of the divine substance against the Arians.[79] It is true, of course, and Erasmus readily grants it, that John 10:30 may serve to "strengthen the conviction of orthodox believers," though he is quick to add that it will not have "the same efficacy

75. Erasmus, *Apology against Certain Spanish Monks*, CWE 75: 68–69. For a contemporary discussion of four readings of this text, see *Romans*, trans. Joseph A. Fitzmeyer, Anchor Bible, vol. 33 (New York: Doubleday, 1992), 548–49. The first "makes Paul proclaim Christ as preeminent among the prerogatives of Israel, even as God (though not *ho theos*), and blest forever." The second, the view of Erasmus ("who introduced the modern discussion of the punctuation"), has "Paul assert the natural descent of Christ from Israel, and then because of it utters a doxology addressed to God as preeminent in the manner of Jewish doxologies. Christ is thus the climax of the prerogatives of the Israelites as Messiah, and Paul praises God for it." The third reading is a variant of the second, in which (with different punctuation) "Paul acknowledge[s] the natural descent of Christ and assert[s] his preeminence among Israel's prerogatives, and then praises God in a doxology because of it." The fourth view, finally, first mentioned by a "sixteenth-century Socinian" and not out of keeping with an Arian perspective, says that "Christ by natural descent is a prerogative of Israel, but that God is the one who is preeminent and blest forever." Only the first reading explicitly identifies Christ with God.

76. Erasmus, *Apology against Certain Spanish Monks*, CWE 75: 66.

77. Erasmus, *Responding to the Annotations of Edward Lee*, CWE 75: 409.

78. Erasmus, *Responding to the Annotations of Edward Lee*, CWE 75: 409. That the words of John 10:30 refer to a "unity of power and operation," see *The Gospel According to John (I-xii)*, trans. Raymond E. Brown, Anchor Bible, vol. 29 (Garden City, NY: Doubleday and Company, 1966), 407.

79. Erasmus, *Responding to the Annotations of Edward Lee*, CWE 75: 409–10. The same holds for the language of oneness in John 17:20–21, 22–23. See, similarly, Erasmus, *Apology against Certain Spanish Monks*, CWE 75: 46.

with obstinate heretics," or for that matter with those who simply disagree. And the heretics would be right, Erasmus adds, as it is not the case that "whenever in Scripture two are said to be one it is understood that they are of one undivided essence."[80]

So Erasmus calls into question, here and elsewhere, the practice of wielding weak or forced arguments against the Arians, first, because it is a style of interpretation that does "violence to Scripture," and second, because it will not have any effect in "weakening the pertinacity of [these] heretics."[81] It may be understandable, he concedes, that the fathers who were caught up in the struggle against heresies would use whatever arguments they could muster, even if some packed greater validity for those who were "favourably disposed" than for those "reluctant to believe." But no one should think, on that account, that such arguments bear great authority and lead to certainty; nor should "orthodox believers" be overly surprised (or "shaken," for that matter) to discover that proof-texts like this can easily be "refuted by men of keen intelligence."[82]

What stands out in Erasmus's handling of these four passages is his steadfast fidelity to the biblical texts, as best they can be retrieved with the critical tools of his day, in a manner that is remarkably independent of the apologetic interests of theological orthodoxy. That does not mean that he is not committed to sound theological understanding, though it seems likely that he would not have addressed Trinitarian questions without being pressed by critics, but it does mean that whatever is said of the dignity and divinity of the Son—certainly an integral dimension of his Christology—should not be based on errant philology, twisted interpretation, and weak rhetoric. The problem with pressing biblical passages into service as weapons against heretics is, in the first place, that the reader is tempted to assume that the words and the phrasing means what is needed for polemical purposes, and thereby the text is

---

80. Erasmus, *Apology against Certain Spanish Monks*, CWE 75: 46. Thus, Erasmus observes, "when Paul writes to the Galatians 'You are all one in Jesus Christ,' [Gal 3:28] he does not speak of substance but of their fellowship in grace. And again, when he writes to the Romans [actually 1 Cor 3:8], 'he who plants and he who waters are one' he speaks of equality in function, not of the same substance." See Erasmus, *Responding to the Annotations of Edward Lee*, CWE 72: 410.

81. Erasmus, *Apology against Certain Spanish Monks*, CWE 75: 46–47.

82. Erasmus, *Apology against Certain Spanish Monks*, CWE 75: 47–48.

forced to say what it does not say. Far better, Erasmus shows, to begin with textual scrutiny (determining, as much as is possible, what is authentic and what is a later corruption of the text) and philological considerations (tending to wording, punctuation, context, and so on), and then to pursue theological questions on that basis. Bent on victory rather than understanding, in the second place, the wielding of biblical texts as weapons against heretics bespeaks an unspoken air of invincibility, though, in fact, it opens the door to a conflict without end. "If we try to exclude every objection of the Arians," Erasmus exclaims more generally, "they would be able to question also 'And the Word was God' and 'My Lord and my God,' and a thousand other passages of this kind."[83]

How much better, Erasmus advises, to approach difficult passages with a capacious sense of theological possibility and thus to interpret in a manner that confidently acknowledges, even as it actively engages, a rich variety of interpretation both within and beyond the pale of established orthodoxy. In practice, as we have seen, Erasmus regularly engages assorted fathers of the early church, squarely facing up to the conflict of interpretation among them, and often conceding that either of the rival interpretations are justifiable. He also proceeds in a manner that is generous and sympathetic to heterodox views, yielding an accommodating posture that allows him to appreciate the worth of Arians readings, even when he finally disagrees with them. Then again, he adds, relying on errant philology and twisted interpretations to ward off the challenge of heretics is rhetorically ineffective, as any thoughtful Arian easily will spot the weakness of such arguments. How much more persuasive it is to tender one's case on the basis of honest scholarship, with a capacious sense of theological possibility, and in a manner that is both generous and sympathetic to one's rivals.

"Tricks of This Sort"

To look at ancient books historically—as Erasmus did in his *Annotations* on Christian scriptures, but also as he did when editing the works of Seneca and Jerome, for example—is to admit that these works

---

83. Erasmus, *Apology against Certain Spanish Monks*, CWE 75: 66.

developed in and through the hands of fallible human beings and their traditions across time. Though it surely is true that Erasmus affirms "the inviolable authority of divine Scripture," he grants without hesitation that the evangelists were "human none the less," and hence they could make mistakes, though, he piously adds, the "credit of the whole of Scripture" is not "imperilled" if an evangelist "by a slip of memory did put one name for another."[84] What is more, the transmission of biblical texts through the hands of countless translators and scribes introduces abundant textual corruptions, and hence it adds even more variation and confusion to biblical materials. All of this is the inevitable result of the very human process of tradition, Erasmus observes.[85] So while one may wish for a pure text without disagreement and corruption, Erasmus adds with perfect honesty, "it never has been the fact, nor, I think, ever will be."[86]

Worse by far are the places and times where scripture is manipulated to promote a doctrine against heretics. Indeed, Erasmus writes

84. Erasmus to Johann Maier von Eck, letter 844, CWE 6: 28. See also Erasmus to Maarten van Dorp, letter 337, CWE 3: 136. Elsewhere, Erasmus cautiously suggests that no harm is done in saying that "the Spirit governed the minds of the apostles in so far as it was present in their meanings; but in their expression it left them to their own ability" ("A Response by Desiderius Erasmus," CWE 73: 165). The same holds for the "Translator" responsible for the authoritative Vulgate text, who Erasmus says makes many mistakes in "correct Latin." As he puts it, however, "Scripture will not immediately become a human artifact if the Translator uses human powers of the mind to translate what he reads" (144).

85. On corruption and changes in scriptural texts, see CWE 72: 76–82. Indeed, Erasmus asks Lee, "who has ever produced either a manuscript or a printed copy of the holy books with such scrupulous care that no corruption can be found in it anywhere?" It is simply impossible, Erasmus insists, which is why the careful editorial work of the biblical critic is so important and so legitimate. In response to the Spanish monks meeting at Valladolid, however, Erasmus points out, somewhat humorously, his own lapse of attention in allowing the phrase "of you" (from Luke 1:35, where the angel says to Mary that "the child to be born [of you] will be holy") to remain in the 1516 edition of the New Testament, even while he had written in his annotation that those two words "are not found in any Greek manuscript nor in Theophylact nor in ancient Latin manuscripts." As Erasmus later discovered, those he had put in charge of "correcting proofs" had reinserted the phrase, as they preferred to follow a "manuscript of the New Testament" provided by Johann Reuchlin ("which was more beautiful than accurate") than the "very old manuscript of Theophylact." Erasmus mocks as "nonsense" his critics' suggestion that "of you" is an important proof-text against the Sabellians, though his response is more interesting (and amusing) as an example of his own editorial error, something he often attributes to careless and ignorant scribes (*Apology against Certain Spanish Monks*, CWE 75: 78–79).

86. Erasmus, "*Apologia* of Desiderius Erasmus," CWE 41: 467. As Erasmus observes in the same context, "the version that is now old was once new; and this new version, if we permit, will at some time in the future be old." See, similarly, Erasmus, *The Chief Points in the Arguments*, CWE 41: 832.

in the *System of True Theology*, "nearly every one of the ancients twists the Scriptures whenever they contend with an adversary;"[87] and, as he adds to Lee, "on no occasion was more violence done to Scripture than in arguments against heretics, when we twist everything to gain a victory."[88] Sometimes the wording itself may be altered, as when—Erasmus surmises—the Greeks added the word "wise" to "the only God" in 1 Timothy 1:17 to counter the Arians "who wanted only the Father to be regarded as the true God,"[89] while on other occasions, a passage will be pressed to thwart a heretical challenge, as when the language of "in the form of God" in Philippians 2:6–7 is "rather forcibly twisted to refer to Christ's [divine] nature" rather than (as Ambrose had it) "to the image and example of one who manifests himself as God in miracles."[90] It is never a good thing, Erasmus declares, that "we should maintain Christ's teaching by tricks of this sort," which is why, as we will see shortly, he labors to rectify these deliberate corruptions of scripture, though for the self-styled defenders of orthodoxy—not unexpectedly—these efforts of Erasmus leave the Arian heresy "unshaken and unassailable" by removing the church's standard arguments against them.[91]

With regard to Trinitarian questions, the most notorious case of orthodox corruption and the most controversial instance where Erasmus moves to restore a scriptural text concerns the so-called Johannine comma,[92] the clause inserted in the middle of 1 John 5:7–8, originating

87. Erasmus, *System of True Theology*, CWE 41: 683–84. See also Erasmus to Archduke Ferdinand, letter 1333, CWE 9: 243.

88. Erasmus, *Responding to the Annotations of Edward Lee*, CWE 72: 394. Only rarely does Erasmus sympathize with ancient writers who wielded twisted arguments against their adversaries, though he quickly adds that such measures were hardly convincing (*Apology against Certain Spanish Monks*, CWE 75: 47).

89. See Erasmus, *Responding to the Annotations of Edward Lee*, CWE 72: 309–11. The passage reads, "To the King of the ages, immortal, invisible, the only God, be honor and glory forever and ever." See Jerry H. Bentley, *Humanists and Holy Writ: New Testament Scholarship in the Renaissance* (Princeton, NJ: Princeton University Press, 1983), 151–52. As Bentley puts it, "the adjective [wise] would qualify the otherwise stark reference to 'the only God' and make it less likely for interpreters to cite the text in an effort to exclude Jesus from the Godhead" (152).

90. Erasmus, *Responding to the Annotations of Edward Lee*, CWE 72: 393–94. In his *Paraphrase on Philippians*, CWE 43: 371, Erasmus instead stresses the "example of perfect modesty" demonstrated by Christ who "was by nature God." In his response to Lee, Erasmus declares that he does not reject either reading. See also Hieronymus Dungersheim to Erasmus, letter 554, CWE 4: 286–91.

91. Erasmus, *Apology against Certain Spanish Monks*, CWE 75: 49–50.

92. With the comma in brackets, the full text of 1 John 5:7–8 would read as follows: "there are

in North Africa and Spain centuries after the composition of this letter, first as a gloss in the margins and then later in the Latin text itself, whereupon it became a convenient proof-text for the doctrine of the Trinity.[93] What could be better, church apologists no doubt thought, than to draw on an explicit reference to the three Persons of the Trinity in Christian scriptures? For the 1516 edition of the New Testament, however, Erasmus records in his *Annotations* that he found no sign of this passage in the Greek manuscripts at his disposal, and hence, he did not include it in the Greek or Latin text of either the 1516 or the 1519 editions.[94]

For Lee and other critics, however, this move directly threatened the received text (the Vulgate) used in the churches, while indirectly undermining the authority of the church by removing a most convenient proof-text for the orthodox doctrine of the Trinity. As Erasmus explains in successive editions of the *Annotations*, he consulted a number of manuscripts available to him, including a "very ancient codex in the Vatican Library, in which there is no mention of the testimony of the Father, Word and Spirit," and the comma is nowhere to be found.[95]

---

three that testify [in heaven, the Father, the Word, and the Holy Ghost. And these three are one. And there are three that give testimony on earth], the Spirit and the water and the blood, and these three agree." On Erasmus's developing comments on this passage, see Rummel, *Erasmus' Annotations on the New Testament*, 132–34.

93. On the origin and history of this passage, see *The Epistles of John*, trans. Raymond E. Brown, Anchor Bible, vol. 30 (Garden City, NY: Doubleday and Company, 1982), 775–87. Today, Brown notes, "scholars are virtually unanimous that the Comma arose well after the first century, as a trinitarian reflection of the original text of 1 John and was added to the biblical MSS. hundreds of years after 1 John was written" (776).

94. "Translation of Erasmus's annotations on the Johannine comma (1516–35)," in Grantley McDonald, *Biblical Criticism in Early Modern Europe: Erasmus, the Johannine Comma and Trinitarian Debate* (Cambridge: Cambridge University Press, 2016), 315. Erasmus includes a paraphrase of the Johannine comma in his *Paraphrase on the First Epistle of John*, trans. John J. Bateman, in *Collected Works of Erasmus: New Testament Scholarship*, vol. 44 (Toronto: University of Toronto Press, 1993), 198. As Bateman observes, Erasmus included the disputed passage because he was paraphrasing the Vulgate which included it (348, n. 9). Oddly enough, in 1526, the Paris theologians took exception to Erasmus's paraphrase on 1 John 5:7–8, suggesting that he had eliminated "the strong testimony for belief in the unity of substance in three persons, [thereby] providing a foothold to defend the heresy of Arius." In response, Erasmus correctly points out that his paraphrase "expressly and clearly professes" this point of orthodoxy (*Clarifications Concerning the Censures*, CWE 82: 146–47).

95. "Translation of Erasmus' annotations on the Johannine comma," 319–20. As he writes in response to Lee, "if I had come across one manuscript that had the reading found in our texts, I *would have* added the phrase in the others on the strength of that one." Instead, he adds, he simply "indicated what was lacking in the Greek texts." See Erasmus, *Responding to the Annotations*

Nor, he continues, did church fathers (like Cyril, Augustine, and Bede) deploy this passage against the Arians, something they surely would have done if this testimony to the Trinity had been included in their versions of 1 John.[96]

When Erasmus later was informed that there was a Greek manuscript of 1 John that contained the comma (the Codex Montfortianus in Ireland), he quickly changed course and included the comma, first in a separate Latin translation printed in 1521 and then in the 1522 edition of the New Testament. As Bietenholz observes, however, this "by no means equalled a retraction" on Erasmus's part, for as he explains in the 1522 *Annotations*, he continued to "suspect that this codex was adapted to agree with the manuscripts of the Latins," and in this regard, he was entirely correct.[97] Whatever his reasons for including the comma in 1522, and those reasons surely were manifold and complex, his move proved to be only a pause—and certainly not a surrender—of his critical posture in studying scriptural texts.[98] However, even with the comma remaining in 1 John, Erasmus counters in typical fashion that

---

of Edward Lee, CWE 72: 404, my italics. As H. J. De Jonge argues, "this is not a promise [to include it later], but a justification after the event of what had happened cast in the unfulfilled conditional." See H. J. De Jonge, "Erasmus and the *Comma Johanneum*," *Ephemerides Theologicae Lovanienses* 56, fasc. 4 (1980): 385.

96. "Translation of Erasmus' annotations on the Johannine comma," 316–17; Erasmus, *Responding to the Annotations of Edward Lee*, CWE 72: 406. See also Erasmus, *An Apologia to Diego López Zúñiga*, CWE 74: 151–54.

97. Bietenholz, *Encounters with a Radical Erasmus*, 236; "Translation of Erasmus' annotations on the Johannine comma," 319. See also Erasmus, *An Apologia to Diego López Zúñiga*, CWE 74: 154–55. McDonald wryly observes that it was a "remarkable coincidence" that this manuscript "should have been presented to Erasmus at the moment when it might make a difference" (*Biblical Criticism in Early Modern Europe*, 33). It is likely, in fact, that this text was produced by British Franciscans under the direction of Lee, though as De Jonge suggests, it is unlikely, or at least unproven, that Erasmus himself suspected that the text was produced "to induce him to include the Comma Johanneum" (De Jonge, "Erasmus and the Comma Johanneum," 386–89).

98. De Jonge argues that Erasmus did not restore the comma to fulfill a promise, as he sometimes is read, but "for the sake of his ideal"—that is, to provide a "new, modern and readable translation of the New Testament in Latin," and, hence, "to make the words of Christ and the apostles accessible to a wide circle"—by removing any impediments to his project ("Erasmus and the Comma Johanneum," 384–85). It may also be the case that Erasmus truly wished "to preserve harmony in the church on a matter not worth fighting about," as Joseph M. Levine points out. See Levine, "Erasmus and the Problem of the Johannine Comma," *Journal of the History of Ideas* 58, no. 4 (October 1977): 593. David M. Whitford rightly adds that, given the surge in anti-Lutheran forces in 1521, something for which Erasmus often was targeted, he "yielded to the pressures of his time" simply (but importantly) "to save his own skin." See Whitford, "Yielding to the Prejudices of His Time: Erasmus and the Comma Johanneum," *Church History and Religious Culture* 95 (2015): 35–40.

it still will not be persuasive to reasonable Arians, as they could simply read the passage as saying that the Father, Son, and Holy Spirit are "one through the consensus of their testimony."[99]

So Erasmus "left both the comma *and* his doubts to posterity," as Levine nicely puts it.[100] The comma endured because the New Testament of Erasmus (with the comma) gave shape to the received Greek text upon which major translations would be based, and the doubts were rekindled with the advent and development of historical critical study of biblical texts, blossoming with force among Protestant scholars in the nineteenth century and finally emerging in Catholic circles in the twentieth century.[101] In his own day, Bietenholz notes, there was a "radical emphasis" in Erasmus's insistence that the Trinity was "not anchored in scripture" by 1 John 5:7–8; though "today it can be taken for granted that Erasmus's judgment was correct."[102] So what was bold for one era is commonplace for another: such are the currents of history. What was bold for his epoch was the conviction that "as philologist, he could not depart from the clear meaning of the words in the Gospel, although his church might do so."[103]

As Rummel points out, Erasmus was "engaged in legitimate textual criticism," and what is more, he was doing so as a devout Christian in the Catholic Church, and this combination was not without its tensions.[104] As Bietenholz observes, with respect to the comma, "one had to choose either truth or untruth," and yet, most importantly, "Erasmus was confident that personally he could remain orthodox and still choose the truth" as a scholar.[105] Managing that, of course, required a sincere but delicate fusion of loyalty to the church and well-crafted qualifications that allowed him both intellectual freedom and personal

99. Erasmus, *Responding to the Annotations of Edward Lee*, CWE 72: 410–11. For the same point, see Erasmus, *Clarifications Concerning the Censures*, CWE 82: 147–48.

100. Levine, "Erasmus and the Problem of the Johannine Comma," 595.

101. Werner Georg Kümmel, *The New Testament: The History of the Investigation of its Problems*, trans. S. McLean Gilmour and Howard C. Kee (Nashville: Abingdon Press, 1970), 40–73.

102. Bietenholz, *Encounters with a Radical Erasmus*, 237.

103. Bietenholz, *Encounters with a Radical Erasmus*, 243.

104. Erika Rummel, "New Perspectives on the Controversy Between Erasmus and Lee," *Nederlands Archief voor Kerkgeschiedenis/Dutch Review of Church History* 74, n. 2 (1994): 227. As Rummel puts it, Erasmus "did not question the nature of the Trinity, but engaged in legitimate textual criticism."

105. Bietenholz, *Encounters with a Radical Erasmus*, 238.

security. So Erasmus typically says that he is offering annotations, not making pronouncements of doctrine;[106] that what he puts forth is for readers' consideration, allowing each to make their own judgment;[107] that critical philological work on biblical materials is a danger to neither faith nor doctrine;[108] and though he regularly declares his willingness to bow to the church's word,[109] he will do so, he tells us, "as soon as [he] hear[s] her clear voice,[110] though, as Erasmus wryly notes, the church is not normally in the business of judging the correct reading of obscure passages.[111]

In all of this, Erasmus anticipates the posture of a modern, critically minded scholar who wishes to make a constructive contribution to theology while fully and responsibly residing within a church setting. Certainly, this is something familiar enough in the modern universities and seminaries of all major Christian churches, yet also something that only came to be after long struggles to overcome the entrenched fear and powerful resistance to critical scholarship on biblical literature.[112]

106. Erasmus, *Responding to the Annotations of Edward Lee*, CWE 72: 48. See Erasmus to Jacob of Hoogstraten, letter 1006, CWE 7: 50, 52;

107. Erasmus, *Responding to the Annotations of Edward Lee*, CWE 72: 34–35. "I am all for discussion, I decide nothing," Erasmus writes to Jacob Hoogstraten, CWE 7: 52. See *Apology against Certain Spanish Monks*, CWE 75: 68.

108. See, for instance, Erasmus, *Apology against Certain Spanish Monks*, CWE 75: 40, where Erasmus insists that good biblical scholarship "has always been done among men of learning and continues to be done, with no detriment to the faith." See also *Responding to the Annotations of Edward Lee*, CWE 72: 34, 40, where Erasmus insists that his work is not a danger to scripture or church authority.

109. Erasmus, *Responding to the Annotations of Edward Lee*, CWE 72: 39.

110. Erasmus, *Apology against Certain Spanish Monks*, CWE 75: 38; see also "Translation of Erasmus' annotations on the Johannine comma," 322.

111. In Erasmus, *Apology against Certain Spanish Monks*, CWE 75: 38–39, Erasmus observes that the "church does not condemn immediately one who in some places is doubtful about the genuineness of a reading, when the manuscripts differ among themselves and when not infrequently orthodox readers both introduce and interpret a threefold reading."

112. On the struggle of modern biblical scholarship within the world of Catholic theology, see Mark Schoof, *A Survey of Catholic Theology, 1800–1970*, trans. N.D. Smith (Paramus, NJ: Paulist Newman Press, 1970), as well as the earlier work by George Tyrrell, *Christianity at the Crossroads* (London: George Allen and Unwin, Ltd., 1963). With respect to Roman Catholic attempts to curtail and control scholarship on the Johannine comma, see Brown, *The Epistles of John*, 780–81. Echoing "the fear of rationalism in exegetical methods ungoverned by tradition or dogma" expressed by Leo XIII in *Providentissimus Deus* (1893), Coogan strangely claims that "Catholic biblical studies" have "only recently and reluctantly" accepted the critical "methodology" inaugurated in the works of Erasmus (Coogan, *Erasmus, Lee and the Correction of the Vulgate*, 24, n. 31). One should rather say that Catholic biblical studies have flourished since the Second Vatican Council, and, too, that their successes have not been reluctant.

Though Erasmus stands toward the beginning of this long process, he nonetheless sets an important principle for anyone who would draw on biblical texts to speak of Christ in Trinitarian terms. In a word, whatever is said of the dignity and divinity of the Son cannot ignore the insights garnered from close textual and historical scholarship on biblical materials, and that means, in sum, squarely facing the fact that the scriptural texts drawn upon to formulate and defend doctrinal statements on the divinity of Christ bear all the expected marks of human handling, including both accidental corruption and deliberate manipulation.

"A Great War of Words"

Looking back at the controversies leading up to the Council of Nicaea, Erasmus opines that—at least as he sees it—the matter simply was "not worth a fight to the finish by East and West, or the shameful sundering of world concord" that resulted from these doctrinal battles. It was, as he wrote in his *Annotation* to Hebrews 1:3, a "great war of words," for the Arians insisted that there were "three *hypostases*" [substances] in the Father, Son, and Holy Spirit, but "they were averse to the term *homoousios*" [of the same essence] proposed by Athanasius and what would become the orthodox party.[113] The latter term, Erasmus points out, was "a word never heard before, it was nowhere read in Scripture, and it was therefore suspect." It surely was reasonable, consequently, for the Arians to dissent from the use of this novel bit of language in a doctrinal decree of an ecumenical council. Because of the resulting fracture, Erasmus asks imaginatively, "would it not have been better for both sides to abandon new terms and to maintain universal concord in the world than to bring all Christianity into the greatest danger?"[114]

Indeed, Erasmus recalls, this "solution was also considered expedient by the most respected bishops and princes of that time"—that

---

113. Erasmus, *Responding to the Annotations of Edward Lee*, CWE 72: 395–96. Hebrews 1:3 reads, "He is the reflection of God's glory and the exact imprint of God's very being, and he sustains all things by his powerful word." The complaint over a "war of words" likely draws on 1 Timothy 6:4 ("disputes about words"); 2 Timothy 2:23 ("stupid and senseless controversies"); and Titus 3:9 ("stupid controversies").

114. Erasmus, *Responding to the Annotations of Edward Lee*, CWE 72: 396.

"the conflict over words ought to be abandoned, provided they could agree on the substance of the faith"—but alas, the consensus collapsed and ecclesial division ensued.[115] Still, Erasmus wonders with the same perfect conditional phrasing, "would it not have been better to accept the loss of two words than to allow such a damaging conflict?" It would seem to have been possible, he muses more positively, for both sides to maintain a "more accommodating" line of thinking, such that, for instance, the Arians might have "embraced with us the three Persons," while the other side might have taught the "equality of Persons" without "the invention of the new word *homoousios*."[116] What Erasmus proposes, in sum, is a more capacious sense of doctrinal orthodoxy, not certainly one that is open to anything whatsoever but definitely one that will be accommodating to the language of others and sympathetic to their sentiments, all the while affirming constructively how both sides are commonly tethered to the "apostolic truth" at stake.[117]

"It is right," Erasmus readily admits, "that we all agree on those things which are handed down to us by the apostles and the Fathers who drew on them. As for the rest," however, "making everything an article of faith is just a seedbed for dissent and a bane for Christian concord," and without that concord, he boldly declares, "we are not Christians."[118] It would be so much better, he says to Lee, "not to provide so many definitions of such matters, which the human mind cannot grasp and language cannot express."[119] This does not mean, we are assured,

115. Erasmus, *Responding to the Annotations of Edward Lee*, CWE 72: 396–97. In fact, Erasmus advises retrospectively, it would have been "better not to know the meaning of words like *homoousios* and *homoeousios* [like in being] with respect to the divine Persons than to defend or attack these terms at the cost of such great upheaval" (400).

116. Erasmus, *Responding to the Annotations of Edward Lee*, CWE 72: 397.

117. Erasmus, *Responding to the Annotations of Edward Lee*, CWE 72: 398–99; Erasmus, *Apology against Certain Spanish Monks*, CWE 75: 36.

118. Erasmus, *Responding to the Annotations of Edward Lee*, CWE 72: 398.

119. Erasmus, *Responding to the Annotations of Edward Lee*, CWE 72: 399. See also Erasmus to Jan Šlechta, letter 1039, CWE 7: 126; Erasmus to Jean de Carondelet, CWE 9: 252. Erasmus concedes, of course, that some creed or summary of doctrines is necessary and helpful for the Christian community over time, and his proposals typically call for something simple, modest, and fairly reflecting the "philosophy of Christ." See, for instance, the brief summary of "the whole of the Christian philosophy" found in Erasmus to Jan Šlechta, letter 1039, CWE 7: 126–27. To correct heretics, Erasmus proposes simply "gospel faith" and "conduct worthy of Christ." See Erasmus, "War is a treat for those who have not tried it," adage IV. i. 1, CWE 35: 433. In debate with Martin Luther, he offers the "Apostles' Creed" as the common doctrine between Catholic and Lutherans (Erasmus, "An Examination Concerning the Faith," CWE 39: 410–47).

that Erasmus "condemn[s] investigation" as such, though, he is quick to add, there are plenty of "subtle and contentious questions about this subject matter" that would be better left to "worship rather than [to] understand."[120]

Trinitarian questions, in a word, are inscrutable and unfathomable, which is why the hyperabstract and interminably contorted speculations of theologians can easily be "ignored without loss of salvation or [simply] left in doubt." Nor for that matter, Erasmus continues, can they "be proved by any satisfactory arguments or grasped by the intellect or even vaguely conceived of by like means,"[121] which is why it is so ironic when Erasmus tells the Spanish monks at Valladolid that "what the Arians deny"—that the Son is one in being with the Father—can only be demonstrated by "speculative reasoning," which in itself is impotent to resolve such questions.[122] All too often, Erasmus complains, both ancient writers and living theologians carry their "dangerous inquisitiveness" about divine mysteries to the point of "irreverent audacity."[123] What Erasmus contributes to these questions, consequently, is a healthy dose of epistemic modesty with respect to Trinitarian doctrine, hardly something very radical but not what is demanded by those who crave certainty for their doctrines. In fact, he suggests in a manner at once skeptical, pious, and yet also humorous, "it would be much more fitting to defer such questions to that time when we shall see God face to face without the mirror and without the mystery."[124]

In the meantime, Erasmus says to Lee, he believes that, first and foremost, "those things chiefly should be taught that are conducive to a pious life." This comment appears after Erasmus mentions various issues that caused "great upheavals" in the early church," including the date for celebrating Easter, the rebaptism of those baptized by heretics,

120. Erasmus, *Apology against Certain Spanish Monks*, CWE 75: 42.

121. Erasmus to Jean de Carondelet, letter 1334, CWE 9: 250–51. Both points were censured by the Paris theologians in 1526. See Erasmus, *Clarifications Concerning the Censures*, CWE 82: 253.

122. Erasmus, *Apology against Certain Spanish Monks*, CWE 75: 44. Compare with Erasmus to Jean de Carondelet, letter 1334, CWE 9: 250–52.

123. Erasmus to Jean de Carondelet, letter 1334, CWE 9: 250–51. Compare the words of Folly on the absurd arrogance of theologians (Erasmus, *Praise of Folly*, CWE 27: 126–30).

124. Erasmus to Jean de Carondelet, letter 1334, CWE 9: 253. The language of Erasmus is drawn from 1 Corinthians 13:12. This sentence also was censured by the Paris theologians, who apparently lacked the necessary humor to appreciate this pious sentiment. See *Clarifications Concerning the Censures*, CWE 82: 266–77.

and arcane discussions of Trinitarian doctrine. None of these issues can compare with the importance of shaping the pious character of human life, Erasmus insists. In that respect, he continues, he "would not be much in favour of philosophizing excessively about fine points [of Trinitarian theology] that have more of showing off about them than practical use, especially if it causes serious upheaval in the Christian commonwealth."[125] So it is practical value upon which Erasmus ultimately wishes to focus attention, which is, to say the least, asking a lot from Trinitarian discussions, and it is discord that he laments as the actual fallout from classical Trinitarian feuds.

With this in mind, he suggests, attention should be placed primarily on what pertains properly to "the realm of Christian piety," for therein lies "the stem and stern of our whole happiness," as he nicely puts it, "that we may become one with God and after the example of divine concord may also be joined together into one among ourselves like members of one body under one head."[126] In that simple statement we find, once again, the integral religious ethic that Erasmus deems the essential point and purpose of Christian life. As we will see in more detail in chapter 8, this is an ethic of peace that speaks to an ideal way of being human before God and with others, though in the present context, Erasmus simply wishes to stress how vastly more important this ethic is for Christian life when compared with questions of Trinitarian theology.

"Perhaps," he muses on the one hand, "it would be better to occupy ourselves in pious studies with the aim of being united with God, than to engage in overly subtle arguments about how the Son is distinguished from the Father, and how the Spirit differs from both."[127] Then again, he asserts on the other hand, no one will be damned for not comprehending the niceties of Trinitarian theology, though—now shifting the focus to the ideal virtues of Christian life—"you will not escape perdition unless you see to it ... that you have the fruits of the Spirit, which are charity, joy, peace, patience, kindness, goodness, forbearance,

125. Erasmus, *Responding to the Annotations of Edward Lee*, CWE 72: 397.

126. Erasmus, *Apology against Certain Spanish Monks*, CWE 75: 43. See Erasmus, "Stem and stern," adage I. i. 8, CWE 31: 56–57.

127. "Translation of Erasmus' annotations on the Johannine comma," 318. Taken from the 1522 edition of the *Annotations*, this became yet another topic of objection from the Spanish monks meeting in Vallalodid. See Erasmus, *Apology against Certain Spanish Monks*, CWE 75: 41.

gentleness, faith, moderation, self-control, and chastity."[128] Whatever one thinks of Trinitarian relations, Erasmus concludes, the most important thing is "to live in harmony with one another in accordance with Jesus Christ, so that with one mind and with one voice we may honour the God and Father of our Lord, Jesus Christ, not torn apart but joined together and made whole in the same understanding and the same feeling."[129] As with the previous three chapters, here again, we find Erasmus highlighting the ethical import of Christological doctrines.

So what, in the end, is the position of Erasmus concerning the dignity and divinity of the Son? Most simply, though admittedly far too simply, Erasmus embraces the orthodox teaching that Christ is one in being with the Father. But then, of course, he writes a good deal beyond that simple confession, though he does so for the most part in response to the challenge of critics and hence in the midst of controversy.[130] More often than not, as we have seen, the focus of his responses to Lee and others centers on textual and philological issues that give rise to theological inquiry when pressed by way of controversy. This is not to say that Erasmus is "founding doctrine exclusively on the historical-philological analysis of Holy Writ," as Cecelia Asso puts it, though it is correct to note that, in the eyes of Erasmus, biblical exegesis should never ignore the textual and grammatical insights garnered from historical and philological analysis of biblical texts.[131]

The fact is that Erasmus did not set out to develop a theology of Christ's divinity in the context of Trinitarian questions, as his abiding purpose was to provide a revised edition of Christian scripture that

128. Erasmus to Jean de Carondelet, letter 1334, CWE 9:251. Erasmus is drawing on Galatians 5:22 for his list of virtues.

129. Erasmus to Alonso Manrique, letter 1967, CWE 75: 10. Alonso Manrique was the inquisitor-general of Spain, but also an important protector of Erasmus. See R. W. Truman, "Alonso Manrique de Lara," COE, vol. 2, 373–75.

130. As Rummel puts it, Erasmus's "comments on doctrinal matters are usually induced by external criticism," which therefore justifies saying that he was "an enthusiastic philologist but a reluctant theologian" (*Erasmus' Annotations on the New Testament*, 183, 185). It is true, however, that some later works of Erasmus dedicated to ecclesial tasks—like the instruction of preachers or explanation of the Apostles' Creed—include brief but basic discussion of Trinitarian doctrine without the pressure of controversy. See, for instance, Erasmus, *Evangelical Preacher* 4, CWE 68: 1026–27, 1065–80; *Explanation of the Creed*, CWE 70: 247–49, 266–69, 283–87, and 317–24.

131. Asso, "Martin Dorp and Edward Lee," 195.

would be "clearer, purer, and more accurate,"[132] and then to supplement the biblical text with philological explanations and other textual details in the notes. Though it is true that the early *Annotations* included some theological observations, these grew in volume and importance as Erasmus was forced to respond to a series of critics. At every step along the way, therefore, he is confronted with uncritical assumptions concerning the meaning of words; twisted and forced use of scriptural texts as arguments against heretics; unwarranted presumptions to knowledge of divine realities; narrow construal of orthodox doctrine mixed with insensitivity toward alternative sentiments; and an emphasis on belief over ethical life. In response, as we have seen throughout this chapter, Erasmus insists that whatever is said about the dignity and divinity of Christ be shaped by fidelity to the sources; honesty with respect to the limits of language; modesty regarding what can be known; a capacious and empathetic sense for doctrinal orthodoxy informed by a rich sense for historical variety; and capped with a concentration on the practical significance of what is said for people's characters and lives together.

132. Erasmus, "*Apologia* of Desiderius Erasmus of Rotterdam," CWE 41: 466. On Erasmus's "trinity of objectives"—"producing a text that was a faithful, intelligible, and idiomatically correct version of the Greek original"—see Rummel, *Erasmus' Annotations on the New Testament*, 89–121.

CHAPTER 5

Christ as the '*Sermo*' of God

In the 1519 edition of the New Testament, Erasmus made a small but seismic change to the Latin translation of the first verse of the Gospel of John. Instead of "In the beginning was the Word (*verbum*)," it now read "In the beginning was the Speech (*sermo*)." What was *logos* in the Greek became *sermo* in Erasmus's Latin, thereby replacing the customary and familiar *verbum* of the Vulgate. As Erasmus reports, the uproar over his perceived novelty was fast and furious, with critics ascending to the pulpit—almost simultaneously, it would seem—to denounce what was deemed to be his "impious error."[1] The "first rumblings" appeared in Britain, Erasmus reports, when a man "respected for his theological qualification, venerable for his religious teaching, and even distinguished by his dignity as a bishop"—namely, the Franciscan Henry Standish—began to preach in the churchyard of St. Paul's Cathedral in

1. Erasmus, "A Defence by Erasmus of Rotterdam Publicly Refuting the Mischievous Clamour of Certain Men among People both Influential and Humble to Whom They Declare that it was an Impiety on his Part to Translate in the Gospel of John: *In principio erat sermo*" (1520a), CWE 73: 14.

London on the subject of Christian charity, only to suddenly "forget all Christian charity" by ranting "intemperately" against Erasmus's translation of the Gospel of John.[2] "At almost the same time in Brussels," Erasmus continues, a "Carmelite and bachelor of theology" warned from the pulpit that "there was a certain Erasmus who was not afraid of correcting the Gospel of John."[3] A "similar commotion" arose in Paris, Erasmus observes, possibly spread abroad through "emissaries,"[4] until the "same nonsense is bandied about everywhere."[5] Convinced that he was facing a conspiracy against humanist scholarship under the false "pretext of Christian religion," Erasmus complains that they all

2. Erasmus, "A Defence by Erasmus of Rotterdam of '*In principio erat sermo*'" (1520b), CWE 73: 16. Appointed bishop of Asaph in 1518, Standish was an outspoken critic of humanist scholarship on biblical and patristic literature. See R.J. Schoeck, "Henry Standish," COE 3: 279–80. Erasmus takes enormous pleasure in telling the story of fierce combat between the Franciscan Standish ("a tireless Scotist who knows not fear") and an Italian Servite, who had put forward a strict rendering of the Franciscan vow of poverty, something Standish thought "stank of heresy," as it no doubt would impoverish his entire order. Full of bluster and spewing abuse, these theological gladiators are called before the cardinal (Thomas Wolsey) to settle the dispute. In what is simultaneously a compliment to Wolsey and some "exceedingly entertaining" mockery of Standish, Erasmus credits the cardinal with the wisdom and humor required to enjoy this absurd battle as an "entertaining spectacle" rather than "serious business," whereupon he "dismissed them both in such terms that it was not yet quite clear which was the stronger man." See Erasmus, "Esernius versus Pacidianus," adage II. v. 98, CWE 33: 286–90.

3. Erasmus, "Defence of 'Word'" (1520b), CWE 73: 16. The bachelor of theology may be the largely unknown Jan Robyns, likely a student of Nicolaas Baechem, the Carmelite theologian at Louvain and later assistant inquisitor of the Netherlands. "Popularly known as the 'Camelite' because of his dull wittedness," Baechem would be "a better man than St. Paul," Erasmus tells us, "if he was as pleasing to Christ as he is to himself" (16). Long an adversary of Erasmus, Baechem offered an ongoing target for Erasmus's criticism and wit. See Marjorie O'Rourke Boyle, "Nicolaas Baechem," COE 1: 81–83. For a vivid yet amusing and satiric account of the "famous discussion" between Erasmus and Baechem before Godschalk Rosemondt, the rector of the University of Louvain, see Erasmus to Thomas More, letter 1162, CWE 8: 91–98

4. Edward Lee may have been one of these emissaries. "It is not surprising," Erasmus writes to John Fisher, "if some rumour has been spread among monks and the unlearned … seeing how Lee does nothing else, as though that were his purpose in life" (Erasmus to John Fisher, letter 1068, CWE 7: 209).

5. Erasmus, "Defence of 'Word'" (1520b), CWE 73: 15–16, 39. Denis L. Drysdall suggests that—given the time lag (about eight months) between Standish's sermon and the release of Erasmus "Defence of 'Word'" (1520a), and given the mention of Lee (and not Standish) in the prefatory letter (Ep. 1072) to this same piece—it "seems likely that the immediate motivation for this publication was not the dispute with Standish but that with Lee," even though, as Drysdall acknowledges, "Lee did not comment on the substitution of *sermo* for *verbum* in John 1:1." The release of "Defence of 'Word'" (1520b), however, with its additional evidence from patristic literature, as well as the more "heated protests against the 'conspiracy' that [Erasmus] is sure is being mounted" against him, would seem to have been a "response to the increasing hostility at Louvain" (Drysdall, "Introduction," CWE 73: xiii–xviii).

"start[ed] crying out in public that the matter was too dreadful for any-one to tolerate and that all should rise immediately as one and stone the author of such an impious crime."[6] The fundamental issue—once again, as in the previous chapter—was the authority of the received transla-tion of Christian scriptures when confronted with critical scholarship on biblical texts, while the immediate question at hand was the substi-tution of *sermo* for *verbum* in John 1:1.

The problem facing Erasmus was, first and foremost, how to deal with critics who broadcast their attacks from the pulpit rather than in published writings, and second, and eventually of greater importance, how to respond to those theologians who lurked in the background while providing inspiration for the public outbursts against his work. To the latter, as we will see shortly, he offers philological arguments and historical evidence for the legitimacy of using *sermo* for Christ. For the likes of Standish, however, who wishes to rouse ordinary peo-ple to action with his brainless "yapping," Erasmus weaves laughter and derision into his account of how the preaching of Standish was received by people of good sense and intelligence.[7] With respect to Standish's sermon in London, a small part of which Erasmus somehow appeared to quote,[8] Erasmus reports that Standish begged the mayor and citizens of London to prevent the spread of "new translations" of

6. Erasmus, "Defence of 'Word'" (1520b), CWE 73: 14–15, 39.

7. Those like Standish, Erasmus writes, "rush to the pulpit, they shout shamelessly, irratio-nally, nor do they stop to think what poor account they give of their reputation as they attack someone else's with such stupid arguments. For if anyone shouts without understanding what he says, how little, I ask you, does he differ from a madman?" Or, as Erasmus rethinks his wording, they do not "argue but yap" (Erasmus, "Defence of 'Word'" (1520b), CWE 73: 37–38). Naturally enough, he adds with a bit of a bite, these shouting preachers are not "ashamed of their brainless ideas," for "they have no brains" (18). On the use of reported "laughter and indignation" as criti-cism, see Rummel, *Erasmus and His Catholic Critics*, vol. 1, 123–24.

8. Erasmus may have received an account of the sermon from one of his English allies, per-haps yielding sufficient detail for him to roughly quote the words of Standish. The latter is said to have composed a collection of his sermons, titled "Several Sermons Preached to the People," as well as a "Treatise against Erasmus, His Translation of the New Testament," though there is no evidence that they were published, and neither apparently exists today. For the reference to these collections, see Anthony Wood, *Athenae Oxonienses: An Exact History of All the Writers and Bishops Who Have Had Their Education in the University of Oxford*, vol. 1 (London, 1815), 92–94. Erasmus complains of both the pamphlets and the public sermons in which theologians (who "profess poverty," so evidently friars) "excoriate one another," referring in the same context to the sermon of Standish, so it is possible, though not in the least confirmed, that Erasmus encoun-tered a pamphlet copy of this piece. See Erasmus to Thomas Wolsey, letter 1060, CWE 7:169–70.

Christian scriptures. Erasmus then adds pointedly that, while Standish "was pleased with himself," the "stupid fellow was laughed at by all the educated people there, and the more sensible among the uneducated were incensed that he should spout such nonsense that had nothing to do with the lives of the people."[9] So Erasmus mirrors Standish's oral attack with a parallel account of the laughter and derision from those who heard his ignorant babbling.

More delicious by far, are the accounts Erasmus gives of Standish's humiliation at court, first in a discussion with two allies of Erasmus, where he is egged on with feigned respect to defend his denunciation of the use of *sermo* in place of *verbum*, though it is clear when questioned that he has not read the "commentaries" of Erasmus; and then again when he is made to see that his abusive treatment of Erasmus was itself "half-way to heresy," since he was making the "suggestion of heresy" against something approved by Pope Leo X.[10] Then secondly, "some time later," Standish is goaded into denouncing—"with a wonderful air of saintliness"—several heresies of Erasmus before the king and queen of England, though when the "defending counsel" of Erasmus "explained the whole thing," the sheer "stupidity" of Standish became clear "for all to see," or at least that is how Erasmus tells the story. Feeling "sorry to see such colossal stupidity pilloried in such exalted company," however, we are told that the king "came to the man's rescue" by changing the subject of discussion.[11] So Erasmus did not need to respond in writing to the oral charges of someone like Standish, when a narrative report highlighting the snickers and embarrassment of those who heard him rant and rave are a perfectly fitting riposte.

For more serious adversaries, as well as for those who may have been sympathetic to his work, Erasmus offers philological arguments

9. Erasmus, "Defence of 'Word'" (1520b), CWE 73: 15–16. For the sermon of the Carmelite preacher in Brussels, Erasmus similarly refrained from a direct response, relying instead on the reported critical response of the congregation. As he tells it, "sensible and educated people were for the most part displeased by the stupid audacity of this young man; ordinary, uneducated folk suspected there was some villainy" (16).

10. Erasmus to Hermannus Buschius, letter 1126, CWE 8: 9–10. The "champions" of Erasmus are unnamed in the text, though they are identified by Bietenholz as the royal chaplain John Stokesley and Erasmus's friend Thomas More. See notes 9 and 10, CWE 8: 356. Compare the slightly different accounts in Erasmus to Martin Luther, letter 1127A, CWE 8: 20.

11. Erasmus to Hermannus Buschius, letter 1126, CWE 8: 10–12. The same story is told in abbreviated form in Erasmus to Martin Luther, letter 1127A, CWE 8: 20.

for the legitimacy of using *sermo* for Christ, bolstered by historical evidence to show that *sermo* was used in early Latin translations of Christian scriptures and in the writings of numerous church fathers. Preliminary to these defenses, however, is the more fundamental task of establishing the legitimate space for biblical scholarship, without threatening the authority of scripture and without overly impinging on the claims of the church. To this end, as we will see in the first section of this chapter, Erasmus insists that his translations and annotations were meant not "for the general public" in the churches, but "for the learned" in their "private reading."[12] But while this distinction of audience is meant to ensure the security of those engaged in scholarly work on biblical literature, Erasmus at the same time affirms that ordinary folk in fact are capable of understanding the fruits of biblical scholarship, if only pastoral educators would explain these matters clearly and effectively, which is something he clearly encourages.

Central to his case is the argument that *sermo* is a more exact translation of the Greek word *logos* than is *verbum*, though he does not entirely reject the latter, as it, too, appears in the "sacred texts" and is used in the churches.[13] Variety and hence flexibility are inherent in the choice of words for divine matters, he insists, as these things naturally outstrip the reach of language, though as we will see in the second section, that fact underscores the necessity and the value of finding the terms that best express what is needed. This grammatical search is augmented by an appeal to traditional usage, as will be evident in the third section, a line of discussion that Erasmus significantly amplifies in "A Defence of 'Word'" (1520b). In what must have been startling to his theological critics, therefore, Erasmus proceeds to show that "Christ is called *sermo* in the canonical Scriptures, in the usage of the church, and in the writings of orthodox Doctors," all of which undermines, as he put it, the "stupid clamour" of his ill-informed critics.[14] Unlike the controversy with Edward Lee, however, these critics do not address the Christological implications of what they take to be Erasmus's impious reading of scripture, and thus they give him little reason to develop the theological

12. Erasmus, "Defence of 'Word'" (1520a), CWE 73: 4–5.
13. Erasmus, "Defence of 'Word'" (1520b), CWE 73: 18–19.
14. Erasmus, "Defence of 'Word'" (1520b), CWE 73: 18–20.

potential of using *sermo* in place of *verbum*. There are a number of interesting hints, however, that, as we will see in the final section of this chapter, are corroborated in other writings of Erasmus—hints enough, that is, to give this controversy its own Christological value.

"The Best Sorts of Learning"

How "mischievous" it is, Erasmus exclaims, when churchmen ascend to the pulpit to scream out their scorn for his translation of the prologue of the Gospel of John "before the ignorant mass of people." What was "intended to be discussed among scholars," he complains, is instead broadcast by these preachers "among tanners, weavers, and mere women."[15] In marking this shift in audience, Erasmus highlights how inappropriate it is to disseminate scholarly work on biblical literature to those who have been deprived of sufficient education to understand the issues and arguments, especially when it pertains to something so sacred and so familiar. Though it is true, as Willis Goth Regier comments, that Erasmus kept "a healthy Horatian distance" from ordinary people,[16] the target of his complaint in this context is not common folk

15. Erasmus, "Defence of 'Word'" (1520b), CWE 73: 17. That Erasmus includes women within what he calls the "undiscriminating crowd" is a reflection of the social system of his day, though the term he uses for woman—"*mulierculas*"—is a "diminutive form of *mulier*" (meaning, little woman), which does not refer to all women, and certainly not "women of high rank and excellent education"; instead, it denotes "less fortunate" or common women. See footnote 40 by Ann Dalzell in CWE 41: 411. It is true, however, that Erasmus certainly knew that women were intellectually capable, something he saw and respected first-hand when meeting the daughters of Thomas More. On the value of giving girls and women a sound education, see Erasmus to Guillaume Budé, letter 1233, CWE 8: 296–98.

16. Willis Goth Regier, "Adages as Insults: Erasmus against the Barbarians," *Erasmus Studies* 40 (2020): 58–59. On the elitist tendency of Erasmus to speak about ordinary folk in pejorative terms, see Paul Jacopin and Jacqueline Lagrée, *Érasme, humanisme et langage* (Paris: Presse Universitaire de France, 1996), 76–77; Chomarat, *Grammaire et rhetorique chez Erasme*, vol. 2: 1057–58. Chomarat cites examples from *Evangelical Preacher* in which Erasmus vividly describes the kind of dissolute, distracted, and disruptive congregations of common folk to which preachers must somehow convey gospel wisdom. See, for instance, Erasmus, *Evangelical Preacher* 1, CWE 67: 438–39. There is, of course, another side to consider, as Erasmus consistently shows great sympathy for the plight of common people, notably in his writings on warfare, where the argument against the justifiability of war from the destructive consequences that overwhelmingly affect ordinary people constitutes one of Erasmus's major lines of thinking against war. See Erasmus, "War is a treat," CWE 35: 404; Erasmus, *A Complaint of Peace Spurned and Rejected by the Whole World*, trans. Betty Radice, CWE 27: 316–17. On Erasmus's argument against war based on the horrendous consequences befalling ordinary people, see Martin, *Truth and Irony*,

but the preachers who abuse the power of the pulpit to deceive and manipulate their listeners.

In fact, as we saw in the first chapter, Erasmus insists that Christian scriptures should be accessible—whether in vernacular translations or through clear and effective preaching—to everyone, including (as he nicely puts it) ploughmen, weavers, skippers, peddlers, and of course, both men and women.[17] The problem, as Erasmus describes it, is that the common people of his day tended to trust the clergy: in his words, they believe "the sacred pulpit from which they are accustomed to hear the word [*sermo*] of Christ not the poison of men," and for that very reason, they were vulnerable to manipulation when clergy abuse their proper function.[18] Indeed, Erasmus writes, even the "foremost courtiers" are "not difficult to deceive," especially when they are confronted with the preacher's well-practiced "prophetic refinement," and what a show that is, including "the severe and frowning brow that might announce a man of worth," the "title of 'reverend,'" and "the shrewd and false appearance of piety, which tricks even exceptionally sensible people."[19] What people take away from listening to these theatrical preachers, consequently, is that Erasmus is "condemning what the Evangelist wrote," when in fact, he insists, his business was purely with the quality of the translation, as he had never proposed changing "the ecclesiastical and public reading" of the Gospel of John.[20]

"Lying with perverse zeal," Erasmus observes, these men of religion distort, slander, and deceive the people with "jugglers' tricks to inflame them" against humanist scholarship generally, and against Erasmus by name.[21] The great danger, we are warned, is that this clerical manipu-

---

102–6. As will be illustrated shortly, Erasmus is quite confident in people's capacity for rational thought, empathetic with their perceptions and judgments, and convinced that they should have ready access to scripture.

17. Recall, once again, the spirited call for scripture to be made accessible to all people in languages they could understand. See Erasmus, *Paraclesis*, CWE 41: 409–12. See also chapter 1, n. 18.

18. Erasmus, "Defence of 'Word'" (1520b), CWE 73: 37.

19. Erasmus, "Defence of 'Word'" (1520b), CWE 73: 17.

20. Erasmus, "Defence of 'Word'" (1520b), CWE 73: 17, 19.

21. Erasmus, "Defence of 'Word'" (1520b), CWE 73: 17. Erasmus often protests the treacherous and incendiary preaching of his day. Appealing to the perspective of "ordinary people," he asks a regular theological adversary—who elsewhere Erasmus calls "a doctor of divinity and a confounded numbskull, who is always barking at me"—"what do you suppose comes into their minds when they see a theologian distinguished by his religious vestments and standing in that

lation of the people will lead to actual violence—in a word, as Erasmus puts it rather graphically—that these crafty clerics will manage to "incite coarse and uneducated common folk to throw stones."[22] And much of that fury and violence, Erasmus understandably fears, is being directed his way, and that is not only dangerous but—as he sees it—both unfair and undeserved. "How wicked it is and how foreign to Christian sincerity," he complains, "to rant against someone else's reputation so odiously and without cause," and how hypocritical when "this is being done by those who claim to be masters of gospel teaching and pillars of religion in its entirety"; how corrupt and vile, moreover, when these self-styled men of God "rouse the credulous and uneducated populace to destroy a neighbour ... from the very place whence the people are accustomed to hear the teachings of the Gospel."[23]

But what is even more contemptible, Erasmus adds with reference to his own scholarly contribution to biblical studies, is that this criticism and violence is being directed toward "a man who, having spent so much effort in vigils and labours, deserves the best of them."[24] Repeatedly Erasmus cast himself, naturally enough, as a "well-deserving man" who "does real good," and hence one who deserves thanks for his scholarship rather than calumny and threats of violence.[25] "What a dreadful injury" it is, he says, returning again to graphic language, "to hand over a well-deserving man to be stoned by the people—as indeed they can—and further, to slaughter a man who not only does no harm but in fact does real good."[26] As much as Erasmus focuses on these undeserved threats against himself, however, he warns that the clerical

---

sacred place, the pulpit in a church ... [who] holds forth with uncontrolled spite and in virulent language against the good name of his neighbours, with blazing eyes and frothing lips and roaring voice, and with the whole posture of his body evincing bitterness and spite?" Certainly, Erasmus answers his own question, the people have sufficient feeling and wisdom to understand that such behavior has nothing to do with authentic piety. See Erasmus to [Vincentius Theoderici], letter 1196, CWE 8: 186; Erasmus to Wolfgang Faber Capito, letter 1165, CWE 8: 101 for the derogatory portrayal of this critic. See also Rummel, *Erasmus and His Catholic Critics*, vol. 1, 132–33.

22. Erasmus, "Defence of 'Word'" (1520b), CWE 73: 36–37.

23. Erasmus, "Defence of 'Word'" (1520b), CWE 73: 36, 39.

24. Erasmus, "Defence of 'Word'" (1520b), CWE 73: 37.

25. Erasmus, "Defence of 'Word'" (1520b), CWE 73: 40. Doing "harm to one who deserves well," Erasmus says again, "is a particular sort of devilish malice." Indeed, he claims, he is "a man who has done his best to deserve well of everyone" (39).

26. Erasmus, "Defence of 'Word'" (1520b), CWE 73: 38–39.

abuse of the pulpit may finally "break out in serious harm to the peace of Christianity" on a larger scale, as rival preachers take up the pulpit to rail against each other.[27] It should not go unnoticed, however, that Erasmus's famous aversion to conflict and violence does not keep him from happily imagining the time when people at last will "come to their senses and drive these blowers of brazen horns off the bridges with stones."[28]

While Erasmus vigorously protests the public attacks on him, he insists repeatedly that his work on biblical literature was meant purely for "private reading" among scholars. He is not the one, he duly notes, who disseminated the substitution of *sermo* for *verbum* to the general public, as he never intended to replace the standard text of scripture used in the churches, nor did he wish to burden ordinary people with his scholarly annotations.[29] His scholarship on biblical books, he insists, was "prepared only with a view to private reading" among scholars,[30] so his critics have shamelessly breached the proper separation of scholarship and ecclesial life with their inflammatory preaching. It would have been more appropriate, we are told, if they had advised him "in person" or had sent him a "written refutation."[31] Certainly that would have been

27. Erasmus, "Defence of 'Word'" (1520b), CWE 73: 39.

28. Erasmus, "Defence of 'Word'" (1520b), CWE 73: 37. As Erasmus explains, to throw someone off the bridge classically meant "to consign older people to idleness, as if they were doting and useless in all walks of life, and to cut them off from the exercise of all occupations." See Erasmus, "To throw the sexagenarians off the bridge," adage I. v. 37, CWE 31: 416–17. While this proverb could refer to "those who owing to the weakness of old age have sought retirement," it also could "be used to express aversion for old age, as useless for anything." In any case, as one of Erasmus's sources indicates, such a statement was understood to be a "bad expression." When Erasmus applies it to his adversaries rather than to people in their sixties—adding, moreover, that they were to be driven from the bridge "with stones"—he gives a decidedly aggressive twist to this notion, at least as a fantasy of retribution.

29. See Erasmus, "Defence of 'Sermo'" (1520b), CWE 73: 19. Erasmus explains in 1519 that he had not changed *verbum* for *sermo* in the 1516 edition of the New Testament "for fear of immediately offending the weak," while in 1522 and later editions, he changed his explanation to say that he was afraid of "giving a handle to those who criticize anything at any opportunity," thereby showing, as Drysdall argues, a shift in attention to meet the challenge of more serious critics at Louvain. See Drysdall, "Introduction," CWE 73: xii; *In Evangelium Ioannis Annotationes Des. Erasmi Roterodami*, ed. E. F. Hovingh, *Opera omnia Desiderii Erasmi Roterodami*, VI - 6 (Amsterdam: Elsevier, 2003), 30. On his critics at Louvain, see Marcel Gielis, "Leuven Theologians as Opponents of Erasmus and of Humanistic Theology," trans. Paul Arblaster, in *Biblical Humanism and Scholasticism in the Age of Erasmus*, 197–214.

30. Erasmus, "Defence of 'Sermo'" (1520b), CWE 73: 18. See also 17, 19, 38, and 40, as well as "Defence of 'Sermo'" (1520a), CWE 73: 3, 5, and 11.

31. Erasmus, "Defence of 'Sermo'" (1520b), CWE 73: 17.

the appropriate procedure among scholars, but, Erasmus complains, "no one offered me advice, no one counselled me, no one convicted me of error." Instead, he continues, as we have heard already, they bark out their accusations to the "inexperienced mob, which for the most part does not judge," in order to do lasting harm to "good scholarship."[32]

As much as Erasmus contends that "the best sorts of learning" should be conducted in private,[33] wherein, he insists, "it is legitimate to read anything," and also where a certain "liberty" of inquiry is allowed,[34] this is not the whole story, for he certainly hopes that his biblical scholarship will have a salutary effect on the life of the church and the conduct of theology.[35] So there are signs of tension between Erasmus's defensive insistence on the private nature of scholarship and his two-fold public interest, first, to provide a clear and accurate text to the church, on the basis of which better theology might develop, and second, to make the scriptures available to everyone, including the most common of people.[36] Though Erasmus continued to uphold this separation, in part because many scholarly exchanges are by their very nature and language

32. Erasmus, "Defence of 'Word'" (1520b), CWE 73: 37, 40.

33. Erasmus, "Defence of 'Word'" (1520b), CWE 73: 14.

34. Erasmus, "Defence of 'Word'" (1520b), CWE 73: 38, 18.

35. Erasmus refers obliquely to these positive outcomes when he speaks of "the public usefulness of scholarship" in the church (Erasmus, "Defence of 'Word'" (1520b), CWE 73: 39). A familiar statement from Erasmus, he wrote in 1516 that he wished "that the labours that I have undertaken for the general good, which were by no means inconsiderable, might prove to be of general use" (Erasmus to Henry Bullock, letter 456, CWE 4: 53).

36. That his biblical scholarship was written for scholars but not for the public, Rummel suggests, stands in tension with "an earlier, more idealistic view that the Gospel text was every Christian's business." See Rummel, *Erasmus and His Catholic Critics*, vol. 1, 124. The "curious contradiction" between scholarship as private and the earlier wish for scriptures to be available to all, Boyle similarly suggests, may be due to an "altered attitude." See Boyle, *Erasmus on Language and Method in Theology*, 6–7. "It is also possible," Boyle more correctly suggests, "that Erasmus wished the New Testament to be available to all, but the debate about certain issues confined to scholars" (156, n. 43). C. A. L. Jarrot similarly suggests that the "propagation of the Word" was meant for everyone, while discussions concerning the "purification of the sources" was intended purely for scholars. See Jarrot, "Erasmus' *In principio era sermo*': A Controversial Translation," *Studies in Philology* 61, no. 1 (January 1964): 39. Though there is some variation in what Erasmus has to say on this question, he persists in hoping that Christian scriptures be readily available to all people. In the *Paraclesis* of 1516, certainly, but also in the preface to the *Paraphrase on Matthew* (1522), and even in a late work like *Explanation of the Apostles' Creed* (1533), Erasmus insists that the philosophy of Christ is something for which "every sex and every age proves an apt pupil." See Erasmus, *Explanation of the Apostles' Creed*, CWE 70: 278–79. As we saw in chapter 1, n. 18, Erasmus's apparent retraction of his endorsement of vernacular translations of the Bible is heavily qualified and quite possibly ironic.

not accessible to larger audiences, and in part to ensure his personal security, he also put forward a more daring proposal—to wit, that the "unlearned" should be calmly and clearly given "the facts" concerning Erasmus's use of *sermo* in John 1: 1, rather than being subjected to the "lies and tricks" of these critics.[37] With this statement, Erasmus gives voice to an abiding confidence that the fruits of critical scholarship on the Bible, even if not the most obscure and technical of matters of his *Annotations*, might be effectively shared with everyone, and he also reveals his conviction that "the public is not too stupid to understand" that "there can be no religion in the heart" that hurls abuse at well-deserving neighbors.[38] The people may be "sheep," he concedes, and they are uneducated at that, but they nonetheless possess "reason," Erasmus adds, so they might truly come to understand that the substitution of *sermo* for *verbum* in John 1:1 was an innocent and justified proposal, were they to enjoy some honest and helpful instruction from their pastors.[39]

Some "Trivial Matters" of Grammar

The would-be defenders of orthodoxy accused Erasmus of adulterating the scriptures, but he met these charges not with a theological rejoinder, as one might expect, but with philological explanations. What was a question of religious orthodoxy for his critics thereby becomes for Erasmus a matter of grammatical accuracy for translating the Greek *logos* into Latin. In taking this tack, Erasmus chooses his ground wisely,

37. Erasmus, "Defence of 'Sermo'" (1520b), CWE 73: 40. Elsewhere, Erasmus powerfully imagines the "murmured comments of women as well as men" who rightfully question the truth and value of what they receive from their preachers, which is largely, it would seem, "a lesson in hatred, jealousy, and bad language." "Why do they keep on telling us that there are men who … correct the Gospel of St. John? If there is anything wrong with these, why cannot they put it right among themselves, instead of calling on us to start throwing stones and rousing subversion among those who are at peace?" Indeed, they conclude, "I shall not entrust my children to them, nor shall I confess to them the secrets of my heart." See Erasmus to [Vincentius Theoderici], letter 1196, CWE 8: 186–87.

38. Erasmus to [Vincentius Theoderici], letter 1196, CWE 8: 186. Such is the wise judgment Erasmus daily hears from "bargemen, carters, and uneducated women," we are told. And "there is no man of intelligence and good will," he adds, "who does not see that their complaint is perfectly justified" (187).

39. Erasmus, "To the Pious Reader," CWE 45: 13. Elsewhere, Erasmus warns "church leaders" that they "should not misuse their authority over the people." It is true that "they are sheep," he writes, "but thinking sheep and to this extent the equals of the bishops; [indeed] sometimes they are even wiser than certain bishops." See Erasmus, "A Letter Concerning the Prohibition on Eating Meat," CWE 73: 87.

as it was "in large part at least," as Denis L. Drysdall puts it, "his philological methods that raised the ire of the traditionalists."[40] What is more, it is a form of analysis in which Erasmus wields expertise that his critics lack, so that he immediately seizes the upper hand;[41] it is also an approach that allows close examination of the text without immediately elevating the dispute to a question of theological orthodoxy.

In the face of such challenges, Erasmus's first move is to establish the legitimacy of using various words for Christ and then, with flexibility of language ensured by this variety, to argue that *sermo* is the fuller and more accurate translation of the Greek word *logos* used in the prologue to the Gospel of John. Since it is "generally agreed that *verbum* and *sermo* mean the same" thing "whenever we are speaking of human things," Erasmus wonders how it could be "irreverent" to call Christ by the name of *sermo*. This is especially the case since, as we saw repeatedly in chapter 4, "no human terms can properly express divine things." If the terms are equivalent, in short, and none are completely adequate, then why is one rather than the other considered so irreverent by these critics? Certainly, we have the right, Erasmus continues, to use "parent" or "procreator" for "God the Father," in addition to the customary title of "Father" since the former terms express "the same thing to us as 'Father.'" And similarly, he asks along the same lines, can the Son not also be called "'child,' 'offspring,' 'seed,' 'progeny,' or something else that has the same force" without someone branding it irreverent? Where is the "fault" in any of this, Erasmus wonders, when the terms generally mean the same thing?[42]

40. Drysdall, "Introduction," CWE 73: xviii.

41. It is not without good reason when Erasmus observes that his scholastic critics often are "those who without grammar have become theologians." See Erasmus, *Apology against Certain Spanish Monks*, CWE 75: 50. Saying this means, as Erasmus sees it, that such theologians lack the rudimentary, and yet foundational, knowledge of the nature and workings of language; therefore, they lack the skills required for sound interpretation of biblical literature. On the meaning of grammar in the Renaissance and its relation to rhetoric, see W. Keith Percival, "Grammar and Rhetoric in the Renaissance," in *Renaissance Eloquence: Studies in the Theory and Practice of Renaissance Rhetoric*, ed. James J. Murphy (Berkeley: University of California Press, 1983), 303–30. In the view of Erasmus, though "knowledge of grammar by itself is not the making of a theologian, ... much less is he made by ignorance of grammar; at the very least, skill in this subject is an aid to the understanding of theology and lack of skill is the reverse" (Erasmus to Henry Bullock, letter 456, CWE 4: 49). On the utility of grammar in the context of Erasmus's defense of using *sermo* in place of *verbum*, see Boyle, *Erasmus on Language and Method in Theology*, 8–12.

42. Erasmus, "Defence of 'Word'" (1520b), CWE 73: 18.

Even if there is a difference in meaning between *sermo* and *verbum*, Erasmus asks, "does it follow directly that Christ is not rightly called *sermo* because he is rightly called *verbum*?" Certainly, Erasmus observes, there is nothing wrong in calling "Christ 'light' or 'truth' because it is correct to call him 'Word' [*verbum*]." The appropriateness of one name does not thereby exclude the utility of using other terms, especially since all of these terms are chosen and applied within the limited "conventions of human speech" so that "our dullness of mind may be more readily led to some knowledge of God."[43] If the terms are equivalent and any such terms are immeasurably surpassed by the infinite goodness of God,[44] then all the more reason, Erasmus concludes, that a rich variety of words are employed.[45]

The question at hand for Erasmus and his critics is which Latin term better captures the meaning expressed by the Greek word *logos*. As Erasmus explains, *logos* has "multiple meanings," including "speech" (*sermo*), "word" (*verbum*), "discourse" (*oratio*), "reasoning" (*ratio*), "wisdom" (*sapienta*), or "calculation" (*computus*).[46] It is a word, clearly enough, that is rich in signification, so choosing the best Latin equivalent is as important as it is difficult. "Latin speakers liked *sermo* or *verbum* best," Erasmus notes, with Jerome apparently finding advantages in each of the above terms, and Augustine considering *verbum* to be "more appropriate than *ratio* or other words to designate the Son of God."[47] Jerome's suggestion is intriguing, but Erasmus does not follow up on its potential; though Augustine's comparison is deemed "irrelevant" to

---

43. Erasmus, "Defence of 'Word'" (1520b), CWE 73: 33.

44. Erasmus, *Paraphrase on John*, CWE 46: 13.

45. On the value of "copious language" for God and Christ in the works of Erasmus, see Boyle, *Erasmus on Language and Method in Theology*, 11–12; Hoffmann, *Rhetoric and Theology*, passim; and Chantraine, *"Mystere" et "Philosophie du Christ" selon Érasme*, 297–301. As O'Malley writes, "Erasmian *pietas* has an accommodating quality to it," and this principle finds expression in the persistent attention showed by Erasmus for the variety (*varietas*) of words and things in proper speaking, good writing, and sound reading; as well as the plenitude found in divine creation and revelation, and thus in the protean character of the life of Christ. See O'Malley, "Introduction," CWE 66: xviii. Of course, Erasmus had long been devoted to the study of rhetorical style, something richly in evidence in *Copia: Foundations of the Abundant Style*, trans. Betty I. Knott, *Collected Works of Erasmus: Literary and Educational Writings*, vol. 24 (Toronto: University of Toronto Press, 1978), 284–659, a long work that eventually became "a textbook of rhetoric in schools and universities throughout northern Europe" (Knott, introductory note, CWE 24, 283).

46. Erasmus, "Defence of 'Word'" (1520b), CWE 73: 18.

47. Erasmus, "Defence of 'Word'" (1520b), CWE 73: 18–19.

Erasmus's concern, as he is comparing *sermo* and *verbum* but not *ratio*, and he prefers "*sermo* without rejecting *verbum*."[48]

In any case, Erasmus suggests, there are several problems with using *verbum* to designate the Son of God, and though he calls these "trivial matters," what emerges is packed with hints of theological significance.[49] In its "narrow sense," he observes, *verbum* is linked with "*rhema*" [verb] or "*lexeis*" [word], though these cognates are not used in the scriptures with reference to the Son, as they are too ordinary and pedestrian in meaning for religious use. It is true, Erasmus continues, that *verbum* sometimes is used for "some short saying such as a proverb or an aphorism," though whenever it is used for something beyond a single word, as in a discourse, for instance, it is put in the plural [*verba*], which while grammatically appropriate would be problematic for Christology, as it might suggest a plurality of Sons.[50] What Erasmus suggests, in sum, is that *verbum* is too limited in its power and range of signification to function well as a translation of the polysemous *logos*. Though he does not reject the word *verbum*, as it is found in the Vulgate and is used the churches, it is, grammatically speaking, not the best of choices.

48. Erasmus, "Defence of 'Word'" (1520b), CWE 73: 19. Here, Erasmus rebuts the appeal apparently made by Standish to the authority of Augustine in order to claim that *verbum* was a superior translation of *logos* than *ratio* (15). The same rebuttal is put in the mouth of one of Erasmus's friends in dialogue with Standish while dining at court. See Erasmus to Hermannus Buschius, letter 1126, CWE 8: 9. As Drysdall notes, Augustine, in fact, claimed that *verbum* (word) was more fittingly said of the Son than *cogitatio* (thought). See Augustine, *On the Trinity*, bk. 15, chap. 16, in *Nicene and Post-Nicene Fathers*, vol. 3, ed. Philip Schaff (New York: Charles Scribner's Sons, 1900), 214.

49. Erasmus, "Defence of 'Word'" (1520b), CWE 73: 19. Erasmus frequently speaks of "trifles" in an ironic manner, so that what appears to be a trivial matter turns out to be of great importance, and conversely, what is taken as serious turns out to be nothing but trifles. Consider, for instance, the ironic play on the trivial and the serious in Erasmus to Thomas More, letter 222, which served as the preface to *The Praise of Folly*, CWE 27: 84; see also the clever response to Budé's apparently serious complaint that Erasmus is wasting his "intellectual gifts" by spending so much time on philological "trivialities," where Erasmus retorts that everything of his is "trifling," including his work on the New Testament, which he calls "those 'trifling trivialities," though they nonetheless are "welcomed by the most authoritative theologians." See Erasmus to Guillaume Budé, letter 421, CWE 3: 306–8, written in response to From Guillaume Budé, letter 403, CWE 3: 279–80. On the dual sense of "trifle" in Erasmus, at once critical (where something serious is reduced to a "mere joke") and yet also positive and revelatory (where "the trifle turns out to be a gem"), see Gordon, *Humanist Play and Belief*, 91.

50. Erasmus, "Defence of 'Word'" (1520b), CWE 73: 19. As in the example given by Erasmus, *verba facere* for "to speak." See Boyle, *Erasmus on Language and Method in Theology*, 8.

As Erasmus says several times, *logos* is "more correctly and commonly expressed in Latin by the word *sermo* than by *verbum*."[51] However, even if the two Latin words are roughly equivalent, the "congruence of gender," he observes, "certainly favors the word *sermo*," as *sermo* is grammatically masculine, which, like the masculine *logos*, accords with the sexual gender associated with a Son, while *verbum* is neuter.[52] Such reasoning might seem odd for English-speaking readers in our day, but it functions more naturally in languages where grammar is inflected with gender. Indeed, as Erasmus explains in a manner that appears to minimize the gender factor, "even a slight additional consideration," like the grammatical gender, "tips the scales one way or the other when a matter is otherwise in balance." Though this is true enough for Erasmus, what he adds immediately after that would seem to indicate that his preference for *sermo* over *verbum* is based on something more than the mere grammatical association of gender.

After noting that "congruence of gender certainly favours the word *sermo*," he continued by saying that "otherwise [he] would almost prefer *oratio* to *sermo* because *sermo* often means conversation when people are chatting in a familiar manner," implying that such a connotation is too mundane to properly express the august discourse of God.[53] The wording of Erasmus—"would almost prefer"—so typical of the subtle hedging often found in his writings, replaces the more deliberate "would prefer" in "A Defence of 'Word'" (1520a).[54] The problem for Erasmus, implied but not stated, is that *oratio* is feminine, so that "slight additional consideration" [sic] also makes *sermo* a more suitable translation of *logos* than *oratio*. Without considering gender, however, Erasmus may well have opted for *oratio*, and the reason, once again, is that *sermo* often means familiar conversation when people are casually chatting with each other; thus, it would seem it lacks some of the plenitude and grandeur implied in *oratio*. What Erasmus appreciates in *sermo* is that it captures some of the range and plenitude of *logos* in a way that *verbum,* as a simple and discrete word, fails to do, and what

---

51. Erasmus, "Defence of 'Word'" (1520b), CWE 73: 19.

52. Erasmus, "Defence of 'Word'" (1520b), CWE 73: 19. On grammatical gender as expressive of a "concern for propriety," see Boyle, *Erasmus on Language and Method in Theology*, 33–35.

53. Erasmus, "Defence of 'Word'" (1520b), CWE 73: 19.

54. Erasmus, "Defence of 'Word'" (1520a), CWE 73: 5.

he finds appealing about *oratio*, along the same lines, is that it conveys a yet fuller and grander form of discourse. If only it was not feminine, or so Erasmus appears to say. What Erasmus is searching for in these philological considerations is a Latin word that will have sufficient range and depth of meaning to serve as a translation of the Greek *logos*, and, other things being equal, *sermo* serves that purpose, even though *oratio* has a greater semantic range. All of this is meant grammatically at this stage, but as we will see shortly, the implications for Christology are not insignificant, as language is needed that can serve to express the breadth and the richness of the *logos* of God.

"Infinite Examples Could be Adduced"

But there is more, Erasmus proceeds to say, for "Christ is called *sermo*" in "the canonical scriptures, in the usage of the church, and in the writings of orthodox Doctors, both ancient and modern."[55] What a surprise this must have been for his critics, when what they took to be an irreverent novelty turns out to be ancient tradition. Indeed, Erasmus adds, Christ is so called "in the very passage these people are raising such an uproar about," namely, in John 1:1. Surely they should have known this, Erasmus chides his critics, unless, of course, they are simply "unversed in Holy Scripture," he muses, or perhaps because they simply are "stupid in not having noticed this, or false accusers in criticizing so provocatively what is shown to be validated by so many authorities."[56] In fact, the evidence Erasmus provides from scripture and tradition does more than shame his shameless critics, as it more importantly offers confirmation of the philological defense of *sermo* and thereby provides an all-important warrant for Christological reflections.

Erasmus turns first to Cyprian (d. 258 CE)—"so ancient, so generally approved" and famous too for his "eloquence," "holiness," and "martyrdom"—for evidence to show that *sermo* was used in early Latin translations of Christian scriptures. There is, in fact, a citation by Cyprian of the prologue of John, translated just as Erasmus has it: "In the beginning was the Word [*sermo*], and the Word [*sermo*] was with God,

55. Erasmus, "Defence of 'Word'" (1520b), CWE 73: 19–20.
56. Erasmus, "Defence of 'Word'" (1520b), CWE 73: 20.

and the Word [*sermo*] was God." In case anyone suspects that Erasmus had doctored this passage, however, he challenges them to "look at the old manuscripts" and consult the various editions of Cyprian's works, because there they would find that the scriptures used by Cyprian clearly refer to Christ as the *sermo* of God.[57] But there is much more evidence, Erasmus proceeds to show, as Cyprian cites numerous Psalms, a bit of Isaiah, as well as a passage from the book of Revelations to show that some early Latin Bibles translated *logos* as *sermo*.[58] Next Erasmus appeals to Tertullian (d. 160 CE), who "calls the Son *sermo* more than once," including in his citation of the prologue of John as *In principio erat sermo*, which shows once again that "it was the practice of Latin speakers to read it like this," though Erasmus awkwardly grants that Tertullian, in fact, "preferred the word *ratio*."[59]

Then, again, there is Augustine (d. 430 CE), who comments that John 17:17 ("your word is truth"), as well as John 1:1, are commonly read with *verbum* as a translation of *logos*, though he acknowledges that "in some codices that the Catholic church used in his time," *sermo* stood in place of *verbum*. Here and elsewhere, Erasmus concludes, "a respected authority [like Augustine] did not shrink from the word *sermo*," as

57. Erasmus, "Defence of 'Word'" (1520b), CWE 73: 20. Erasmus was well-prepared to level this challenge, as he had recently published a first edition of the works of Cyprian, an undertaking that saw Erasmus working with existing print editions, as well as some "very ancient manuscript" containing writings of Cyprian that he secured from the abbey of Gembloux in 1519. See Erasmus's request for the materials and the gracious response of Antoine Papin, the abbot of Gembloux, in Erasmus to Antoinie Papin (letter 975) and From Antoine Papin to Erasmus (letter 984), CWE 6: 385–86, 983. On Erasmus's editions of the works of Cyprian, see C. S. M. Rademaker, "Cypriani Opera, Introduction," *Opera omnia Desiderii Erasmi Roterdami*, VIII - 1 (Leiden: Brill, 2019), 321–24.

58. Erasmus, "Defence of 'Word'" (1520b), CWE 73: 20–21. Erasmus cites Psalm 106 (107), among others, which says, "He sent His Word [*sermonem suum*] and healed them." A bit murkier, Erasmus cites Cyprian's rendering of "*sermonem breviatum*," as found through the allusion in Romans 9:28 ("the Lord will make the sentence shortened on the earth," from the NRSV). Then too, Erasmus observes that Revelations 19:13 as cited by Cyprian calls the one riding the white horse "the Word of God [*sermo Dei*]."

59. Erasmus, "Defence of 'Word'" (1520b), CWE 73: 22. Pelikan notes that the use of *sermo* for *logos* "in some of the earliest Latin versions of the New Testament" provides indication of "the presence within Christian teaching of a doctrine of the *Logos* not primarily determined by Greek cosmological speculation." Pelikan cites examples from Tertullian, Cyprian, and Novatian (d. 258 CE) (Pelikan, *The Emergence of the Catholic Tradition*, 186–87). On the Christology of Tertullian, including his preference for *sermo* to describe the *logos*, see Aloys Grillmeier, *Christ in Christian Tradition: From the Apostolic Age to Chalcedon (451)*, trans. J. S. Bowden (New York: Sheed and Ward, 1965), 144–57.

it was evidently in common use in certain versions of the scriptures during that period of Christian history. Indeed, modern scholars argue, an independent strand of Old Latin manuscripts existed in North Africa, offering some "divergences from the generally received text" and "on the whole" agreeing with "the quotations of Tertullian and Cyprian."[60] So it turns out that Erasmus is on firm ground when he appeals to Cyprian, Tertullian, and Augustine to show that *sermo* was used in the scriptural texts cited by these very church fathers.

It also is not unheard of, Erasmus continues, for "holy and orthodox writers" from the early church to use *sermo* for the Son of God in their own works. Erasmus starts with Hilary of Poitiers (d. 368 CE), who in some rather strained Trinitarian discussions, calls "Christ the 'eternal Word' [*sermo*], proceeding tirelessly from the eternal mind of the Father." Unlike human speech [*sermo humanus*], Erasmus explains on behalf of Hilary, where speech is a "movement" produced by "bodily organs" and that "comes to an end," Christ is the eternal *sermo* of the Father.[61] Then Erasmus draws material from Ambrose to show that Christ is the world-creating speaking [*sermo*] of God, though he is aware in part that some of his sources may be from other authors.[62] Following this, Erasmus quotes from Jerome's commentary on Ephesians to show that Jerome did not have "any scruple here in calling the Son of God *sermo*," as well as Lactantius (d. 320 CE), who also "preferred *sermo* to *verbum*," though he found the Greek *logos* to be superior to either Latin word, "for *logos* means 'speech' [*sermo*] and 'reasoning' [*ratio*] because it is the voice [*vox*] and the wisdom of God." Erasmus continues with citations showing the use of *sermo* from what he takes to be the works of Anselm (which, as Drysdall notes, are from St. Martin of León [d. 1203 CE] and Augustine) and from Remigius (which is from Haimo of Auxerre).

---

60. Bruce M. Metzger, *The Early Versions of the New Testament: Their Origin, Transmission, and Limitations* (Oxford: Clarendon Press, 1977), 325–27. Augustine complains about the "innumerable" translations of scriptures from Greek into Latin, often by people with questionable "facility in both languages" (Augustine, *On Christian Doctrine*, II. 16. 44).

61. Erasmus, "Defence of 'Word'" (1520b), CWE 73: 27–28.

62. Erasmus, "Defence of 'Word'" (1520b), CWE 73: 28–30. As Erasmus acknowledges, the material he thinks is from the hand of Ambrose is "certainly [by] Remigius [d. 533 CE] or someone not very different," who Drysdall identifies as Haimo of Auxerre (d. 855 CE).

All these references, Erasmus concludes, "must be amply sufficient to refute those who clamour that it is impious to call the Son of God *sermo*," though "if anyone had the time to investigate the passages," he is sure that "infinite examples could be adduced" to show that "approved Doctors of the church were not deterred by any scruple from calling Christ the *sermo* of the Father." For good measure, however, Erasmus points to the early Christian poet Prudentius (d. 413 CE), whose hymn "the choir sings in church": "Come, supreme Father, whom none has ever seen, and Christ, the Word [*sermo*] of the Father, [and] kindly Spirit." So the accusers of Erasmus may well have sung *"sermo"* of Christ themselves, without even noticing what they were saying.[63] He caps off the turn to tradition, however, by citing the words of Thomas Aquinas—one of the most celebrated heroes of the scholastic critics of Erasmus—to show that "this author [also] makes no distinction between *sermo* and *verbum*."[64] On that historical note, Erasmus rests his case.

The Erasmian turn to tradition, in sum, is a strategic continuation of his philological analysis, which deals with common and correct usage of select Latin terms, but now what is apt and correct in grammatical principle is confirmed in actual use where it matters—in the traditions that took biblical sources seriously and used them to think and converse about Christ. Indeed, Erasmus concludes, that *sermo* is a correct and suitable translation of *logos* is now "validated by so many authorities" drawn from the history of Christian thought.[65] With that said, Erasmus challenges his accusers to draw out the logical conclusion of their indictment. As he put it,

> if it is impious, if it is blasphemous, if it is a capital offence to call Christ *sermo*, they must condemn before me or with me so many

---

63. Erasmus, "Defence of 'Word'" (1520b), CWE 73: 30–33.

64. Erasmus, "Defence of 'Word'" (1520b), CWE 73: 24–26. Erasmus also gives evidence from other medieval commentators, including Nicolas of Lyra (d. 1349 CE) and Hugh of Saint-Cher (d. 1263 CE), to show the use of *sermo* in biblical commentaries of the medieval era. Erasmus cites these sources, he tells us, because he is "dealing with people for whom these writers have authority."

65. Erasmus, "Defence of 'Word'" (1520b), CWE 73: 20. As Boyle puts it, "the apology for *sermo* demonstrate the mastery through grammar of the texts that comprise Christian tradition" (Boyle, *Erasmus on Language and Method in Theology*, 15).

outstanding princes of the church: Cyprian, Ambrose, Jerome, Augustine, Hilary, Prudentius, Lactantius, and with those Thomas, Nicolas of Lyra, Hugh, the Glossa ordinaria, no, rather the whole church.[66]

All of which is to say, using *sermo* for Christ is not impious, and thereby, the case is firmly closed.

In making this argument, however, Erasmus is by no means making a "submissive appeal to Christian tradition," as Boyle strangely puts it,[67] but rather is deliberately engaging its plentiful voices, just as good theologians of all stripes have always done, in search of confirmation or correction. It is true, of course, that Standish and others did not challenge Erasmus for Christological errors, as Lee and the Spanish monks meeting at Valladolid did, so there was no explicit prompt to theological reflections by way of the controversy over *sermo*.[68] And yet, controversy has again served Erasmus well, as Boyle observes, for in responding to his critics' insistence on the orthodox usage of *verbum* by cleverly turning to argue grammatically that *sermo* best conveys what needs to be expressed as a translation of *logos*, he proceeds to a creative rendering of the orthodox claim that Christ is God's full and eternal revelation; better yet, he manages this move in a way that is licensed by learned and venerable sources from Christian tradition. In sum, a grammatically exact reading of scripture is bolstered by the voices of tradition in a way that opens the door for Christological insight. More subtly perhaps, but true nonetheless, as we will see in the final section of this chapter, Erasmus again has moved from philology to theology by way of the arguments necessary to succeed in controversy.

---

66. Erasmus, "Defence of 'Word'" (1520b), CWE 73: 38. Earlier, Erasmus asks, "if any try to show by sophistical subtleties that Christ is correctly called *verbum* and incorrectly called *sermo*, what are they doing but making so many distinguished princes of the church blasphemers and lunatics?" (33).

67. Boyle, *Erasmus on Language and Method in Theology*, 8.

68. Nor did the theologians of the faculty of theology at the University of Paris raise Christological objections to the use of *sermo* in place of *verbum*. Instead, they complain only that Erasmus "departs from the ordinary usage of the church" in paraphrasing John 1:1. Erasmus responds, much as he does in "Defence of 'Word'" that he never introduced a new reading for public use in the churches and that *sermo* frequently appears "in older and more recent Doctors and also nowadays in the liturgy of the church." See Erasmus, *Clarifications Concerning the Censures*, CWE 82: 145–46.

"Eternal Word of the Eternal Mind"

One stepping-off point for considering how Erasmus's reflections on *sermo* contribute to Christology appears, oddly enough, in his response to the "syllogism of a theologian" designed to show that Christ cannot be called *sermo*. "*Verbum*," this theologian apparently declares, "is a silent concept. But if Christ is correctly said to be *sermo*," he continues, "it will follow that *sermo* too is a silent concept," which would leave us with a "patently absurd" conclusion, since *sermo*, at least as he sees it, "is a concept uttered by the voice."[69] This is such a "silly syllogism," as Boyle aptly puts it, that one might think with good reason that Erasmus concocted it as a bit of satire, though elsewhere he attributes roughly the same point to a "Spanish Franciscan" who is not further identified.[70] This illustration of the sickly arguments leveled by his critics provides Erasmus an occasion to remind his readers of the inadequacy of human terms for speaking of intra-trinitarian relations, as "the Son of God is neither a silent concept nor [one] uttered by a voice," even though these notions might be stretched analogically to apply to the divine life, so that the former might refer at best to "Christ abiding in the Father" and the latter could point metaphorically to "Christ eternally born of the Father."[71]

But, in addition, because this strange little syllogism draws upon a distinction well-known in the works of Augustine, that between an unspoken word and one given sound externally, responding to his theo-

---

69. Erasmus, "Defence of 'Word'" (1520b), CWE 73: 33.

70. See Boyle, *Erasmus on Language and Method in Theology*, 18. In "Defence of 'Word'" (1520b), CWE 73: 33, Erasmus notes that this was "the syllogism of a theologian, distinguished in the judgment of a few others and in his own in particular, a syllogism that he was not ashamed to put forward in the company of men of both the highest dignity and the highest learning." The latter context matches the accounts we have heard that describe the humiliation of Standish in England, though in Erasmus to Martin Luther, letter 1127a, CWE 8: 20, the syllogism on *sermo* is attributed to a "Spanish Franciscan," while the stories of "that well-known madman Standish" are set off in a following paragraph, after the queen had given the Spanish Franciscan "leave to go." Drysdall, however, suggests that the theologian wielding this syllogism may be the "notoriously vain Baechem," perhaps because Erasmus accents that this is a man who is distinguished "in particular" in his own judgment. See Denis L. Drysdall, "The Two Versions of Erasmus's *Apologia de In principio erat sermo* and the Role of Edward Lee," in *Acta Conventus Neo-Latini Upsaliensis*, vol. 1, ed. Astrid Steiner-Weber (Leiden: Brill, 2012), 370.

71. Erasmus, "Defence of 'Word'" (1520b), CWE 73: 33. See Boyle, *Erasmus on Language and Method in Theology*, 17–21.

logical critics' feeble attempt at reasoning also gives Erasmus the opportunity to engage Augustine in a manner that is both critical and yet appreciative. What Erasmus insists, on the one hand, is that Augustine's basic distinction is far too limiting, as it appears to consign the spoken word of God solely to the human life that was assumed, though Erasmus willingly grants, on the other hand, that in other places, Augustine shows that he is aware that the "eternal Word" [*verbum*] "emanate[s] from the Father" in a transcendent and mysterious manner that "cannot be understood literally as meaning the human form he took on." Because "the thought of the Father is eternal," Erasmus concludes in a way that highlights the enormous breadth of divine speech, it must be understood as "being uttered from the mind of the Father in several ways"—from eternity "when Christ is begotten," then "when through it the Father created all things," and then, too, "most plainly and in the way most familiar to us when he took on human form and spoke to us in human speech."[72]

With this statement, Erasmus outlines the broad range of divine speaking—from eternity through creation to the incarnation in Jesus—though even here, admittedly, the *sermo* of God is cast in a way that suggests temporally discrete moments of utterance; this is, it would seem, the inevitable pitfall of all efforts to speak about God in narrative language. These same separated instances of speaking are described in *The Tongue*, as well, in which Erasmus, in fact, accents that God "speaks most seldom and most briefly."[73] How different is the account given

72. Erasmus, "Defence of 'Word'" (1520b), CWE 73: 34–35. In *Evangelical Preacher*, Erasmus follows the same traditional format in describing the different ways in which God the Father speaks. "Before all ages," Erasmus writes, "God the Father used to talk to himself, so to speak, through the Son in the presence of the Holy Spirit." "But when the world was created through the Son, he began in another way to speak through the Son, and in another way he, so to speak, begat the Son, since according to that supreme philosophy, 'uttering his word' was the same for the Father as 'begetting the Son.'" Then, "when mortals' minds had been prepared as best they could, he spoke to us in a most intimate manner through his Son born from the Virgin, for now the Word, which was God with God the Father without beginning, could be touched by us and revealed to all our senses" (*Evangelical Preacher* 4, CWE 68: 1081–83). "Speaking" here translates forms of "*loquetor*," and the Son is called "*verbum*," though earlier in this same section, the Son is called "'Word' or 'speech'" (*verbum aut sermo*); see Erasmus, *Ecclesiastes sive de ratione concionandi*, ed. Jacques Chomarat, *Opera omnia Desiderii Erasmi Roterodami*, V - 5 (Amsterdam: Elsevier, 1994), 370–72, 366, respectively. In *Evangelical Preacher* 1, CWE 68: 253, Erasmus also speaks of the Son of God as "the Word or Speech [*verbum aut sermo*] of God."

73. Erasmus, *The Tongue*, CWE 29: 323. In this context, however, Erasmus emphasizes God's "brevity of speech" in order to contrast the divine pledge of "trust and love" with the "infinite

in the *Paraphrase on John,* where Erasmus speaks of the divine Word (*sermo*) as "forever coming to birth from" God the Father, "everlasting from everlasting … in short, God from God … eternal word of the eternal mind [*aeternae mentis sermo aeternus*], whereby the Father forever speaks with himself as in mystic [*arcana*] thought, even before the creation of the world." Indeed, Erasmus continues in paraphrase of John, "there was never a time when he had not brought forth for himself the all-powerful word [*sermonem omnipotentem*].["](74)

So what we discover in these statements, as Christine Christ-Von Wedel puts it, is "a continuous intra-trinitarian colloquy,"[75] wherein the "everlasting word" (*sermo … aeternus*) of God comes "continually forth from the Father without ever departing from the Father."[76] But just as it is with human beings, when we want to communicate the "will of our heart" to someone else, this is "accomplished by nothing more surely or swiftly than by speech" (*oratio*), so, too, for God the Father, who "from his innate goodness" created the world and everything in it "by means of his Son and word" (*sermonem*), so that "through it he might become known to us in speaking." And then, again, the Father brought forth "his word [*sermonem*] to us a second time" with the birth and life of Jesus Christ to reconcile the created world to God.[77]

---

talkativeness carried on through the "forms and rituals" of institutional religion. Much of *The Tongue*, after all, bemoans the "disease of chattering" and talkativeness, so it is only natural that Erasmus would emphasize discretion and brevity when depicting divine speech. In this context, Erasmus uses *verbum* and *sermo* interchangeably. See Erasmus, *Lingua*, ed. F. Schalk, *Opera omnia Erasmi Roterdami*, IV - 1, ed. F. Schalk (Amsterdam: North Holland Publishing Company, 1974), 294.

74. Erasmus, *Paraphrase on John*, CWE 46: 16. See Boyle, *Erasmus on Language and Method in Theology*, 23.

75. Christ-Von Wedel, *Erasmus of Rotterdam*, 135. Christ-Von Wedel taps into the language of love from the afterword Erasmus added to the *Paraphrase of John* in 1524 to argue that Erasmus understands this "continuous intra-trinitarian colloquy" as an "intra-trinitarian community of love" (CWE 46: 141). In the afterword, "To the pious reader," Erasmus writes that "this sacred triad, firmly united within itself and returning into itself, is the prime example of absolute love and harmony" (CWE 46: 226). With that language in hand, she concludes, Erasmus conceives of "the sole, eternal, and immutable divine essence" as "a constantly renewed and conversing community of love that reveals itself voluntarily to humans in love, and wants to be loved voluntarily by humankind in return" (Christ-Von Wedel, *Erasmus of Rotterdam*, 144).

76. Erasmus, *Paraphrase on John*, CWE 46: 17. "Coeternal" with the Father, Erasmus continues with the same thought, and hence "equal in all things" and only distinguished by "the particularity of begetter and begotten, of utterer and utterance delivered," this "one word from the one speaker" (*unicus sermo ab unico promente*) was "forever proceeding from his Father's mind without ever departing from it," and what is more, this same dynamic process is "without end."

77. Erasmus, *Paraphrase on John*, CWE 46: 16–18.

These reflections are, to be sure, the most focused and concentrated effort from Erasmus to articulate the immense scope of divine speech, emphasizing not only that the divine *sermo* is "pre-existent" (as many classical Christologies insisted) but truly eternal, and hence also spoken in this very moment and forever into the future. It is true, nonetheless, that Erasmus here is working exegetically with just one short passage, and too, as is his custom, that he does not pursue the hidden meanings of this notion of divine speech in a speculative manner.[78] With that said, however, these reflections on the eternal *sermo* of God square nicely with the philological reasons given by Erasmus for preferring *sermo* over *verbum*, and they also connect in some interesting ways with other places in which Erasmus stresses the broad and copious character of the divine *sermo*, as we will see presently.

As we heard earlier from Erasmus, *sermo* is a more correct and more apt translation of the Greek *logos* than *verbum*, and his reasons for this preference were strictly philological, in short, because its semantic range is broader and fuller and it happens to be masculine, as well. What ultimately attracts Erasmus to *sermo*, however, and indeed, what almost would make *oratio* even better is that it better conveys the kind of breadth and plentitude required for adequately speaking of divine speech. A philological reason, therefore, pays a theological dividend in this regard, since one may now speak more suitably of the scope and fullness of the eloquent oration of God. Certainly, the prologue to the Gospel of John opens the way in speaking—as Erasmus contends in the *Paraphrase on John*—of the emanation of the word of God as eternal; then again, with respect to the "admirable text of creation" and the living presence of Christ incarnate in human life, the utterance of God is not one solitary word but an elaborate discourse or a copious oration, one that is, in any case, rich, ample, plentiful, and complete.

"Because the *Logos* is the copious discourse of the Father," and indeed

78. Christ-Von Wedel acknowledges that Erasmus is rightly "restrained" in speaking about the preexistent *logos*, given his aversion to speculative theology. It appears in a "unique and prominent way" in the *Paraphrase on John*, she observes, precisely because "John's prologue is a text that specifically encourages the Christ-centered, dynamic vision of the Trinity that Erasmus developed in the Paraphrase." "That Erasmus refrained from systematizing his doctrine of the *logos* and using speculation as a foundation for his theology shows his integrity as an exegete," she rightly suggests, since the notion is not mentioned in the Synoptic Gospels (Christ-Von Wedel, *Erasmus of Rotterdam*, 141).

"the sufficient revealing oration," as Boyle describes it, "*verbum* is [simply] inadequate to designate him," as it is too narrow and particular in its signification.[79] There is so much more of God's speech to be heard, after all, in "the traces of divine power, wisdom, and goodness [which] cast a dim glow in the created universe";[80] there is also so much more to be gleaned through the incarnation of the divine *sermo*—an entire gospel philosophy for authentic life—than one mere word. Of course, someone may retort that this range and plenitude already was intended within the traditional notion of the *logos* of God, and they would be right, though as Erasmus surely would respond, *verbum* is semantically ill-suited to convey this universal scope and the wealth of this philosophy, so the original richness of intention was diminished in the translation to *verbum*.

It is obvious, nonetheless, that Christian tradition in the Latin west recoiled from *sermo* and *oratio* in favor of *verbum*, and by so doing, it tended to constrict the plenitude of revelation with a concentrated focus on the singularity and uniqueness of the incarnate person of Jesus Christ. The fixation on oneness in the formative centuries of Christian history, however, something classically on display in Cyprian's "The Unity of the Catholic Church," served to exclude alternative voices in order to ensure a uniform orthodoxy centered in one church under the authority of a solitary leader, namely, the successor of Peter.[81] What the insistence on unity did to Christology, however, was to harden the emphasis on the exclusive particularity of the divine word in a manner that eclipsed "the ancient faith in a Christ who is the Father's eloquent discourse" to the world; it is precisely that faith, however, that Erasmus works to retrieve and defend. The broad notion of revelation conveyed by *sermo* or *oratio*, in other words, was sublated by the "doctrine of the only-begotten" Son, as Boyle observes, "so that one Son has been

79. Boyle, *Erasmus on Language and Method in Theology*, 23, 9.

80. Erasmus, *Paraphrase on John*, CWE 46: 13. Erasmus is typically cautious in this passage concerning the knowledge of God drawn from the nature of the created world. And yet he does not rule out such inferences from nature to the power and goodness of God as creator. See, for instance, Erasmus, "The Godly Feast," CWE 39: 179.

81. See Cyprian, "The Unity of the Catholic Church," in *St. Cyprian, The Lapsed and The Unity of the Catholic Church*, trans. Maurice Bévenot (Westminster, MD: Newman Press, 1957). Cyprian's treatise naturally relies on the biblical warrant of Ephesians 4:4–6 ("There is one body and one Spirit, just as you were called to the one hope of your calling, one Lord, one faith, one baptism, one God and Father of all, who is above all and through all and in all.")

conceptualized with [the idea of] one Word."[82] It is certainly true, of course, that Erasmus did avow "only one personal Son," as Boyle rightly makes clear, but he also conceived of this Son as a "complete oration" or an "eloquent speech" rather than a single and simple word. Indeed, as Boyle writes, Erasmus "might have retorted that the unity of the second Person would not have been compromised by *sermo* any more than the unity of an oration is compromised by its composition of many words."[83] The divine oration can be heard, Erasmus cautiously suggests, across the span of creation, and the message it entails is a copious philosophy of life that is made up of many words, even if it has its origin in a single teacher.

The accent on the revelatory breadth and eternal plenitude of the divine *sermo* is not a matter for speculation, as Erasmus sees it, but a topic of great and enduring practical significance for the living of a pious and virtuous life. It is true, of course, that theologians with metaphysical talents often have feasted on the speculative richness of these Trinitarian notions, but the interest of Erasmus characteristically turns instead to the effective power of the divine word for the transformation of twisted and distorted human lives. What that means, plainly enough, is that one must listen attentively to the copious speech of God where it most vibrantly lives and breathes—and that, Erasmus tells us, is in Christian scriptures interpreted soundly and preached persuasively. With this in mind, he writes to Pope Leo X in the preface to the 1516 edition of the New Testament, that

> all those who profess the Christian philosophy the whole world over should above all absorb the principles laid down by their Founder from the writings of the evangelists and the apostles, in which that heavenly Word, which once came down to us from the heart of the Father, still lives and breathes for us, and acts and speaks with more immediate efficacy, in my opinion, than in any other way.[84]

---

82. Boyle, *Erasmus on Language and Method in Theology*, 28.

83. Boyle, *Erasmus on Language and Method in Theology*, 30–31.

84. Erasmus to Leo X, letter 384, CWE 41: 769. As Sider notes, Erasmus used *verbum* when this letter served as the preface to the 1516 edition of the New Testament, though it was fittingly changed to *sermo* in the preface to the edition of 1519.

With this little passage, Erasmus manages to combine many of the key elements that we have seen regularly in his Christological reflections.

Christ as *sermo*, to begin with, speaks to humanity with the "principles" of a "philosophy," which as we saw in the first chapter amounts to the integral religious ethic of godly and virtuous life he bequeathed to his followers. The philosophy of Christ, moreover, is a "heavenly Word," which descended "from the heart of the Father." So what is very much a *scopus* laid out before human beings for a godly and virtuous life has its origin in the eternal *sermo* of the Father, since Christ as *sermo* springs eternally from the Father, while Christ as *scopus* beckons us toward the transformation of our lives. What is heavenly in origin, in short, is ethical in substance; additionally, what is said eternally is very much contemporary in its import—as Christ the divine *sermo*, we are told, still "lives and breathes" today, inasmuch as it "acts and speaks" on people with incomparably "immediate efficacy" through the living words of scriptural teaching. Far from a speculative matter for Erasmus, speaking of Christ as *sermo* is first a question of grammar, which then makes way with the supporting precedents of Christian tradition for theological insight, the substance of which leads back to the philosophy of Christ as the *scopus* for human life.

To speak of Christ as *sermo*, in sum, addresses a Trinitarian question—how one might think of the relation of the Son to the Father—and yet, in the hands of Erasmus, it also and more importantly points to the Gospel message of Christ, that redemptive discourse transmitted by Christ incarnate that provides an ethical *scopus* for the transformation of human existence. By ethical, once again, I do not mean merely a set of moral guidelines but rather a full-fledged ideal for enhancing the very character of human life. While much more will be said about this ethic in the final chapter of this book, for now it is enough to stress how the Trinitarian notion of Christ as *sermo* issues in a pastoral mandate and an ethical challenge for those who would follow the philosophy put forward in Christian scriptures. For starters, as Erasmus writes in the *Paraphrase on Matthew*, just as everything Christ taught "emanated from the heavenly Father," so too, then, "apostolic men" were charged to "bring forth only what they had received from Christ." The responsibility of gospel preachers, in short, is to set out "simple gospel teaching" in a manner that is faithful to what they had received and persuasive to those who would listen.[85] Such is the dignity and the purpose of the "evangelical orator," Erasmus writes in the *Evangelical Preacher*, whose entire duty is to "dispense the Lord's own word [*verbum*] to his flock."[86] In essence, therefore, the good Christian pastor is to function as a living conduit of the eternal *sermo* of God incarnate.

Roughly the same thing is true, of course, for everyone else as well, those of us who are challenged to respond in word and action to the lure of Christ as *scopus* by actively participating in the divine conversation that is Christ as *sermo*. What is remarkable in this regard is the transition Erasmus charts from the metaphysical heights of divine eternity—by way of the philosophy taught by Christ embedded in scripture—to the heart of human life in the world, where people are invited by the divine *sermo* to imitate the reconciling words of Christ with lives centered in piety and the gospel virtues of "charity, joy, peace, patience, kindness, goodness, forbearance, gentleness, faith, moderation, self-control, and chastity."[87] It is exactly this kind of life, as we will see in more detail in chapter 8, that Erasmus depicts in certain characters of the *Colloquies*, those whose lives are filled with joy and peace, whose hearts exude faith and kindness, and whose words beam with intelligence and respect.

Chapters 4 and 5 have dealt with the most transcendental issues in Christology: to wit, the dignity and divinity of the Son, and with that, the relation of the divine word to God the Father. These are lofty matters, indeed, which is why Erasmus never tires of reminding us of the limits of human language for speaking of such things. Despite these warnings, however, Erasmus is pressed to address these questions through the challenges of controversy, and he responds, as we have seen, with exegetical arguments rooted in philological considerations and supported by the

---

85. Erasmus, *Paraphrase on Matthew*, CWE 45: 227. Erasmus here imaginatively paraphrases Matthew 14:19. On the "mirroring" of thought as an Erasmian metaphor for the divine *sermo* and as "moral obligation incumbent on all Christians," see Eric MacPhail, "Erasmus and Christian Humanist Latin," *Reformation* 22, no. 2 (2017): 78–79.

86. Erasmus, *Evangelical Preacher* 1, CWE 67: 252–53. In the same context, however, Erasmus speaks of "that highest *ecclesiastes*, the Son of God" as being "the Word or Speech of God" (*verbum aut sermo*) (253).

87. Erasmus to Jean de Carondelet, letter 1334, CWE 9: 252. For this list of virtues, Erasmus draws on Galatians 5:22.

precedents of tradition, yielding thereby some theological insights that ultimately focus on the religious and ethical transformation of human life. The following two chapters turn to address Erasmus's treatment of the humanity of Christ. The final impulse of the Christology of Erasmus, as we will see, is the affirmation of the full incarnation of Christ in human existence, eschewing—as much as is possible for anyone wrestling with Christological questions—traces of docetic insulation of the divine from the travails of human life. Ultimately, for Erasmus, Christ embodies the merciful and healing embrace of humanity by God and a compelling model of reconciling love for those willing to live according to this gospel philosophy.

CHAPTER 6

The Humiliation of Christ

In July of 1517, Erasmus reports to Thomas More that he will be respond-ing in print to the criticism leveled by the French humanist Jacques Lefèvre d'Etaples against his handling of Hebrews 2:7 in the *Annotations* on the New Testament.[1] The criticism of Lefèvre—to wit, that Erasmus's commentary on the language of Psalm 8:5, which is embedded in He-brews 2:6–9, was "heretical [*impium*] and most unworthy of Christ and God"—was a charge of such severity that it apparently caught Erasmus by surprise, as he had been confident that he was on friendly terms with the venerable French humanist.[2] Both were well-known and celebrated scholars, after all, and up to that point, they had spoken of each other with respect and praise.[3] It is true, as Erasmus readily acknowledges,

1. Erasmus to Thomas More, letter 597, CWE 5: 11. For similar announcements of his pend-ing response to the "unfriendly" attacks of Lefèvre, see Erasmus to Cuthbert Tunstall, letter 607, CWE 5: 31; Erasmus to Pierre Barbier, letter 608, CWE 5: 34; and Erasmus to Beatus Rhenanus, letter 628, CWE 5: 72–73.

2. For Lefèvre's charge, see appendix four, *Opera omnia Desiderii Erasmi Roterdami*, IX - 3 (Amsterdam: Elsevier, 1996), 210. Erasmus quotes Lefèvre's hostile words in Erasmus, *Apology against Lefèvre*, CWE: 83: 33. The full indictment also states that the opinion of Erasmus is "con-trary to the spirit and adhering to the letter which destroys."

3. In October of 1514, for example, Lefèvre sent warm words of praise and thanks to Eras-mus. See From Jacques Lefèvre d'Étaples, letter 315, CWE 3: 49. For his part, Erasmus praised

that he had offered a number of critical comments on Lefèvre's translation and commentary on the Epistles of Paul (1512)—some in the *Annotations* of 1516, and others in three letters (now lost)[4] written directly to
Lefèvre[5]—though Erasmus heard by correspondence that Lefèvre was
not disturbed by his remarks.[6]

It seems that this was not the case, however, as Erasmus would
discover in the summer of 1517 that the second edition of Lefèvre's
Commentaries on the Epistles of St. Paul, which apparently had been in
circulation for some time without Erasmus's knowing of it, included a
"lengthy dispute" with Erasmus concerning the proper rendering of the
second chapter of Hebrews.[7] As Lefèvre sees it, Hebrews was written

---

Lefèvre as "a scholar of uncommon erudition … a man of high character … and a close friend,"
though he adds in passing some reservations about the "quality" of Lefèvre's work. See Erasmus,
"To the Reader," letter 326, CWE 3: 71, a letter serving as the preface to the second volume of
Erasmus's edition of Jerome. Similarly, in late 1516 and early 1517, Guillaume Budé passes along
"greetings" from Lefèvre, who apparently was too ill at the time to write to Erasmus (Guillaume
Budé to Erasmus, letter 493, CWE 4: 151–52). Erasmus responds to Budé with regret upon hearing of Lefèvre's ill-health, who he praises as "a man of such saintly character, so civilized and so
scholarly, and has done so much for learning and all who wish to learn, that he deserves never to
grow old or die" (Erasmus to Guillaume Budé, letter 531, CWE 4: 242).

4. On the three letters, see Erasmus, *Apology against Lefèvre,* CWE 83: 9 and n. 28.

5. Erasmus concedes in the *Apology against Lefèvre* that he may have provoked Lefèvre with
the comments and questions scattered throughout the *Annotations,* though he insists that disagreements are not insults, and hence do not deserve such a "contentious" reply. See CWE 83: 7,
11. Lefèvre's response, Erasmus contends, was simply disproportionate. "I merely mentioned in a
restrained manner and without any exaggeration that you had slipped up in certain particulars,"
Erasmus declares. "You, on the other hand, charge me with impiety even where I have committed
no error" (98). Late in the *Apology against Lefèvre,* Erasmus recalls in detail a number of Lefèvre's
confusions and mistakes that he had mentioned in the *Annotations.* See CWE 83: 87–92. The ma-
jority of such comments in the *Annotations* are entirely innocuous, however, whether observing
that Lefèvre has a different translation, raising a question about Lefèvre's rendering, or offering
an occasional correction. See, for examples, *Annotations on Romans,* CWE 56: 125, 178, 181, 189,
192, and 304, as well as Erasmus, *Annotations on Galatians and Ephesians, Collected Works of
Erasmus: New Testament Scholarship,* vol. 58, trans. Riemer A. Faber (Toronto: University of
Toronto Press, 2017), 39, 175, and 202–3. More striking is the praise of Lefèvre's character and
erudition in the first edition of the *Annotations on Romans* (1516), CWE 56: 28, after which Erasmus reminds his readers (and Lefèvre as well) that even the most gifted (like Augustine) must
sometimes retract their errors, as everyone (including Lefèvre and Erasmus) should be open to
friendly disagreement. For Erasmus's annotation of Hebrews 2:7 that clearly did offend Lefèvre,
see appendix 3, ASD IX - 3: 203–5.

6. Erasmus received second-hand assurance that Lefèvre did "not resent in the slightest" the
criticisms of Erasmus. See Karel Ofhuys to Erasmus, letter 480a, CWE 4: 113; Thomas Grey to
Erasmus, letter 445, CWE 3: 345. Indeed, Erasmus notes, Lefèvre never gave "so much as a hint,
either by letter or through some close friend" that there was a problem. See Erasmus, *Apology
against Lefèvre,* CWE 83: 33.

7. On Erasmus's belated discovery of Lefèvre's second edition, dated as published in 1515

by Paul in Hebrew, and thus it stays faithful to the original language of Psalm 8:5, which Lefèvre translates as "you have made them a little lower than God (*Eloim*)." When this psalm is applied Christologically in Hebrews 2, therefore, Lefèvre in turn translates that Christ was made "a little lower than God."[8] For his part, Erasmus dissents both from Lefèvre's assumptions regarding authorship and from his translation, leading him to render the passage from the Greek in Hebrews as saying that Christ was made "for a little while lower than the angels." These shifts, as we will see in this chapter, demonstrate two central features of the Christology of Erasmus: the vital part played by rigorous critical scholarship and the resolute affirmation of the humanity of Christ.

Jacques Lefèvre d'Étaples (Faber Stapulensis) was a fascinating and intriguing figure of importance for his day. A Catholic priest from Étaples-sur-mer in what is now the far north department of Pas-de-Calais, Lefèvre was professor of philosophy and the arts at the Collège du Cardinal-Lemoin in Paris from 1490 until 1508, whereupon he moved but a short distance to the abbey of Saint-Germain-des-Prés, where he could concentrate on scholarly projects under the patronage of his friend and the abbot, Guillaume Briçonnet. Lefèvre's intellectual interests were richly eclectic, including mathematics and magic, though his most notable efforts reflected the humanist penchant for the recovery, purification, and dissemination of ancient, patristic, and medieval texts.[9] Lefèvre is no doubt most famous in this regard for his efforts

---

but shown to Erasmus in July 1517, see *Apology against Lefèvre*, CWE 83: 4, 10–11. Erasmus surmises that the dating of Lefèvre's second edition as 1515, even though it included his response to Erasmus's *Annotations* of 1516, was likely a printer's error (which probably is correct), though he wonders (rather fancifully) whether an ally of Lefèvre might have changed the publication date to underscore Lefèvre's independence. The *Apology against Lefèvre* was published in Louvain by Dirk Martens in 1517, along with Erasmus's annotation on Hebrews 2:7 and Lefèvre's critical note, now called the "*Disputatio*." On the confusion surrounding the dating of Lefèvre's second edition, see above all Steenbeek, "Introduction," ASD IX - 3: 60–64, but also Margaret Mann, *Érasme et les débuts de la réforme française, 1517–1536* (Paris: Librairie Ancienne Honoré Champion, 1934), 30; H. Feld, "Der Humanistern-Streit um Hebräer, 2, 7 (Ps 8,6)," *Archiv für Reformationsgeschichte* 61 (1970): 6–7, 17–20.

8. For Lefèvre's 1512 translation and annotation of Hebrews 2:7, see ASD IX - 3: 201–2, appendix 2. For the same rendering of Psalm 8:6, see ASD IX - 3: 197–200, appendix 1.

9. On the life and work of Lefèvre, see Augustin Renaudet, "Un problème historique: La pensée religieuse de J. Lefèvre d'Étaples," in *Humanisme et Renaissance* (Genève: Librairie E. Droz, 1958), 201–16; Eugene F. Rice, Jr., "Introduction," in *The Prefatory Epistles of Jacques Lefèvre d'Etaples and Related Texts*, ed. Eugene F. Rice (New York: Columbia University Press, 1972), xi–xxv; and Guy Bedouelle, "Jacques Lefèvre d'Étaples," *The Reformation Theologians: An*

to retrieve a "pure Aristotelian philosophy," something to be rendered anew in its original purity and eloquence and made available to readers through Lefèvre's "translations, commentaries, introductions, paraphrases and dialogues."[10] More pertinent for understanding Lefèvre's religious thinking, however, is his extensive work in editing and promulgating mystical literature from Christian tradition, above all, Pseudo-Dionysius (fifth century), who Lefèvre mistakenly thought was Dionysius the Areopagite of Acts 17:34, but also Raymond Lull (d. 1316), John of Ruusbroec (d. 1381), and Nicholas of Cusa (d. 1464), among others.[11]

Central to his life-work, however, are the various commentaries on biblical literature, increasingly prepared for the spiritual benefit of ordinary readers, and culminating in French translations of Christian scriptures in 1523 and of the entire Bible in 1530.[12] Lefèvre left Paris in 1521 to join Bishop Briçonnet's efforts at church reform in the diocese of Meaux,[13] though as Eugene F. Rice, Jr. observes, "the fortuitous

---

Introduction to Theology in the Early Modern Period, ed. Carter Lindberg (Oxford: Blackwell, 2002), 19–33.

10. Eugene F. Rice, Jr., "Humanist Aristotelianism in France: Jacques Lefèvre d'Étaples and his Circle," in *Humanism in France at the End of the Middle Ages and in the Early Renaissance*, ed. A. H. T. Levi (Manchester: Manchester University Press, 1970), 132–49. Though Lefèvre's return to the original sources helped to free Aristotle from its Thomistic cast, the end result was nonetheless an Aristotle "bathed in a Christian vocabulary and in Christian associations" (140). See also Philip Edgcumbe Hughes, *Lefèvre: Pioneer of Ecclesiastical Renewal in France* (Grand Rapids, MI: Eerdmans, 1984), 1–6.

11. On the importance of Christian mystics for Lefèvre, see Eugene F. Rice, Jr., "Jacques Lefèvre d'Étaples and the Medieval Christian Mystics," in *Florilegium Historiale: Essays Presented to Wallace K. Ferguson*, ed. J. G. Rowe and W. H. Stockdale (Toronto: University of Toronto Press, 1971), 89–124. On Lefèvre's embrace of the legend of Dionysius as a contemporary of Paul and the first apostle to the Gauls, see *Prefatory Epistles of Lefèvre*, 65–66; Guy Bedouelle, *Lefèvre D'Étaples et l'intelligence des écritures* (Genève: Librairie Droz, 1976), 42–45; and, especially, Jean-Pierre Massaut, *Critique et tradition à la veille de la réforme en France* (Paris: Librairie philosophique J. Vrin, 1974), 179–87. Appealing to Lorenzo Valla (d. 1457), whose works on Christian scriptures Erasmus had published in 1505, Erasmus denied that the author of the mystical *Hierarchies* (fifth century) is the same Dionysius mentioned in Acts 17:34. See Erasmus, *Annotationes in Acta Apostolorum*, ed. P. F. Hovingh, ASD VI - 6: 288–91. Erasmus makes the same point in Erasmus to Erard de la Marck, letter 916, CWE 6: 238, and he later defended this judgment against the charges from the faculty of theology in Paris. See *Clarifications Concerning the Censures*, CWE 82: 242–44.

12. The prefaces to Lefèvre's vernacular translations of the Gospels and Epistles (1523–24) are addressed appropriately "to all Christian men and women." See *Prefatory Epistles of Lefèvre*, 449–70. Showing his evangelical passions, Lefèvre asks in one such preface, "Who, then, is the person who will not reckon it a thing right and consistent with salvation to have this New Testament in their own languages?" (465); translation from Hughes, *Lefèvre*, 159.

13. On the reform movement at Meaux, see Bedouelle, *Lefèvre d'Étaples*, 90–103. Debates

coincidence of this experiment in reform with the first penetration of Lutheranism in France focused the [ominous] attention of the faculty of theology on his exegetical works."[14] With Francis I held captive in Madrid after the defeat of his forces at Pavia in 1525, the faculty of theology and the Parlement of Paris were emboldened to act aggressively against the reformers at Meaux, moving initially to condemn new Latin and French versions of the Bible, and then to arraign individuals suspected of heresy, which naturally included Lefèvre.[15] In order to avoid arrest, Lefèvre fled Meaux for Strasbourg, where he was welcomed into the company of fellow émigrés, local scholars, and various reformers.[16] Six months later, however, he was recalled to France by Francis I, who had recently been freed from captivity in Spain.[17] After a visit to Oecolampadius and possibly Erasmus in Basle,[18] Lefèvre settled first in Blois

------

persist whether Lefèvre was an architect or a spectator of the Reformation and, too, whether he was Catholic or Protestant. Such questions overlook the inherent complexity of the issues, for as Lucien Febvre observes, these questions do not allow for simple and unequivocal answers. See Febvre, "Une question mal posée: Les origines de la réforme et le problème des causes de la réforme," in *Au coeur religieux du XVIe siècle*, deuxième édition (Paris: Écoles Pratiques des Hautes Études, 1957), 7–95, especially 23–35. See also Richard Stauffer, "Lefèvre d'Etaples, artisan ou spectateur de la réforme?" reprinted in *Interprètes de la Bible* (Paris: Beauchesne, 1980), 11–29; Henry Heller, "The Evangelicalism of Lefèvre d'Etaples," *Studies in the Renaissance* 19 (1972): 42–77; and Richard M. Cameron, "The Charges of Lutheranism Brought against Jacques Lefèvre d'Etaples (1520–29)," *The Harvard Theological Review* 63, no. 1 (January 1970), 119–49.

14. *Prefatory Epistles of Lefèvre*, xiv. The documents from the Parlement of Paris offer a fascinating account of the concerted efforts to bring judicial power against the circle of Meaux—including investigations of individuals, legal and financial pressures against the bishop, and (remarkably enough) a warrant for the arrest of "the composer of songs in Meaux that are critical of the Catholic faith." See the documents from 1525 in *Religion, Reformation, and Repression in the Reign of Francis I: Documents from the Parlement of Paris, 1515–1547*, vol. 1, ed. James K. Farge (Toronto: Pontifical Institute of Medieval Studies, 2015), 87–242.

15. See James K. Farge, *Orthodoxy and Reform in Early Reformation France: The Faculty of Theology of Paris, 1500–1543* (Leiden: Brill, 1985), 177–85; Hughes, *Lefèvre*, 141–50. On the Parlement's ban on vernacular translations of the Bible, see *Religion, Reformation, and Repression*, document 131, 197–99; document 184, 249–51. Document 137 calls for the arrest of four individuals associated with Meaux and for Lefèvre to appear before the court (*Religion, Reformation, and Repression*, 217–19).

16. On Lefèvre's exile to Strasbourg in 1525, see Hughes, *Lefèvre*, 171–73; Bedouelle, *Lefèvre d'Étaples*, 107–9. Apparently, Lefèvre used an "assumed name" (Antonius Peregrinus) during his escape, a fact that Erasmus comically compares with a character in a comedy of Terence who does the same to avoid his wife with a "terrible temper." See Erasmus to Jan (II) Laski, letter 1674, CWE 12: 72; *The Comedies of Terence*, vol. 2, trans. John Sargeaunt (Cambridge, MA: Harvard University Press, 1983), 83–85, "Phormio," act 5, scene 1.

17. Erasmus reports that Lefèvre has been "summoned back to the [royal] court" after fleeing France in fear because he had translated the Gospels into French (Erasmus to Willibald Pirckheimer, letter 1717, CWE 12: 223).

18. See Bedouelle, *Lefèvre d'Étaples*, 110. Erasmus mentions a visit to Basle by Lefèvre in

(1526), where he was commissioned with organizing the royal library, and then in Nérac (1531) at the court of Marguerite d'Angoulême, the evangelical sister of the king, where he enjoyed a "tranquil retirement," withdrawn from the religious conflicts sweeping France until his death in 1536, the same year as Erasmus.[19]

Despite their controversy over Hebrews 2, Erasmus and Lefèvre shared a great deal in common, and yet, as will become clear in this chapter, at many points of convergence, significant differences arise.[20] When the *Apology against Lefèvre* is read against this backdrop, in fact, features of the Christology of Erasmus that were not evident in chapters 4 and 5 of this work clearly come to the fore. To begin with, Erasmus devotes a good number of pages to offer a justification for responding to Lefèvre's charges—his *Apology* requires an apology, so to speak—and his correspondence of 1517–1518 reflects the same preoccupation and anxiety. What emerges from these efforts, as we will see in the first section of this chapter, is a distinctive and decidedly modern call for theology to be guided by scholarship that is critically minded in handling texts, capacious in considering and preserving alternative readings, and civil in the course of debate.

When Erasmus turns to explain his handling of Hebrews 2:7, it is exactly these methodological qualities that drive his defense, though, as will be apparent in the second section, Lefèvre's pious desire to ensure the dignity of Christ throws their exchange headlong into some of the largely intractable conundrums so common in Christology, specifically, in this case, how the infinite gap between Creator and creation can be bridged by one who somehow is both divine and human. It is true,

---

Erasmus to Jacques Toussain, letter 1713, CWE 12: 211, though Bietenholz observes that the letter does not indicate that Erasmus and Lefèvre actually met. See Peter G. Bietenholz, *Basle and France in the Sixteenth Century: The Basle Humanists and Printers in Their Contacts with Francophone Culture* (Geneva: Librairie Droz, 1971), 181–82, n. 4. Interestingly enough, a letter from an influential friend in the papal curia suggests that Erasmus may have sought support in Rome on Lefèvre's behalf. See Gian Matteo Giberti to Erasmus, letter 1650a, CWE 11: 385. Here again, however, Bietenholz notes that this letter does not confirm that Giberti's mention of support was responding to a request from Erasmus (181–82, n. 4). Intriguing though they are, letters suggesting friendly relations between Erasmus and Lefèvre at this time need to be read with caution.

19. Lefèvre's decision to retire in silence was voluntary and principled. "Pursued in Paris, tracked down in Meaux, suspect in Blois," Bedouelle observes, "Lefèvre decides to keep quiet not from fear but for dignity" (Bedouelle, *Lefèvre d'Étaples*, 131).

20. See Mann, *Érasme et les débuts de la réforme française*, 10–20.

nonetheless, that Christ is absolutely central to the religious thought of Lefèvre and Erasmus, though as the third section will illustrate, Lefèvre consistently emphasizes the transcendent sublimity of Christ, while Erasmus accents the full humanity of Christ. It is here, in fact, that we discover Erasmus's characteristic insistence that theology must squarely face the "extraordinary diminution of Christ," which is why, at the same time, he challenges the docetic tendencies in Lefèvre's decidedly high Christology.[21] Despite these differences, both Lefèvre and Erasmus conceive the redemptive work of Christ in terms that accent the fundamental transformation of human life, though as will be evident in the final section of this chapter, Lefèvre conceives this change in spiritual or mystical terms, while Erasmus once again points to a robust ethical reorientation of personal and social life.

"Writing Annotations not Doctrine"

The exchange with Lefèvre once again illustrates how Erasmus moves from philological questions to theological reflection by way of the push and pull of controversy, only on this occasion, as Jean-Pierre Massaut suggests, differences over the language of Hebrews 2:7 furnish only the "initial opportunity" for what very quickly becomes a "theological debate." In fact, it is fair to say that for Lefèvre, thinking of Christ as just a "little lower than God" was from the start a "concern of piety" rather than a question of correct translation, and that is precisely why he speaks so vehemently against what he takes to be Erasmus's "impious" diminishment of Christ.[22] Lefèvre's less-developed critical sensibility does not serve him well in this regard, for there is little to restrain his tendency to dogmatically turn simple disagreement into a matter of orthodoxy or heresy.[23] But, Erasmus rightly wonders, is it really nec-

---

21. Erasmus, *Apology against Lefèvre*, CWE 83: 38.

22. Massaut, *Critique et tradition*, 61. Renaudet speaks of Lefèvre as "a writer without genius, but passionate for the interior life," a portrayal that aptly explains why Lefèvre throws himself with what Hughes calls a "misconceived zeal" into a feud over doctrine with Erasmus. See Renaudet, "Un problème historique," 201; Hughes, *Lefèvre*, 115.

23. The "limits of his critical sense" are illustrated, among other places, where he regards the correspondence of Paul and Seneca as authentic, even if not canonical, and as well when he attributes the fifth-century "Epistle to the Laodiceans" to Paul. See Bedouelle, *Lefèvre d'Étaples*, 205; Irena Backus, "Renaissance Attitudes to New Testament Apocryphal Writings: Jacques

essary to turn every disagreement into a capital case? It would seem, in fact, that Lefèvre is "fabricating" a dispute where there was no need whatsoever, for as Erasmus insists in his defense, he simply pointed out that there were two readings—Christ as "a little lower than God" or Christ as "for a little while lower than the angels"—"without rejecting either" one.[24] Certainly neither view is heretical, he insists, and both deserve a fair and impartial hearing, and yet, he adds, difficulties "seem to remain" for both readings.

With remarkable neutrality and critical objectivity, Erasmus assumes a methodological posture that could not be more different than Lefèvre's. In the oft-repeated words of Erasmus, he is "writing annotations not doctrine,"[25] and that means, we are told, that he wishes to "place before the reader a variety of material" for consideration, to point out "obstacles" that may attend alternative readings, and to offer possible solutions for removing exegetical difficulties, all the while leaving the reader "free to choose between [the] readings according to his own judgment."[26] This is to be done, most importantly, while maintaining a "neutral stance"—which with respect to Hebrews 2:7 means registering "both readings without rejecting either"—rather than definitively insisting on one interpretation over the other, since doing that might entail (as it clearly did for Lefèvre) "repudiating the other as impious and heretical."[27]

Throughout this process, Erasmus adds, his suggestions carry no more than "the weight of probable proofs," so it is entirely unfair to attack his notes, as Lefèvre has done, as though he had "offered each

---

Lefèvre d'Étaples and his Epigones," *Renaissance Quarterly* 51 (1998): 1169–98. It is Erasmus who in early 1518 complained of Lefèvre's tendency to turn those with different opinions about some truly obscure exegetical questions—"the three Magdalens and Christ's three-day sojourn" in the tomb—into "an adversary of the Christian faith, the Gospels, and every aspect of truth" (Erasmus to Guillaume Budé, letter 778, CWE 5: 311). As Erasmus sees it, Lefèvre "conducts his case as if he either wished to use the knife himself or it must be used against him" (Erasmus to Edward Lee, letter 765, CWE 5: 282). See also Erasmus to Henricus Glareanus, letter 766, CWE 5: 283–84.

24. Erasmus, *Apology against Lefèvre*, CWE 83: 24. See also 16, 69. Of the "alternative readings," Erasmus writes, both "enjoy the support of such great authorities" and "neither deserves to be rejected out of hand, and each is in its own way acceptable, provided that the word *Eloim* in Hebrew can be singular or plural, and sometimes mean God, sometimes gods, sometimes judges, sometimes angels" (69).

25. Erasmus, *Apology against Lefèvre*, CWE 83: 15.

26. Erasmus, *Apology against Lefèvre*, CWE 83: 76, 16, and 25.

27. Erasmus, *Apology against Lefèvre*, CWE 83: 87, 24.

one as an authoritative statement."[28] It is true, of course, that Erasmus includes his own preferences for resolving sticky exegetical problems, but this is done "on the principle that each person should be free to make his own judgment."[29] It is only in response to Lefèvre's indictment, however, that Erasmus gives voice to his own theological stance, though even then, he does not abandon his even-handed regard for the position he chose not to favor. The aim of Erasmus, as we will see throughout this chapter, is not to establish orthodoxy but to reimagine the contours of exegetical debate in a manner that does not run roughshod over other possibly legitimate readings. Erasmus operates, in short, with a tempered sense of doctrinal self-certainty and a robust capacity for engaging alternative views, and this methodological posture reflects the even-handedness typical of the ancient Academics, even as it anticipates what will come to be regarded as a modern and pluralistic manner of theological scholarship,[30] though in fact—as Margaret Mann has noted—this posture also stems from the charitable and inclusive sentiments of the philosophy of Christ, which is the very heart of the piety of Erasmus.[31]

In the course of the *Apology against Lefèvre*, it becomes clear that Erasmus is not comfortable with the task he has undertaken; and thus, even as he engages Lefèvre over their Christological differences, he must also justify making a reply at all. In fact, Erasmus tells us with clear regret, this is "a necessary but distasteful business."[32] It is necessary to defend himself in part for reasons of practical security, and this is required—naturally enough—because of the doctrinal gravity of the charges. It is one thing to be called "stupid, a rock, a brute, a pumpkin, [or] a fool," Erasmus says with a bit of humor, but it is another thing altogether to be charged with having "an ill opinion of Christ."[33] That is "one kind of insult," he continues, that cannot be tolerated, for "to remain silent against a charge of sacrilege is itself sacrilege."[34] Such a

---

28. Erasmus, *Apology against Lefèvre*, CWE 83: 30–31, 17.

29. Erasmus, *Apology against Lefèvre*, CWE 83: 15.

30. See Martin, "Heresy and Humanity," 5–32.

31. Mann, *Érasme et les débuts de la réforme française*, 36.

32. Erasmus, *Apology against Lefèvre*, CWE 83: 15. As Erasmus put it later, he "undertook this *Apologia* unwillingly and my nature shuns nothing more than confrontations of this sort" (55).

33. Erasmus, *Apology against Lefèvre*, CWE 83: 55. Erasmus later rejects the charge of stupidity as well (73–74).

34. Erasmus, *Apology against Lefèvre*, CWE 83: 13. As Erasmus puts it a bit later, "silence on

statement vividly shows the urgency and indignation that drive Erasmus to defend himself against Lefèvre's charge of impiety.[35]

Doing so, however, is thoroughly distasteful for Erasmus, and this reaction also stems from his piety, though in a very different sense. What Lefèvre has done with his accusation, we are told, is to force Erasmus to write against a "friend" on questions of biblical exegesis, and that in itself is a breach of another side of piety, one that concerns the practical life with others rather than questions of doctrinal belief.[36] When Erasmus speaks of a friendship with Lefèvre, of course, he is referring to what he takes to be their shared commitments to humanist scholarship. In their commonly held labor of love for biblical literature, Erasmus says to Lefèvre, "both of us together ... stand at centre stage," where we are to proceed, at least ideally, with mutual respect and generosity for the "public good" in such a way as "not to harm in the slightest the reputation of a friend."[37] But Lefèvre has changed all that; now, Erasmus finds himself drawn into the fray—practically "a full-scale war," he calls it with considerable exaggeration—and the entire affair is utterly unpleasant, precisely because we lose "our dearest possession, and that is friendship." If theological work demands such a loss, he declares forthrightly, then he wishes to "quit the field and reject the terms of combat."[38] Anything less would violate the piety of friendship among Christian scholars.

---

my part could be construed as an admission of guilt" (89). The same point is made with some variation, when Erasmus says that "to admit a charge of irreligion is forbidden in the first place by religion itself," and again, "to lay down one's life for a friend is honourable; but for a friend's sake to be counted a blasphemer against Christ is not only absolutely mad but grossly impious" (Erasmus to Guillaume Budé, letter 778, CWE 5: 307, 309).

35. On Erasmus's "sincerity, emotion, and indignation" over the charge of impiety, see Massaut, *Critique et tradition*, 63–65.

36. "Piety," for Erasmus, is an encompassing term that combines the interior life of belief and devotion with the interpersonal or social life. In other words, it always includes both the relation to God (including faith, devotion, or what Erasmus calls "godliness") and the relation with others (especially the virtues of practical, social life). On the range of this term in the works of Erasmus, see O'Malley, "Introduction," CWE 66: xi–xxi.

37. Erasmus, *Apology against Lefèvre*, CWE 83: 6–8.

38. Erasmus, *Apology against Lefèvre*, CWE 83: 97–98. As Erasmus puts it, "that kind of battle belongs to gladiators, not to theologians." See also CWE 83: 92. On the centrality of friendship for building and maintaining communities of shared labor, see Kathy Eden, *Friends Hold All Things in Common: Tradition, Intellectual Property, and the Adages of Erasmus* (New Haven, CT: Yale University Press, 2001), 25–31, 142–73. See also Yvonne Charlier, *Érasme et l'amitié d'après sa correspondance* (Paris: Les Belles Lettres, 1977).

How inappropriate it is, Erasmus writes, that "the din of human passions should obtrude" in discussions "where all is divine and heavenly," that is, where dealing with an ultimate and even sacred issue like the nature and range of divine incarnation. But it is worse yet, he adds, with an eye on the controversy in which he and Lefèvre are embroiled, "that we should appear less than temperate and impartial in our treatment of these Books which alone make us truly virtuous and worthy."[39] Though Lefèvre clearly believes he is battling for the purity of doctrinal faith, Erasmus consistently stresses that Christian life does not depend on the "thorny niceties" that so often infest Christological disputes.[40] In fact, as Mann observes, Erasmus does not attach much importance to the precise words debated by theologians, as long as there is consensus concerning the substance at stake.[41] Besides, as he often says, "human discourse is inadequate for explaining the sublimity of things of this kind."[42] What that means, as Mann aptly puts it, is that doctrinal questions are not "as serious for Erasmus as for his adversary," since "the truth according to Erasmus is to be found elsewhere"—specifically, in the lived piety and moral life, rather than in the "abstract ideas" debated among theologians.[43]

So how unfitting it truly was, Erasmus complains, when Lefèvre assailed him "in a tone more bitter, more strident, and more dramatic than either the topic itself or our friendship warranted."[44] All Erasmus did in his *Annotations*, he recalls, was to "correct a friend's mistake," just as he would like to be corrected in turn, while Lefèvre proceeds to "virtually drown in spite a friend" as if he were an "enemy."[45] Scholarly conversation thereby was subverted by open hostility, and, with good reason, Erasmus doubts very much whether "Christ would be pleased

---

39. Erasmus, *Apology against Lefèvre*, CWE 83: 6.

40. Erasmus to Wolfgang Faber Capito, letter 734, CWE 5: 233. The same thing is said of Trinitarian speculation, as we saw in chapter 4, in Erasmus to Jean de Carondelet, letter 1334, CWE 9: 252.

41. See, for instance, Erasmus, *Apology against Lefèvre*, CWE 83: 31, in which Erasmus insists that "for those who are truly pious it ought to be a simple matter to agree in matters of terminology as long as there is no dispute over substance."

42. Erasmus, *Apology against Lefèvre*, CWE 83: 31. See Mann, *Érasme et les débuts de la réforme française*, 34.

43. Mann, *Érasme et les débuts de la réforme française*, 36.

44. Erasmus, *Apology against Lefèvre*, CWE 83: 5.

45. Erasmus, *Apology against Lefèvre*, CWE 83: 102, 104.

to have his dignity defended if it means that we ruin our reputations as Christians" by such a squabble.[46] Over the course of the *Apology against Lefèvre*, Erasmus makes the same claim for his manner of answering Lefèvre's assaults—that he has "defended [his] innocence in a polite and open manner" by way of argument rather than abuse[47]—and, with the exception of an occasional blunt comment and a number of sarcastic quips, it is fair to say that Erasmus has managed to produce a remarkably civil answer to Lefèvre,[48] though not everyone agreed.[49]

What is important to see in this regard is that—while Erasmus pays serious attention to the Christological issues at stake in the interpretation of Hebrews 2:7, as will be clear shortly—the manner in which their exchange transpires, whether amicably or with acrimony, makes all the difference in the world for Erasmus, since only the former is an authentic expression of true Christian piety. "The only thing left," Erasmus says to Lefèvre in closing, "is for both us to join together in

46. Erasmus, *Apology against Lefèvre*, CWE 83: 97.

47. Erasmus, *Apology against Lefèvre*, CWE 83: 89.

48. Erasmus correctly defends the measured character of his reply to Lefèvre, though he could be quite blunt, as when he calls out Lefèvre for his credulous acceptance of apocryphal texts, or later, when he observes that "the field of translation and annotation" is not exactly Lefèvre's "forte," or again, by his own admission, when he suggests that a "deep slumber" must have fallen upon Lefèvre when he mistranslated a passage from Titus (Erasmus, *Apology against Lefèvre*, CWE 83: 84, 104, and 86). Occasionally, too, Erasmus could write sarcastically against Lefèvre. See CWE 83: 55–56, 58.

49. Erasmus received plenty of criticism for the hostile tone of his response to Lefèvre, though that was often from allies or friends of Lefèvre. See, for instance, the letter written from Meaux in 1524 that—while lamenting the "complicated quarrels" among humanists—complains that Erasmus has "criticized Lefèvre excessively" (Jean Lange to Erasmus, CWE 10: 147–48). See also the friendly and eloquent warnings from Guillaume Budé that, in responding to Lefèvre, Erasmus put too much trust in "disputatiousness and dreary pamphlets full of argument," when he should have "stood [his] ground in silence" (Guillaume Budè to Erasmus, letters 774 and 810, CWE 5: 247, 370–71). For a review of both laudatory and critical judgments about the tone of the *Apology against Lefèvre*, see Rummel, *Erasmus and His Catholic Critics*, vol. 1, 53–59. Contemporary scholars also have faulted the tone of Erasmus's response. Bedouelle says, for instance, that while the *Apology against Lefèvre* reads like a "learned dialogue," the tone of Erasmus can be "sharp, vehement, and even biting." His corrections of Lefèvre, Bedouelle continues, constitute a "harshly administered lesson" ("Introduction," CWE 83: xiii, xxii). Elsewhere, Bedouelle speaks of Erasmus's demonstrations of the errors of Lefèvre as "cruel" ("Jacques Lefèvre d'Étaples," 25). Massaut similarly suggests that Erasmus's argument from tradition is handled with "ferocity" so that Lefèvre will feel its "cruelty" (*Critique et tradition*, 66). See also Hughes, *Lefèvre*, 115, where the style of Erasmus is called "hard-hitting." Whatever these comments say about the performance of Erasmus, they certainly also say a great deal about the sensitivities of contemporary scholars, for by the standards of sixteenth-century polemics, the *Apology against Lefèvre* is remarkably tame.

repairing the damage" by returning to "the learning and discovering we do together," though he adds a word of warning if Lefèvre persists "in attacking a friend in unfriendly fashion."[50] For his part, Lefèvre never responds, and their exchange comes to an abrupt close—this despite three letters from Erasmus to Lefèvre appealing for "an end of this impious disputation," what Erasmus amazingly calls a "mad orgy of personal abuse" that is the cause of "discord among Christians" and a source of delight to "the devotees of primeval ignorance" who oppose "liberal studies."[51] In turn, Lefèvre remains silent. With that strange ending,[52] we miss the chance to find Erasmus and Lefèvre pursuing a productive resolution of their controversy, though for the purposes of this chapter, the *Apology against Lefèvre* provides ample illustration of the manner in which Erasmus turns his Christology to affirm the humanity of Christ.

50. Erasmus, *Apology against Lefèvre*, CWE 83: 106–7.

51. See Erasmus to Jacques Lefèvre d'Étaples," letter 659, CWE 5: 115–16; Erasmus to Jacques Lefèvre d'Étaples," letter 724, CWE 5: 215–16; and Erasmus to Jacques Lefèvre d'Étaples," letter 814, CWE 5: 387–88.

52. In one limited respect, the controversy continued, since Erasmus included the key challenges of the *Apology against Lefèvre* in the 1519 edition of the *Annotations*, and Lefèvre made no changes to his rendering of Hebrews 2:7 in the third edition of his *Commentaries on the Epistles of Paul*. See Mann, *Érasme et les débuts de la réforme française*, 45; Rummel, *Erasmus and His Catholic Critics*, vol. 1, 52. On a positive note, which suggests but does not confirm a rapprochement of sorts, Peter Gillis reported to Erasmus that Lefèvre was "sorry that he ever annoyed you and will never publish a reply till the Greek calends"—which signifies a time that will never happen. Charming as this is, Gillis's report comes not directly from Lefèvre but third-hand from the Parisian printer Josse Bade over a dinner with Gillis. See Pieter Gillis to Erasmus, letter 849, CWE 6: 42–43. For his part, Erasmus similarly expresses regret for his dispute with Lefèvre, while reporting in vague terms that "steps are being taken, and there is good hope that this surface wound will soon heal over" (Erasmus to Willibald Pirckheimer, letter 856, CWE 6: 69). Then again, Erasmus reports to Juan Luis Vives in 1520 that his "skirmish" with Lefèvre has been "long since forgotten," so much so that he would "listen impatiently to anyone who spoke of him otherwise than one would of a most upright and most learned man" (letter 1111, CWE 7: 309). And Erasmus writes in 1525 that Lefèvre "acknowledged he was wrong" and "our friendship has never been interrupted," though the comment is made in a joke about three men named "Jacobus" who "have published books which are wildly insulting" (Erasmus to Jacopo Sadoleto, letter 1555, CWE 11: 59–60). In a cordial letter of 1527, Erasmus offers Lefèvre the wish that his "old age may be blessed with peace and quiet" (Erasmus to Jacques Lefèvre d'Étaples, letter 1795, CWE 12: 496). No letters from Lefèvre to Erasmus during these years are extant, though apparently Lefèvre did change his translation of Hebrews 2:7 to "than the angels" in the 1524 edition of his French translation of the New Testament. See Hughes, *Lefèvre*, 115, in which this change is taken as a sign of Lefèvre's humble concession to the view of Erasmus. In contrast, Steenbeek suggests that this change was made to conceal his identity as the translator ("Introduction," ASD IX - 3: 14).

"For a Little While Lower than the Angels"

In celebrating the majesty of God over the created world, Psalm 8 of
Hebrew scriptures marvels at the uniquely elevated status graciously
given to human beings. How amazing it is, the psalm proclaims, that
God has "made them a little lower than the gods [*elohim*], and crowned
them with glory and honor." What is more, it continues with an echo
of Genesis 1:26, people have been given "dominion" over all other living things, including beasts of all sorts, as well as birds and fish. On
its own terms, as Erasmus rightly observes, this psalm applies to all
people as a hymn to their elevated position in creation.[53] When the
Greek-speaking Christian author of Hebrews coopted this psalm from
the Greek Septuagint of Psalm 8, the focus was turned toward Jesus,
who in Hebrews 2:9 is said to have been made "lower than the angels."
For his part, however, Lefèvre follows Jerome in referring the psalm to
Christ alone and in translating Hebrews 2:7 and 9 (as if they were from
a Hebrew text) as saying that Christ was made "a little lower than God,"
thereby taking *elohim* in the singular to avoid the apparently impious
suggestion that Christ was diminished below even the angels. There is
plenty of irony in this situation: to begin with, that a psalm focused on
the elevated status of human beings is transformed (in the Greek of Hebrews) into a statement of the diminishment of Christ, but then again,
oddly enough, that a Christian exegete (Lefèvre) renders the language
of Hebrews 2:7 through the Hebrew lens of Psalm 8 in order to lessen
that diminishment as much as possible. For Lefèvre to accomplish this,
however, *elohim* must be translated as "God" rather than as "gods" (as
the NRSV is translated above), or as "angels" (as Erasmus puts it).

In his *Annotations* on Hebrews, Erasmus reminds Lefèvre that he
merely pointed out that "there are two readings [of Hebrews 2:7 and 9]:
Jerome's and the Septuagint," that he did "not reject either of the two
opinions," and that he seems, in fact, to favor the former, which is fan-
cied by Lefèvre.[54] Nonetheless, Erasmus observes, the "same difficulty
seems to remain" for either reading, and while that difficulty has philological and exegetical roots, it ultimately is theological—in the words of

---

53. Erasmus, *Apology against Lefèvre*, CWE 83: 75.
54. Erasmus, *Apology against Lefèvre*, CWE 83: 15–16, 24.

Erasmus, "that Jesus Christ, as far as his human condition is concerned and the manner of life he lived on earth, would seem to have been diminished not only below God, but below the angels and most of mankind as well."[55] Following the consensus of church tradition, Erasmus opts for the fuller sense of diminishment,[56] though he offers a solution in translation that he feels might mitigate Lefèvre's pious concern that Christ is being diminished too much. In brief, he suggests, the Greek for "a little" (*brachu ti*) should be taken as referring not to the "degree" of Christ's debasement but to the "length of time" he was diminished, so that Hebrews 2:7 and 9 would read—as they do in modern translations like the NRSV—"for a little while lower than the angels."[57] It is doubtful, however, that Lefèvre would find this proposal very satisfying, as any such diminution of Christ—even for a short while—is for him questionable and thus impious. Therefore, we have a situation where Erasmus, speaking with the neutrality and objectivity expected of an annotator, proceeds by way of close philological observation to answer the theologically charged objections of Lefèvre with a Christological suggestion of his own: in a nutshell, that Christians ought not to flinch at the idea that Christ was greatly diminished in the human life he took upon himself.

It is precisely here, in fact, that Erasmus begins to address some of the most difficult—and likely intractable—of Christological conundrums. The problems arise, clearly enough, from the murkiness of language drawn from Hebrews—specifically, "lower than" or "a little lower than"—for speaking about the relation of something divine and something human. "Is it 'a little' that he descends who comes down as God to man," Erasmus asks, "when human nature is by infinite degrees lower than divine nature?"[58] That would seem, in fact, to be very much more than a little, to say the least, as any bit of an infinite is itself infinite. The language for degrees of distinction in this case—especially a "little lower"—is inherently muddled, Erasmus observes, as the distinction between the nature that assumed (divine) and the nature that was assumed

---

55. Erasmus, *Apology against Lefèvre*, CWE 83: 16.
56. Erasmus, *Apology against Lefèvre*, CWE 83: 19, 23.
57. Erasmus, *Apology against Lefèvre*, CWE 83: 32. See also CWE 83: 57, 61–62, 70, and 80.
58. Erasmus, *Apology against Lefèvre*, CWE 83: 17.

(human) is simply "immense," if not incommensurable.[59] But what is deeply problematic for Lefèvre—that Christ would suffer an undignified diminishment—is for Erasmus not a "problem" at all but (as Massaut puts it) "the substance of the mystery" of the incarnation.[60]

Rather than play down the diminution of Christ in order to preserve his transcendent sublimity, Erasmus fully embraces the logic of divine incarnation. In his words, "to the extent that he was a man," Christ "was far inferior to God the Father," and thus by no means "just a little diminished"; then again, "to the extent that he was a man and subject to the misfortunes which afflict a mortal nature," Christ also was "to some degree inferior to the angels, at any rate with respect to his body."[61] It certainly is rare to find Erasmus engaging in this kind of theological acrobatics, yet it becomes necessary to answer Lefèvre's hesitations regarding the diminished status implied in the life of Jesus. When, for instance, Lefèvre suggests that there is a relation of "identity and equality" between Christ and the divine nature—perhaps drawing on a text like John 10:30 ("I and the Father are one")—Erasmus wonders quizzically who "ever heard of a relation which consists in identity," or for that matter, "who has ever proposed a relation between infinity and infinity?"[62] But more seriously, he asks, if there is a "relation of identity between the Son of Man and God," then "how is he said to be lower than God," even if just a little or for a little while, as demanded by

59. Erasmus, *Apology against Lefèvre*, CWE 83: 26, 70.

60. Massaut, *Critique et tradition*, 62.

61. Erasmus, *Apology against Lefèvre*, CWE 83: 32. After chastising both Lefèvre and Erasmus for their venomous dispute, Symphorien Champier, an admirer of Lefèvre but filled with respect for Erasmus, amazingly suggests as a possible mediating position that Christ was made "lower than God, but not so low as an angel; rather, a little lower in the direction of the angels, or better, a little less low than the angels" (Symphorien Champier to Erasmus, letter 680a, CWE 5: 142–45).

62. Erasmus, *Apology against Lefèvre*, CWE 83: 49. In support of this point, Erasmus cites Aristotle, a move meant to poke fun at Lefèvre, the long-time scholar of Aristotle. Bedouelle rightly suggests that Erasmus was thinking of Aristotle's *Physics* 8. 1 (252a10–19) and *On the Heavens* 1. 6 (273b27–274a18), though in both places Aristotle is speaking of the rational order of the natural world, where the infinite finds no place whatsoever. In the passage from the *Physics*, Aristotle is arguing that there is no *ratio* (measure) between an infinite time of change and an infinite time of rest in the natural order of things, and in *On the Heavens*, he is discussing the impossibility of bodies of infinite weight or lightness. See Aristotle, *Physics*, trans. R. P. Hardie and R. K. Gaye, *The Complete Works of Aristotle*, ed. Jonathan Barnes, vol. 1 (Princeton, NJ: Princeton University Press, 1984), 421; Aristotle, *On the Heavens*, trans. J. L. Stocks, *Complete Works of Aristotle*, 455.

Hebrews 2:7 and 9?[63] If there is absolutely no diminution in the incarnate life of Christ, then there is no such thing as the incarnation, and the consequences of that for Christian piety would not be insignificant. The alternative from Erasmus is to fully affirm what is expressed in Hebrews, that in assuming a human life, Christ became lower than the angels and lower even than a good part of humanity.

What this mean, Erasmus observes, is that Christ took upon himself human nature, and it is precisely Erasmus's positive handling of that fundamental but still truly inscrutable notion that Lefèvre finds difficult to accept. In the words of Erasmus, Lefèvre was "too severe" when condemning as impious Erasmus's statement "that with respect to the attributes which belong to Christ as God and as man, something can be predicated of Christ incarnate which need not be predicated of him in his other form." A bit later, Erasmus readily concedes that his words may have been expressed with "too little caution," but that was an "incidental slip" he insists, whereas Lefèvre certainly "knew all along what in fact [Erasmus] had meant."[64] What Erasmus, in fact, meant by "Christ incarnate" was simply the "humanity of Christ," in which case certain things may have been experienced by Christ "with respect to his body" that "need not be predicated of him in his other [that is, divine] form."[65]

The explanations of Erasmus in this context certainly are strained, though, admittedly, the topic itself does not lend itself to great clarity. In any case, Lefèvre apparently thought that Erasmus was with these words undermining the "essential oneness of the substance of Jesus Christ." So in turn, Erasmus responds by means of some traditional Christological reasoning—what is called the "*communicatio idiomatum*" (exchange of properties)—to argue that things attributed to Christ's divinity or humanity can be "predicated of him under either title" precisely because of the unity of his person.[66] This is something "every neophyte in theology knows,"[67] Erasmus reminds us, though it surely must remain baffling

---

63. As a counter to John 10:30, Erasmus refers Lefèvre to the words of Christ in John 14:28, "My Father is greater than I" (Erasmus, *Apology against Lefèvre*, CWE 83: 49).

64. Erasmus, *Apology against Lefèvre*, CWE 83: 30, 31.

65. Erasmus, *Apology against Lefèvre*, CWE 83: 27–28.

66. Erasmus, *Apology against Lefèvre*, CWE 83: 26–27.

67. Erasmus, *Apology against Lefèvre*, CWE 83: 27.

to anyone who gives it serious consideration, in a word, that a coherent identity could be maintained amid such vastly divergent natures, such that things said of both divinity and humanity could be communicated intelligibly of one and the same person. But that is precisely what orthodox Christology demands, and it is why the reasoning involved in juggling the oppositions implied in various biblical passages about Christ is so strenuous and precarious.

Thus, for example, though Christ is said to have "certain attributes by reason of his divine nature and others by reason of his human nature," nevertheless, Erasmus observes, they can be legitimately "predicated of him under either title, on account of the oneness of his hypostasis" or person. This means, to cite one example from Erasmus, that Christ "may be called God when he is said to have wept, and sorrowed, and died," and "in turn may be called man when he is said to be equal to God the Father."[68] Such speech is naturally confusing and very often misleading, though this very conundrum serves to illustrate the kind of linguistic agility required in Christological discussions, even while it also makes plain how much forbearance is needed when judging the language preferred by someone else. Even Augustine "spoke rather clumsily," Erasmus points out, when speaking of the "mingling" rather than the "union" of natures in Christ, though surely it is delusional and pretentious to think that there is any greater clarity or precision in speaking of a "union" of two natures.[69]

---

68. Erasmus, *Apology against Lefèvre*, CWE 83: 26–27. As Erasmus explains it, legitimate pronouncements can be made "concerning one or the other of Christ's natures" when "the same thing applies to him taken as a whole"—thus, for instance, "Christ's humanity has taught us to despise the affairs of man, his divinity will raise us up to things eternal." And yet, "by the same token," nothing prevents us "from using something which belongs to Christ as a whole to apply to one or other of his hypostases separately," so that one might say that "the body of Christ was afflicted with blows for our sins, the spirit of Christ sorrowed for our misfortunes, [and] the divine nature conquered death" (28–29).

69. Erasmus, *Apology against Lefèvre*, CWE 83: 30–31. For his part, Erasmus was forced to defend himself from the suggestion of Ludwig Baer that he had written that Christ was a "composite being," which Erasmus repeatedly denies, while wondering whether Baer had even read the *Apology against Lefèvre*. See Erasmus to Ludwig Baer, letter 730, CWE 5: 225; Erasmus to Wolfgang Faber Capito, letter 731, CWE 5: 227; and Erasmus to Beatus Rhenanus, letter 731, CWE 5: 230. Erasmus answers more thoroughly, and with remarkable facility for Christological reasoning, that he had, in fact, denied both that Christ should be "taken as two" and that he was "one composed of two" (Erasmus to Wolfgang Faber Capito, letter 734, CWE 5: 232). Erasmus is correct in his defense, as he had called the idea of a composite being "ridiculous." See *Apology against Lefèvre*, CWE 83: 41. For what it is worth, Erasmus prefers to say of Christ's natures that

"Human discourse" of any kind, Erasmus reminds Lefèvre and his readers, "is inadequate for explaining the sublimity of things of this kind," which is exactly why it is always better to offer someone else "instruction rather than criticism."[70] What Erasmus has received from Lefèvre, however, is abusive criticism, and this concerning not his own choice of terms but the biblical language of Psalm 8 and Hebrews 2, specifically, that Christ may be said to have been "made lower" than God (in Lefèvre's rendering) or than the angels (as Erasmus has it). What this phrase means, Erasmus tells us once again, is "nothing other than the taking on of human nature," and that is something that both Lefèvre and Erasmus fully affirm in principle.[71] Where they differ significantly, however, as we will see in the next section, concerns the meaning and the degree of the diminishment involved in the incarnate life of Christ.

"The Extraordinary Diminution of Christ"

It was the signal achievement of the Council of Chalcedon (450 CE) to have produced a rough but largely workable fusion of the rival sentiments of the two schools of classical Christology, one associated with Alexandria, which magnified the unity of Christ by means of his divine nature, the other linked with Antioch, which sought above all to preserve the full humanity of Christ.[72] Remarkably enough, both impulses survived within the doctrinal formula of Chalcedon, albeit in tension and thus, somewhat awkwardly, and as a result, the very same strains persisted in later Christologies that were developed within the matrix of Chalcedon. Thus, for instance, medieval sources often accent the transcendent divinity of Christ, while modern works often highlight the humanity of Jesus, yet both strands of Christology coexist within

---

he was "a divine [nature] which has taken to itself the human" (CWE 5: 230, 227). If truth be told, Erasmus adds with a familiar point, all "human speech" on such matters is "mere stammering," so one rightly may wonder whether there is any "peril" in someone saying that "Christ was composite" (CWE 5: 232).

70. Erasmus, *Apology against Lefèvre*, CWE 83: 31.

71. Erasmus, *Apology against Lefèvre*, CWE 83: 30.

72. On the classical Christological debates between the rival schools of thought culminating in the Chalcedonian dogma of the two natures in the person of Christ, see Pelikan, *The Emergence of the Catholic Tradition*, 226–66; Grillmeier, *Christ in Christian Tradition*, 363–487.

the expansive framework of Chalcedonian thinking, even as they often pull against each other or at times push beyond the outer lines of this classical blueprint for orthodoxy. The controversy of Erasmus and Lefèvre also fits well within this larger framework, and it does so precisely insofar as these two biblical humanists move in opposite directions with their competing views of the incarnation of Christ.

There are countless examples from scriptures that proclaim "the boundless excellence of the Word of God," Erasmus observes, even while so many other passages "make exceedingly plain the lower estate into which the Divine Word [*sermo divinus*] cast himself down for our sake."[73] Said once again, many passages speak to the "sublimity of Christ," though many others "testify to his lowliness." In a word, both perspectives are amply illustrated in Christian scriptures, both in principle fall within the Chalcedonian framework, and hence both demand a place in sound Christology, though if truth be told, Erasmus reminds us yet again, both emphases are "beyond the power of any human mind to fathom and any human thought to grasp." With that caveat in hand, however, Erasmus correctly observes that Lefèvre typically prefers to "extoll the sublimity of Christ," while Erasmus generally insists that "Christ in his humble state" has "more relevance for us."[74]

Though both views have scriptural backing and traditional legitimacy, we are told, Erasmus opts to stress "as much as possible the lowliness Christ assumed of his own accord for our sakes."[75] To that end, therefore, he magnifies the language of Hebrews 2:7 and 9 to assert that the divine Word "descended and cast himself down far below the angels to the extent that he took on a body and a soul that were subject to death and tortures and pains." Indeed, Erasmus notes with graphic detail, "the Son of God was not content simply to take on our nature, but took upon himself almost all the misfortunes of this life—toil, pains, sweat, hunger, thirst, weariness, insults, bonds, whippings, and the cross—misfortunes that most men escape, even though they might deserve them."[76] It is far from sufficient, in other words, to say

73. Erasmus, *Apology against Lefèvre*, CWE 83: 35.
74. Erasmus, *Apology against Lefèvre*, CWE 83: 34–35.
75. Erasmus, *Apology against Lefèvre*, CWE 83: 33.
76. Erasmus, *Apology against Lefèvre*, CWE 83: 34.

that Christ was made lower than God or the angels when, in fact, Erasmus firmly insists, Christ "descended to some degree far below even the lowest of men."[77]

So why is it, Erasmus asks Lefèvre, that "the word 'exaltation' is the only one that pleases you?"[78] Surely there is nothing impious "in saying that Christ degraded himself below even the lowliest of men," Erasmus insists, and within that humble estate, there is nothing that detracts from "the dignity of Christ,"[79] though Lefèvre surely would disagree on both counts. That Christ was poor, that he lived in "dire hardship," and that he suffered a painful death amid disgrace, none of this—remarkably enough—"detracts from Christ's loftiness," Erasmus contends, but "in fact it makes his sublimity all the greater by exalting the goodness and wisdom which make him great in our eyes no less than does his power."[80] The heart of the Christology of Erasmus resides precisely here, where the "extraordinary diminution of Christ" is firmly rooted in divine beneficence for a twisted and corrupted world.[81]

As Erasmus puts it, the Son of God is "greater by infinite degrees than every creature," and yet this same Christ "at one time descended for our sake to a condition inferior to that of the angels," and "even to that of many men," whereupon he took upon himself "not only a nature that was subject to thirst, hunger, weariness, insults, pain, and death, but also so many of the injustices of human life."[82] It is Paul in Philippians 2:7–9, Erasmus grants, who gives him the confidence to speak like this, that is, to affirm that Christ was "made desolate," which means in short that he "humbled himself to the greatest degree possible," for which God in turn exalted him in "divine glory." In contrast to Lefèvre, consequently, Erasmus emphasizes that "Christ was diminished not just a little but a great deal," and as well, that the "utter humiliation of Christ" means not only that he assumed human nature

---

77. Erasmus, *Apology against Lefèvre*, CWE 83: 34. Erasmus later makes the same point, when insisting that "it is not at all heretical to say that for a time Christ was made lower than most, in fact all, men, seeing that he took upon himself more afflictions than any man ever suffered or would be able to bear" (56).

78. Erasmus, *Apology against Lefèvre*, CWE 83: 41.

79. Erasmus, *Apology against Lefèvre*, CWE 83: 37.

80. Erasmus, *Apology against Lefèvre*, CWE 83: 36–37, 71.

81. Erasmus, *Apology against Lefèvre*, CWE 83: 38.

82. Erasmus, *Apology against Lefèvre*, CWE 83: 36.

but that he willingly took upon himself an "extreme degree of diminution."[83] As further support, Erasmus cites Ambrose and Augustine to bolster his claim that the diminution of Christ was a function not only of his becoming human but more truly because of "his humiliation through suffering."[84]

Exactly this idea was impossible for Lefèvre, who with a "principle of dignity" mandating what can and cannot be said of Christ, refuses to admit the strong language of diminishment that Erasmus heartily embraces. It is true, of course, that Lefèvre also affirms that the Son of God humbled himself as described in Philippians 2:7, and yet, unlike Erasmus, Lefèvre consistently hedges the degree to which Christ may be said to be diminished by extolling his transcendent sublimity. He was at most made just a little lower than God, according to Lefèvre's rendering of Hebrews 2:7 and 9, so the dignity of Christ is well assured; in fact, if the judgment of the Stoics is to be believed, someone with power who subjected himself to beatings and death for the good of his people should be considered "far more worthy of honor."[85] As Lefèvre sees it, the negative things said of Christ—being called a "worm" in Psalm 22:6–7, for instance—are simply "the estimation of the Jews"; then again, that Christ is described as being abandoned, degraded, and helpless is, according to Lefèvre, simply "the estimation and judgment of the priests, the Scribes, and the Pharisees."[86]

---

83. Erasmus, *Apology against Lefèvre*, CWE 83: 60–61, 38–39. Erasmus received a letter in March 1517 challenging his reading of Philippians 2:6–7. See Hieronymous Dungersheim to Erasmus, letter 554, CWE 4: 286–90. The concern for Dungersheim was that Erasmus applied the Pauline phrase "thought it not robbery to be equal with God" to "Christ, inasmuch as He is man," when, in fact, "the Apostle is speaking of the divinity of Christ." What Paul meant, Dungersheim continues, is that "Christ did not think it robbery to be equal with God according to the form of His deity, in which He is the same with God the Father." There could be no robbery, in short, if he was already equal with the Father in "the essence of His deity." In support of his complaint, Dungersheim observes that many "Fathers of the Church" (including Augustine, Jerome, Hilary, Ambrose, and Pope Leo) and some "famous scholars" (including Valla and Lefèvre) supported this reading, since the alternative (that "Christ is said to have been unwilling to think Himself equal to the Father") leads straight into the "rankest Arianism." As Rummel notes, Erasmus "augmented the note in response to Dungersheim's query," though he maintained his translation, which emphasized the humbling of Christ in "human form." See *Erasmus and His Catholic Critics*, vol. 1, 46–47.

84. Erasmus, *Apology against Lefèvre*, CWE 83: 38–39.

85. Erasmus, *Apology against Lefèvre*, CWE 83: 38–39, 40. See Lefèvre, *Disputatio*, ASD IX - 3: 214, lines 261–64; see Steenbeek, "Introduction," ASD IX - 3: 28–31.

86. Erasmus, *Apology against Lefèvre*, CWE 83: 42; see also 72. See Lefèvre, *Disputatio*, ASD IX - 3: 211, lines 165–67.

But it is not the case, Erasmus counters in response, that the "entire psalm has to do with the estimation of Jews," for Christ was "forsaken in fact, not in opinion." When, for instance, Christ was "flayed with whips, spit upon, bound, accused, condemned, abused with insults, and crucified between two criminals," Erasmus asks, "does all this not belong to the realm of fact, not the estimation of the Jews?" It is not the case, Erasmus insists, that Christ was made "worthless only in speech," as Lefèvre would have it, since what was said—that "he was made worthless beneath the most worthless of men"—"was true," not merely as a manner of speaking or a figure of speech. The danger of Lefèvre's reading, Erasmus continues, is that there will be no answer to those who think "Christ suffered not in reality but [merely] in his imagination."[87] In a word, there is a creeping docetism at work in the denials of Lefèvre, such that the humiliation of Christ is taken as a mere appearance rather than a brutal fact. But if that is the case, Erasmus wonders, for what were the women and disciples weeping at the crucifixion? And why, as Lefèvre himself puts it, was "the heart of the Virgin ... struck by his suffering as by a sword?" "Were they weeping over the Word of God who is always equal to the Father," Erasmus asks incredulously, or for "a man who was suffering terribly for the sake of us all?"[88] Of course, for Erasmus, there is no uncertainty as to the proper answer to these questions, which is why he resolutely affirms the full humanity of Christ against what he calls Lefèvre's "principle of opinion."

The controversy with Lefèvre provides Erasmus with a perfect opportunity to affirm the humanity of Christ, and in that, we come to the very heart of his Christology. Having said that, however, it nonetheless is true that Erasmus also hesitates when thinking about the mortal life of Christ incarnate, exactly as all traditional Christologies have done in one way or another, and where only the most modern readings of the life of Jesus have refrained from at least some hint of docetism. When

87. Erasmus, *Apology against Lefèvre*, CWE 83: 45. When Lefèvre writes that "it is in the estimation of the Jews that Christ was abandoned by the Father," Erasmus retorts that this is not only "feeble" but also "differs from the view of all ancient commentators."

88. Erasmus, *Apology against Lefèvre*, CWE 83: 46. "What lack of learning," Erasmus responds harshly, "indeed what impiety is evident in your argument that Christ was not humiliated in his suffering on the cross" (56). On Lefèvre's move "in the direction of docetism," see J. B. Payne, "Erasmus and Lefèvre d'Etaples as Interpreters of Paul," *Archiv für Reformationsgeschichte* 65 (1974): 78.

speaking of the incarnation as described in Hebrews 2, for instance, Erasmus pulls back from the idea of an absolute or thorough-going diminution of Christ. It is legitimate, he contends, to speak of Christ as "degraded," as "illustrious writers" like Augustine and Hilary have done, and yet, Erasmus contends, no one should sink "to such a degree of impiety, nay madness, as to ascribe imperfection, unworthiness, or disgrace to Christ." Nor should anyone dare to think of Christ as succumbing to "conscious misdeeds," as wicked people do habitually.[89] Christ incarnate embraced human existence, Erasmus insists, but there are limits to the range and degree in which even Erasmus will say that Christ was fully human.

For starters, as Erasmus sees it, Christ seems to have been immune from moral struggle, and with that, as well, he was never susceptible to moral failure, though both struggle and failure are all too familiar features of human existence. More remarkably, the figure described by Erasmus seems not to have suffered from confusion or fallen into ignorance. Repeatedly in fact, as Erasmus tells it in the *Paraphrase on Matthew*, we find an apparently human Jesus who yet somehow is equipped with divine foreknowledge of future events and a preternatural clairvoyance of what others are thinking.[90] And while he conceals his divinity to "make clear the reality of his human nature," we are told, he sometimes reverses course in order to prove his divinity with miraculous interventions in nature or by mighty acts against ferocious demons.[91] Astonishingly enough, as Erasmus puts it, this figure "could

89. Erasmus, *Apology against Lefèvre*, CWE 83: 39. Erasmus here follows the tradition rooted in Paul's Romans 8:3, where the Son of God is described as existing only "in the likeness of sinful flesh." In his *Paraphrases on Romans*, Erasmus observes that Christ was "dressed in the same flesh in which other sinners are clothed," though he was, in fact, "a stranger to all contagion of sin." Hedging his language, Erasmus speaks of Christ adopting "the mask of sin, so to speak" (CWE 42: 45). In his annotation on this passage, Erasmus similarly writes of Christ's assumption of "the role of a sinner" as a "kind of play-acting, if you will forgive the expression." He added a sentence in 1535 to emphasize that what was "unreal" was purely his being "under the appearance of the flesh subject to sin" (*Annotations on Romans*, CWE 56: 201–2).

90. "As a human being," Erasmus writes, Jesus "allowed them to report [the death of John the Baptist] as if he did not know about it, though he had known beforehand, even before it was done" (*Paraphrase on Matthew*, CWE 45: 224). Later, Jesus indicates to his disciples that there would be those who "would betray the gospel message," and, moreover, "to show clearly that absolutely nothing escaped him, and so that at the same time the conscience of his betrayer thus stung might turn to repentance," announces that one of them will betray him" (346–47).

91. Erasmus, *Paraphrase on Matthew*, CWE 45: 247. As Erasmus puts it, the Jesus of Matthew

have repressed" his adversaries "in some hateful manner," or "he could have overcome them with miracles" or even "destroyed" them, had he chosen to wield his divine power.[92]

This is no ordinary human being, to say the least; in fact, this is not someone who seems to have dealt with the full range of human experience. What we have from Erasmus, it seems, are conflicting signals, though they surely are not his alone, as the Chaledonian model for thinking of Christ invites just these odd and awkward juxtapositions, and Christologies crafted in this manner have always shunned the idea of ascribing cognitive limits or moral weakness to Christ. When it comes to the divinity and the humanity of Christ, finally, Erasmus affirms that "both things belong to Christ," as he never "ceased for a while to be the highest and most blessed," even when "he took these misfortunes upon himself of his own accord."[93] No matter how odd and inscrutable this combination is, Erasmus concludes, the divinity of Christ incarnate is not impugned by the frailty of human existence; though unlike Lefèvre, the divine dignity of Christ also does not eclipse the fact of his human suffering.

"The Unspeakable Love Which He Had for Us"

The emphasis by Erasmus on the humanity of Christ is far from an exercise in what is sometimes called "ontological" Christology, where someone tries to work out theoretically the convergence and coherence of the dual natures in the personal life of Christ. Instead, as the earlier chapters of this book have shown, the interest of Erasmus concerns the "functional" significance of Christ for human existence, where

---

"rebuked the winds and the sea," while turning the "troubled sea" into "supreme tranquility," so "it would be obvious that it was not accomplished by human strength, but by divine power" (147–48). Then again, we are told, Jesus demonstrated his "divine power" when he drew out the ferocious demons from two men possessed and placed these demons in the swine (149–50). Thus, Erasmus writes, Jesus "proves by his miracles that his powers were greater than human" (82).

92. Erasmus, *Paraphrase on Matthew*, CWE 45: 196.

93. Erasmus, *Apology against Lefèvre*, CWE 83: 34. Thus, Erasmus writes, "both things belong to Christ through his divine nature, in which he was always God, and through his human nature, which he thought it worthy to assume for a while" (35). See also CWE 83: 71, where Erasmus reaffirms that Christ could be called "most afflicted and most blessed" because of "his opposite natures united in the same substance."

reflection centers on the redemptive significance and practical implications of the exemplary humility in Christ's gracious assumption of the burdens of human life. It is true, of course, as we saw in chapters 4 and 5, that Erasmus piously affirms the "transcendence and majesty" of Christ, though, as has been evident in the controversy with Lefèvre, he places far greater weight on his "immanence and humanity." It is "one and the same Christ," as he puts it, "each from a different perspective," though Erasmus immediately adds, it is from the humanity of Christ that "more profit is to be gained for the present."

Erasmus is not explicit about what he means by "more profit," any more than when he declares that "Christ in his humble state" has "more relevance for us" than the heavenly Christ.[94] But what is clear, as Bedouelle observes, is that for Erasmus, it is "Christ's incarnation and passion"—not simply his transcendent sublimity—that serve as "the very source of [human] redemption."[95] The "extreme lowliness of Christ" not only "redound[s] to the glory of Christ," Erasmus explains, but more importantly, it serves as living "testimony to the unspeakable love which he had for us."[96] Indeed, he writes in a very traditional vein, Christ "cast himself down ... for our sake," and then in turn, again echoing Philippians 2:9, he "was raised up above all things." With respect to the incomparable example of humility, Erasmus declares, "we see *what we must imitate*," and in the vindication of Christ in his glory, we discover "*what we may hope for*."[97] The model of perfect humility, in short, provides a goal and measure for the ethical transformation of human life, while the exaltation of Christ offers an eschatological promise of redeemed life.

Here, once again, as has been the case in each of the previous chapters, the upshot of the Christology of Erasmus is to be found in the ethical transformation of human life. By "ethics" here, once again, I do not mean a simple set of moral prescriptions for good behavior but rather the ideal character of being human before God and with others. It is exactly that, after all—a religious ethics rooted in faith and flowering

---

94. Erasmus, *Apology against Lefèvre*, CWE 83: 35.
95. Bedouelle, "Introduction," CWE 83: xxi.
96. Erasmus, *Apology against Lefèvre*, CWE 83: 33–34.
97. Erasmus, *Apology against Lefèvre*, CWE 83: 41, my italics.

in assorted social virtues—that defines the essence of the philosophy of Christ, which, as we saw in the first chapter, constitutes the ultimate goal and measure (*scopus*) of human existence. In the context of the controversy with Lefèvre, this ethical dimension is not developed in much detail, though the seeds of it are clearly at play.

First and foremost, Erasmus writes, Christ is an exemplary model of humility. In brief, his self-abasement was, in the words of Erasmus, to "the highest degree remarkable and genuine."[98] What is more, he adds elsewhere, Christ's entire life was an "endless display of mercy to all," and with that, too, his whole teaching was dedicated to nothing but "concord and mutual love."[99] The point and purpose of the incarnation of Christ, in short, is the embodied revelation of an ethic of humility, mercy, friendship, and peace. This ethic will comprise the central focus of the final chapter of this book, as the peace of Christ for Erasmus offers the transformative goal and measure for a redeemed life, precisely what is so lacking in the twisted and corrupted world as it actually exists. In the context of the *Apology against Lefèvre*, we encounter a sign of this ethic where Erasmus puts forth earnest appeals that scholarly communications might aspire to the ideals of friendship, civility, and concord. In imitation of Christ's paradigmatic humility, therefore, Erasmus counsels "Christian modesty" as the font from which civil and amicable discussions might flow.[100] After all, Erasmus complains to Lefèvre, to "raise a storm" over someone else's language is "contrary to Christian charity" and thus a violation of the peaceful relations possible among scholarly friends.[101]

"What can be hoped for"—a redeemed life in Christ, or something to that effect—is not addressed in the *Apology against Lefèvre*, though it is clear that Erasmus understands the redemption of the human world less as a majestic act of supernatural power than as a merciful act of divine humility which in its exemplary expression of love offers

---

98. Erasmus, *Sermon on the Immense Mercy of God*," CWE 70: 118.

99. Erasmus, *Complaint of Peace*, CWE 27: 299; "War is a Treat," CWE 35: 425.

100. See Erasmus, *Apology against Lefèvre*, CWE 83: 55, on Christian modesty. When Erasmus complains of Lefèvre's "abusive language," for instance, he in turn endorses a "polite and open manner" of discussion (89). And when disagreement arises, Erasmus encourages "an amicable form" of exchange (8).

101. Erasmus, *Apology against Lefèvre*, CWE 83: 93.

a transformative pattern for a life shaped by modesty and kindness. Though Erasmus can be found speaking of an other-worldly salvation in heaven, mostly when reflecting on particular biblical texts or working with church doctrine, it is true in the end that Erasmus thinks of Christ primarily as one who brings redemption to the life in the world itself.[102] In the *Paraphrase on Matthew*, for instance, Christ is introduced as a "master teacher" of a "truly salvific and efficacious philosophy" by which all people can attain "true godliness and true happiness."[103] Then again, drawing on the many and varied miracle stories, he is presented as a healer who not only overthrows "every disease" but especially as a "physician of souls" who offers to "purify" everyone of their "disease[s] of the mind."[104] Finally, too, we find Erasmus describing the death of Christ as a "salvific sacrifice for everyone," whereby his selfless yet freely chosen sacrifice of life was offered to "redeem the entire world" when confirmed with "divine power by his resurrection."[105] Erasmus works with each of these images of the redeemer—Christ as wise teacher, merciful healer, and model of self-sacrificial love—as each contributes something to flush out the means by which Christ's diminishment can be understood to have "profit" or "relevance" for human life.

102. See, for instance, Erasmus, *Paraphrase on Matthew*, CWE 45: 66, 85, in which Erasmus takes up the notion of "heavenly rewards" or a "heavenly kingdom" found in the biblical text. The synoptic gospels speak of "eternal life" as an experience in the future granted at the final judgment (see Mk 10:30 and Mt 18:8–9), though John speaks of it as an already achieved present possibility (see Jn 5:24). For the latter, see Erasmus, *Paraphrase on John*, CWE 46: 67–68. In a pastoral writing like *Preparing for Death*, consequently, Erasmus advises the reader to prepare for death by "contemplating eternal and heavenly things," so that "we learn to think little of the temporary and earthly." Though this is said to be an "important part of Christian philosophy," most of this writing, in fact, is dedicated to calming measures to be practiced throughout one's life. See Erasmus, *Preparing for Death*, trans. John N. Grant, CWE 70: 396. In reflecting on the Apostles' Creed, moreover, Erasmus discusses the meaning of the "resurrection of the body" at "the end the world." See Erasmus, *Explanation of the Apostles' Creed*, CWE 70: 345–48. The Apostles' Creed, he writes, concerns "what must necessarily be believed by all to gain eternal salvation"—and that, in short, amounts to a "heavenly philosophy," whose "matter is a holy life" and "its goal is heavenly life" (246). This brief creed shows "the road by which one must reach eternal glory," though the faith which it teaches, Erasmus again emphasizes, is of "the greatest importance for a holy and happy life" in this world, for which Christ is the "personal example" (304, 276, and 357).

103. Erasmus, *Paraphrase on Matthew*, CWE 45: 72, 30. See also CWE 45: 83, 58.

104. Erasmus, *Paraphrase on Matthew*, CWE 45: 82, 140–42, 150, 155, and 164.

105. Erasmus, *Paraphrase on Matthew*, CWE 45: 249, 294, 341, 343, 349, and 370. See Payne, *Erasmus: His Theology of the Sacraments*, 64–66.

The key in this regard is to see that Christ's embrace of humanity has directly to do with life as we live it, in a word, it addresses the twisted inversions that infect so much of life with teaching, example, and guidance for a new way of being human. What is at stake in the diminution of Christ described in Hebrews 2 and Philippians 2, therefore, is the possibility of transforming the very character of human life through the imitation of Christ's "extraordinary virtues."[106] This is a task to be pursued throughout life, we are told, though the strenuous pursuit is a response to the powerful allure of Christ, who in his humanity beckons people to follow even as he models the virtues to imitate. This is, in the end, the "profit" to be "gained for the present," that is, where the actual lives of men and women are transformed through the diligent imitation of Christ. In making this point, Erasmus draws on the language from Paul, which describes the shift from a life animated by self-interest to one where Christ may be said to "live in them" through their acts of mercy, kindness, and friendship.[107]

It is interesting to note at this point that Lefèvre also emphasizes the manner in which a life of humble service prepares one for a "true assimilation of Christ in us."[108] In Lefèvre's case, however, the imitation of Christ is recast as a mystical "adherence to Christ"—a full-fledged "*Christiformitas*," in Lefèvre's language—whereby Christ comes to abide in us and we find ourselves anew in Christ.[109] Likely influenced by Nicholas of Cusa,[110] Lefèvre's thinking yields "a mysticism very far from the Philosophy of Christ" found in Erasmus, as Mann notes.[111] Despite the difference in their thinking, it remains true that the transformation conceived by Erasmus also involves a seismic shift in the

---

106. Erasmus, *Paraphrase on Matthew*, CWE 45: 127. It is important to note that Erasmus does not exhort Christians to literally imitate the passion of Christ.

107. Thus, Paul writes in Galatians 2:20, "it is no longer I that lives, but it is Christ who lives in me." See Erasmus, *Paraphrase on Galatians*, CWE 42: 107.

108. Bedouelle, *Lefèvre d'Étaples*, 228.

109. J. Dagens, "Humanisme et évangélisme chez Lefèvre d'Étaples," in *Courants religieux et humanisme*, 129. On "*Christiformitas*" in Lefèvre, see Steenbeek, "Introduction," ASD IX - 3, 31–35; Bedouelle, "Jacques Lefèvre d'Étaples," 227–31;

110. On Lefèvre's interest in Nicholas of Cusa, see Bedouelle, *Lefèvre d'Étaples*, 60–70; Hughes, *Lefèvre*, 44–47. On possible sources in the works of Nicholas, see "On the Vision of God," in *Nicholas of Cusa: Selected Spiritual Writings*, trans. H. Lawrence Bond (New York: Paulist Press, 1997), chap. 9, 34, 250; "On Learned Ignorance," *Nicholas of Cusa*, chap. 11, 252, 200.

111. Mann, *Érasme et les débuts de la réforme française*, 73.

fundamental character of personal life, so there could have been an interesting conversation contrasting the ethical and the mystical works of Christ had Lefèvre and Erasmus managed to turn their attention in that direction. What is most important for Erasmus, in any case, is the affirmation of Christ's humble assumption of the difficult course of human life, for that is the all-important condition for the possibility of the ethical renewal of human character.

CHAPTER 7

Jesus the Truly Human Christ

It was in late 1499, while visiting England for the first of six times, that Erasmus engaged the preacher and educator John Colet in a friendly, though apparently rather spirited, discussion over the meaning of those parallel passages from the Gospels that depict the dread and distress felt by Jesus in the garden of Gethsemane as his arrest and execution loomed.[1] Mark and Matthew recount that Jesus was both "troubled" and "sorrowful" as he went to pray, while all three synoptic Gospels record Jesus' desperate plea that his Father "remove this cup from [him]," followed by an obedient concession to the Father's will.[2] These and similar stories have long been problematic for Christian thinking about the divine mission accorded to Jesus—how was it possible, in a word, for Christ to have feared his own death when this event was to be so central to God's plan of redemption? And how do such familiar human

---

1. Erasmus refers to "our sparring match yesterday afternoon," the details of which he records in Erasmus to John Colet, letter 109, CWE 1: 206–11. On the life and work of Colet, see John B. Gleason, *John Colet* (Berkeley: University of California Press, 1989); J. B. Trapp, "John Colet," COE 1: 324–28.

2. See Mark 14:32–36, Matthew 26:36–39, and Luke 22: 39–42.

emotions square with the omnipotence and omniscience commonly linked with the Christ figure?

It is these questions that Erasmus and Colet debated at St. Mary's College (Oxford) in the presence of prior Richard Charnock, the details of which were recalled by Erasmus in a brief exchange of letters with Colet.[3] In the eyes of Colet, Christ's agony in the garden, and specifically his plea that the Father spare him "this cup," does not signal fear of his own death, but rather—apparently following Jerome—a loving concern for the Jews for whom his execution will in turn "be a cause of death."[4] In response, Erasmus objects to Colet's "forced or strained" interpretation of a passage that lacks any reference to the Jews, opting instead for a simpler and more natural reading that acknowledges what the narratives "loudly proclaim"—"that here is a man who stands in fear of death."[5] Shortly after this exchange of letters, Erasmus expanded their debate in what became *A Short Debate Concerning the Distress, Alarm, and Sorrow of Jesus*, a compact treatise in which Erasmus seizes the opportunity to explore and defend what will be some enduring Christological preferences regarding the humanity of Christ.[6]

3. The extant correspondence on these issues opens with Erasmus to John Colet, letter 108, CWE 1: 202–6, which later prefaces Erasmus, *A Short Debate Concerning the Distress, Alarm, and Sorrow of Jesus*, trans. Michael J. Heath, CWE 70: 9–12. In Erasmus to John Colet, letter 109, CWE 1: 206–11, Erasmus moves to "record the entire controversy in writing." Colet replies in John Colet to Erasmus, letter 110, CWE 1: 211–12, followed by a rejoinder from Erasmus in letter 111, CWE 1: 212–19. On some confusion in the ordering of these letters, see G. J. Fokke, "An Aspect of the Christology of Erasmus of Rotterdam," *Ephemerides theologicae Lovanienses* 54 (1978): 161–72. R. J. Schoeck claims that "there are few exchanges in the history of Biblical criticism that are quite so warm yet challenging, so filled with a sense of excitement of exploring the meaning of key scriptural passages, as the letters that passed between Colet and Erasmus in the autumn months of 1499." See Schoeck, *Erasmus of Europe: The Making of a Humanist, 1467–1500* (Edinburgh: Edinburgh University Press, 1990), 228.

4. Erasmus to John Colet, letter 111, CWE 1: 214, 215. See also Erasmus, *The Distress of Jesus*, CWE 70: 16, 22.

5. Erasmus to John Colet, letter 111, CWE 1: 214–15. As Erasmus later writes, "no small leap of the imagination . . . is required to make the facts and the words apply to the destruction of the Jews" (*The Distress of Jesus*, CWE 70: 18). For a similar challenge, see CWE 70: 22. Citing John 18:11 ("the cup that my Father has given me"), Erasmus argues that "the Father gives the Son the cup to drink, and the Son, as a man . . . weak with the woes of humanity, is filled with genuine dread of imminent death and begs his Father to take the cup from him." Erasmus reads the words from John through the lens of the synoptic Gospels, even though in John there is not the slightest sign of fear and dread before death. In that context, in fact, Jesus faces his impending death obediently and resolutely, as Erasmus later emphasizes in the *Paraphrase on John*, CWE 46: 200.

6. Erasmus, *The Distress of Jesus*, CWE 70: 1–67, was first published along with *The Handbook of the Christian Soldier* as part of the *Lucubratiunculae* (Antwerp: Thierry Martens, 1503).

Unlike the works of Erasmus dealt with in the previous three chapters, *The Distress of Jesus* is not an apology designed to fend off hostile criticism, nor does it concern theological issues generated from philological disputes. Those types of works will not arrive for over a decade, after Erasmus has issued his ground-breaking work on Christian scriptures. The original discussion with Colet, in fact, was a "dispute between friends," as John B. Gleason puts it, a remarkably civil and amicable exchange if judged from their letters that only becomes a bit heated due to Colet's habitual self-certainty and occasional bad temper over disagreement.[7] After a pause of communication between the two, Erasmus writes to Colet in late 1504, informing him that he has thrown himself into the study of "sacred literature"—"full sail, full gallop," as he puts it—now equipped with Greek and a familiarity with Origen.[8]

Along with this letter, Erasmus sends "a small literary gift," including the "debate on the fear of Christ" that they shared in England; only now, Erasmus cautions, "it is so much altered that you would hardly recognize it."[9] The latter comment is exactly right, as *The Distress of Jesus* is a literary creation in its own right, in which the original debate is greatly expanded and superseded in the thoroughness with which arguments are developed and delivered. One can still discern the positions

7. Gleason, *John Colet*, 95. Alternatively, Heath describes the tone of *The Distress of Jesus* as "far from amicable" (introductory note, CWE 70: 5). Erasmus certainly discovered that Colet's convictions often "proved impervious to reason" (Gleason, *John Colet*, 105–11). Consider also Erasmus's vivid description of Colet's high-handed and frenzied loss of good temper at another gathering: "he seemed to become intoxicated with a sort of holy frenzy, and to exhibit in his bearing something of superhuman exaltation and majesty. His voice was altered, his eyes had a different look, and his features and expression were transformed" (Erasmus to Johannes Sixtinus, letter 116, CWE 1: 230).

8. Erasmus to John Colet, letter 181, CWE 2: 86–87. For the proverbial expression used by Erasmus, see "With sail and horse," adage I. iv. 17, CWE 31: 332–33. In the fall of 1499, Colet had encouraged Erasmus to lecture on scriptures, a task that he declined as being "too great for my powers" (Erasmus to John Colet, letter 108, CWE 1: 205). Though scholars used to emphasize Colet's influence in turning Erasmus to biblical studies, it seems, in fact, that Erasmus intentionally turned away from Colet's approach to the Bible by working to learn Greek—something that would pay rich dividends in both his collection of adages and the work on Christian scriptures. See Erika Rummel, *Erasmus' Annotations on the New Testament*, 10–12; Phillips, "La '*Philosophia Christi*' reflétée dan les 'Adages' d'Érasme," in *Courants religieux et humanisme*, 57; and Gleason, *John Colet*, 112–14. Erasmus is thinking of theologians in general when he mocks the folly of interpreting "Holy Scripture untaught and unpracticed" in ancient languages ("With unwashed hands," adage I. ix. 55, CWE 32: 212). In June 1516, Colet tells Erasmus that he has set himself to learning Greek (John Colet to Erasmus, letter 423, CWE3: 312–13). See Gleason, *John Colet*, 58–59.

9. Erasmus to John Colet, letter 181, CWE 2: 86–87.

of Erasmus and Colet as recounted in their letters of 1499, though Erasmus has taken huge strides forward in thinking through how one may coherently say that Jesus dreaded his impending death while still being divine, even while he greatly augments the objections and counterarguments wielded by the literary version of Colet. What we have, in sum, is roughly a literary dialogue between Erasmus and "Colet"[10]—a text modeled, as Erasmus notes, on "the traditional method of argument used in the Academy"—that allows Erasmus to articulate his views in the give and take of well-argued conversation while coyly concealing his creative embellishment of the arguments from both sides.[11]

Though *The Distress of Jesus* is an early work in the career of Erasmus—for instance, it is amply sprinkled with classical allusions, even as it lacks the kind of philological precision found in more mature writings—it nonetheless makes a compelling and truly novel contribution to Christology. What is crystal clear from the very start is the readiness of Erasmus to enter the "maze of Christological issues" surrounding Jesus' agony in the garden of Gethsemane, where, as O'Malley aptly puts it, "so many have lost their way."[12] In fact, as we will see in the first section, Erasmus handles the dialectical complexities of Christological language—that Jesus did and did not dread his own death, for

10. As Erasmus tells us in the opening paragraph of *The Distress of Jesus*, a passage lifted directly from the start of his summary of their exchange in letter 109 to Colet, he stepped back after their debate in order to look at the issues in "a harder and more concentrated way." Trying to free himself from "every shred of prejudice," he continues, he "put together and weighed the arguments on both sides"—so much so, in fact, that he imaginatively "altered things round so as to adopt your arguments exactly as if they were my own and to criticize my own no less severely than if they had been yours" (CWE 70: 14). As Ross Dealy observes, this imaginative method of composition allowed Erasmus to portray "what Colet *could* have said in the debate, considering his basic outlook, rather than what he had actually said," and with that, as well, we find arguments from Erasmus that are richer and more sophisticated than anything he might have uttered when face to face with Colet. See Dealy, *The Stoic Origins of Erasmus' Philosophy of Christ*, 152. Following Dealy's lead, "Colet" will signify the literary persona rather than the man himself.

11. Erasmus, *The Distress of Jesus*, CWE 70: 23. Erasmus later recalls his preference for the dialogue format, that "free and easy form of discussion the ancients used," in contrast to the "newfangled method of disputation" used by theologians (66). Though he had misgivings about the scholastic genre of "disputed questions," O'Malley rightly notes the playful irony of Erasmus's chosen title—a "little disputation" (*disputatiuncula*)—given as "short debate" in the CWE translation ("Introduction," CWE 70: xi). On Erasmus's penchant for the "dialogue structure," see A. Godin, "Introduction," *Opera omnia Desiderii Erasmi Roterodami*, V - 7 (Leiden: Brill, 2013), 196; Terence J. Martin, *Living Words: Studies in Dialogues about Religion* (Atlanta, Ga.: Scholars Press, 1998), 249–316.

12. O'Malley, "Introduction," CWE 70: xi.

example—in a manner that preserves the awkward but necessary oppositions brought on by insisting on the full humanity of Jesus, something that "Colet" (and many traditional theologians like him) collapse by ignoring the natural humanity of the man. It is precisely here where we see the distinctive quality of Erasmus's thinking, as he resolutely seeks to affirm the "capacity and dignity" of Jesus' humanity, in contrast to so many theologians (including Colet) who in one way or another insist upon the "weakness and depravity" of human existence.[13]

To this end, as will be apparent in the second section, Erasmus shows impressive philosophical creativity—with the help of a revised Stoic framework, as Ross Dealy has shown—in accounting for Jesus' natural disinclination to death.[14] What emerges, significantly enough, is a robust Christological affirmation of the humanity of Jesus. To bolster his case for what will be an enduring point of emphasis, as will be evident in the third section, Erasmus contests the various efforts of "Colet" to render Jesus somehow exempt from full-fledged emotional dread of death. In this regard, Erasmus strongly opposes "Colet's" assorted docetic strategies designed to insulate the dignity of Christ from injurious emotions, even though he occasionally relents to the pressures of tradition to accent the transcendent dignity of Christ.[15] It is the contention of "Colet," however, that any sign that Jesus feared for his own well-being will diminish his broader love for others, including the Jews who persecuted him. In response, as we will see in the final section of this chapter, Erasmus argues that Jesus' incomparable emotional

13. Eugene F. Rice, Jr., "John Colet and the Annihilation of the Natural," *The Harvard Theological Review* 45, no. 3 (July, 1952): 141. Rice describes Colet as an "ascetic reformer," an educator of importance, "profoundly Christian," and yet "not a humanist" ("John Colet and the Annihilation of the Natural," 141–12). That Colet does "not merit the name of humanist," see also Germain Marc'hadour, "Érasme et John Colet," in *Colloquia Erasmiana Tyronensia*, vol. 2 (Paris: Librairie philosophique J. Vrin, 1972), 767.

14. Dealy, *The Stoic Origins*, 101–50.

15. See Fokke, "An Aspect of the Christology of Erasmus," 183. Docetism is that tendency in Christology which denies the reality of the incarnation by deeming Jesus' bodily existence (and hence his agony) as a mere appearance or as something unreal. Classically found in Gnostic circles of early Christian history, the same tendency often reappears in Monophysitic (one nature) and Monophylitic (one will) Christologies, which emphasize the divine nature and will of Christ at the expense of the human nature and will. On docetism in Gnostic sources, see Grillmeier, *Christ in Christian Tradition*, 93–110, 115–16; Pelikan, *Emergence of the Catholic Tradition*, 89–90. On the background of Gnostic thinking, see Hans Jonas, *The Gnostic Religion: The Message of the Alien God and the Beginnings of Christianity*, 2nd ed. (Boston: Beacon Press, 1963).

suffering is the surest evidence of his "inestimable charity" for humanity, by means of which people receive an exemplary pattern of "charity and gentleness" for the living of a transformed life of love.[16]

"Confusing and Conflicting Ideas"

The agony of Jesus in the garden of Gethsemane—especially what certainly appears to be a desperate plea to be freed from a torturous death— has spawned centuries of Christological dismay. How, on the one hand, can someone who is marked by divine sonship show such signs of human weakness and fear? How, in other words, can such apparently irreconcilable opposites—divinity and humanity, as the tradition came to conceive them—be coherently combined in the same person? In addressing these questions, on the other hand, we might also wonder how we are to understand this figure's life, as he seems to have been—at the same time—both very much like us and yet drastically unlike us. How, in short, are we to understand such a life, when what is familiar is inextricably bound up with what is unquestionably alien, and vice versa? These are perennial questions in the history of Christology: the first set of questions concern the character of Christ's identity, and these require dialectical finesse in handling the unsettled equipoise of opposing natures in a single person; while the second kind of questions have to do with the relative weight given to what is recognizably familiar in comparison with what is intractably different, and to sort through these matters requires considerable skill in analogical reasoning. Every Christology must grapple with both sets of questions, but the way they are resolved makes all the difference in the world for the theological result.

In *The Distress of Jesus*, Erasmus confronts his readers with a veritable "clash of Christologies," and the skirmish laid out before us is fought over exactly these questions.[17] On the one side stands the Christology defended by "Colet," in which the view of so-called "modern theologians," who claim that Christ feared "the cruel and terrible ordeal that drew ever closer," is firmly opposed. Though "Colet" affirms the reality of the incarnation, such that Jesus is said to have experienced true emotions,

16. Erasmus, *The Distress of Jesus*, CWE 70: 64–65.
17. Gleason, *John Colet*, 105.

it is for "Colet" "patently absurd to claim that Christ shuddered at either the infamy or the pain of the cross," since as the divine embodiment of "true love," he "had come for no other purpose."[18] The view of Colet (and "Colet") is simple and largely without complications, though it pays a price for so stressing the singular dominance of the divine will over the human nature of Jesus, namely, what Eugene F. Rice graphically calls, "the annihilation of the natural," and that is a very steep price to pay.[19]

Erasmus counters with an unflinching affirmation of the natural humanity of Jesus, while trying not to compromise the divine presence in his words and actions. "Through the frailty of the condition he had assumed," Erasmus writes, Jesus "shrank from approaching death," even while "he went on to face it with all steadfastness" by means of "divine aid and the strength of his obedience."[20] In opposition to the "monophylitic" habits of "Colet" that exempt Jesus from the human emotions of fear and dread by giving preeminence to his divine will, Erasmus insists that Christ was "a complete and real human being." It was, we are told, by "the nature he received" in human birth that he "dreaded and shrank from his own death." In turn, it was "human emotion" that "made him pray for deliverance" and "human will" that "made him refuse" approaching death. And yet, Erasmus continues, "all this in no way detracts from his obedience," which was "entire and perfect," nor does it diminish "his love for us, which was greater than any love could be."[21] What Erasmus offers us, therefore, is a more balanced approach to Christology, though as we will see presently, the price to be paid for that effort is the inevitably contorted language involved in granting weakness and fear to a divine person.

In fact, the dialogue with "Colet" offers a rare opportunity to witness Erasmus grappling with the analogical and dialectical conundrums written into the fabric of Christology. By "analogical" puzzles, I refer to the manner and degree with which Jesus is deemed to be "like us" (and "unlike" us) in our human experiences. In contrast with "Colet," who privileges the great degree in which Jesus is unlike us by reason of his divinity, Erasmus offers up a full-throated affirmation of Jesus'

18. Erasmus, *The Distress of Jesus*, CWE 70: 14–15, 21.
19. Rice, "John Colet and the Annihilation of the Natural," 162.
20. Erasmus, *The Distress of Jesus*, CWE 70: 19.
21. Erasmus, *The Distress of Jesus*, CWE 70: 23.

human nature, though as with any Christology developed within the pale of Chalcedonian standards, there are counternotes of divinity that add both complexity and confusion. As Erasmus puts it,

> Jesus took on the complete nature of a man, with all the feelings that would have existed in Adam had he continued in his original state: a sensible body and a sensible soul subject to the natural passions.[22]

What is more, Erasmus continues, "Jesus deigned to take on not only a human nature, but even one that was subject to many of our afflictions," specifically, those forms of weakness and disability that plague the sinful state of current humanity.

Curiously enough, Jesus is said by Erasmus to have been "immune" to those afflictions "that befall us as individuals"—such as "diseases" and "deformities"—as these would have been "an affront to his dignity and immaterial to our salvation." Still, Erasmus insists, Jesus assumed "many, but not all" of our "universal afflictions," like the "helplessness of childhood" (which he would have known) and the "frailty of old age" (which, of course, he never faced). But Jesus certainly knew "thirst, hunger, weariness, sorrow, pain, drowsiness, and the thousand trials of our earthly life," all of which "arise from sin," we are told, though "they are not in themselves sins." In line with Christian tradition, however, Erasmus excludes both "inclination toward sinfulness" and "lack of knowledge" from the natural human life of Jesus, though he leaves "undecided" the "necessity of dying."[23]

---

22. Erasmus, *The Distress of Jesus*, CWE 70: 23.

23. Erasmus, *The Distress of Jesus*, CWE 70: 24. Regarding the degree to which Jesus assumed the various afflictions of fallen humanity, the view of Erasmus is not far removed from medieval theologians, whom he refers to as "moderns." See Bonaventure, *Breviloquium*, *The Works of Bonaventure*, vol. 2, trans. Jose de Vinck (Paterson, NJ: St. Anthony Guild Press, 1963), 167–69; Thomas Aquinas, *Summa Theologica*, vol. 2, trans. Fathers of the English Dominican Province (New York: Benziger Brothers, n.d.), part III, qu. 46, art. 5. This is a good example of the way in which the early Erasmus sometimes follows "rather faithfully in the track of his predecessors," as James D. Tracy puts it. See Tracy, "Humanists Among the Scholastics: Erasmus, More, Lefèvre d'Étaples on the Humanity of Christ," *Erasmus of Rotterdam Society Yearbook* 5 (1985): 42; see also Dealy, *The Stoic Origins*, 231–32. It remains true, however, as will be apparent in the pages that follow, that *The Distress of Jesus* involves "a serious and fundamental revision of concepts which had achieved a high degree of consensus in earlier periods." See Daniel T. Lochman, "Colet and Erasmus: The *Disputatiuncula* and the Controversy of Letter and Spirit," *Sixteenth Century Journal* 20, no. 1 (1989): 87. "Far from being an unoriginal work," Dealy writes along the same lines, "*De taedio Jesu* radicalizes virtually every subject it takes up" (*The Stoic Origins*, 104).

Realizing the sensitivity of these issues, Erasmus has "Colet" object that Erasmus is giving Christ "those troublesome urges that impel the rest of us towards wickedness." But that would mean that Christ could sin, which is not something Erasmus would ever assert. In order to respond effectively to this charge, consequently, Erasmus must underscore the manner in which Jesus was not like us, even while continuing to affirm—over and against "Colet"—that Jesus was very much like us in the range of his experiences. It is true, Erasmus writes, that Christ "possessed the same emotions, but not in the same way or with the same effects." The passions felt by people everywhere, we are told, are those that have suffered a "corruption of nature," so now "in their blindness [they] gravitate towards what should be shunned."[24] Quite differently, however, Christ assumed a perfect "nature as created in the beginning," along with some of the afflictions given as punishments for the original sin of human beings, yet, Erasmus suggests, he did not assume a "nature corrupted by sin," so he "could not in fact be lured towards evil." As Erasmus puts it,

> since Christ took nothing from fallen nature except the handicaps imposed on us as chastisement, and there was in him no capacity for sin, I shall boldly ascribe to him the natural passions appropriate to mind and body respectively: grief, joy, hatred, fear, and anger in the mind; in body, hunger, thirst, drowsiness, weariness, suffering, [and] death.[25]

There is no good reason, then, not to ascribe natural passions of mind and body to Christ, as these existed independently of their corrupted form so familiar to the rest of us.

At the same time Erasmus insists on the ways Christ was like us in our natural passions, however, he also underscores how much he was unlike us, most basically, as we have heard, in the nature he assumed, which was uncorrupted by sin and hence not at all the human nature as we know it. But Christ also was unlike other human beings in a more positive sense, as we will see later in more detail, because his "unique love" for humanity meant that he felt all fear and pain far more keenly

24. Erasmus, *The Distress of Jesus*, CWE 70: 38–39.
25. Erasmus, *The Distress of Jesus*, CWE 70: 39.

than others.[26] In this last respect, curiously enough, Christ was unlike us precisely because he was more like us than we are, which is another way of saying that he assumed a prelapsarian version of human nature, which—frankly put—is something completely foreign to actual human experience.

To say the least, Erasmus finds himself deep in a thicket of "confusing and conflicting ideas," though the problems involved are by no means unique to Erasmus, as they are endemic to all Christologies crafted within a Chalcedonian framework.[27] Because of this, it is not uncommon—in fact, it is necessary—for Erasmus to compose the kind of intriguing yet perplexing combinations required in Christology. Thus, for example, as mentioned above, Jesus assumed a "child's helplessness" as an inevitable part of the human condition, though simultaneously, Erasmus adds with some dialectical awkwardness, Jesus enjoyed "perfect wisdom" throughout his days.[28] More pertinent to the questions arising from Christ's passion, however, Erasmus boldly claims that Jesus "feared death, and did not fear it. He dreaded it, and did not. He desired it, and did not." For an explanation, Erasmus suggests that Jesus feared death "not as we do, out of necessity, but voluntarily, and yet he was truly afraid."[29]

So even the explanation carries the complexity of an odd juxtaposition! "He was unwilling to die because death is in itself evil and inimical to the nature he assumed," which refers to the prelapsarian nature he adopted, and yet, he also could have feared from the "afflictions" he assumed without just desert. Now accenting the divine quality of his love, however, Jesus is said to have been "willing to die because it would procure salvation for those he loved." There is no need to hesitate in attributing such incongruous combinations to Christ, Erasmus concludes, including "complete dread and perfect eagerness, sublime joy and intense pain, supreme bliss and extreme suffering," precisely because "Christ's fear, dread, and alarm belong to the category of human

26. Erasmus, *The Distress of Jesus*, CWE 70: 64, 54–55.
27. Erasmus, *The Distress of Jesus*, CWE 70: 52.
28. Erasmus, *The Distress of Jesus*, CWE 70: 24.
29. Erasmus, *The Distress of Jesus*, CWE 70: 52. "Unlike others Christ *chose* … to be bound by natural instincts and other human disabilities. He chose this path notwithstanding spotless innocence, plenitude of grace, and enjoyment of divinity" (Dealy, *The Stoic Origins*, 179, my italics).

woes that the Redeemer took to himself without guilt." Even then, Erasmus adds with a bit of reassurance that also complicates things yet further, "these emotions dwelt within him quite separately from his divine nature," and thus—remarkably enough—they did not "in any way disturb his composure" or "dim the joy his soul found in endless contemplation of the divine."[30] With these dual affirmations, Erasmus takes up the kind of grammatical acrobatics required in orthodox Christology, which means affirming Christ's humanity without impugning his divinity, and vice versa.

"A Complete and Real Human Being"

While it is not unusual in Christian tradition to find theologians affirming the humanity of Christ, the explanations offered by Erasmus are creative, novel, and bold. "Our redeemer Jesus," we are told, "took on the complete nature of a man, with all the feelings that would have existed in Adam had he continued in his original state," and that would have included "a sensible body and a sensible soul subject to the natural passions." That does not mean, once again, that Jesus assumed human nature as current people know it, since that version of nature is said to be corrupted and hence is prone to sin; though, as we saw earlier, Erasmus grants that Jesus took on many of the afflictions of human life that were added to the original state of human nature as punishments for sin. What is most interesting here is not the notion that Jesus assumed some of the afflictions which now curse human existence but rather the hypothetical formulation of Erasmus, that Jesus took on human nature as it "would have existed" *if* Adam had "continued in the original state." So, one might ask, what feelings and passions would have been included in this prelapsarian existence?

To respond to this question, Erasmus steps back to speak a "little more philosophically," as he puts it—thereby bracketing theological

---

30. Erasmus, *The Distress of Jesus*, CWE 70: 53. It is worth noting that Erasmus maintains a rough separation of the two natures to insulate the "composure" of Christ's divinity. Though this is not uncommon in Christologies framed in Chalcedonian terms, where there is a clear interest in protecting the dignity of the Son, it also introduces language that the formula of Chalcedon wished to exclude by insisting that the one person of Christ existed "without division, without separation." See "The Chalcedonian Decree," *Christology of the Later Fathers*, 373.

concerns for the moment, including the "question of sin," and apparently also the notion of the "fall"—whereupon he "venture[s] to say" that "it is only human nature to dread death; and that, such is the human condition, there would have been a place for it even in the state of innocence."[31] What a remarkable suggestion that is, given that traditional church teaching has long claimed that death—much less the dread of death—did not exist before the fall from innocence with Adam's sin. In this regard, Erasmus piously grants that "death is truly the offspring of sin,"[32] but he then adds, "philosophically" speaking, that death also is "the enemy of nature, which yearns to live forever." Indeed, Erasmus continues, it is the natural role of death to "bring extinction," and from that, "every living being shrinks." Certainly "brute beasts" are terrified by the threat of death, but even plants, if Aristotle is to be believed, "recoil at nature's urging from anything hostile or dangerous."[33]

In fact, Erasmus notes, "even the most rudimentary creatures can sense very quickly the approach of danger and, as if filled with dread, draw themselves in," precisely the reaction found in sponges who, as Aristotle testifies, "cling on more tightly" when they "sense the sounds of fishermen."[34] In which case, Erasmus cleverly inquires of "Colet," "if nature implanted dread of extinction in sponges, will you deny it to a human?"[35] The answer, clearly enough, is negative, or, to put the point more positively, Erasmus asserts, "nature implanted in us an affection for the essentials of life, teaching us to pursue whatever is conducive

31. Erasmus, *The Distress of Jesus*, CWE 70: 25.

32. Erasmus here echoes Romans 5:12 ("just as sin came into the world through one man, and death came through sin, and so death spread to all because all have sinned.") and James 1: 14–15 ("one is tempted by one's own desire, being lured and enticed by it; then, when that desire has conceived, it gives birth to sin, and that sin, when it is fully grown, gives birth to death").

33. Erasmus, *The Distress of Jesus*, CWE 70: 25. See Aristotle, *On the Soul (De Anima)*, trans. J. A. Smith, *Complete Works of Aristotle*, vol. 1, 657–61, bk. 2, chaps. 2–4. In *On the Soul*, 413a 25–34, Aristotle speaks of the "originative power"—which includes the "power of self-nutrition"— through which plants "increase or decrease in all spatial directions." As the power "in virtue of which all are said to have life," the "nutritive soul" is the only "psychic power" found in plants (415a 23–25). However, Aristotle also surmises that those who study the "constitution of plants" will discover a sense in which their "natural bodies" are "organs of the soul," to which and for which they grow (415b 15–20). See also Aristotle, *History of Animals (Historia Animalium)*, trans. A. W. Thompson, *Complete Works of Aristotle*, vol. 1, 922, bk. 4, chap. 30, 588b.

34. Erasmus, *The Distress of Jesus*, CWE 70: 32–33. See Aristotle, *History of Animals*, 866, bk. 5, chap. 16, 548b11–15. Aristotle also observes that sponges react in the same way in "windy and boisterous weather."

35. Erasmus, *The Distress of Jesus*, CWE 70: 33.

to survival and to recoil from whatever harms us."[36] It is only natural, therefore, for people to cling to life and to dread its extinction in death, and those same reactions, interestingly enough, would have found their proper place even "in the state of innocence."[37]

Erasmus's philosophical interlude is designed to defend the integrity of some basic impulses that naturally animate human psychology, and that very much includes the fear of death. To this end, as Dealy argues, Erasmus taps into certain currents of Stoic thinking in order to underscore the presence of a "self-preservation instinct" (*oikeiosis*) that is naturally given at birth.[38] Erasmus signals his debt to the Stoics in this regard, even as he distances himself from some well-known Stoic habits of thinking. Thus, he writes, while it is true that the Stoics "generally expect rather more of their wise man than human frailty can bear," they nonetheless "allow him this dread of death," and what is more, they even give this emotion "the leading place among the 'first principles of nature.'"[39] What Erasmus combines in this statement were in fact discrete though overlapping strands of the centuries-long Stoic tradition.

But while he demurs at the traditional Stoic ideal of a mental equanimity that remains undisturbed (*apatheia*) when faced with the turbulence of the passions, he readily embraces the later Stoic notion of a natural instinct for survival. One of the "earliest lessons that nature teaches us," he declares, "is to avoid, at first instinctively but later by reasoning too, anything that threatens her gentle rule, and still more anything that may destroy it entirely."[40] Nature teaches us from the beginning, in short, "to protect and cherish our existence," so it is entirely natural "to dread some evil that is yet to come."[41] With these statements, Erasmus

36. Erasmus, *The Distress of Jesus*, CWE 70: 27.

37. Erasmus, *The Distress of Jesus*, CWE 70: 25. For that reason, Dealy wryly comments that Erasmus describes "a state of innocence less innocent that ever imagined," as it would have been "built from intractable mental and physical instincts," like the attraction to life and the dread of death (*The Stoic Origins*, 240). As Dealy notes, the suggestion of Erasmus runs counter to the traditional tenet that "fear of death, like death itself, came about as a result ... of Adam's fall" (105).

38. Dealy, *The Stoic Origins*, 7, 67, and 135.

39. Erasmus, *The Distress of Jesus*, CWE 70: 25. For the classical use of this phrase, see *The Attic Nights of Aulus Gellius*, vol. 2, trans. John C. Rolfe (Cambridge, MA: Harvard University Press, 1960), 12.5.7. See Dealy, *The Stoic Origins*, 106.

40. Erasmus, *The Distress of Jesus*, CWE 70: 25; Gellius, *Attic Nights*, 12.5.7–8.

41. Erasmus, *The Distress of Jesus*, CWE 70: 25, 32. Thus, Erasmus writes, "nature planted this

draws heartily on Stoic philosophy, as Dealy demonstrates; or, to be more precise, again with Dealy's help, Erasmus taps into one slice of later Stoic thought, which he then creatively adapts to help to explain why a human being—any human being, but including Jesus—would naturally dread impending death.[42] What these sources offer to Erasmus, in sum, is a way of understanding human existence that will help to make sense out of the Christological puzzles generated by the stories of Christ's passion.

A common depiction of human existence in Christian tradition, one often found in the works of Erasmus, speak of a basic division between the "two parts of our soul"—"one, dwelling down amid the grosser bodily organs and anchored in the flesh, is brutish and inclined towards evil; the other shines like a beacon amid the smoky fogs of instinct, and always strives towards good."[43] The latter is linked with reason by philosophers, while the former usually is named with reference to the passions and appetites for worldly or "fleshly" things, and though human beings are "endowed with a single will," Erasmus grants, it is not uncommon for people to "feel conflicting impulses," one drawing us toward the "right thing" and another "tugging in a different direction."[44] But then, he quickly adds, "no one is so irreverent as to attribute to Christ" this kind of "dissension and endless strife between reason and passion," since such interior tumult "originates in sin and entices us to sin" and is therefore "incompatible with the Redeemer's dignity."[45]

In place of this two-fold schema, consequently, Erasmus suggests that there, in fact, are "three different kinds of impulses in the human mind." There is, once again, a division between "spirit" (which from

principle all the more firmly in us because, in her judgment, it is vital for survival to avoid anything that might harm us." See also CWE 70: 27. The same account of "self-preservation" as "the very first instinct instilled by nature in living creatures" appears in Erasmus, *Warrior Shielding a Discussion 2*, CWE 77: 622–23.

42. Though "built from Stoicism," Dealy argues, the thoughts of Erasmus on the natural instinct for self-preservation is "ultimately out of sync with orthodox Stoicism," which famously insists upon the undisturbed tranquility of the wise man. The natural "love and affection for ourselves" that is helpful for the "perpetuation of the human race" is found in Gellius, *Attic Nights*, 12.5.7, but Dealy suggests that Erasmus did not take "fear of death as a first principle from Gellius" but from other sources, possibly Antiochus of Ascalon. See Dealy, *The Stoic Origins*, 109–12.

43. Erasmus, *The Distress of Jesus*, CWE 70: 58–59. For a similar discussion, see Erasmus, *Handbook of a Christian Soldier*, CWE 66: 41–43.

44. Erasmus, *The Distress of Jesus*, CWE 70: 58.

45. Erasmus, *The Distress of Jesus*, CWE 70: 59.

"judgment and grace" turn to "the invisible, the good, and the eternal") and "flesh" (which from corruption grasps at "evil simply because it is evil"). But "midway between the two," Erasmus suggests, are certain "feelings of inclination" that—from "natural instinct"—incline "toward anything that is favourable to nature" while recoiling from "anything that threatens our survival, or even our peace of mind." With this suggestion, Erasmus carves out independent space for natural instincts and their corresponding emotions between the terrain of spirit and flesh. In making this move, as Dealy notes, Erasmus creatively transforms "a significant part of what had been flesh" in philosophical and theological tradition "into a soul consisting of natural instincts."[46] What that means, in short, is that emotions like fear of something violent or dread of impending death, while not laudatory in their own right, are also not blameworthy, as there can be no culpability for what is an entirely natural fact of life.

These natural instincts, Erasmus concludes, surely exist "even in the best of us, and ultimately even in Christ."[47] It was, for example, a natural sense of dread that Peter felt before his martyrdom, Erasmus tells us, a common feeling of anxious trepidation that is "deeply implanted in us by natural instinct" in response to "anything that is inimical to nature." When Christ appeared "unwilling to die," similarly, it was "simply a natural dread of death" and not at all a violation of the spirit or something rooted in the interests of the flesh. That he "shrank from death was a sign of weakness"—there is no denying that—but it was an entirely natural sign of frailty and not at all something blameworthy. Indeed, Erasmus adds, such "natural weakness" is the "surest evidence of humanity," something Christ "deliberately and willingly" assumed "for love of us."[48] It is precisely this natural frailty, these deeply rooted "promptings of nature," that are on display when Jesus pleads to the Father to let the cup of death pass from him.

---

46. Dealy, *The Stoic Origins*, 140. As Dealy puts it, "while early Stoics considered emotion false reasoning and later Stoics tended to see emotion as something that needs to be subordinated to reason, Erasmus makes emotion a natural and ineradicable instinct and places it among things that are in Stoicism 'indifferent'"—which is to say, among things that are neither noble and good nor base and evil (104). See also 126–32.

47. Erasmus, *The Distress of Jesus*, CWE 70: 60.

48. Erasmus, *The Distress of Jesus*, CWE 70: 61.

But, of course, that is only half of the Christological story, though it is the dimension so often ignored by those in a hurry to magnify the divine power of Christ; hence, it is to Erasmus's credit for rehabilitating the natural emotions in depicting the character of Jesus. As a "complete and real human being," Jesus "suffered ineradicable natural instincts," as Dealy puts it, even as his spirit thirsted for death because it sought "the salvation of the human race."[49] For that reason, Erasmus concludes, Jesus was "both willing and unwilling to die," the former for the "restoration of humanity" and the latter because of his natural abhorrence of death.[50]

"Nothing Bold and Fearless"

Erasmus is true to his word when he says that *The Distress of Jesus* is modeled after that "free and easy form of discussion the ancients used," as a considerable amount of this little disputation is devoted to engaging and answering the ways in which "Colet" seeks to render Christ immune from the kind of emotional strain evident in the synoptic stories of Jesus in the garden of Gethsemane.[51] These counterarguments to Erasmus's efforts to affirm the natural reality of Jesus' agony are familiar throughout Christian tradition; indeed, there has never been a shortage of such attempts in Christian theology which seek—by hook or by crook—to insulate Christ's dignity from even a hint of weakness. Though some of these sentiments likely were held by Colet himself, it is a credit to Erasmus's skill in crafting his literary interlocutor that he gives "Colet" many things to say that the man himself would never have been able to muster, and doing that, in turn, gives Erasmus the opportunity to defend the natural humanity of Christ in yet greater depth. In response to "Colet's" efforts to explain away the fear and distress of Christ, as we will now see, Erasmus rejects the idea that Jesus somehow

49. Dealy, *The Stoic Origins*, 82; Erasmus, *The Distress of Jesus*, CWE 70: 62, 23.

50. Erasmus, *The Distress of Jesus*, CWE 70: 62–63. Erasmus adds some complexity, however, when he claims that "even in the higher part of soul, which was always in perfect harmony with the Godhead, Christ seems to have been, to some extent, reluctant to die," as he was displeased by death since it was the "penalty for sin," and "sin displeased him, as did the author of sin, the devil" (*The Distress of Jesus*, CWE 70: 62).

51. Erasmus, *The Distress of Jesus*, CWE 70: 66.

rose above such emotional trauma by means of heroic bravery, Stoic fearlessness, or the joyful eagerness displayed by martyrs. Each of these options, Erasmus suggests, is an unwarranted invention designed to deny the obvious fact that Christ assumed human nature with its impulse for survival and hence that he shrank from death, as anyone would do.

It is inconceivable, "Colet" contends, that "someone so very brave as Christ" could come to "dread a death that was to be glorious and salutary." But how can Christ be called a "brave man," "Colet" asks, when we see his "shaking limbs ooze bloody drops of sweat" and we hear his "prayer for deliverance from death?"[52] In response, Erasmus points out that "Colet" has misunderstood the meaning of bravery. To be brave, after all, is not being "insensible to things that are dangerous and hostile to nature," but rather having "the ability to endure and overcome them with a steadfast heart." A person faced with danger is not lacking in bravery if "he shudders inwardly, his face turns pale, his heart beats faster, his blood ebbs away, and his suffering wrings from him a groan," as these things are simply the natural effects of encountering danger. "It is natural to be afraid and natural also to feel pain," Erasmus insists, so "anyone unmoved by the imminent threat of some terrible danger is either unaware of his peril or simply brutish and stupid; [and] anyone insensible to pain when it starts is like a block of wood (*stipitis*), less than human, in fact barely alive."[53]

The "virtuous heroes" of classical history and literature, after all, were certainly brave, and yet they were by no means free from fear and dread, even as they remained steadfast in their self-sacrificial loyalty to the greater good which they served.[54] Truly, they were brave, and certainly they were terrified, though the feeling of terror does not nullify the bravery, as it is simply a natural expression of being human. Too often, Erasmus observes, the "very essence" of bravery is misunderstood because of excessive reliance on a person's external demeanor, for instance, a "man fighting bravely in the line" is deemed a coward because "his hair stood on end" and "he let out a groan," or, as an opposite

<hr>

52. Erasmus, *The Distress of Jesus*, CWE 70: 26–27.
53. Erasmus, *The Distress of Jesus*, CWE 70: 27–28.
54. See Erasmus, *The Distress of Jesus*, CWE 70: 28–30.

example, when "pitiful felons" who go to the scaffold smiling and joking, acting as if they were "merely drunk," are counted as brave, when in fact they are "mindless, brutish, and stupid."[55] "Signs of fear and fearlessness," in sum, are not reliable indicators of authentic bravery.[56] When it comes to Christ, therefore, it surely is foolish to deny the trepidation he felt as death loomed, for such things are born from natural instinct, as we have seen. Besides, Erasmus quips, such a denial would seem to ascribe to Christ "an impassive nature completely incapable of feeling pain," something at odds not only with the Gospel narratives but also with centuries of church teaching affirming his humanity.[57]

There may be rare individuals who have "sufficient strength of character to face death with a calm and resolute countenance," Erasmus concedes, men like the Athenian general Phocion and the philosopher Socrates, whose examples prove that "the human spirit may remain unconquered," especially among "the wise and the good."[58] Even if this is the case, however, Erasmus insists that individuals like these do not provide a useful measure for determining the presence of bravery, as their remarkable composure owes more to their unique "natural inclinations" and physical "make-up" than to some "moral principles" to which they cling. In any case, Erasmus observes, neither example fits the synoptic portrayals of Jesus' agony in the garden of Gethsemane, since Jesus appears to have been overwhelmed with dread, leading him to cry out with sheer despair. But neither dread nor despair are evident in the sporting demeanor of Phocion or the steadfast manner of Socrates, as both appear to have risen above this kind of emotional response as their executions approached. Jesus, by way of contrast, would seem to have had an emotional meltdown, if we are to go by the accounts in the synoptic gospels, so there is no point in comparing him with these illustrious ancients.

Perhaps there is a better parallel to be found in the classical story of the Stoic philosopher caught in a monstrous storm at sea.[59] As the tale is told by Aulus Gellius, when "ceaseless gales were hammering

---

55. Erasmus, *The Distress of Jesus*, CWE 70: 30–31.

56. See Erasmus, *The Distress of Jesus*, CWE 70: 34.

57. Erasmus, *The Distress of Jesus*, CWE 70: 32.

58. Erasmus, *The Distress of Jesus*, CWE 70: 33–34.

59. Erasmus takes the story and explanation from *Attic Nights*, 19.1.6–13.

the ship" and "typhoons threatening to send the ship under at any moment," the Stoic "turned white" with fear, even while a "nameless rogue" and worthless "libertine" who also was on board remained "quite unmoved by the danger." "Colet" is not impressed that the Stoic "turned pale," so Erasmus reminds him that—wise, learned, and brave though he was—the Stoic "could not, even so, cease to be human" in showing the emotional strain caused by the terrible tempest at sea.[60] A bit later, in fact, Erasmus has "Colet" defend the orthodox Stoic ideal of the unperturbed wise man who refuses "assent" to the forces of danger. And what "Colet" proposes is entirely in line with the explanation offered by Gellius, which he claims to be the "opinions and utterances" of Epictetus, to wit, that "the wise man, after being affected for a short time and slightly in his colour and expression, 'does not assent,' but retains the steadfastness and strength of the opinion" that such fearsome experiences ("visions") are "in no wise to be feared but excite terror by a false appearance and vain alarms."[61]

"The wise man may sometimes be terrified," "Colet" admits, but only "when some sudden vision of great evil assaults the senses and stirs up disorder in the mind before its ruler, reason, can pass judgment on it." But the wise Stoic "fears nothing," "Colet" continues, "since he believes nothing need be feared except evil," and death—which is "as natural as birth"—is "to be feared only by fools."[62] Against this backdrop, therefore, "Colet" complains that Erasmus has demeaned Christ by foisting a "dread of death" on him, though his death was "a work more pleasing to God and more meritorious than any other."[63] Besides, "Colet" continues, Jesus simply could not be terrified, since "nothing unexpected could assail his senses, as he had complete knowledge of everything." What appear to be cries of fear and agony, therefore, must be explained in other and nobler terms—perhaps that he agonized over

60. Erasmus, *The Distress of Jesus*, CWE 70: 29.

61. *Attic Nights*, 19.1.20. Gellius says that the Stoic who had survived the storm at sea showed him the "fifth book of the *Discourses* of the philosopher Epictetus" so that he would better understand the Stoic explanation why the Stoic at sea had suffered "that brief but inevitable and natural fear" (*Attic Nights*, 19.1.14). The account of Gellius is the only surviving source for this book purportedly from Epictetus.

62. Erasmus, *The Distress of Jesus*, CWE 70: 36.

63. Erasmus, *The Distress of Jesus*, CWE 70: 35–37.

the fate of the Jews, for instance, or that he feared for the destiny of his followers.[64]

The reply of Erasmus is complex but clever. He begins, interestingly enough, by requesting permission to "deviate" from Stoic teaching, which in this case would mean rethinking whether the Stoic ideal of the unperturbed wise man with which "Colet" is so enamored is suitable for understanding Christ's response to impending death. There is plenty of irony in Erasmus's request, for starters, as Dealy notes, because it is Erasmus himself who has constructed this dialogue between traditional and revised versions of Stoicism,[65] and again insofar as Erasmus's response to "Colet's" lengthy defense of traditional Stoic doctrine is a mirror image of "Colet's" impatient retort to Erasmus's Stoic-inspired argument that fear and dread are natural instincts. "Colet" had complained, "what are the Stoics to me, ... when I am discussing Christ?" Erasmus then responds to "Colet's" Stoic argument that death is not to be feared by asking, "how does that affect my case," when "Scripture teaches me that death is evil?"

So Erasmus knows well with whom he is arguing, and it certainly is not Colet but rather a Stoic-inspired theology that seeks—as does "Colet"—to immunize Christ from the emotional tarnish of fear and dread. In response, as we have seen, Erasmus offers an explanation that more fully captures what the biblical narratives recount, which is that, "as a real man" equipped with "the natural passions appropriate to mind and body," "Christ shrank from death as from something evil in itself,"[66] just as the Stoic wise man aboard the ship in the storm naturally turned pale because he very much was afraid for his life.[67] The standard Stoic ideal

64. Erasmus, *The Distress of Jesus*, CWE 70: 36–37.

65. Erasmus orchestrates a debate between "his own employment of Stoicism" and "the standpoint of orthodox Stoicism," as Dealy observes. The purpose of this debate, however, is not so much about Stoicism but in the service of Christology (Dealy, *The Stoic Origins*, 154, 163).

66. Erasmus, *The Distress of Jesus*, CWE 70: 37, 39. The same account is given of Jesus' "dread of death" in later works. See, for instance, Erasmus, *Paraphrase on Matthew*, CWE 45: 353–55; *Paraphrase on Mark*, trans. Erika Rummel, in *Collected Works of Erasmus: New Testament Scholarship*, vol. 49 (Toronto: University of Toronto Press, 1988), 163; and especially, *Paraphrase on Luke*, CWE 48: 198–99.

67. Erasmus effectively rewrites Gellius's story of the Stoic in the storm by insisting that the wise man underwent a full-blown emotional reaction to the tremendous danger. See Dealy, *The Stoic Origins*, 170–73.

of emotional equanimity, in sum, is ill-suited to explain the experiences of both Jesus and the Stoic in the storm.

The most stunning way in which "Colet" tries to deny that Jesus truly feared for his life appears when he compares Jesus' demise with the eager joy (*alacritas*) attributed to Christian martyrs as they heroically faced their executions. In the mind of "Colet," Jesus was "super-brave, a martyr of martyrs," as Dealy puts it, so that he overcame the fear of death with that "spirit of eagerness" typical of the martyr's "powerful love."[68] It is simply inconceivable, as "Colet" sees things, for Jesus to have "dreaded his own death," as then "his love for us would have been diminished" by being so selfishly focused on his personal welfare.[69] In response, Erasmus warns that it would have been "hard to believe that his death was real, had not his obvious dread of it been set before our eyes," and yet that is exactly what "Colet" denies when he pictures Jesus going through "the ordeal with eager joy on his face."[70]

The specter of docetism is clearly evident in "Colet's" efforts to equate Jesus and the martyrs, just as it was when he appealed to heroic bravery or Stoic constancy to describe Jesus' state of mind as death approached. All in all, it is nearly impossible for "Colet" to imagine that Jesus actually underwent the kind of natural experiences of fear and dread that mark the actual lives of human beings. But there is nothing in the Gospels to compare with "all the tales told of martyrs," Erasmus counters, though these same narratives go into some detail on Jesus' "grief, distress, [and] sweat."[71] Unlike "Colet," therefore, Erasmus highlights the terror exhibited by Jesus, recalling, for instance, that "Christ sweated blood, not just from his face but from every pore, and so freely that the drops trickled to the ground."[72] What is more, Erasmus adds, "his boundless charity made the pain of death no whit more bearable, so nothing lessened the intensity of his dread."[73] In the end, therefore, there is nothing of the eager joy attributed to martyrs to be found in the

---

68. Dealy, *The Stoic Origins*, 119; Erasmus, *The Distress of Jesus*, CWE 70: 44.

69. Erasmus, *The Distress of Jesus*, CWE 70: 44.

70. Erasmus, *The Distress of Jesus*, CWE 70: 65. See Dealy, *The Stoic Origins*, 142–47.

71. Erasmus, *The Distress of Jesus*, CWE 70: 46.

72. Erasmus, *The Distress of Jesus*, CWE 70: 44.

73. Erasmus, *The Distress of Jesus*, CWE 70: 47.

passion of Jesus. In fact, Erasmus observes, "the martyrs prayed for the very thing that the Saviour prayed to escape."[74]

With each of these arguments, Erasmus moves to challenge the kind of docetic denials at work—sometimes explicitly, sometimes subtly—in centuries of traditional Christology. While it is true, Erasmus grants, that some medieval theologians taught that Christ knew suffering beyond measure,[75] he rejects their view (which originated with Jerome) that Christ suffered only the beginnings of passion (called "propassion") rather than "full-fledged passions."[76] The trepidation and the pain that Jesus felt, Erasmus insists, not only "overtook" his mind, but "most violently overwhelmed it."[77] Even his initial sorrow was "as deep as could be and left him only along with life itself," so it makes no sense to say that his fear and despair were something small, preliminary, or limited. What is more, Erasmus suggests, with far more than his customary taste for speculative questions, Jesus' "divine nature was temporarily suspended and its redundance withdrawn," which would seem to mean that the divine powers resident "in his rational part did not overflow [*redundare*] into the sensible part of his soul."[78] In this "exceptional case," we are told, the "rational part" of his soul was "filled with matchless joy by his death," since it was "destined to ensure our salvation," and yet, Erasmus insists in a manner that once again seeks to affirm the integrity of human emotions, it "did not overflow into the sensible part of his soul" in order to diminish the natural dread of death.[79]

In fact, Erasmus contends, Jesus "had reason to fear death … even more keenly than anyone else," in part because of the incomparable

74. Erasmus, *The Distress of Jesus*, CWE 70: 46.

75. Bonaventure, for instance, argues that Christ suffered "a passion most comprehensive." *Breviloquium*, 170; see Thomas Aquinas, *The Summa Theologica*, part III, qu. 46, art. 6, titled "whether the pain of Christ's passion was greater than all other pains."

76. Dealy, *The Stoic Origins*, 156, 163, 185, and 221–30.

77. Erasmus, *The Distress of Jesus*, CWE 70: 56.

78. Erasmus, *The Distress of Jesus*, CWE 70: 57, 63–64. See also 54. As Fokke writes, "the *suspensio divinitas* and the *privatio redundantiae*" are the "key-stones in the structure of Erasmus's christology," as they are the "essence of Christ's kenosis for our sake in its two main aspects" ("An Aspect of the Christology of Erasmus," 183).

79. Erasmus, *The Distress of Jesus*, CWE 70: 64. Unlike "Colet," Erasmus denies Jesus the outward signs of "eager joy," though he insists that we "must allow to him, and to him alone, an inward joy unmatched by all the martyrs" (23). Erasmus later writes that Jesus "rejoiced inwardly" that the time had come "when by his death he would reconcile humankind to himself as God" (57). Here Erasmus introduces a remarkable degree of insulation—certainly bordering on separation—between the human and the divine in the psychology of Jesus.

nobility of his life and in part because of his "complete foreknowledge of every detail of his torments."[80] What is more, we are told quite remarkably, Jesus took on a body that was "less tolerant of cold, heat, fatigue, hunger, and pain than any body has ever been," and he "assumed a soul that was endowed with the most acute sensitivity in every one of it faculties."[81] To make matters yet more severe, Erasmus insists that Jesus did not allow himself any of the natural means—born of "human constancy and strength of mind"—by which "he might have banished, or eased considerably, the dejection and perhaps even the pain he felt."[82] Nor, Erasmus continues, did Jesus "avail himself of the blessing with which ... he was richly endowed," including "the enjoyment of divinity," to lessen the intensity of his suffering.[83]

Such statements from Erasmus clearly serve to magnify the "physical ailment" and "mental anguish" felt by Jesus, especially with both natural and divine remedies excluded, so it is understandable that "Colet" would demand to know—"somewhat testily," Erasmus observes—"what is the point ... of heaping upon Christ this pile of heart-rending woes?" The answer of Erasmus is two-fold. On the one hand, as we will see in the final section of this chapter, magnifying the degree of Christ's suffering serves to underscore the "incomparable charity" by which human beings are redeemed.[84] On the other hand, in direct response to the tendency of "Colet" to minimize the agony of Christ's passion, Erasmus hopes to remove as much as possible any traces of docetic denial of the humanity of Christ.

80. Erasmus, *The Distress of Jesus*, CWE 70: 25–26.

81. Erasmus, *The Distress of Jesus*, CWE 70: 54. As Erasmus puts it with amazing emphasis and detail, "his body took the full impact of every single blow; a thousand fell on him and he felt each one, every single one, as though it were the only one. He felt every conceivable bodily ailment as keenly as if his mind were suffering nothing; likewise, he felt every kind of mental anguish as keenly as if his body were not in pain" (54–55).

82. Erasmus, *The Distress of Jesus*, CWE 70: 54. As Erasmus points out, "we find various ways to soften the blows of everyday misfortune: we find reasons or precedents that encourage us to bear them more bravely, we divert our thoughts from troubles towards something more pleasant, or we contemplate the rewards of suffering, or the merits of the one for whose love we are suffering." Indeed, he continues, there is a "natural, commonplace 'redundance' [overflow]... through which pain yields to pleasure, or one pain blots out another. For example, you do not notice the loss of a penny if you have just made ten pounds, and you do not feel a pinprick if simultaneously your arm is broken with a cudgel" (54).

83. Erasmus, *The Distress of Jesus*, CWE 70: 55.

84. Erasmus, *The Distress of Jesus*, CWE 70: 55–57, 47.

And yet, curiously enough, these very efforts to highlight the humanity of Christ make him increasingly and uniquely unlike us even in the very experiences that make him so recognizably human. There is clearly something extraordinary at work in this figure, even as he is thoroughly human in his emotional life, and yet, we get a glimpse of his divine character, Erasmus suggests, only when attending to the unusually intense human suffering he endured. When Erasmus dares to offer an accounting of this most perplexing fact—ultimately the most mysterious, if not simply the most inscrutable of Christological questions— he appears to backtrack somewhat in his campaign against docetism.

It is true, Erasmus writes, that Christ took on "human woes" like "fear, dread, and alarm," though "all these emotions dwelt within him quite separately from his divine nature and in no way impeded the readiness of his spirit." Nor, Erasmus continues in the same vein, did they "in any way disturb his composure" or "dim the joy his soul found in endless contemplation of the divine." Nor, for that matter, did these traumatic passions "diminish the pleasure his soul felt at the prospect of humanity's salvation."[85] So there appears to be a significant separation—a psychological firewall, as it were—between the human agony and the divine spirit that remains perfectly serene and joyful.[86] And yet, Erasmus quickly adds in a manner that shows his confidence in the logic of Chalcedonian Christology, one need not fear trying to "combine in him complete dread and perfect eagerness, sublime joy and intense pain, supreme bliss and extreme suffering," though he is well aware of just how difficult it can be to make sense out of all such combinations without allowing at least some degree of separation; precisely this kind of tension remains evident in his own accounts.

In a nod to the kind of Christology favored by Colet, in fact, where the dignity of the divine stands well above the squalid world of human weakness and suffering, Erasmus readily grants that Christ "*could have* avoided any such burden of fear," as he already possessed "the perfect knowledge, contemplation, and enjoyment of the Godhead." Then again, in the same tone, these same "delights *might easily have*

---

85. Erasmus, *The Distress of Jesus*, CWE 70: 53.
86. On the presence of this Christological firewall in *The Distress of Jesus*, see Dealy, *The Stoic Origins*, 182–83, 243–44.

lifted all such burdens from both body and mind," had he "not chosen to make an exception, in his pity for us, and to spare himself nothing to relieve the misery of our human condition." Certainly, too, Erasmus asserts, "the fiery flames of love so filled his mind that … they alone *would have* sufficed to banish from him not only fear but any feeling of pain." Then, again, we are told, the "powerful joy" that "filled his mind" because "humankind was to be restored," "*could easily have* driven out all troublesome thoughts."[87]

So "Colet" is correct, as far as it goes, in accentuating the divinity of Christ and emphasizing his potential immunity from fear and pain, and thus, Erasmus surely grants (again using the past tense modal), that Christ *could have* avoided the fear and agony of a gruesome death *if* he had wished to do so. But then—most importantly and returning to his usual points of emphasis—Erasmus asserts that Jesus did not avail himself of this power. Instead, as we have seen throughout this chapter, Christ embraces human life with all its natural passions and problems, and he does so, as we shall now see, with incomparable charity.

"Extraordinary Generosity"

The Distress of Jesus culminates as a debate between two contrasting views of the immense love of God for humankind at work in the life and death of Jesus. To be sure, as we have seen, many other things are addressed in detail: the presence or absence of fear and dread in the emotional life of Jesus; whether or not divinity serves to mitigate or intensify his suffering; and the status of nature, especially of natural instinct, in his cry of despair as execution loomed. The take of Erasmus on these topics, clearly enough, involves a resolute affirmation of the natural humanity of Jesus. He "leaves nature unscathed,"[88] Erasmus declares with some pride, but also with a bit of overstatement, as this is no small accomplishment in Christology, where the temptation to let the divine overwhelm the natural is commonplace. It is interesting to note, however, that both "Colet" and Erasmus place divine love at the center of their accounts of Jesus' passion and death, though for "Colet," divine

87. Erasmus, *The Distress of Jesus*, CWE 70: 53–54, my italics.
88. Erasmus, *The Distress of Jesus*, CWE 70: 66.

love overrides all human weakness, while for Erasmus, the frailty of Jesus' humanity serves as the optimal portal for discerning the immense love of God. Though *The Distress of Jesus* is an early work of Erasmus, it nonetheless gives an excellent account of what will be an enduring insistence on the humanity of Christ, and with that, it initiates what will be a lasting emphasis on the transformative impact of Christ's love for living a life of gentleness, patience, and kindness.

In their early conversations, Colet found Erasmus to be a "clever and eloquent man," someone whose arguments were "brilliantly expressed and resourceful, rather than true."[89] Erasmus was a talented rhetorician, in other words, but wide of the mark when it comes to questions of piety. In *The Distress of Jesus*, "Colet" once again compliments Erasmus's "pretty speech," wryly noting that it makes "the best of a bad case," but then complaining that it commits a "slight on Jesus' perfect charity" by suggesting that Jesus "dreaded his own death." It may be natural to dread one's death, "Colet" concedes, but "the role of charity is to surmount nature and bring it to perfection."[90] "Hunger is one of nature's sternest tests," for example, "but exceptional love can shrug off its pangs," just as it can "make death itself desirable and even pleasant."[91] But if that is true for ordinary lovers, "Colet" argues, then it must be all the more true for Christ, whose love was "so warm and so immense that all the loves of the whole human race fused into one could not compare." Indeed, "Colet" concludes, "the power of love" drove out all the human frailty assumed by Christ, thereby producing for him "a quite different kind of existence." "Perfect charity and craven

---

89. John Colet to Erasmus, letter 110, CWE 1: 211–12.

90. Erasmus, *The Distress of Jesus*, CWE 70: 41. Elsewhere, Colet speaks of Christ as the "measure" and "standard" for the one striving for perfection. See *John Colet's Commentary on First Corinthians*, trans. Bernard O'Kelly and Catherine A. L. Jarrott (Binghamton, NY: Medieval and Renaissance Texts and Studies, 1985), 141. Commenting on 1 Corinthians 13, Colet writes that "charity inflames us to perfection, that being perfect we may be pleasing to God." And "perfection is, indeed, charity" (*John Colet's Commentary*, 257–59). See also John Colet, *An Exposition of St. Paul's Epistle to the Romans*, trans. J. H. Lupton (Eugene, Ore.: Wipf and Stock; replicated from the edition by Bell and Daldy, 1873), 28–29, 68–70. The ideal of perfection in the spirituality of Colet is well-expressed in John Colet to Erasmus, letter 593, CWE 4: 398, where he writes, "My dear Erasmus, of books and knowledge there is no end. Nothing can be better, in view of this brief life of ours, than that we should live a holy and pure life and use our best endeavours every day to become pure and enlightened and perfect"—something that proceeds only "by the fervent love and imitation of Jesus."

91. Erasmus, *The Distress of Jesus*, CWE 70: 41.

fear" simply do not mix, "Colet" adds, but that is what Erasmus has done with his "impertinent case" dressed up in all "the fine colours of rhetoric."[92]

After dismissing "Colet's" quip concerning his eloquence, Erasmus offers an alternative conception of Christ's love that is designed not to overcome pain and dread but to voluntarily enter into it with patience and endurance. For starters, Erasmus grants that "it is the nature of love to make things appear sweet that are intrinsically bitter," and he concurs that "Christ's charity was so much more complete than ours that they cannot be compared."[93] "Colet" goes wrong, Erasmus argues, when he combines these two propositions. "If you measure Christ's charity by its effectiveness in blotting out painful sensations," he writes to "Colet," then you in fact are "belittling his love by your diligent but ill-advised efforts to extol it," first, because boldly facing danger and gladly accepting pain are things any crazed lover might manage, so the comparison does nothing to magnify the perfection of Christ's love; second, because in fact Christ showed terror and agony more than even the "greatest coward" might have done, so that would leave him among some unsavory company; and third, because Christ demonstrated none of that "eager joy" for which the martyrs are so famous, which curiously enough, would mean that "the martyrs love more ardently than Christ."[94] What this adds up to, Erasmus concludes, is that "Christ's incomparable charity cannot properly be judged by the criteria" suggested by "Colet."[95] A "more reliable criterion," Erasmus suggests, is to be found in the "underlying cause" that moved Christ to love "in the face of insults and abuse" and then ultimately "to pay, freely, with his death." His love is "sublime," as Erasmus puts it, precisely because it chose voluntarily to "coexist with extreme pain" and "extreme dread" for the sake of humankind.[96]

It is a central contention of "Colet" that Christ's prayer for "deliverance from the cup of death" is attributable "to anything but the dread of

90. Erasmus, *The Distress of Jesus*, CWE 70: 42.
93. Erasmus, *The Distress of Jesus*, CWE 70: 42–43.
94. Erasmus, *The Distress of Jesus*, CWE 70: 43–47.
95. Erasmus, *The Distress of Jesus*, CWE 70: 47.
96. Erasmus, *The Distress of Jesus*, CWE 70: 48–49. See Godin, "Introduction," ASD V - 7: 199–200.

death." Because it is "one of love's unique and fundamental qualities" to "take thought of others" while neglecting one's "own concerns," "Colet" concludes that it would be a "slight to the Redeemer's charity" if his concern was first and foremost for himself.[97] Praying for deliverance from death, in fact, would suggest a "man who was self-centered," and that would hardly be "evidence of an all-consuming love."[98] In response, Erasmus recalls that the distress and dread shown by Jesus were integral to the natural condition he assumed, though at this point he joins "Colet" in acknowledging that Christ "recoiled from his own death, but for our sake, not his own." The same is true, by way of example, when Jesus was hungry, as his hunger certainly was part of the nature he assumed," even while he assumed it "willingly for our sake—and also for love."[99] "Whatever disabilities" that came with the nature he adopted, including "his dread, his distress, [and] his bloody sweat," "cannot but be attributed to his free will and to his spontaneous love." In fact, Erasmus insists with particular emphasis, "the more woes you assign to him (though not those tainted with sin or shame), the more you increase and glorify the Saviour's love."[100] The "disabilities" that came with the nature he assumed—the very things from which "Colet" would like to insulate Christ—must be attributed to his free and gracious love.[101] For Erasmus, finally, everything about the incarnation finally is rooted in divine love.

It is exactly at this point that Erasmus issues the ultimate challenge in his dialogue with "Colet." "Which one of us," he asks, "is diminishing his love?" Is it "Colet," who denies that he felt "dread of death?" Or is it Erasmus, who holds that, "for love of us, he did not refuse even that?" Posing the same challenge again, but now set against a larger contrast between docetic and orthodox Christologies, Erasmus inquires who

---

97. Erasmus, *The Distress of Jesus*, CWE 70: 15, 41. "Colet" normally says that Jesus feared that his death would "prove fatal to the Jews" (15–16). More broadly put, he is made to ascribe to Jesus a concern for "the death of the Jews, the destruction of Jerusalem, the desertion of the shocked disciples, and the suffering of the martyrs" (22).

98. Erasmus, *The Distress of Jesus*, CWE 70: 49, 22. As Fokke puts it, Colet's yardstick for "true moral greatness" pivots on the distinction between love of self and lover for others, so he can only account for Christ's distress in terms of his love for "his kinspeople the Jews" ("An Aspect of the Christology of Erasmus," 180).

99. Erasmus, *The Distress of Jesus*, CWE 70: 49.

100. Erasmus, *The Distress of Jesus*, CWE 70: 49–50.

101. Erasmus, *The Distress of Jesus*, CWE 70: 50.

did "the most harm to his love": was it those who "ascribe to him a body and a soul insensible to pain?" Or is it those who insist that one cannot subtract emotions like fear and dread from the total without "belittling the Redeemer's love?" Erasmus's preference for the latter is clear, though it is interesting to find him at this point willing to agree with "Colet" that it does great justice to Christ's love to say that he was "exceedingly glad of his death, but grieved for the destruction of the Jews and the desertion of the disciples."

Both are true, Erasmus acknowledges, though he would go further by asserting, along the lines of "Colet's" thinking, that "Jesus' mind was less deeply troubled by the pain that racked his body than he was by our sins," and, too, that "he was more profoundly grieved by the loss of a single soul than by the scourges, the nails, [and] the cross."[102] So Erasmus readily includes the kind of broader loves cited by "Colet," because along with the "natural cause" for Jesus' sorrow, they "flow from the same source, namely, charity." His "grief over the death of other people" surely was "an act of love," Erasmus agrees, but so, too, were "his alarm and distress when, as a vulnerable human being, he saw death draw near to him." And it is precisely here that we discover an important key to the Christology of Erasmus, to wit, that "the greater his vulnerability, his despair, [and] his acceptance of our common frailty, the greater the love he showed in assuming it of his own free will."[103] In a word, the fuller and deeper the incarnation, the greater the love that is revealed.

The ultimate purpose of Christ's death, Erasmus tells us in traditional language, "was to atone for many other deaths and to wash away the sins of the world."[104] He does not provide an explanation as to the meaning of this "atonement," any more than he pursues a theoretical account of the claim that the death of Jesus was "destined to ensure our salvation."[105] As we have seen throughout this book, Erasmus freely

102. Erasmus, *The Distress of Jesus*, CWE 70: 50.

103. Erasmus, *The Distress of Jesus*, CWE 70: 50. In this regard, A. Godin rightly observes that Erasmus underscores "the realism of the Incarnation," thereby initiating—as we saw in chapter 6—a discussion on the very "truth of the Incarnation" that was revisited in Erasmus's controversy with Lefèvre ("Introduction," ASD V - 7: 203).

104. Erasmus, *The Distress of Jesus*, CWE 70: 55–56.

105. Erasmus, *The Distress of Jesus*, CWE 70: 64. A very brief explanation is found in the *Explanation of the Creed*, where Erasmus says that Christ's love was bent on wiping out "all the crimes of the human race" but also to "show the road by which one must reach eternal glory"

employs all sorts of language drawn from scripture and tradition, without being wed for systematic reasons to each and every term. This is a most open and varied approach, to be sure, but it is not one that will satisfy the demands of those hungry for systematic precision. With that said, however, it is clear that an Erasmian understanding of redemption—meaning, the manner in which the life, teaching, and death of Christ are said to function in a salvific manner for human beings—consistently lays emphasis on what he calls the "restoration of humanity."[106] What this entails will be discussed in detail in the final chapter of this book, where the focus will rest on the various senses of peace offered by Christ. Ultimately, as we will see, these forms of peace are the ethical substance of the *scopus* for life that is embodied in Christ, and hence the antidote for the corrupt inversions of human existence discussed in the first chapter. For now, however, it should be emphasized that, in Erasmus's view of things, the death of Jesus, like his life and teachings, bears a transformative impact on human life as actually lived.

The death of Jesus is described by Erasmus, somewhat paradoxically, as the "wellspring of life" for humankind.[107] What is curious in this statement, of course, is that a grizzly execution is said to be the source of something truly life-giving, though once again Erasmus takes no steps to explain this reversal of meaning with a traditional theory of atonement. Instead, as we have seen, he speaks of Jesus' dread of death as an extraordinary "*example* of gentleness, patience, and obedience," thereby "setting us an *example* to love and to emulate." In his agony and death, Erasmus continues, we encounter an *example* of "charity and gentleness"—the very "lineaments of humanity," as he calls it—"not the

---

(*Explanation of the Creed*, CWE 70: 303–4). Erasmus freely admits, however, that he is simply "dealing with the basics, not with the high points," since this text is meant for "instructing a catechumen, not a theologian." So there is no attempt made to clarify what is meant by "eternal glory" (300). Brief discussions of "eternal life" and "heavenly salvation" are scattered throughout the *Paraphrases*, though they remain largely exegetical by reflecting the text being read. See, for instance, Erasmus, *Paraphrase on John*, CWE 46: 49 on "everlasting life" in John 3:16; the repeated references to the "treasure in heaven" for those who believe in the "divine and salvific philosophy" of Christ in *Paraphrase on Matthew*, CWE 45: 121, 164, 167, and 187, for instance; ubiquitous mention of "eternal salvation" in Erasmus, *Paraphrase on Luke*, CWE 47: 17, 33, 65, 154, 275, for instance; and *Paraphrase on Luke*, CWE 48: 9, 94, 124, 156, 177, 202, and 219. For a brief review of the soteriology of Erasmus, See Payne, *Erasmus: His Theology of the Sacraments*, 71–97.

106. Erasmus, *The Distress of Jesus*, CWE 70: 63.

107. Erasmus, *The Distress of Jesus*, CWE 70: 64.

trappings of divinity" and certainly not a spectacular show of power.[108] In speaking of Jesus' agony and death as an example, Erasmus most certainly is not extolling the virtues of pain and death, as if these things were worthy of imitation;[109] but neither, in using the word "example," does he intend a mere instance of love or even a simple role model to be copied. He means, instead, that the incomparable love for humanity embodied in Christ's voluntary and gracious self-sacrifice is a paradigm for imitation with the power to transform the shape of human life.

It is, as we have seen in the preceding chapters, each of which deals with later works than *The Distress of Jesus*, a most robust kind of example, one that embodies the capacity to affect people in a transformative way. Christ's "extraordinary generosity," for starters, is said to be "a powerful example" given "to *inspire* even the coldest of hearts to love, and *encourage* the most sluggish to emulate it for the health of their souls."[110] Along the same lines, Erasmus adds, Christ's "charity toward us"—his "inestimable charity" and the "boundless love" with which he dove into the frailty and misery of human life—"*inspires* [us] to love him in return," thereby *inviting* people into a relationship of imitation in which we emulate his charity in the way we live with others.[111]

Far from being a mere sketch of the life we should live, therefore, the divine love incarnate in the agony and death of Jesus is said by Erasmus to be a "powerful, salutary, and life-saving medicine" delivered for the "restoration of humanity."[112] What Erasmus means by a "medicine," however, is not a magical elixir for the human condition, the kind of miraculous remedies expected by many Christians, but rather an

---

108. Erasmus, *The Distress of Jesus*, CWE 70: 64, my italics. See Dealy, *The Stoic Origins*, 180–81.

109. Unlike certain currents of popular piety and devotional literature of the day, where physical suffering was encouraged in the imitation of Christ, Erasmus places the emphasis on the emulation of self-giving love and not on the active pursuit of pain. In this respect, as O'Malley observes, *The Distress of Jesus* served as a "silent criticism of the darker aspects of popular piety in his day" ("Introduction," CWE 70: xiii). See also Dealy, *The Stoic Origins*, 246–55.

110. Erasmus, *The Distress of Jesus*, CWE 70: 55–56, my italics. Christ's love was "kenotic in all its aspects as a sign of his absolute humility. He wanted to be an example of complete humanity for mankind, not a superhuman being" (Fokke, "An Aspect of the Christology of Erasmus," 180).

111. Erasmus, *The Distress of Jesus*, CWE 70: 64, my italics. On Christ's "example of meekness, obedience, patience and peace" as the founding source of "a sound, moral life," see Fokke, "An Aspect of the Christology of Erasmus," 183.

112. Erasmus, *The Distress of Jesus*, CWE 70: 63–64.

inspiring invitation and supportive encouragement to active imitation of the love shown by Christ for humanity. What Erasmus has in mind by this "restoration," as we will see in the next chapter, is both a gift, in as much as its revelation is the fruit of God's "charity toward us," and a task, insofar as it remains an ideal possibility to be realized through active endeavor. What is more, as a "restoration," it points backwards (so to speak) as a recovery of a lost state of human innocence displayed in living form as a "perfect man" in Jesus, and it points forward, as a goal for the ethical transformation of human life.

CHAPTER 8

The Peace of Christ and the Christ of Peace

The Christology of Erasmus culminates in reflection on the ways in which Christ may be said to redeem or rectify the corrupted condition of human life. This, in a nutshell, is the point of Christology for Erasmus: to speak of the "works" of Christ in a manner that highlights their potential for transforming the twisted and broken character of human existence, while second-order discussions concerning the divinity and humanity of Christ (the topics addressed in chapters 4 through 7) serve mainly to undergird the salutary potential for redemption found in Christ's life and death. To speak of redemption, of course, assumes a world in need of rescue and rejuvenation, and this is precisely where the reflections of Erasmus begin, as we saw in the first chapter. Recall from that point of departure how, for Erasmus, the world as we find it is twisted, inverted, and corrupted; for exactly those reasons, it should be noted, the world also is marked by pervasive and persistent conflict which seriously diminishes human life across the board.

Think, for instance, of the brutality and devastation of military warfare, which Erasmus describes in graphic detail,[1] but consider, as well, the manifold forms of hostility infecting social life; the virulent disputes over the reform of religious life; the "feuds and quarrels" plaguing monastic culture; the "secret dissension and rivalry" at work in the courts of princes; the "insane" warfare fought by scholars with their "poisoned pens"; and the strife so apparent in many marriages.[2] What is more, Erasmus adds, individuals suffer from a "battlefield within," where "reason is at war with the passions and these are in conflict with each other."[3] So at its very core, we come to see, human existence is marked by a chronic condition of hostility and conflict—both personally and socially—and given that twisted and fractured state of being, it is sundered from God as well. All in all, as Erasmus describes it, humanity stands in desperate need of remediation, and, as we have come to expect, he directs us to Christ as the source of that restoration.

Erasmus frequently speaks of the redemptive impact of Christ on human existence, and he does so—as is his manner—with an ample variety of imagery drawn from traditional sources. Christ is "our victory," Erasmus writes in a pastoral vein, "our hope and security," who took upon himself "all the evils that were owed to us," and having "diminished their strength and having given us the extra strength of the spirit," points "the way to [our] victory" over mortal afflictions.[4] Elsewhere,

1. Erasmus, *Complaint of Peace*, CWE 27: 296, where Erasmus vividly describes people's "frenzy for mutual extinction." Indeed, Erasmus writes, "the princes wage war unscathed and their generals thrive on it, while the main flood of misfortune"—namely, "pillaging, bloodshed, disaster, and destruction"—"sweeps over the peasants and humble citizens, who have no interest in war and gave no occasion for it" (312). Compare Erasmus, "War is a treat," CWE 35: 403–4. On Erasmus's criticisms of war, see Ross Dealy, "The Dynamics of Erasmus' Thought on War," *Erasmus of Rotterdam Society Yearbook* 4, no. 1 (1984): 53–67.

2. Erasmus, *Complaint of Peace*, CWE 27: 296–98. Recall also Erasmus's account through Folly's clever eyes of "the countless hordes of mortals" quarreling and bickering among themselves, a wild show that is sometimes funny, often pathetic, though frequently alarming" (*Praise of Folly*, CWE 27: 122). Erasmus gives the battles of humanity a linguistic turn, when he notes how "the deadly sickness of a malicious tongue has infected the whole world with its awful venom, pervading the courts of princes, the homes of commoners, theological schools, monastic brotherhoods, colleges of priests, regiments of soldiers, and the cottages of peasants." See Erasmus to Krzysztof Szydlowiecki, letter 1593 and dedicatory letter to *The Tongue*, CWE 29: 259.

3. Erasmus, *Complaint of Peace*, CWE 27: 298–99. On the interior battle against vices, see Erasmus, "War is a treat," CWE 35: 424. Much earlier, Erasmus describes the life of individuals as consumed with "unremitting warfare," where one is attacked from without by the vices of the world and threatened from within by our own worst instincts. See Erasmus, *Handbook of the Christian Soldier*, CWE 66: 24–25.

4. Erasmus, *Preparing for Death*, CWE 70: 399.

Erasmus speaks figuratively of Jesus as "our good physician"—indeed, as that "heavenly physician"—who with "indescribable mercy" and "all-welcoming goodness" heals those suffering from various "diseases of the soul" by exorcizing the vicious demons that possess them.[5] Then again, quite often in fact, Erasmus deems Christ as "the teacher of salvific philosophy," that "truly salvific and efficacious philosophy" by which people can "attain true godliness and true happiness."[6]

The fact is that Erasmus freely employs each of these images, and many more, to convey the restorative works of Christ, though some (like Christ the teacher) garner more emphasis, while others (Christ our victory, to name just one) are piously mentioned but never come to play a central role in his Christology. However, one way by which Erasmus depicts the works of Christ—namely, that Christ is the *scopus* of human life—proves to be especially well suited to getting at the heart of what Erasmus thinks of the redemptive significance of Christ's life and death.[7] When Erasmus speaks of Christ as the *scopus* for human life, after all—at once its ultimate goal, its most effective pattern, and its enduring measure—he indicates a possibility for reversing the crippling inversions which plague human life, as we saw in the first chapter, but his choice of terms also highlights a process for healing the fractious divisions and pacifying the furious conflicts so common in human affairs. The substance of Christ as *scopus*—its essential meaning and ultimate character, in short—is peace with God, peace within oneself, and peace between people.

The purpose of this chapter, consequently, is to engage Erasmus's understanding of the "gospel of peace"[8] and specifically to clarify how

---

5. Erasmus, *Paraphrase on Luke*, CWE 47: 154–59, 169–78. The miracles of Jesus, Erasmus writes, "contained a figure and representation of what was being carried out in human hearts," so his readings of these stories naturally stress the pattern of Jesus' healing activity. On Jesus as the "purifier of all" and the one who takes away the "diseases of the soul," see Erasmus, *Paraphrase on Matthew*, CWE 45: 140–45, 150, and 155–56.

6. Erasmus, *Paraphrase on Matthew*, CWE 45: 30, 83. Reflecting his own view of sound education, Erasmus notes of Jesus' pedagogy that "it is the mark of a good teacher to lower himself to the capacity of those who he is instructing" (77). See also CWE 45: 157–58. Erasmus speaks in a similar manner of Jesus as an "extraordinary and mighty teacher" in *Paraphrase on Luke*, CWE 47: 144.

7. Recall the passages on Christ as *scopus* discussed in chapter 1 of this book, including Erasmus to Paul Volz, CWE 6: 82, 90; *Paraphrase on Philippians*, CWE 43: 384; and *Handbook of the Christian Soldier*, CWE 66: 61.

8. See Erasmus to Archduke Ferdinand, letter 1333, CWE 9: 242.

the Christ of peace, as the *scopus* of human life, may be said to transform, redeem, and enhance human existence. Discerning exactly what this means, however, is anything but simple, as Christ is revealed in startling guises and through puzzling figures, as we saw in chapters 2 and 3, and, what is more, speculative debates on the transcendent sublimity of Christ do little to explain the potential for redemption offered in his life and death, as was evident in chapter 4. What is clear, however, is the manner in which Erasmus repeatedly and emphatically seeks to affirm the incarnational trajectory of divine love for the sake of restoring the corrupted condition of humanity. Indeed, as chapter 5 showed, the "heavenly Word (*sermo*)" which springs eternally from the Father, is rendered by Erasmus as a living and breathing *scopus* that beckons people to a godly and virtuous life; then again, as we have seen in chapters 6 and 7, Erasmus offers a robust affirmation of the humanity of Christ, where his immense mercy and incomparable love for humanity bequeath to us an exemplary model of gentleness, patience, and kindness for the living of radically transformed lives. The peace of Christ, in other words, represents a very different way of being human, and the Christ of peace, as Erasmus explains it, is the incarnate source by which the goal and measure for such a life are set before us as invitation and challenge.

What Erasmus has in mind by the life of peace is both complex and multifaceted, but fundamentally, it is a manner of handling our lives—within the confines of individual conscience, through the social interchanges of our lives together, and in the spiritual life before God—that enriches and ennobles human life and culture. Erasmus takes his start with recourse to the scriptural accounts of the life and death of Jesus. This is the bedrock of Erasmus's Christology of peace, where the teachings of Jesus are read as a "lesson in concord and mutual love,"[9] yielding thereby an ethic of "friendship among many people,"[10] though, as we will see in the first section of this chapter, Erasmus also must come to terms with the stories of conflict and statements of division attributed to Jesus. The peace bestowed on humanity by Christ, as

---

9. Erasmus, *Complaint of Peace*, CWE 27: 299, 300. See also Erasmus, "War is a treat," CWE 35: 425.

10. Erasmus, "War is a treat," CWE 35: 412.

Erasmus describes it, is said to be a fundamental "restoration" of human nature[11]—what the tradition generally has deemed "salvation"—and this transformation carries both ethical and eschatological senses. Rooted in what Erasmus calls the "immense mercy of God," this transformative peace is conveyed through the prompting and stirring of a divine exemplar incarnate in human life, as well as by the scriptural testimonies to his life and message, though, as we will see in the second section, it is for Erasmus a gracious form of divine agency that must be met with at least some degree of human resolve and effort.

Erasmus describes what the resulting life of peace might look like on both a personal and a social level, and in both cases, his proposals are highly promising and yet extraordinarily demanding. For individuals, the peace of Christ is described by Erasmus as the peace of a good conscience, something received in faith and then flowering in love for others, and, as will be evident in the third section, Erasmus offers us vivid profiles of this manner of living—what he audaciously depicts as Christian Epicureans—in selected *Colloquies*. On a far broader scale, as we will see in the final section of this chapter and this book, Erasmus depicts peace as the dynamic flourishing of life across the spheres of human endeavor; to that end, he counsels the cultivation of those virtues that allow for the tempering of hostility and the bridging of differences between nations. With this material, we encounter the political import of the Christology of Erasmus.

"A True and Perfect Friendship"

"Survey the life of Christ from start to finish," Erasmus asks in the *Complaint of Peace*, and what else is it but a lesson in concord and mutual love?" Or, put a bit differently, "what else did he teach and expound but peace?"[12] With these rhetorical questions, Erasmus underscores the centrality of peace in the teachings and actions of Jesus. In fact, Erasmus insists with yet another such question: was it not the entire purpose of the incarnation of the "Son of God" to function as a divine

---

11. Recall Erasmus, *The Distress of Jesus*, CWE 70: 63.

12. Erasmus, *Complaint of Peace*, CWE 27: 299–300. Compare the similar statement in Erasmus, "War is a treat," CWE 35: 417.

agent of peace; "to reconcile the world with the Father"; "to bind men together with mutual and indestructible love"; and "finally, to make men his own friend?"[13]

The first element in this description points to the fundamentally transcendent (and likely eschatological) reconciliation of the world to God "through Christ's ministry." By dissolving the penalty for past sins, Erasmus explains in quite traditional terms, God restores "to newness the world he had once created through him."[14] With the second element, however, Erasmus highlights what is for him a central and ever-recurring emphasis on Christ's love as the force that "binds men together" in a community of peace. It is "peace with unanimity" that Christ encourages through gentleness and mutual forgiveness, Erasmus emphasizes, so those who would live in imitation of Christ are to live together in loving harmony.[15] But then, additionally, Erasmus adds a third reason for the incarnation, to wit, that Christ wished "to make men his own friend." With this point, Erasmus employs the language of "friendship," which, as we will see shortly, is essential to his understanding of the life of peace, but he does so in this context specifically to underscore that "Christ asks for his people a special sort of concord," one in which "they unite among themselves to foster peace" through concerted action.[16] The peace of Christ, in short, is to have a revitalizing effect on the entire course of human life, such that those who join with Christ as friends commit themselves in "common purpose" to social "concord" through tolerance, love, and gentleness.[17]

The Christ of peace, as Erasmus tell it, is the incarnate exemplar of a way of life premised on forgiveness and love; as such, we are told, Christ points the way to ultimate peace—that "sum total of happiness"—with

13. Erasmus, *Complaint of Peace*, CWE 27: 300.

14. Erasmus, *Paraphrase on Second Corinthians*, CWE 43: 232. Erasmus similarly calls Jesus the "supremely good shepherd who has reconciled the fallen human race to the Father, paying out of his own resources the penalty that we earned" (*Paraphrase on Luke*, CWE 48: 71–72).

15. Erasmus, *Complaint of Peace*, CWE 27: 302–3. On the centrality of forgiveness in Erasmus's reading of the Lord's Prayer, see Hilmar M. Pabel, "The Prince of Peace: Erasmus' Conception of Jesus," in *The Unbounded Community; Papers in Christian Ecumenism in Honor of Jaroslav Pelikan*, ed. William Cafferro and Duncan G. Fisher (New York: Garland Publishing, 1996), 137–39.

16. Erasmus, *Complaint of Peace*, CWE 27: 300–301. Thus, Erasmus writes in paraphrase of Christ in John 15:13–16, "I have called you friends because I have once and for all shared the whole intention of my heart with you" (*Paraphrase on John*, CWE 46: 179).

17. Erasmus, *Complaint of Peace*, CWE 27: 302–3; "War is a treat," CWE 35: 417.

an exhortation to live together in friendship and harmony. As thoroughly positive as this description certainly is meant to be, Erasmus is fully aware that the Gospel narratives do not always cast Jesus in such a rosy light. Luke and Matthew, for example, depict Jesus confronting his listeners with the stark declaration that he has come not to bring peace but to stir up division, with Matthew remarking that he does this with a "sword" (Mt 10:34), while Luke adds ominously that he had brought "fire" to the earth (Lk 12:51). Both Gospels continue by stressing that such divisions will rip through households, separating those otherwise united in the most familiar bond. Neither of these passages sound gentle and loving, to say the least; in fact, they sound downright aggressive and hostile. Along the same lines, moreover, one must not overlook the accounts of Jesus' many rancorous exchanges with the Pharisees, where he routinely rebukes their arrogance and hypocrisy. Here again, it must be acknowledged, Jesus appears more aggressive and combative than gentle and kind.

When Erasmus deals with these passages, however, the words of Jesus are not read as failures of his message of peace, as if his cause was not what it purports to be but rather as the inevitable frictions generated from the challenge posed by the peace of Christ for what he calls "the peace that this world loves,"[18] that kind of false concord dreamed up by the powerful and benefitting only the wicked. "The gospel in and of itself," Erasmus writes in paraphrase of Matthew, is "an instrument of peace," though "great divisions" naturally will arise when those "who passionately love this world" with its manifold injustices rooted in arrogance and greed are challenged by others who are "touched by the fire of gospel love."[19] It is not, to be sure, that the world is somehow to be shunned as evil in itself but rather that the "evil peace" that reigns in life as we know it, where stability and security are defined by the self-serving accords of the powerful, is confronted by a starkly divergent way of life. A "salutary discord will arise," Erasmus writes in paraphrase of Luke, where the peace of Christ moves to reverse the twisted inversions of the world's unjust order.[20] And it is precisely this that is

18. Erasmus, *Paraphrase on Luke*, CWE 47: 43.
19. Erasmus, *Paraphrase on Matthew*, CWE 45: 176–77.
20. Erasmus, *Paraphrase on Luke*, CWE 48: 43. See Pabel, "The Prince of Peace," 133–34.

evident in the sharp yet revealing exchanges of Jesus and the Pharisees, in which Jesus proposes to substitute humility and sincerity for the arrogance and hypocrisy evident in the behavior of established religious authorities.[21]

What Erasmus says about the peace of Christ primarily derives from the teachings and actions attributed to Jesus; most often, as we have seen, these lessons are meant to apply directly and with transformative power to actual human life. Having said that, however, it also is true that Erasmus treats the death of Jesus as a source of redemption, and when taking this line, he often focuses on the manner in which Jesus is said to have approached his death, rendering it as a supreme example of humility and forbearance to be imitated in present life.[22] Once again, therefore, we find Erasmus stressing the ethical transformation arising from Christ as the perfect model of selfless love for others.

At other times, however, the redemptive peace brought forth in Jesus' death is given an eschatological meaning, to wit, that the cross of Christ bestows eternal salvation on fallen humanity. It is clear, in this regard, that Erasmus is entirely comfortable with the traditional claim that, in his freely chosen death, Jesus is "the renewer and redeemer of a fallen race."[23] But Erasmus certainly does not attempt to explain the

21. Erasmus consistently highlights Jesus' rebuke of the Pharisees' arrogance, malice, and wickedness; their inverted sense of what makes for religious life; and their hypocrisy and sanctimony. See, among other places, Erasmus, *Paraphrase on Matthew*, CWE 45: 111–12, 128–29, 134–36, 156, 192–94, 232–35, 241–42, 312–14, and 317–20; *Paraphrase on Luke*, CWE 47: 226–29; and *Paraphrase on Luke*, CWE 48: 51, 59–60, 95–97, 104, 119–20, 155–56, and 184. In these scenes of conflict, however, it cannot be denied that Erasmus inherits and reflects a widespread and long-standing anti-Judaic trope from Christian tradition. See, for instance, *Paraphrase on Luke*, CWE 48: 158 and 164, where Erasmus speaks more broadly of the "Godless conscience" and "pretended righteousness of the Jews." See also CWE 48: 223. At the same time, however, Erasmus is thinking as much about the behavior of Christian teachers and leaders in his own day as of the Pharisees of old, as when he laments that "this kind of actor were not so omnipresent among Christians, compared to whom the Pharisees could seem straightforward and sincere" (*Paraphrase on Matthew*, CWE 45: 314).

22. See, for example, Erasmus, *Paraphrase on Luke*, CWE 47: 133–34, 152, and 173; *Paraphrase on Luke*, CWE 48: 192–93, 217.

23. Erasmus, *Paraphrase on Luke*, CWE 47: 123. For similar language, see Erasmus, *Paraphrase on Matthew*, CWE 45: 249, 256, 294, and 343. Payne is correct in objecting to those who claim that Erasmus reduces Christ to a "moralist" teacher or mere example, since, as Payne writes, Erasmus "was not only a moralist; he was also a Catholic Christian who knew how to speak about Christ as redeemer" (*Erasmus: His Theology of the Sacraments*, 64–65). At the same time, however, those who stress the traditional religious dimension of Erasmus's thinking often overlook the vibrant ethical impulse animating so much of his writing: precisely the kind of

kind of causality involved in such a renewal, except to recite the traditional image of Jesus as "the most pure lamb, who would be sacrificed for the salvation of the world."[24] By undergoing this sacrifice, we are told, Jesus' death "atone[s] for the sins of the world, freely reconciling to God anyone who professed this [new] covenant."[25] The peace that flows from this proxy sacrifice is described repeatedly by Erasmus as an eternal state of life, or even as "eternal happiness" and "eternal bliss,"[26] though in the absence of such peace, he does not hesitate to speak of "eternal death," or even of "eternal punishment."[27]

In speaking of the peace of Christ in these terms, as redemption stemming from a sacrificial atonement and resulting in eschatological life, Erasmus dutifully reflects the biblical text even as he piously echoes the religious tradition in which he lives. He is at ease with such language, clearly enough, though he shows no interest in speculating about the exact meaning of this atonement, perhaps because such matters lie well beyond the grasp of human understanding, but also because such questions lack the practical urgency and ethical importance found in clarifying how the peace of Christ might transform the course of actual human life. The best that might be said is that, for Erasmus, the death of Christ represents an extraordinary act of divine mercy, and it is such mercy for humanity—as we will see in the next section of this chapter—that constitutes the ultimate source of redemptive peace. Rather than speculating about how the death of Jesus atones for human sin, therefore,

---

thing emphasized by Febvre and Renaudet. Both dimensions are integral to the Christology of Erasmus, as has been argued throughout this book, so that it is insufficient to ignore the fact that Erasmus renders redemption as both the healing restoration of peace with God resulting from Christ's loving sacrifice on the cross and a fundamental renewal of human life issuing from the ethically transformative agency of the target (*scopus*) and measure embodied in the person of Christ and broadcast through his teachings.

24. Erasmus, *Paraphrase on Luke*, CWE 48: 186. As the sacrificial lamb, Erasmus writes elsewhere, Jesus "would redeem with his most holy blood the entire world from the tyranny of sin" (*Paraphrase on Matthew*, CWE 45: 341). The "mystery of the cross," Erasmus emphasizes, was an "extraordinary sacrifice for the salvation of the human race" (*Paraphrase on Luke*, CWE 48: 125, 145).

25. Erasmus, *Paraphrase on Luke*, CWE 48: 71–72; *Paraphrase on Matthew*, CWE 45: 349.

26. Talk of "eternal life" and "eternal salvation" is widespread in the Paraphrases on the synoptic Gospels. For mention of "eternal happiness," see Erasmus, *Paraphrase on Matthew*, CWE 45: 205; for "eternal bliss," see Erasmus, *Paraphrase on Luke*, CWE 48: 39, 91.

27. For language of "eternal death," see Erasmus, *Paraphrase on Luke*, CWE 47: 33; *Paraphrase on Luke*, CWE 48: 144. For mention of "eternal punishment," see Erasmus, *Paraphrase on Matthew*, CWE 45: 265.

Erasmus insists that this death embodies, even as it reveals, the depth of Christ's incarnational love and the range of his self-sacrificial humility.[28] It conveys with finality, in other words, the peace of Christ that was enacted and taught throughout his life.

The Christ of peace, in sum, is for Erasmus the living medium through which God reconciles the world to himself through the forgiveness of sins. It is peace with God—what the tradition has long called salvation—that Christ graciously offers to humanity through his life and death.[29] People thereby are invited in turn to reconcile with each other in what Pabel calls a "friendship based on [mutual] forgiveness,"[30] and as friends with Christ, as we heard earlier, they are prompted to "foster peace" in the world around them.[31] The peace of Christ, therefore, is meant to have a transformative and salutary effect on the actual course of human life, effectively building toward the consummation of the life of peace, what Erasmus calls "a true and perfect friendship" in Christ and with others.[32]

Human beings thrive in the harmonies possible between friends, he insists, which is why it is found to be so unbearable when the pleasure and profit of friendship are diminished due to time or distance, and it is why life is so impoverished when friendships dissolve in acrimony and conflict.[33] Human life, in short, is greatly enriched by the happiness and

28. In this regard, Payne rightly observes that Erasmus favors the "Abelardian motif" that emphasizes divine love as the force of redemption in Christ, as opposed to the "Anselmian" theme of atonement by Christ's death. See Payne, *Erasmus: His Theology of the Sacraments*, 64–66.

29. So Erasmus writes, in paraphrase of Peter in Acts 10:36, that God "has now at last fulfilled what he promised, making it known … though his only Son Jesus Christ, offering the abolition of sins and reconciliation to himself through faith and obedience to the one he sent." See Erasmus, *Paraphrase on the Acts of the Apostles*, trans. Robert D. Sider, in *Collected Works of Erasmus: New Testament Scholarship*, vol. 50 (Toronto: University of Toronto Press, 1995), 73.

30. On the Erasmian equation of peace with forgiveness, reconciliation, and friendship, see Pabel, "The Prince of Peace," 143.

31. Recall Erasmus, *Complaint of Peace*, CWE 27: 300–301.

32. Erasmus to Richard Foxe, letter 187, CWE 2: 103. When Erasmus speaks of friendship, he praises it as an invaluable and enduring community of lives freely linked together with amity, benevolence, and tolerance, and perhaps, too, by a bit of folly. On these elements of friendship, see Erasmus, "Where there are friends, there is wealth," adage I. iii. 24, CWE 31: 256; "Friendships should last forever," adage IV. v. 26, CWE 36: 157–58; "Between friends all is common," adage I. i. 1, CWE 31: 29–30; "The cup of friendship," adage IV. iii. 96, CWE 36: 58; "A Formula for the Composition of Letters," trans. Charles Fantazzi, CWE 25: 139; "Know your friend's weaknesses but hate them not," adage II. v. 96, CWE 33: 285; and *Praise of Folly*, CWE 27: 96–97.

33. See the commentary of Erasmus in "A friend is more necessary than fire and water,"

pleasure arising from friendship, and for this very reason, it is from the experience of friendship that Erasmus draws one of the root metaphors for the redeemed life of peace across the spheres of human existence and beyond. The peace of Christ, as the divinely bestowed *scopus* for human existence, represents an ideal life comprised of the kindness and tolerance uniquely possible between friends.

"Endless Display of Mercy to All"

In September 1524, Erasmus issued a *Discussion of Free Will* from the presses of Johann Froben in Basel, thereby launching—in the remarkably tempered and even-handed manner of classical deliberative rhetoric—what soon would become a regrettably hostile and finally intractable exchange with Martin Luther.[34] The same year also would see the release of two other works in which Erasmus speaks to the brewing religious questions of the day: first, "An Examination Concerning the Faith," a truly irenic dialogue in which a Lutheran is shown—much to the surprise of the Catholic character—not to be heretical,[35] and second, *A Sermon on the Immense Mercy of God*, a little studied but certainly profound discussion of the power and range of divine love in the redemption of humanity. It is in the latter work especially, as we will see in this section, that Erasmus develops his understanding of the range and depth of God's redemptive love, something, he works to show, that is vividly on display in God's beneficence in creation, repeatedly extolled in "every single book of the old covenant," and supremely manifest in "the whole story of Christ's life," which as Erasmus puts it, is an "endless display of mercy to all."[36]

---

adage II. ii. 75, CWE 33: 114–15; "Friends dwelling far away are no true friends," adage II. iii. 86, CWE 33: 181–82.

34. Erasmus, *Discussion of Free Will*, CWE 76: 5–89. On the rhetorical tone and purpose of this work, see Boyle, *Rhetoric and Reform*, 5–42. What was a "collation" for Erasmus, a "sort of comparison" to be handled with deliberative rhetoric, becomes a "collision" for Luther, something to be adjudicated in a juridical manner (44–66).

35. Erasmus, "An Examination Concerning the Faith," CWE 39: 419–47. On the meaning and importance of this dialogue, see Craig R. Thompson, *Inquisitio de Fide: A Colloquy* (Hamden, CT: Archon Books, 1975), 38–49; Martin, *Living Words*, 284–88.

36. Erasmus, *Sermon on the Immense Mercy of God*, CWE 70: 84, 91–92 on creation; 117 on Hebrew scriptures; and 118 on the life of Christ. For helpful discussions of the *Sermon on Mercy*,

Written under the guise of a homily, the *Sermon on the Immense Mercy* quietly proceeds along the same path as the *Discussion of Free Will*, though without personal reference to Luther and freed from the rancorous tone that creeps into the responses to Luther's *The Bondage of the Will* in the second volume of *Warrior Shielding a Discourse*.[37] Instead, Erasmus addresses what he calls "two particular diseases," the first of which burdens people with "persistent stiff-knecked pride" in their own capacities for achieving a final and secure peace, while the second leads people to "despair of forgiveness" altogether, convinced of their own unworthiness before the severe judgment of an all-powerful God.[38] One must, Erasmus insists, steer clear of both the "arrogance" of self-sufficiency and the "despair of forgiveness," as the former is blind to the necessity and the latter misses the ready availability of divine mercy as the source of eternal salvation for all.[39]

As a pure gift, Erasmus argues, the peace of Christ is not an accomplishment on the part of the recipient, so the view that affirms the power of human agency to fulfill God's commands—a position traditionally linked with what came to be deemed the heretical stance of Pelagius

---

see C. S. M. Rademaker, introduction to *De immensa Dei misericordia concio*, ASD V - 7: 3–28; Michael J. Heath, introductory note to the *Sermon on the Immense Mercy*, CWE 70: 70–75.

37. Erasmus complains a great deal about the "insults and slanders" arising from Luther's pen in *Warrior Shielding a Discourse 1*, CWE 76: 124–25, as well as 137, 140, 141, 160, 162, 166, 278, and 295. The same complaints appear in Erasmus, *Warrior Shielding a Discourse 2*, CWE 77: 453–54, 636, for example, though Erasmus can be found ably returning the favor in this second volume. See Erasmus, *Warrior Shielding a Discourse 2*, 379, 393, 403, 464, 578, 621, and 655. In July 1524, Christoph von Utenheim, the Catholic bishop of Basel, advised Erasmus not to add anything to the *Sermon on the Immense Mercy* "that might excite the Lutherans or those who observe the genuine old-fashioned faith, or even upset their stomach, and might exhibit us as followers of this or that sect." Keen that he and Erasmus not be found to be offensive to either party, therefore, the bishop urges Erasmus to remove the "additions at the end of the book" (Christoph von Utenheim to Erasmus, letter 1464, CWE 10: 300). It would seem that Erasmus followed this advice, as Heath observes, since there is nothing at the end of the *Sermon on the Immense Mercy* to offend either camp, "and the work does not appear to have attracted criticism from anyone" (introductory note, CWE 70: 300, n. 3). At the same time, Luther must have winced at the suggestion by Erasmus that acts of kindness might "extract" divine mercy, and defenders of Catholic orthodoxy likely took exception to the lack of discussion of the ecclesial forms of penance. See Rademaker, "Introduction," ASD V - 7: 17.

38. On the disease of arrogance, see Erasmus, *Sermon on the Immense Mercy*, CWE 70: 79, 104, and 105–9; from the same source, see 82, 109, and 120–21 on the disease of despair.

39. Erasmus, *Sermon on the Immense Mercy*, CWE 70: 78, 81. One must avoid the "Scylla of arrogance," Erasmus writes elsewhere, as well as the "Charybdis of despair" (*Discussion of Free Will*, CWE 76: 87). See also Erasmus, *Warrior Shielding a Discourse 1*, CWE 76: 140–46.

(d. 418 CE)—is quickly rejected by Erasmus. But neither is redemption in Christ something about which to despair, Erasmus assures his readers, as the "immense and ineffable mercy of God" is "always and everywhere so close at hand."[40] The *Sermon on the Immense Mercy* does not name the proponents of the view that would cause despair, but the *Discussion of Free Will* and both volumes of *Warrior Shielding a Discourse* make it clear that Erasmus is thinking primarily of Luther, first and most generally, for what Erasmus regards as Luther's hyperbolic negativity in exaggerating human wickedness[41] and second, for Luther's insistence that human will can do nothing but sin.[42] Additional reasons for despair, Erasmus argues in these same writings, appear when Luther asserts that God rules with "sheer necessity," so that someone might be damned who does not, in fact, deserve it,[43] but also when Luther contends that God prescribes things while knowing they cannot be fulfilled.[44]

40. Erasmus, *Sermon on the Immense Mercy*, CWE 70: 88, 120.

41. Referring to Luther as "our hyperbolic fellow," Erasmus repeatedly complains of Luther's exaggeration of human wickedness (*Warrior Shielding a Discourse 2*, CWE 77: 464 and 578, but also 355, 394, and 66). See as well *Warrior Shielding a Discourse 1*, CWE 76: 186 and 192–93. Erasmus especially objects to what he takes to be Luther's excessive depiction of the human condition as wicked, exaggerating original sin, and stressing sinfulness so much as to render human beings no different than Satan. See Erasmus, *Discussion of Free Will*, CWE 76: 84; *Warrior Shielding a Discourse 2*, CWE 77: 373, 394, 571, 591, 700–701, 716, and 721. In response, Erasmus proposes a more nuanced view, where nature is said to contain not only "an inclination to vice" but also "seeds of great virtue" (*Warrior Shielding a Discourse 2*, CWE 77: 700). And moreover, Erasmus writes, while "the whole gamut of wrongdoings fall upon the whole human race, … each single feature does not apply to each individual" (655). Indeed, he says with an interesting empirical note, while human viciousness certainly is evident for all to see, "what is most outstanding in mankind" is not people doing wicked deeds, but those who have "honoured their parents, loved their children and wives, [and] supported the poor, sick, and afflicted" (648).

42. For Erasmus's rejection of the notion that the human will can do nothing but sin, see Erasmus, *Warrior Shielding a Discourse 2*, CWE 77: 468, 480, 579, 596, and 662.

43. Erasmus rejects the notion that God governs the world with absolute necessity. See Erasmus, *Discussion of Free Will*, CWE 76: 82; *Warrior Shielding a Discourse 2*, CWE 77: 422, 429, and 496. Indeed, Erasmus writes, it is wicked to "say that God damns anyone who does not deserve it," and such a notion would throw people into despair (561, 659).

44. Erasmus here refers to Luther's notion that the "whole Law" accomplishes "no more than to make mankind know that it can fulfil nothing that is commanded, even in the presence of grace" (*Warrior Shielding a Discourse 2*, CWE 77: 361). While Luther claims that the Law was given by God "to taunt our pride and to show that we can do nothing but sin," Erasmus counters that "the single aim of God's Law was the avoidance of baseness and the pursuit of honourable conduct" (362–63). Calling Luther's "negative" use of the Law an "absolutely stupid fabrication," Erasmus complains that Luther's view "throws some into despair," while "some it makes brutally cruel" (356, 389).

When responding to these counsels for despair, Erasmus shows himself at his "humane best," as Michael J. Heath puts it, but he also appears at his theologically most exuberant, as his overriding aim is to highlight the unbounded abundance and universal availability of divine mercy.[45] There is no good reason to "abandon hope in salvation," Erasmus declares with words of assurance, for "the Lord's mercies are without number and without measure."[46] Such is the testimony of Hebrew scripture to "the wondrous, unparalleled abundance of God's mercy."[47] And such, too, is the Gospel of Christ—"the uniquely astounding miracle of his mercy"—when "the immense power of divine mercy" lay hidden "beneath [the] weakness" of human form, spreading the "promise of mercy" through his teaching, and sacrificing himself "to atone for each and every sin of all."[48] With that exuberant magnification of the redemptive scope of Christ's life and death, Erasmus celebrates the restoration of humanity to "the eternal joys of the life everlasting" by means of "mercy that knows no bounds."[49]

45. Heath, introductory note to the *Sermon on the Immense Mercy*, CWE 70: 70.

46. Erasmus, *Sermon on the Immense Mercy*, CWE 70: 104.

47. Erasmus, *Sermon on the Immense Mercy*, CWE 70: 89. Erasmus makes extensive use of Hebrew scriptures in the *Sermon on the Immense Mercy*, as Chomarat notes. See Jacques Chomarat, "Érasme: La miséricorde de Dieu, Sermon. Présentation," *Moreana* 32, no. 122 (June 1995) 6–7; Rademaker, "Introduction," ASD V - 7: 11–12. Indeed, Erasmus writes, "every single book of the old covenant proclaims, hymns, and insists upon the mercy of God." Against those "delirious" heretics who portrayed the God of Hebrew scriptures as "merely just and not also good," Erasmus insists that "he is the same God, the God of both laws, the same truth, the same mercy, through Jesus Christ our Lord, except that what is mere shadow in Moses's law becomes truth in the gospel" (117–18; see also 85–89).

48. Erasmus, *Sermon on the Immense Mercy*, CWE 70: 85, 118–19. On the unbounded mercy of God as the basis for a "theology of consolation and hope for eternal salvation," see Rademaker, "Introduction," ASD V - 7: 6. For a discussion of the appeal of Erasmus's "theology of the open heaven," see Silvana Seidel Menchi, *Erasmus als Ketzer: Reformation und Inquisition im Italien des 16. Jahrhunderts* (Leiden: E. J. Brill, 1993), 169–203.

49. Erasmus, *Sermon on the Immense Mercy*, CWE 70: 100, 89. Erasmus praises the notion of Origen that "even the evil demons and the damned must one day, after long aeons, be restored to grace." While Erasmus acknowledges that "the orthodox Fathers" condemned this view, he mentions it "to show how magnificent an opinion of God's mercy was held by those great scholars who spent their days and nights immersed in the holy books and who proclaim, celebrate, and sing in praise of almost nothing but the mercy of God" (98). For the view of Origen that "the goodness of God through Christ will restore the entire creation to one end, even his enemies being conquered and subdued," see Origen, *On First Principles*, trans. G. W. Butterworth (Gloucester, MA: Peter Smith, 1973), chap. 6, 52. While the Latin translation of Rufinus leaves "the salvation of the devil and his angels an open question," Jerome reports that Origen taught the "one restoration of all things," including the devil. See Origen, *On First Principles*, 57, n. 1. See also Pelikan, *The Emergence of the Catholic Tradition (100–600)*, 151.

"There is nothing that faith cannot obtain from Christ," Erasmus writes with another note of assurance, and what is more, he adds, "there is nowhere that his mercy is not available."[50] Given that ready and universal availability of divine mercy, Erasmus wonders why anyone would despair. Indeed, he asks quizzically, "is anyone so mad as to refuse to be saved?"[51] The answer from the *Sermon on the Immense Mercy* is that there is no good reason why anyone would resolutely renounce God's gracious offer, as "the portals of mercy are opened equally for all" and one's "past life will not count against you," "*so long as you are penitent,*" that is.[52] With that last qualification, Erasmus allows that there is something expected of the recipient of Christ's mercy, though that is not to say that people are able to earn or merit God's grace by means of some "work," as Luther would put it critically; nor, along the same line, does it mean that mercy is something that might be "bought" by an "exchange of money," as Chomarat seems to wonder when commenting on the *Sermon on the Immense Mercy.*[53]

What is required, as Erasmus sees it, is an appropriate personal stance—an interior disposition of character or a fundamental orientation of the heart—on the part of the recipient of such a momentous gift. When Erasmus sets about describing this demeanor, it is clear, above all, that he excludes any form of self-confidence or despair, as the former would make it seem that the gift of mercy is deserved and the latter would make a lie of the promise of forgiveness. To properly receive Christ's mercy, Erasmus declares in the first place, requires an open and "contrite heart." "Simply keep your heart's ears open for it," he says, which interestingly is very much the way Luther speaks of faith,[54] and

50. Erasmus, *Sermon on the Immense Mercy*, CWE 70: 119. That God's mercy is universally available is clearly expressed in the *Sermon on the Immense Mercy*, though he chides Jews and philosophers ("or rather, morosophers," as he puts it) for closing their ears to the divine appeal. A more explicit acknowledgment of the faith and "inborn power that seeks virtue" among "pagan philosophers" and followers of the Law is evident toward the end of *Warrior Shielding a Discourse 2*, CWE 77: 734–43.

51. Erasmus, *Sermon on the Immense Mercy*, CWE 70: 122

52. Erasmus, *Sermon on the Immense Mercy*, CWE 70: 123, my italics.

53. Chomarat, "Érasme: La miséricorde de Dieu, sermon," 7.

54. Erasmus, *Sermon on the Immense Mercy*, CWE 70: 122. "Trust in the merciful one," Erasmus writes, "and you shall know mercy" (119). For Luther's exposition of the powers and gifts of faith, see Martin Luther, "The Freedom of a Christian," trans. W. A. Lambert and Harold J. Grimm, in *Luther's Works: Career of the Reformer 1*, vol. 31, ed. Harold J. Grimm (Philadelphia: Fortress Press, 1957), 343–77.

with that, as well, maintain a keen sense of one's "endless capacity of sin," while being "truly sorry" for one's actual sins and ready to "change [one's] inclinations."[55] Then again, in the second place, a person is most fittingly receptive of divine mercy when performing "service" for neighbors "out of the goodness of [their] heart"—not, once again, in the sense that one might earn mercy as a reward for acts of kindness but because charitable living (unlike prideful self-absorption of one or another sort) constitutes the fertile ground necessary for the appropriate reception of divine mercy.[56] One simply is not ready to receive the gift of Christ's mercy, or any gift for that matter, if one is wrapped up contentedly in one's own self-interest.

With its emphasis on faith, contrition, and kindness, the *Sermon on the Immense Mercy* makes "an oblique contribution to the debate over free will," as Heath puts it, though it does so, it is important to stress, by maintaining a primary emphasis on the extensive range and redemptive agency of divine mercy.[57] When scripture speaks of God's mercy, Erasmus observes, it does so with great variety: it "sometimes implies munificence, sometimes prevenient grace, or elevating grace, and quite often consoling grace; elsewhere it implies medicinal grace, but very often pardoning grace, or even punishing grace."[58] What we see in this statement, first of all, is the appreciation for variety at the center of Erasmus's temperate deliberation on theological questions.[59]

---

55. Erasmus, *Sermon on the Immense Mercy*, CWE 70: 126–27, 115. On the "remedy of repentance" and confessing one's sins to God, see CWE 70: 114–15, 123–24, and 126–27. Chomarat calls attention to the fact that Erasmus stresses repentance before God, without mentioning ritual confession in the church (Chomarat, "Érasme: la miséricorde de Dieu, sermon," 7).

56. Erasmus, *Sermon on the Immense Mercy*, CWE 70: 132–33. On contrition and charity as conditions for receiving God's forgiveness, see Payne, *Erasmus: His Theology of the Sacraments*, 194–95. Erasmus stumbles over his own wording when he asserts that "kindness to one's neighbor will also *extract*" God's mercy, though he quickly adds "*so to speak*" in order to indicate the inappropriateness of that phrasing.

57. See Heath, introductory note to the *Sermon on the Immense Mercy*, CWE 70: 72. Rademaker also notes that the *Sermon on the Immense Mercy* "complements the book on free will" ("Introduction," ASD V - 7: 15–16). For the same point, see Seidel Menchi, *Erasmus als Ketzer*, 184. On parallels between the *Sermon on the Immense Mercy* and the *Discussion of Free Will*, see Rademaker, "Introduction," ASD V - 7: 16–17.

58. Erasmus, *Sermon on the Immense Mercy*, CWE 70: 91.

59. Recall, once again, Erasmus's emphasis on open and civil consideration of rival viewpoints in theological disputes. See Erasmus, *Discussion of Free Will*, CWE 76: 8. On the importance of "civil conversation" in the theological method of Erasmus, see B. A. Gerrish, "*De Libero Arbitrio* (1524)," 187–209.

Along with the attentiveness to variety, however, there is secondly an emphasis on "the *functions* of divine mercy depicted in Scriptures," as Heath rightly observes.[60]

In reviewing the various forms of mercy, consequently, Erasmus consistently stresses the activity of God by means of the suitable verbal locution: for instance, God is said to "[*urge*] us to be good," though divine mercy also "*assists* us in our efforts, *accompanies* us on the journey, and finally *enables* us to complete a task that is beyond human power to achieve."[61] When focused on the "pardoning mercy" of God, alternatively, Erasmus observes how God "patiently *bears with* our frailty … *invites* us to repent, [and] quietly *remits* every offence to those who change their ways."[62] When applied to Christ, moreover, Erasmus again emphasizes that the mercy of Christ "*protects* us on every side," even as he "*elevates*, *consoles*, and *enriches* us."[63] Or, as Erasmus puts in the *Discussion of Free Will*, "mankind owes an immense debt to their redeemer," as Christ "*free*[*s*] them from hell, *shines* upon them with the light of faith, *inflames* them with the fire of charity, [and] *transforms* them into sons of God. He does not," moreover, "extinguish the good he finds but *perfects* it; he does not destroy nature but *completes* it. He *arouses* the sleepy, *setting right* what is depraved, *making up for* what is lacking."[64] The redemptive mercy of Christ, in short, is an effective form of agency, one that, in a great variety of ways, touches, affects, or moves one and all, as long as their lives are to some degree open, penitent, and filled with kindness.

What this ultimately means, for Erasmus is that the peace of Christ is to have an evident effect on actual life. As the universal *scopus* for human life, the Christ of peace lures and beckons, even as he enables, supports, and measures the transformation and reorientation of human existence toward an ample and vibrant life of peace. To respond to

60. Erasmus, *Sermon on the Immense Mercy*, CWE 70: 91, n. 73.

61. Erasmus, *Sermon on the Immense Mercy*, CWE 70: 93, my italics.

62. Erasmus, *Sermon on the Immense Mercy*, CWE 70: 97, my italics; see also 98.

63. Erasmus, *Sermon on the Immense Mercy*, CWE 70: 101, my italics. In the speech of Jesus to the two disciples on the road to Emmaus, we are told, similarly, that Christ "*pricked* his hearers, *moved* them, *carried* them out of themselves, *seared* them, *set them* afire, left sparks and darts in their hearts" (*Paraphrase on Luke*, CWE 48: 272, my italics).

64. Erasmus, *Discussion of Free Will*, CWE 76: 592, my italics. "The impelling grace of God," Erasmus writes, "*stimulates* this desire [for virtue] in thousands of ways to lead it to justification, *egging on* a person's latent, feeble impulse" (*Warrior Shielding a Discourse* 2, CWE 77: 732, my italics).

such a gracious target with energetic effort, we are told, is "to undergo a complete change of character," that is, as Erasmus puts it, "to become sober instead of drunken, chaste instead of debauched, careful instead of spendthrift, generous instead of grasping, truthful instead of lying, kind instead of derogatory, open instead of devious, gentle instead of vengeful, [and] merciful instead of cruel."[65] To enjoy the peace of Christ, in other words, is to experience a thoroughgoing ethical transformation, one in which "ethical" includes not only specific alterations of behavior, like changing from being drunken to sober, for instance, but also fundamental shifts in character that involve the defining points for the shape and course of a person's life, like moving from being derogatory and cruel, for example, to being kind and merciful. Such changes for Erasmus are also, to be sure, essentially religious, as they originate in the agency of divine mercy, manifest themselves in active lives of mercy for others, and ultimately are eschatological in significance as Erasmus sees it. It is understandable, therefore, that Erasmus speaks of such a shift in the character of one's being as "redemption," though, as one would expect, he does so with a variety of synonyms, alternatively speaking of "reformation, renewal, restoration, reparation, and … revival."[66]

Regardless of the terms used to speak of this kind of transformation, it is clear that for Erasmus, the redemptive peace of Christ involves a fundamental affirmation and ennoblement of human existence. As he writes repeatedly in his exchanges with Luther, the "natural desire for virtue" and the "light of nature" (reason) were "overwhelmed" and "darkened" by human sinfulness, but they were not "completely extinguished in us."[67] What sin introduced into human life, therefore, was "impaired vision, not blindness; lameness, not destruction; it inflicted a wound, not death; it brought weakness, not annihilation."[68] And that

---

65. Erasmus, *Sermon on the Immense Mercy*, CWE 70: 136.

66. Erasmus, *Warrior Shielding a Discourse 2*, CWE 77: 624. In *Paraphrase on Matthew*, CWE 45: 166, Erasmus speaks of Christ's aim to "restore the whole world to gospel philosophy." See also *Paraphrase on Matthew*, CWE 45: 58 on redemption as being "renewed."

67. Erasmus, *Discussion of Free Will*, CWE 76: 23; *Warrior Shielding a Discourse 1*, CWE 76: 271–75; from the same volume, see 271–72, 280, and 290, as well as *Warrior Shielding a Discourse 2*, CWE 77: 339, 465, 593–94, 658, 711, 722, and 736.

68. Erasmus, *Discussion of Free Will*, CWE 76: 27; *Warrior Shielding a Discourse 1*, CWE 76: 290. See also Erasmus, *Warrior Shielding a Discourse 2*, CWE 77: 722.

means, consequently, that the redemptive mercy of Christ can be said to "transform" what is an existing, though corrupted and twisted, human good. As Erasmus puts it, when Christ "shines upon them with the light of faith" and "inflames them with the fire of charity," he "does not extinguish the good he finds but perfects it; he does not destroy nature but completes it."[69]

Though Erasmus concedes that God can "transform a person suddenly," moreover, he prefers to render the change as a gradual process—"in imitation of nature"—through which life is restored and renewed.[70] Casting redemption in this manner, of course, mandates a nuanced treatment of the complex manner in which divine agency (grace) and human initiative (will) cooperate in the reformation of human life. Thus, we find Erasmus arguing throughout the second volume of *Warrior Shielding a Discourse* that "the action of grace is combined with the action of free will,"[71] even if it is "only a little" that is allotted to human effort,[72] and even though "the human will is ineffective in achieving salvation without grace."[73] The pay-off of this view, Erasmus argues, is that it "leaves a person the opportunity of serious moral endeavor" but without "making any claims for his own powers."[74] Erasmus makes roughly the same point in the *Sermon on the Immense Mercy*, in which, while affirming that "all our sufficiency is from God,"[75] he concludes by endorsing a religious ethic of peace centered on the resolute imitation of divine mercy, where goodness and love are to be freely

69. Erasmus, *Warrior Shielding a Discourse 2*, CWE 77: 592; see also 707.

70. Erasmus, *Warrior Shielding a Discourse 2*, CWE 77: 624. "We come off well enough," Erasmus writes, "if Christ grows gradually in us" (699). On the process of rebirth, the stages of healing, and the levels of justification, see CWE 77: 730–31.

71. Erasmus, *Warrior Shielding a Discourse 2*, CWE 77: 388. See, similarly, CWE 77: 382, 420, 431, and 466.

72. Erasmus, *Warrior Shielding a Discourse 2*, CWE 77: 399. For similar descriptions, see Erasmus, *Warrior Shielding a Discourse 1*, CWE 76: 186, 192; *Warrior Shielding a Discourse 2*, CWE 77: 399, 623, 627, and 743.

73. *Warrior Shielding a Discourse 2*, CWE 77: 594; see also 471, 564.

74. Erasmus, *Discussion of Free Will*, CWE 76: 32; *Warrior Shielding a Discourse 2*, CWE 77: 375. Appealing to scriptural injunctions and exhortations, Erasmus wonders "how someone can be said to endeavor earnestly and with diligent effort if he does absolutely nothing but is merely subject to the action of grace" (*Warrior Shielding a Discourse 2*, CWE 77: 437, 445). See also *Warrior Shielding a Discourse 1*, CWE 76: 36, 41, and 76.

75. Erasmus, *Sermon on the Immense Mercy*, CWE 70: 104. Divine mercy is said to accompany and enable completion of tasks beyond our capacity. See CWE 70: 93.

shown to neighbors near and far. The incarnate presence of divine mercy in Christ, in sum, constitutes a *scopus* for imitation in living a life filled with mercy and peace, something Erasmus describes in both personal and social terms, as we will see in the remainder of this chapter.

"Of All States Both the Best and Most Joyful"

While it is true that Erasmus is better known for his complaint on behalf of peace against the ravages of international warfare, his reflections on the peace of Christ refer first and most basically to the *scopus* of individual life. So much of personal life, recall once again, is topsy-turvy and fractured by conflict, both within and with others. This condition, in turn, leaves individuals mired in psychological turmoil and snared by moral turbulence, wondering what good or goods might be truly worthy of life's aspiration and service. In response, as we have seen, Erasmus points to the mercy of God in Christ as the source of personal rectification, and the resulting state of being—the condition of redeemed life, as it were—is cast as a personal life of peace filled with happiness and joy.[76] In the *Sermon on the Immense Mercy*, Erasmus describes this kind of peace as "that complete innocence of life without which there can be no friendship with God or true harmony with our brothers."[77]

What Erasmus has in mind by an "innocence of life" is a root orientation of the individual self—what he calls the "pure heart"—which is "robust in faith, ablaze with love, [and] inspired by the heavenly Spirit."[78] "Innocence of heart,"[79] we are told in a kind of biblical collage, is

> a heart at peace from every tumult of evil passions; a heart that
> shuns contact with everything that might stain mental purity; a

---

76. Erasmus, *Sermon on the Immense Mercy*, CWE 70: 100–101.

77. *Warrior Shielding a Discourse 2*, CWE 77: 94. Erasmus derives the language of peace by some imaginative interpretations of the salutations at the beginnings of 1 Timothy and 2 Timothy. See 1 Timothy 1:2 and 2 Timothy 1:2, where "Paul" writes, "Grace, mercy, and peace from God the Father and Christ Jesus our Lord." For a parallel discussion, see Erasmus, *Paraphrase on First Timothy*, trans. John J. Bateman, CWE 44: 6.

78. Erasmus, *Paraphrase on Luke*, CWE 48: 173, 112.

79. Erasmus, *Paraphrase on Luke*, CWE 48: 21. In speaking of the "innocence of heart," Erasmus puts the emphasis on the interior condition of life (thus, a "purity of heart"), as opposed to that "warped judgment" that relegates purity to external rituals of cleansing (21).

heart wreathed in faith, love, humility, purity; a heart that always refrains from all evil doing; a heart that always yearns towards its heavenly native land; a heart that is a temple and guest house for the Holy Spirit; a heart always offering itself as a pure and pleasing sacrifice to God; a heart free from every stain through faith in the gospel; a heart detached from everything of this world and dedicating itself completely to things of God; [and] a heart fully observant of the things that gospel teaching commands and requires.[80]

In such a life, Erasmus boldly declares in paraphrase of Luke 17:21, where the heart is purified with the faith and love of gospel teaching, "there is the kingdom of God," or in the terms of this chapter, there is the peace of Christ, embodied in those who preserve their "peace of mind" by means of lives filled with "gospel gentleness."[81] Unlike those embroiled in the turbulent affairs of the world, where the prizes go to "the proud, haughty, arrogant, and self-confident," those who turn to Christ discover "what truly calms the mind," Erasmus avers, as a "meek and gentle heart is the source of all human tranquility." For what can "disturb or unsettle such a mind," Erasmus affirms with a question, "if the conscience is clear and the mind devoid of every care," and "if there is an unshakeable confidence concerning the rewards of eternal life?"[82]

The redeemed life, in short, or what amounts to the same thing for Erasmus—a personal life of peace—is defined by the tranquility of a

80. Erasmus, *Paraphrase on Luke*, CWE 47: 185–86.

81. Erasmus, *Paraphrase on Matthew*, CWE 45: 86. Unlike the turbulent emotions underlying cruelty and revenge, Erasmus writes, in "friendliness and tolerance" one will not lose their "peace of mind" (109).

82. Erasmus, *Paraphrase on Matthew*, CWE 45: 190–91, n. 37. Tranquility of conscience is an ideal found throughout the works of Erasmus. Thus, we find him writing in 1503 that "no pleasure is lacking when there is a tranquil conscience. But no misery is absent when an unhappy conscience torments us" (*Handbook of the Christian Soldier*, CWE 66: 59). See also *Paraphrase on Luke*, CWE 47: 64, 81; *Paraphrase on Luke*, CWE 48: 191. The possibility of a conscience at peace, of course, is a central bone of contention in the controversy between Erasmus and Luther. For his part, Luther concedes that "even if [he] lived to eternity, [his] conscience would never be assured and certain how much it ought to do to satisfy God." "Anxious doubt" remains as long as salvation depends on human efforts, whereas for Luther, "God has taken [my] salvation out of [my] hands into his, making it depend on his choice and not mine." See Martin Luther, *The Bondage of the Will* (1526), trans. Philip S. Watson, *Luther's Works*, vol. 33 (Philadelphia: Fortress Press, 1972), 288–89. Erasmus wonders in response, "who can be sure about his conscience when it is uncertain"—in Luther's theological scheme—"whether he is numbered among those God selected to be saved?" (*Warrior Shielding a Discourse 2*, CWE 77: 704–5). "God is merciful," Erasmus continues, "he forgives sins, but does so only for the repentant, for those who counter-balance their malefactions with good deeds" (705).

godly and righteous conscience. "Nothing is more disquieting than a bad conscience," Erasmus has his lead character say in "The Old Men's Chat," and nothing is more vital to "true serenity" than "being at peace with God."[83] These two sentiments often converge in the works of Erasmus, as they serve to underscore how the personal life of peace is comprised of both religious and ethical dimensions, while also emphasizing that such a life is marked by remarkable tranquility and joy. Most people "seek a pleasant life in external things,"[84] Erasmus observes in "The Epicurean," whether that be the "riches and honours" promised to the successful, or the physical pleasures linked with food, drink, and sex.[85] But these are merely the "deceitful shadows" of real goods, Erasmus counters in a traditional vein, in pursuit of which people "bring real torment upon themselves," not just the physical "discomforts" and mental anxieties attendant on a debauched life but especially the "agony of conscience," that regular "companion of unlawful pleasure."[86]

In stark contrast to this sorry but familiar sort of life, Erasmus puts forward an alternative possibility, one imprinted with the peace of Christ to the extent possible in a human life. Christ the "helper" or "guide" (*epikouros*), Erasmus writes with a bit of Epicurean flare, "alone shows the most enjoyable life of all and the most full of pleasure."[87] So the "godly man," as Erasmus puts it, "take[s] refuge in God's mercy,"

83. Erasmus, "The Old Men's Chat, or the Carriage," CWE 39: 453. For the same point, see Erasmus, "Nothing is more miserable than a guilty conscience," adage IV. x. 40, CWE 36: 507–8, in which Erasmus cites Horace's observation (from *Epistles* I. 1. 61) that "happiness consists in 'a conscience that does not accuse, no guilty thought to pale one's cheek,'" as well as the Hebrew saying (from Prov 15:15) that "a cheerful heart has a continual feast." See also Erasmus, "Conscience is a thousand witnesses," adage I. x. 91, CWE 32: 277.

84. Erasmus, "The Epicurean," CWE 40: 1087.

85. Erasmus, "The Epicurean," CWE 40: 1077–78.

86. Erasmus, "The Epicurean," CWE 40: 1078–79, 1083, and 1081. In comparison with the "tortures of a guilty conscience," which follow when "the world entices [people] with its painted imitations of good things," Erasmus asks in 1512, "what happiness can be compared with that of the mind which has gained its freedom from error and from emotion, which is secure and continually rejoicing in the witness of conscience, which is worn by no cares, which is lofty, raised high and next to the sky, already beyond the human lot, which is supported by Christ the highest rock?" (*Homily on the Child Jesus*, CWE 29: 69).

87. Erasmus, "The Epicurean," CWE 40: 1086. For the classical roots of the contrast of a good and bad conscience, see 1 Timothy 1:5; 1:18–19; and 3:9; Acts 23:1; and from Seneca, letters 43, 105.8, 122.14, and 97.12–15, in which Seneca credits Epicurus for this point. See *Seneca ad Lucilium Epistulae Morales*, 3 vols., trans. Richard M. Gummere (Cambridge, MA: Harvard University, 1934). On the pleasures of a conscience at peace in Erasmus, see Bietenholz, *Encounters with a Radical Erasmus*, 109–40; Marie Delcourt et Marcelle Derwa, "Trois aspects humanistes de

which "knows neither bound nor limit,"[88] while avoiding "that horrible pain caused by a bad conscience" by living in a righteous manner unburdened by guilt and regret.[89] "None live more enjoyably than those who live righteously," Erasmus twice writes, as they enjoy the fruits of a "good conscience,"[90] and "the truly rich man," Erasmus adds with a religious note, is "one who has God's favour," for "where God, the fount of all joy, is present, there insuperable happiness exists."[91] A redeemed life, in sum, is filled with the righteous pleasure of a sound conscience and the pious joy of being reconciled with God.

Erasmus provides excellent portraits of the life of peace in two brief *Colloquies*: first, "The Old Men's Chat," a charming dialogue of old friends who share their varied life stories after forty-two years without contact, and second, "The Funeral," a brief diptych contrasting the deaths of two very different men. In the first, we meet Glycion, who has lived moderately, "honourably and agreeably," shunning all conflicts and quarrels, while being kindly and pleasant to everyone around him. Unlike Polygamus, who has feasted on "hard drinking ... endless amours, and unrestrained sexuality," not nearly as frisky as Pampirus, who has bounced from one religious order to another with great freedom but little purpose, but also not as boring as the perfectly proper Eusebius, Glycion's life has been rich and full, though modest and decent. Above all, we are told, he has sought to avoid "wrongdoing," as "nothing is more disquieting than a bad conscience," and thus has enjoyed that "true serenity" that comes from being reconciled with God.[92]

In "The Funeral," we encounter a similar character in Cornelius, who faces his impending death with calm and quiet confidence. He has no interest in purchasing extra merits for salvation, we are told, as "there is sufficient abundance of merits in Christ," and—sounding just like Erasmus himself—he has faith in God's "boundless and inexpressible

---

l'Épicurisme Chrétien," in *Colloquium Erasmianum: Actes du Colloque International réuni à Mons du 26 au 29 octobre 1967* (Mons: Centre Universitaire de L'État, 1968), 119–33.

88. Erasmus, "The Epicurean," CWE 40: 1087.

89. Erasmus, "On Disdaining the World," trans. Erika Rummel, CWE 66: 166–67.

90. Erasmus, "The Epicurean," CWE 40: 1077, 1086.

91. Erasmus, "The Epicurean," CWE 40: 1082. "Wherever is a pure heart," Erasmus has Hedonius continue, "there God is. Wherever God is, there is paradise, heaven, happiness. Where happiness is, there is true gladness and unfeigned cheerfulness" (1083).

92. Erasmus, "Old Men's Chat," CWE 39: 453.

mercy." Unlike the rich and powerful George, whose elaborate funer-
ary plans are designed for perpetual self-aggrandizement while keeping
God very much "in his debt," Cornelius feels no need to be visited by
more priests, and he declines a final confession, as he simply has "no
lingering anxieties on his mind." Approaching his death with a "good
conscience," therefore, Cornelius dies exactly as he lived, "without being
burdensome to anyone," while showing kindness to his wife and children.[93] The characters of Glycion and Cornelius, in sum, offer a window
into an often-overlooked dimension of Erasmus's notion of peace, in
which the focus centers on the individual's experience of the peace and
joy of Christ—essentially, a serenity of conscience—that arises from the
abundant mercy of God matched with lives that are resolutely modest,
humble, trusting, and kind. While the Christological connection is not
well-developed in these colloquies, it is clear that both figures embody
the purity of heart and righteous living that Erasmus associates with the
redemptive peace of Christ.

The personal life of peace, of course, is always for Erasmus something that must be lived among and with other people, and therein lies
the problem, as the many perturbations of social existence make serenity of mind and peace of heart enormously fragile. When, for instance,
Erasmus advises readers who are "clear in [their] own conscience" not
to "retaliate against abuse by returning it," but rather—in imitation of
Christ—to "either fall silent or satisfy the accuser with calm speech,"
he is well aware how difficult nonretaliation can be in practice.[94] That
does not, however, prevent Erasmus from imagining what the peace
of Christ might promise—in the pinnacle of its perfection—for interpersonal life, and that is exactly what he presents in "The Godly Feast,"
truly an ideal banquet among friends where most everything is imaginatively reconciled in balanced and fruitful harmony.[95] What a sump-
tuous feast, the host exclaims, "at once equally learned and devout,"[96] as

---

93. Erasmus, "The Funeral," CWE 40: 776–79. On "The Funeral," see Terence J. Martin,
"'The Funeral': An Erasmian Sketch for Enhanced Life," *Responsibility and the Enhancement of
Life*, 147–56.

94. Erasmus, *The Tongue*, CWE 29: 396.

95. Boyle rightly refers to this colloquy as a "microcosm of the Christian commonwealth"
(*Erasmus on Language and Method in Theology*, 140).

96. Erasmus, "The Godly Feast," CWE 39: 204.

each speaker freely offers his reading of a scriptural text, complementing those of the others without a hint of competition or conflict. This luncheon among friends, in sum, bears many of the ideal marks of the life of peace—harmony, balance, pleasure, piety, and intelligence—lived out in a miniature example of interpersonal life. It is safe to say that, for Erasmus, Christ truly is present in this convivial feast, and in answering their prayer, he has "rejoice[d]" their "hearts by his presence."[97]

"Friendship Among Many People"

What the peace of Christ might mean on larger scales, beyond a simple gathering of friends, is another and far more difficult question. And yet, amazingly enough, for Erasmus the Christ of peace, which is to say, the personal embodiment of the life-enhancing virtues that comprise the philosophy of Christ, also serves as the *scopus* for the common life in the world of international relations, and that becomes especially important, he observes, in those times and places where nations conflict with each other militarily. It is there, after all, in the savage clash of armies and the widespread carnage that results—all "started in the interests of princes and carried on with great suffering for the people"— that the sorry and sinful condition of the human world is so brutally evident.[98] What a "pitiable spectacle" this is, he exclaims, as "crops [are] trampled far and wide, farms burnt out, villages set on fire, cattle driven away, virgins raped, old men dragged off in captivity, churches sacked, and robbery, pillaging, violence and confusion everywhere."[99] The upshot of such horrors is that existing life is seriously degraded, and future possibilities for living well are severely diminished, or, as he puts it with his customary eloquence, when nations turn to war, "prosperity immediately declines, increase dwindles, towers are undermined, sound foundations are destroyed, and sweetness is embittered."[100]

So the key question becomes, how might the Christ of peace serve to rectify such a fractured state of existence? And what would it mean

97. Erasmus, "The Godly Feast," CWE 39: 183.
98. Erasmus, *Complaint of Peace*, CWE 27: 307, 312; "War is a treat," CWE 35: 403–4.
99. Erasmus, *Complaint of Peace*, CWE 27: 316; "War is a treat," CWE 35: 404.
100. Erasmus, *Complaint of Peace*, CWE 27: 293.

for the redemptive peace of Christ to transform the destructive condition of international life? Is such a thing possible, or even conceivable, for that matter? And if it is possible, how might it transpire?

When Erasmus takes up these questions, he turns from the psychological terms used to construe personal peace as serenity of conscience and purity of heart to the social language of friendship in order to depict what peaceful relations might mean for international relations. If it is true that there is nothing "better or sweeter" in "the whole world" than friendship, and Erasmus insists that this is very much the case, then "how great the happiness will be"—indeed, how much greater will it be—if "kingdom is united with kingdom and nation with nation in bonds of friendship."[101] As a kind of friendship between nations, therefore, peace on this grand scale represents first and foremost "the source of all human happiness." It is, he tells us, "the mother and nurse of all that is good"—at once, therefore, the social "fount and source," but equally "the sustainer, amplifier, and preserver of all the good things of heaven and earth."[102] Peace in this foundational sense, in short, is the necessary ground from which other human goods may blossom and upon which they may continue to flower, including, as Erasmus tells it, prosperity, security, purity, and pleasure: where such conditions are absent, those goods are undermined and nullified.

As Erasmus sees it, however, peace in the world is not only the condition for the possibility of these developments; it also is—far more significantly—a way of living together on friendly terms, such that people thrive in the activities that define their lives and the goods that fulfil them. The life of peace, in sum, is the active embodiment of the things that make human existence full and rich, and unlike the ravages of war, as Erasmus points out, the "advantages of peace" spread "very quickly," and "most people have a share in them."[103] Countries at peace, he observes, are places where "pleasures are nurtured, law is in repute, statecraft flourishes, religion is fervent, justice reigns, goodwill prevails, artisans practice their crafts with skill, the earnings of the poor are greater

---

101. Erasmus, "War is a treat," CWE 35: 412–13. For background on Erasmus's view of friendship, see Charlier, *Érasme et l'amitié d'apres sa correspondance*, 31–64.

102. Erasmus, *Complaint of Peace*, CWE 27: 293; "War is a treat," CWE 35: 412.

103. Erasmus, "War is a treat," CWE 35: 414.

and the opulence of the rich more splendid."[104] What this rhetorical flourish signals is both the breadth and the vitality of the life of peace. Peace is a way of living together in which people in each sphere of life excel in the activities that define their realm. When war overtakes the world, these very activities are thwarted, the goods are nullified, and life is diminished. By way of contrast, Erasmus insists, peace is a manner of living in which people become happier and better; consequently, it is "of all states both the best and most joyful."[105]

When Erasmus considers how the life of peace might be realized in a world of conflicting nations, he directs his appeals to those with the power to shape events—princes, kings, popes, and emperors—and he often does so with effusive praise for their commitment to peace, even when it is not in the least deserved, set against an idealized portrait of a wise and beneficent ruler.[106] Though the ideal may appear naive and the flattery sound unctuous, Erasmus explains that, in fact, he has landed on a "novel strategem" for reforming the powerful, one that involves crediting them with "possessing already in large measure the attractive qualities" he urges "them to cultivate." More precept than praise, therefore, though "under the guise of praise," good rulers could be improved and bad ones reformed, while even the "hopelessly vicious" might be made to "feel some inward stirrings of shame."[107] With this approach—at once courteous but with a satiric sting and strenuous moral challenge—Erasmus paints an extraordinarily rigorous portrait of the good prince as one who "does everything and allows everything" that will contribute to "continuous peace in his country."[108]

---

104. Erasmus, "War is a treat," CWE 35: 413. Compare with Erasmus, *Complaint of Peace*, CWE 27: 314 15; *Panegyric for Archduke Philip of Austria*, trans. Betty Radice, CWE 27: 53.

105. Erasmus, "War is a treat," CWE 35: 414–15.

106. For praise of pope Leo as peacemaker, see Erasmus to Leo X, letter 335, CWE 3:102; on Francis I for energetically working to quell "the tumults of war in perpetuity," see Erasmus to Francis I, letter 533, CWE 4: 269; on Henry VIII for zealously seeking the "restoration of the peace of the world," see Erasmus to Henry VIII, letter 964, CWE 6: 356–62; and on both Ferdinand and Charles V for their youthful openness to the "gospel of peace," see Erasmus to Archduke Ferdinand, letter 1333, CWE 9: 231–45.

107. On moral admonishment under the guise of praise, see Erasmus to Nicolas Ruistre, letter 179; Erasmus to Jean Desmarez, letter 180; and Erasmus to John Colet, letter 181, CWE 2: 77–89.

108. Erasmus, *The Education of a Christian Prince*, CWE 27: 225. On a prince's ideal duty, see Erasmus, "Sparta is your portion; do your best for her," adage II. v. 1, CWE 33: 238–39. See also Erasmus to Dukes Frederick and George of Saxony, letter 586, CWE 4: 573–83. To ascribe such virtues to monarchs and princes who clearly lack them is, as José Chapiro puts it, "the trick

A good ruler must be marked by "the highest integrity of character," we are told, that is, with a life that is rooted in wisdom, animated with beneficence, guided by virtues of restraint, and active in service for the public good.[109] Such a ruler will clearly see and understand that the ultimate good toward which all of his policies and actions should lead is the "welfare of his people," and, too, he will "warmly love his people," always "taking pleasure" in their well-being, and caring especially for "those who are cast down."[110] What this ideal sketch ultimately demands—astonishingly enough, given the lives and policies of actual princes—is a thorough-going eclipse of self-interest and an unflinching commitment to the common good. In a word, the prince "must take account of the other people's interests and disregard his own," something Erasmus's royal audience surely would regard with skeptical amazement, if not stunned incredulity.[111] It is exactly the intention of Erasmus, however, to confront the powerful with vivid images of the highest ideal, even while he challenges them to face the glaring shortfall in their own character.

Erasmus supplements this satiric prodding of the powerful with some practical proposals meant to foster the life of peace, yet here again, we find him goading political leaders to undertake policies that reflect the ethical ideals of the philosophy of Christ. When at peace, for instance, the good prince should maintain laws that are "just, fair, and conducive to the common good."[112] "The whole purpose of the law," Erasmus writes, "should be to protect everyone, rich or poor, noble or humble, serf or free man, public official or private citizen," though he

---

of a good comedian" who manages to make them appear "even more ridiculous than [if] he had showed them to be evil." See *Erasmus and Our Struggle for Peace* (Boston: Beacon Press, 1950), 71.

109. Erasmus, *Education of a Christian Prince*, CWE 27: 238.

110. Erasmus, *Education of a Christian Prince*, CWE 27: 213, 278, 240, and 263–64. The prince is, after all, only a single "free man ruling [many] free men," and consequently, Erasmus adds with considerable boldness, his power should be wielded in a manner that honors the humanity and "consent of his subjects" (229, 232). Similarly, see Erasmus, "A city and no city," adage V. ii. 6, CWE 36: 600.

111. Erasmus, *Education of a Christian Prince*, CWE 27: 238. Erasmus here draws on Paul's 1 Corinthians 10:24 and 33, as well as Philippians 2:3–4. Taking this evangelical reversal of roles yet further, Erasmus insists that the "ultimate intention of the good prince" is not simply "to guard the present well-being of the state" but to "hand it over in a more flourishing condition than that in which he received it," so the greater good to which the powerful are responsible is, in fact, a life of peace ranging far beyond their own lives (258).

112. Erasmus, *Education of a Christian Prince*, CWE 27: 264.

repeatedly insists that special effort should be made in "helping the weaker element" in society, since the life of "humble men" is exposed "more easily to danger."[113] When it comes to economic matters, we are told, princes should take care that "discrepancies in wealth are not excessive." Indeed, he suggests, some measures should be taken—essentially a progressive tax policy—to "prevent the wealth of the many from being allocated to the few."[114] In addition, Erasmus notes, it is in the prince's interest to make sure that the country's children are educated, and on the other end of life, that those "broken by illness or old age" are cared for in "state institutions."[115] There is, Erasmus observes, no shortage of practical projects for the prince who truly wishes to serve the public good by "increasing the prosperity of the realm."[116] If there should be war, however, then Erasmus counsels the good prince to take disputes to "arbitration," or alternatively to enter "sincere negotiations" with the adversary, where "personal interest"—once again—"will yield to general welfare."[117] With each of these points, Erasmus issues a counsel of humility and an imperative to the common good, exactly the virtues necessary if political power is to be wielded in a manner that promotes the realization of peace on an international scale.

What Erasmus proposes, in essence, would amount to a reversal of the world's twisted inversions of value that generate conflict and carnage across the span of human life. It ultimately promises a thoroughgoing transformation of the world as it has come to be, and thus an opening for redeemed life together where people might thrive in the activities that define their lives and the goods that fulfil them. All of this, in sum, is the point and purpose of the Christology of Erasmus: to clearly and persuasively articulate the redemptive capacity of the Christ of peace and then to indicate how and where this amelioration of life should take place. Earlier in this chapter, we saw how Erasmus conceives the effects of this transformation in the serenity of conscience evident in individuals like Glycion and Cornelius, and now, in this

113. Erasmus, *Education of a Christian Prince*, CWE 27: 269.
114. Erasmus, *Education of a Christian Prince*, CWE 27: 260–61.
115. Erasmus, *Education of a Christian Prince*, CWE 27: 259, 267.
116. Erasmus, *Education of a Christian Prince*, CWE 27: 280–81.
117. Erasmus, *Education of a Christian Prince*, CWE 27: 284; *Complaint of Peace*, CWE 27: 321. See also "War is a treat," CWE 35: 430–31.

section, we have heard Erasmus challenge the political order of his day with the ideals of the philosophy of Christ.

The latter is a radical proposal, to be sure, as it is designed to prompt the powerful to come to terms with the fact that the peace they enjoy, one that favors them in every way, is twisted and corrupt, and with that, to jolt, prod, and spur these individuals to embrace and practice the humility and love that is so central to the philosophy of Christ. In speaking like this, of course, Erasmus pins his hopes for the pacification of the international order on the virtuous actions of select individuals, largely because—as he sees it—it is the political elite who control the means for averting war and for fostering peace on the broadest of scales. And this is precisely why it is so important for Erasmus that the Christ of peace be held up before powerful leaders as the *scopus* for wise and beneficent governance, so that, like Glycion and Cornelius, they might come to possess hearts that are "above the riches, the pleasures, the honours of the world," and thus that they will become keenly attuned to the goal of restoring the world in imitation of the peace of Christ.[118]

It seems certain that princes of the day would find all this to be painfully unrealistic, just as many today—and, no doubt, many reading this very book—surely will complain of the idealistic tenor of these proposals, and in one sense, Erasmus would agree. Though the philosophy of Christ is "in and of itself ... an instrument of peace," he writes, its ideal vision of life is fundamentally at odds with the practical realities of the world, thus posing stark "divisions" with customary ways of thinking.[119] The world has its own sense of peace, Erasmus writes in paraphrase of *John*, though this is an "untrustworthy peace" designed to preserve the current shape of things as it is enjoyed by those with power and privilege. Thus, understandably enough, those comfortable with such a peace will be quick to dismiss and disparage the idealism of the peace of Christ.[120] Perhaps that is why Erasmus echoes some biblical traditions in speaking of the redemption of the world as an eschatological "transformation of things," where the mighty finally will be

---

118. Erasmus, *Paraphrase on Luke*, CWE 48: 112.

119. "Happy is the dividing," Erasmus writes, "that promotes what is sound, and cuts away what is rotten" (*Paraphrase on Matthew*, CWE 45: 176–77, 85). See also Erasmus, *Paraphrase on Luke*, CWE 48: 14, 42–44.

120. Erasmus, *Paraphrase on John*, CWE 46: 174.

"dragged down" and the needy raised up, and where religious insiders will be exposed as godless while "strangers to religion" will be shown to be "nearer to true religion."[121]

More typically and more interestingly, however, as we have seen throughout this book, Erasmus persists in speaking of the peace of Christ—truly an "amazing reversal of human affairs"[122]—as an ideal possibility for renewed ethical life brought forth and made manifest in Christ's life and teachings and thus as a living *scopus* to be held up for imitation throughout human life, both individual and collective. No doubt, once again, this very ideal will be met with dismissive skepticism by two groups of people, as Erasmus well knew, first, by those who cynically reject the possibility of any such transformation, and second, by those who are comfortable with the current state of the world and thus confidently reject the need for renewal. The former, as we heard earlier, despair of redemption, while the latter rest confident in their own capacities for achieving a life of peace.

In response, as we have seen, Erasmus recalls the immense mercy of God as the antidote to despair, even while he insists on the complementary role of human endeavor. The redemptive capacity of the Christ of peace, in short, offers serenity, amity, and joy to everyone, prompting and inviting people to respond with effort and zeal to this merciful appeal with lives shaped by the imitation of the virtues of Christ. As "true children of God," consequently, people are called to the imitation of God's abundant mercy, which means they are to aspire to "perfect virtue" by being "generous not only to our friends, relations, and supporters, but also to strangers, and even to our enemies and rivals."[123] The Gospel ethic of peace, after all, addresses not just what is allowed or realistic in the world as we find it to be but "what goal we must strive for with all our might," as Erasmus puts it,[124] and that goal (*scopus*)—as the consummation of the life of peace among nations—is an unusually extensive "friendship among many people."[125]

---

121. Erasmus, *Paraphrase on Luke*, CWE 47: 55, 88. See also *Paraphrase on Luke*, CWE 48: 55, 62, 98, 100, and 193.
122. Erasmus, *Paraphrase on Luke*, CWE 48: 138.
123. Erasmus, *Sermon on the Immense Mercy*, CWE 70: 98, 132–33.
124. Erasmus, "War is a treat," CWE 35: 426.
125. Erasmus, "War is a treat," CWE 35: 412.

BIBLIOGRAPHY

"Acts of John." *The Apocryphal New Testament*. Translated by M. R. James. Oxford: Clarendon Press, 1924.

Aelian. *Historical Miscellany*. Translated by N. G. Wilson. Cambridge, MA: Harvard University Press, 1997.

Amiel, Émilie. *Un libre-penseur du XVI siecle: Érasme*. Paris, 1899.

Aristotle. *The Complete Works of Aristotle*. Edited by Jonathan Barnes. 2 vols. Princeton, NJ: Princeton University Press, 1984.

Aquinas, Thomas. *Summa Theologica*. Translated by Fathers of the English Dominican Province. 3 vols. New York: Benziger Brothers, n.d.

Asso, Cecilia. "Martin Dorp and Edward Lee." Translated by Denis Robichaud. In *Biblical Humanism and Scholasticism in the Age of Erasmus*, edited by Erika Rummel, 174–95. Leiden: Brill, 2008.

Athanasius. "On the Incarnation of the Word." In *Christology of the Later Fathers*, edited by Edward Rochie Hardy, 55–110. Philadelphia: Westminster Press, 1954.

Augustine. *Expositions on the Psalms*. In *Nicene and Post-Nicene Fathers*. Series 1, vol. 8, translated by Philip Schaff. Grand Rapids, MI: Eerdmans, 1996.

———. *On Christian Doctrine*. Translated by D. W. Robertson, Jr. Indianapolis, IN: Bobbs-Merrill, 1958.

———. "On the Holy Trinity." In *Nicene and Post-Nicene Fathers of the Christian Church*, vol. 3, edited by Philip Schaff. New York: Charles Scribner's Sons, 1900.

———. *The City of God against the Pagans*. Translated by R. W. Dyson. Cambridge: Cambridge University Press, 1998.

Backus, Irena. "Deux cas d'évolution théologique dans les *Paraphrases* d'Erasme." In *Actes du colloque international Erasme*, Tours, 1986. Travaux d'Humanisme et Renaissance 239 (1990): 141–51.

———. "Renaissance Attitudes to New Testament Apocryphal Writings: Jacques Lefèvre d'Étaples and his Epigones." *Renaissance Quarterly* 51 (1998): 1169–98.

Baker-Smith, Dominic. Review of *Erasmus, Lee and the Correction of the Vulgate: The Shaking of the Foundations*, by Robert Coogan. *Moreana* 39, no. 149 (March 2002): 147–56.

Barker, William. "Implied Ethics in the *Adagia* of Erasmus: An Index of *Felicitas*." *Renaissance and Reformation; Renaissance et Réforme* 30, no. 1 (2006): 87–102.

———. *Erasmus of Rotterdam: The Spirit of a Scholar*. London: Reaktion Books, 2021.

Bedouelle, Guy. *Lefèvre D'Étaples et l'intelligence des écritures*. Genève: Librairie Droz, 1976.

———. "Jacques Lefèvre d'Étaples." In *The Reformation Theologians: An Introduction to Theology in the Early Modern Period*, edited by Carter Lindberg, 19–33. Oxford: Blackwell, 2002.

———. "Attacks on the Biblical Humanism of Jacques Lefèvre d'Étaples." Translated by Anna Machado-Matheson. In *Biblical Humanism and Scholasticism in the Age of Erasmus*, edited by Erika Rummel, 117–41. Leiden: Brill, 2008.

Bentley, J. H. *Humanists and Holy Writ*. Princeton, NJ: Princeton University Press, 1983.

Benz, Ernst. "Christus und die Silene des Alcibiades." In *Christliche Wirklichkeitsschau. Aus der Welt der Religion*, edited by Heinrich Frick, 1–31. Berlin: Alfred Töpelmann, 1940.

Bietenholz, Peter G. *History and Biography in the Work of Erasmus of Rotterdam*. Genève: Librairie Droz, 1966.

———. *Basle and France in the Sixteenth Century: The Basle Humanists and Printers in Their Contacts with Francophone Culture*. Genève: Librairie Droz, 1971.

———. *Encounters with a Radical Erasmus: Erasmus' Work as a Source of Radical Thought in Early Modern Europe*. Toronto: University of Toronto Press, 2009.

Bietenholz, Peter G., ed. *Contemporaries of Erasmus: A Biographical*

Register of the Renaissance and Reformation. 3 vols. Toronto: University of Toronto Press, 1987.

Bloemendal, Jan. "Erasmus and Biblical Scholarship." In *A Companion to Erasmus*, edited by Eric MacPhail, 68–89. Leiden: Brill, 2023.

———. "Erasmus' Paraphrases on the New Testament: Introduction." *Erasmus Studies*, 36 (2016): 105–22.

———. "Exegesis and Hermeneutics in Erasmus' *Paraphrases on Luke.*" *Erasmus Studies* 36 (2016): 148–62.

Bonaventure. *Breviloquium.* In *The Works of Bonaventure*, vol. 2, translated by José de Vinck. Paterson, NJ: St. Anthony Guild Press, 1963.

Bouyer, Louis. *Autour d'Erasme: Études sur le christianisme des humanistes catholique.* Paris, 1955.

———. *Erasmus and His Times.* Westminster, MD: Newman, 1959.

———. *Erasmus and the Humanist Experiment.* Translated by Francis X. Murphy. London: Geoffrey Chapman, 1959.

Boyle, Marjorie O'Rourke. *Erasmus on Language and Method in Theology.* Toronto: University of Toronto Press, 1977.

———. *Rhetoric and Reform: Erasmus' Civil Dispute with Luther.* Cambridge, MA: Harvard University Press, 1983.

Brush, J. W. "Lefèvre d'Étaples: Three Phases of his Life and Work." In *Reformation Studies: Essays in Honor of Roland H. Bainton*, edited by Franklin H. Littell, 117–28. Richmond, VA: John Knox Press, 1962.

Cameron, Richard M. "The Charges of Lutheranism Brought against Jacques Lefèvre d'Étaples (1520–1529)." *The Harvard Theological Review* 63, no. 1 (January 1970), 119–49.

Carrington, Laurel. "The Writer and His Style: Erasmus' Clash with Guillaume Budé. *Erasmus of Rotterdam Society Yearbook* 10 (1990): 61–82.

Chantraine, Georges. *'Mystère' et 'Philosophie du Christ' selon Erasme.* Namur Gembloux, 1971.

Chantraine, Georges G. "The *Ratio Verae Theologiae* (1518)." In *Essays on the Works of Erasmus*, edited by Richard L. DeMolen, 179–85. New Haven, CT: Yale University Press, 1978.

Chapiro, José. *Erasmus and Our Struggle for Peace.* Boston: Beacon Press, 1950.

Charlier, Yvonne. *Érasme et l'amitié d'apres sa correspondance.* Paris: Les Belles Lettres, 1977.

Chomarat, Jacques. *Grammaire et rhétorique chez Érasme.* 2 vols. Paris: Belles Lettres, 1981.

———. "Érasme: La misércorde de Dieu, sermon. Présentation," *Moreana* 32, no. 122 (June 1995): 5–8.

Christ-Von Wedel, Christine. *Erasmus of Rotterdam: Advocate of a New Christianity*. Toronto: University of Toronto Press, 2013.

Christian, Lynda Gregorian. "The Figure of Socrates in Erasmus' Work." *Sixteenth Century Journal* 3, no. 2 (October 1972): 1–10.

Cicero. *The Letters to His Friends*. Vol. 1. Translated by W. Glynn Williams. London: William Heinemann, 1927.

Colet, John. *An Exposition of St. Paul's Epistle to the Romans*. Translated by J. H. Lupton. Eugene. OR: Wipf and Stock, 2007; replicated from the edition by Bell and Daldy, 1873.

———. *John Colet's Commentary on First Corinthians*. Edited by Bernard O'Kelly and Catherine A. L. Jarrott. Binghampton, NY: Medieval and Renaissance Texts and Studies, 1985.

Coogan, Robert. *Erasmus, Lee and the Correction of the Vulgate: The Shaking of the Foundations*. Genève: Librairie Droz, 1992.

———. "The Pharisee Against the Hellenist: Edward Lee Versus Erasmus." *Renaissance Quarterly* 39, no. 3 (Autumn 1986): 476–506.

Coppens, J. "Où en est le portrait d'Érasme théologien?" In *Scrinium Erasmianum*, vol. 2, edited by J. Coppens, 569–93. Leiden: Brill, 1969.

Cullmann, Oscar. *Christ and Time: The Primitive Christian Conception of Time and History*. Revised edition. Translated by Floyd V. Filson. Philadelphia: Westminster Press, 1964.

Cummings, Brian. "Erasmus, Sacred Literature, and Literary Theory." In *Erasmus on Literature: His Ratio or "System" of 1518/1519*, edited by Mark Vessey, 48–62. Toronto: University of Toronto Press, 2021.

Curtius, E. R. *European Literature and the Latin Middle Ages*. Translated by W. R. Trask. Princeton, NJ: Princeton University Press, 2013.

Cyprian. "The Unity of the Catholic Church." In *St. Cyprian, The Lapsed and The Unity of the Catholic Church*, translated by Maurice Bévenot, 43–68. Westminster, MD: Newman Press, 1957.

Dagens, J. "Humanisme et évangélisme chez Lefèvre d'Étaples." In *Courants religieux et humanisme à la fin du XVe et au début du XVIe siècle*, 121–34. Paris: Universitaires de France, 1959.

Dealy, Ross. "The Dynamics of Erasmus' Thought on War." *Erasmus of Rotterdam Society Yearbook* 4, no. 1 (1984): 53–67.

———. *The Stoic Origins of Erasmus' Philosophy of Christ*. Toronto: University of Toronto Press, 2017.

The Deipnosophists. Or Banquet of the Learned Athenaeus. Translated by
C. D. Yonge. London: Henry G. Bohn, 1854.

De Jonge, H. J. "Erasmus and the Comma Johanneum." *Ephemerides
Theologicae Lovanienses* 56 (1980): 381–89.

———. "Introduction." In *Opera omnia Desiderii Erasmi Roterdami*,
IX - 2, edited by H. J. De Jonge, 3–58. Amsterdam: North-Holland
Publishing, 1983.

———. "The Character of Erasmus' Translation from the New Testament
as Reflected in His Translation of Heb. 9." *The Journal of Medieval and
Renaissance Studies* 14, no. 1 (1984): 81–87.

De Jonge, Henk J. "The Relationship of Erasmus' Translation of the
New Testament to that of the Pauline Epistles by Lefèvre d'Étaples."
Erasmus in English, May 1984: 1–7.

Delcourt, Marie, and Marcelle Derwa. "Trois aspects humanistes de
l'épicurisme chrétien." In *Colloquium Erasmianum: Actes du colloque
internationale réuni à Mons du 26 au 29 octobre 1967*, 119–33. Mons:
Centre Universitaire de L'État, 1968.

De la Garanderie, Marie-Madeleine. "Qui était Guillaume Budé?" *Bulletin
de l'Association Guillaume Budé*, no. 2 (June 1967): 192–11.

Delaruelle, Louis. "Une amitié d'humanistes, Étude sur les relations de
Budé et d'Érasme d'après leur correspondance." *Musée Belge* (1905):
321–51.

DeMolen, Richard. "*Puero Christi Imitatio*: The Festival of the Boy-Bishop
in Tutor England." *Moreana* 12, no. 1 (1975): 17–28.

DeMolen, Richard L. *The Spirituality of Erasmus of Rotterdam*. Nieuwkoop: De Graaf Publishers, 1987.

Diodorus of Sicily. *Library of History*. Translated by C. H. Oldfather.
Cambridge, MA: Harvard University Press, 1961.

Diogenes Laertius: Lives and Opinions of Eminent Philosophers. 10 vols.
London: William Heinemann, 1925.

Drysdall, Denis L. "Erasmus on Tyranny and Terrorism: *Scarabaeus aquilam quaerit* and the *Institutio principis christiani*." *Erasmus of Rotterdam Society Yearbook* 29 (2009): 89–102.

———. "The Two Versions of Erasmus's *Apologia De In Principio Erat
Sermo* and the Role of Edward Lee." In *Acta Conventus Neo-Latini Upsaliensis*, vol. 1, edited by Alejandro Coroleu and Domenico Defilipps,
363–72. Leiden: Brill., 2009

Eden, Kathy. *Friends Hold All Things in Common: Tradition, Intellectual*

Property, and the Adages of Erasmus. New Haven, CT: Yale University Press, 2001.

Encyclopedia of Comparative Iconography. Edited by Helene E. Roberts. Chicago: Fitzroy Dearborn, 1998.

The Epistles of John. Translated by Raymond E. Brown. In Anchor Bible, vol. 30. Garden City, NY: Doubleday and Company, 1982.

Erasmus, Desiderius. *The Collected Works of Erasmus*. Toronto: University of Toronto Press, 1974–.

———. *Opus epistolarum Desiderius Erasmi Roterodami*. 12 vols. Edited by P. S. Allen. London: Oxford University Press, 1913.

———. *Opera omnia Desiderii Erasmi Roterdami*. Amsterdam, 1969–.

Erasmus, Desiderius. *Praise of Folly*. Translated by Clarence H. Miller. New Haven, CT: Yale University Press, 1979.

Essary, Kirk. *Erasmus and Calvin on the Foolishness of God: Reason and Emotion in the Christian Philosophy*. Toronto: University of Toronto Press, 2017.

Etienne, Jacques. "La médiation des écritures selon Érasme." In *Scrinium Erasmianum*, vol. 2, edited by J. Coppens, 4–11. Leiden: Brill, 1969.

Farge, James K. *Orthodoxy and Reform in Early Reformation France: The Faculty of Theology of Paris, 1500–1543*. Leiden: Brill, 1985.

Farge, James K. "Noël Béda and the Defense of the Tradition." In *Biblical Humanism and Scholasticism in the Age of Erasmus*, edited by Erika Rummel, 143–64. Leiden: Brill, 2008.

Farge, James K., ed. *Religion, Reformation, and Repression in the Reign of Francis I: Documents from the Parlement of Paris, 1515–1547*. Vol. 1. Toronto: Pontifical Institute of Medieval Studies, 2015.

Febvre, Lucien. "Une question mal posée: Les origines de la réforme et le problème des causes de la réforme." In *Au coeur religieux du XVIe siècle*, deuxième édition, 7–95. Paris: École Pratique des Hautes Études, 1957. Originally published in 1929.

———. *The Problem of Unbelief in the Sixteenth Century: The Religion of Rabelais*. Translated by Beatrice Gottlieb. Cambridge, MA: Harvard University, 1982.

Feld, H. "Der Humanistern-Streit um Hebräer, 2, 7 (Psalm 8, 6)." *Archiv für Reformationsgeschichte* 61 (1970): 5–35.

Fernández, José A. "Erasmus on Just War." *Journal of the History of Ideas* 34, no. 2 (April–June 1973): 209–26.

Fokke, G. J. "An Aspect of the Christology of Erasmus of Rotterdam." *Ephemerides Theologicae Lovanienses* 54 (1978): 161–87.

Freudenburg, Kirk. *The Walking Muse: Horace on the Theory of Satire.* Princeton, NJ: Princeton University Press, 1993.

Gardet, L. "Actualité d'Érasme." *Revue Thomiste* 47, no. 3 (1947): 550–60.

Gellius, Aulus. *The Attic Nights of Aulus Gellius.* Vol. 2. Translated by John C. Rolfe. Cambridge, MA: Harvard University Press, 1960.

Gerrish, B. A. "*De Libero Arbitrio* (1524): Erasmus on Piety, Theology, and the Lutheran Dogma." In *Essays on the Works of Erasmus*, edited by Richard L. DeMolen, 187–209. New Haven, CT: Yale University Press, 1978.

Gieles, Marcel. "Leuven Theologians as Opponents of Erasmus and of Humanistic Theology." Translated by Paul Arblaster. In *Biblical Humanism and Scholasticism in the Age of Erasmus*, edited by Erika Rummel, 197–214. Leiden: Brill, 2008.

Gleason, John B. *John Colet.* Berkeley: University of California Press, 1989.

Godin, André. *Érasme, lecteur d'Origène.* Genève: Librairie Droz, 1982.

———. "The *Enchiridion Militis Christiani*: The Modes of an Origenian Appropriation." *Erasmus of Rotterdam Society Yearbook* 2 (1982): 47–79.

Gordon, Walter M. *Humanist Play and Belief: The Seriocomic Art of Desiderius Erasmus.* Toronto: University of Toronto, 1990.

The Gospel According to John (i–xii). In Anchor Bible, vol. 29, translated by Raymond E. Brown. Garden City, NY: Doubleday and Company, 1966.

Graham, Richard Homer. "Erasmus and Stunica." *Erasmus of Rotterdam Society Yearbook* 10, no. 1 (1990): 9–60.

Grant, John N. "Erasmus' Adages." In *Collected Works of Erasmus: Prolegomena to the Adages*, vol. 30, 1–38. Toronto: University of Toronto Press, 2017.

Gredley, Bernard. "Dance and Greek Drama." In *Drama, Dance, and Music*, edited by James Redmond. Vol. 3 of *Themes in Drama*. Cambridge: Cambridge University Press, 1981.

The Greek Anthology. 3 vols. Edited by E. Capps, T. E. Page, and W. H. D. Rouse. London: William Heinemann, 1915.

Gregory of Nyssa. "An Answer to Ablabius: That We Should Not Think of Saying There Are Three Gods." In *Christology of the Later Fathers,* edited by Edward Rochie Hardy, 256–67. Philadelphia: Westminster Press, 1954.

Grendler, Paul F. "How to Get a Degree in Fifteen Days: Erasmus' Doctorate in Theology from the University of Turin." *Erasmus of Rotterdam Society Yearbook* 18 (1998): 40–69.

Grillmeier, Aloys. *Christ in Christian Tradition: From the Apostolic Age to Chalcedon (451)*. Translated by J. S. Bowden. New York: Sheed and Ward, 1965.

Gustafson, James M. *Christ and the Moral Life*. Chicago: University of Chicago Press, 1968, Midway reprint, 1976.

Hadot, J. "La critique textuelle dans l'édition du Nouveau Testament d'Érasme." In *Colloquia Erasmiana Turonensia*, vol. 2, 749–60. Paris: Librairie Philosophique J. Vrin, 1972.

Hanson, R. P. C. *The Search for The Christian Doctrine of God: The Arian Controversy, 318–381*. Grand Rapids, MI: Baker Academic, 1988.

Heath, Michael J. "Twelfth Annual Bainton Lecture: Erasmus and the Infidel." *Erasmus of Rotterdam Society Yearbook* 16 (1996): 19–33.

Hauser, Henri. *Études sur la réforme française*. Paris: Alphonse Picard et Fils, 1909.

Heller, Henry. "The Evangelicalism of Lefèvre d'Étaples." *Studies in the Renaissance* 19 (1972): 42–77.

Hoffmann, Manfred. "Erasmus and Religious Toleration." *Erasmus of Rotterdam Society Yearbook* 2, no. 1 (January 1982): 80–106.

———. *Rhetoric and Theology: The Hermeneutic of Erasmus*. Toronto: University of Toronto Press, 1994.

Homza, Lu Ann. "Erasmus as Hero, or Heretic? Spanish Humanism and the Valladolid Assembly of 1527." *Renaissance Quarterly* 50, no. 1 (1997): 78–118.

Horace. *The Odes and Epodes of Horace*. Translated by Joseph P. Clancy. Chicago: University of Chicago Press, 1960.

Housely, Norman. *Religious Warfare in Europe, 1400–1536*. Oxford: Oxford University Press, 2002.

Hughes, Philip Edgcumbe. *Lefèvre: Pioneer of Ecclesiastical Renewal in France*. Grand Rapids, MI: William B. Eerdmans Publishing, 1984.

Jacopin, Paul, and Jacqueline Lagrée. *Érasme, humanisme et langage*. Paris: Presse Universitaires de France, 1996.

Jaeger, Werner. *Aristotle: Fundamentals of the History of His Development.*

Translated by Richard Robinson. 2nd ed. London: Oxford University Press, 1962.

Jarrott, C. A. L. "Erasmus' *In principio erat sermo*: A Controversial Translation." *Studies in Philology* 61 (1964): 35–40.

———. "Erasmus' Biblical Humanism." *Studies in the Renaissance* 17 (1970): 119–52.

Jarrott, Catherine A. L. "Erasmus' Annotations and Colet's Commentaries on Paul: A Comparison of Some Theological Themes." In *Essays on the Works of Erasmus*, edited by Richard L. DeMolen, 125–44. New Haven, CT: Yale University Press, 1978.

Jonas, Hans. *The Gnostic Religion: The Message of the Alien God and the Beginnings of Christianity.* 2nd ed. Boston: Beacon Press, 1963.

Kohls, Ernst-Wilhelm. *Die Theologie des Erasmus: Textband.* Basel: Friedrich Reinhardt Verlag, 1966.

Kümmel, Werner Georg. *The New Testament: The History of the Investigation of its Problems.* Translated by S. McLean Gilmour and Howard C. Kee. Nashville: Abingdon Press, 1970.

Lear, Jonathan. *A Case for Irony.* Cambridge, MA: Harvard University Press, 2011.

Lefèvre d'Étaples, Jacques. *The Prefatory Epistles of Jacques Lefèvre d'Étaples and Related Texts.* Edited by Eugene F. Rice, Jr. New York: Columbia University Press, 1972.

Le Normand, Antoinette. "Le triomphe de Silène de Jules Dalou." *La Revue du Louvre et des Musées de France* 30, no. 3 (1980): 166–67.

Levine, Joseph M. "Erasmus and the Problem of the Johannine Comma." *Journal of the History of Ideas* 58, no. 4 (October 1997): 573–96.

Llinarè, Armand. "Le Lullisme de Lefèvre d'Étaples et de ses amis humanistes." In *L'humanisme français au début de la renaissance*, 127–36. Colloque International de Tours. Paris: Librairie Philosophique J. Vrin, 1973.

Lochman, Daniel T. "Colet and Erasmus: The *Disputatiuncula* and the Controversy of Letter and Spirit." *The Sixteenth Century Journal* 20, no. 1 (Spring 1989): 77–88.

Lucian. "Icaromenippus, or the Sky-Man." In *Lucian*, vol. 2, translated by A. M. Harmon, 268–323. Cambridge, MA: Harvard University Press, 1988.

Lupton, J. H. *A Life of John Colet, D.D.* London: George Bell and Sons, 1887; Hamden, CT: The Shoe String Press, 1961.

Luther, Martin. *The Bondage of the Will*. Translated by Philip S. Watson.
     Vol. 33 of *Luther's Works: Career of the Reformer 3*. Edited by Philip S.
     Watson. Philadelphia: Fortress Press, 1972.
———. "The Freedom of a Christian." In *Career of the Reformer 1*, edited
     by Harold J. Grimm, 343–77. Vol. 31 of *Luther's Works*. Translated by
     W. A. Lambert and Harold J. Grimm. Philadelphia: Fortress Press,
     1957.
———. *Luther's Works: Table Talk*. Vol. 54. Translated by Theodore G.
     Tappert. Philadelphia: Fortress Press, 1967.
MacPhail, Eric. "Erasmus and Christian Humanist Latin." *Reformation* 22,
     no. 2 (2017): 67–81.
McConica, James Kelsey. "Erasmus and the Grammar of Consent." In
     Scrinium Erasmianum, vol. 2, edited by J. Coppens, 77–99. Leiden:
     E. J. Brill, 1969.
McDonald, Grantley Robert. *Biblical Criticism in Early Modern Europe:
     Erasmus, the Johannine Comma, and Trinitarian Debate*. Cambridge:
     Cambridge University Press, 2016.
McNeil, David O. *Guillaume Budé and Humanism in the Reign of Francis
     I*. Travaux d'humanisme et renaissance, no. 142. Geneva: Droz, 1975.
Mann, Margaret. *Érasme et les débuts de la réforme française (1517–1536)*.
     Paris: Librairie Ancienne Honoré Champion, 1934.
Mansfield, Bruce. *Phoenix of His Age: Interpretations of Erasmus,
     c. 1550–1750*. Toronto: University of Toronto Press, 1979.
———. *Man on His Own: Interpretations of Erasmus, c. 1750–1920*. Toron-
     to: University of Toronto Press, 1992.
———. *Erasmus in the Twentieth Century: Interpretations c. 1920–2000*.
     Toronto: University of Toronto Press, 2003.
Marc'hadour, Germain. "Érasme et John Colet." In *Colloquia Erasmiana
     Tyronensia*, vol. 2, 761–69. Paris: Librairie philosophique J. Vrin, 1972.
Martin, Terence J. *Living Words: Studies in Dialogues about Religion*.
     Atlanta, Ga.: Scholars Press, 1998.
———. "The Intractable Dialectic of Tyranny and Terror: A Reading of
     an Erasmian Adage." *Soundings: An Interdisciplinary Journal* 98, no. 2
     (May 2015): 163–91.
———. *Truth and Irony: Philosophical Meditations on Erasmus*. Washing-
     ton, DC: The Catholic University of America Press, 2015.
———. "The Prospects for Holy War: A Reading of a 'Consultation' from
     Erasmus." *Erasmus Studies* 36, no. 2 (October 2016): 195–217.

———. "'The Funeral': An Erasmian Sketch for Enhanced Life." In *Responsibility and the Enhancement of Life: Essays in Honor of William Schweiker*, edited by Günter Thomas and Heike Springhart, 147–56. Leipzig: Evangelische Verlagsanstalt, 2017.

———. "Heresy and Humanity: Erasmian Retrievals and Overtures." *Erasmus Studies* 41 (2021): 1–28.

Massaut, Jean-Pierre. *Critique et tradition à la veille de la réforme en France: étude suivie de textes inédits traduits et annotés*. Paris: Librairie philosophique J. Vrin, 1974.

Mesnard, Pierre. "Un texte important d'Erasme touchant sa 'Philosophie chrétienne.'" *Revue Thomiste* 47, no. 3 (1947): 524–33.

Metzger, Bruce M. *The Early Versions of the New Testament: Their Origin, Transmission, and Limitations*. Oxford: Clarendon Press, 1977.

Mohl, Ruth. *The Three Estates in Medieval and Renaissance Literature*. New York: Columbia University Press, 1933.

The New Oxford Annotated Bible: New Revised Standard Version. 4th ed. Edited by Michael D. Coogan. Oxford: Oxford University Press, 2010.

Nicholas of Cusa: Selected Spiritual Writings. Translated by H. Lawrence Bond. New York: Paulist Press, 1997.

Nietzsche, Friedrich. *The Birth of Tragedy and The Genealogy of Morals*. Translated by Francis Golffing. Garden City, NY: Doubleday and Company, 1956.

Nonnus. *Dionysiaca*. Translated by W. H. D. Rouse. Cambridge, MA: Harvard University Press, 1956.

Olin, J. "Erasmus and the Church Fathers." In *Six Essays on Erasmus*, 33–48. New York: Fordham University Press, 1979.

Origen. *On First Principles*. Translated by G. W. Butterworth. Gloucester, MA: Peter Smith, 1973.

Ovid. *Fasti*. Translated by James George Frazer. Cambridge, MA: Harvard University Press, 1931.

———. *Metamorphoses*. Translated by A. D. Melville. Oxford: Oxford University Press, 1986.

Pabel, Hilmar M. "The Prince of Peace: Erasmus' Conception of Jesus." In *The Unbounded Community; Papers in Christian Ecumenism in Honor of Jaroslav Pelikan*, edited by William Cafferro and Duncan G. Fisher, 127–48. New York and London: Garland Publishing, 1996.

Pausanias. *Descriptions of Greece*. Translated by W. H. S. Jones. Cambridge, MA: Harvard University Press, 1960.

Payne, John B. *Erasmus: His Theology of the Sacraments*. Richmond, Va.: John Knox, 1970.

———. "Erasmus and Lefèvre d'Étaples as Interpreters of Paul." *Archiv für Reformationsgeschichte* 65 (1974): 54–82.

Pelikan, Jaroslav. *The Emergence of the Catholic Tradition (100–600)*. Vol. 1 of *The Christian Tradition: A History of the Development of Doctrine*. Chicago: University of Chicago Press, 1971.

Pelikan, Jaroslav. *Jesus Through the Centuries: His Place in the History of Culture*. New York: Harper and Row, 1985.

Percival, W. Keith. "Grammar and Rhetoric in the Renaissance." In *Renaissance Eloquence: Studies in the Theory and Practice of Renaissance Rhetoric*, edited by James J. Murphy, 303–30. Berkeley: University of California Press, 1983.

Phillips, Margaret Mann. "La '*Philosophia Christi*' reflétée dan les 'Adages' d'Érasme." In *Courants religieux et humanisme à la fin du XVe et au début du XVIe siècle*, 53–71. Paris: Universitaires de France, 1959.

———. "The Character and Growth of the 'Adages.'" In *The 'Adages' of Erasmus: A Study with Translations*. Cambridge: Cambridge University Press, 1964.

———. "Some Last Words of Erasmus." In *Luther, Erasmus and the Reformation: A Catholic-Protestant Reappraisal*, edited by John C. Olin, James D. Smart, and Robert E. McNally, 87–113. New York: Fordham University, 1969.

———. "Visages d'Érasme." In *Colloque Érasmien de Liège*, 17–33. Paris: Les Belles Lettres, 1987.

Philostratus (the Elder). *Imagines*. Translated by Arthur Fairbanks. Cambridge, MA: Harvard University Press, 1960.

Pineau, P.-B. *Érasme: Sa pensée religieuse*. Paris: Les Presses Universitaires de France, 1924.

Plutarch. "A Letter of Condolence to Apollonius." In *Plutarch's Moralia*, translated by Frank Cole Babbitt, 105–211. London: William Heinemann, 1928.

Quintilian. *Institutio oratoria*. 3 vols. Translated by H. E. Butler. Cambridge, MA: Harvard University Press, 1933.

Rabil, Jr., Albert. "Erasmus's Paraphrases of the New Testament." In *Essays on the Works of Erasmus*, edited by Richard L. DeMolen, 145–61. New Haven, CT: Yale University, 1978.

Plato. *The Collected Dialogues of Plato.* Edited by Edith Hamilton and Huntington Cairns. Princeton, NJ: Princeton University Press, 1961.

———. *The Republic of Plato.* Translated by Francis MacDonald Cornford. New York: Oxford University Press, 1945,

———. *The Symposium and The Phaedrus: Plato's Erotic Dialogues.* Translated by William S. Cobb. Albany: State University of New York Press, 1993.

Rahner, Karl. *Foundations of Christian Faith: An Introduction to the Idea of Christianity.* Translated by William V. Dych. New York: Seabury Press, 1978.

Regier, Willis Goth. "Adages as Insults: Erasmus against the Barbarians." *Erasmus Studies* 40 (2020): 58–59.

Renaudet, Augustin. *Préreforme et humanisme à Paris pendant les premières guerres d'Italie (1497–1517).* Paris: Librairie Ancienne Honoré Champion, 1916.

———. *Études Érasmiennes (1521–1529).* Paris: Librairie E. Droz, 1939.

———. "Autour d'une définition de l'humanisme." In *Humanisme et Renaissance*, 32–53. Genève: Librairie E. Droz, 1958.

———. "Un problème historique: La pensée religieuse de J. Lefèvre d'Étaples," In *Humanisme et Renaissance*, 201–16. Genève: Librairie E. Droz, 1958.

Reventlow, Henning Graf. *The Authority of the Bible and the Rise of the Modern World.* Philadelphia: Fortress Press, 1985.

Rice, Jr., Eugene F. "John Colet and the Annihilation of the Natural." *The Harvard Theological Review* 45, no. 3 (July 1952): 141–63.

———. "The Humanist Idea of Christian Antiquity: Lefèvre D'Étaples and his Circle." *Studies in the Renaissance* 9 (1962): 126–60.

———. "Humanist Aristotelianism in France: Jacque Lefèvre d'Étaples and his Circle." In *Humanism in France at the End of the Middle Ages and in the Early Renaissance*, edited by A. H. T. Levi, 132–49. Manchester: Manchester University Press, 1970.

———. "Jacques Lefèvre d'Étaples and the Medieval Christian Mystics." In *Florilegium Historiale: Essays Presented to Wallace K. Ferguson*, edited by J. G. Rowe and W. H. Stockdale, 89–124. Toronto: University of Toronto Press, 1971.

———. *Saint Jerome in the Renaissance.* Baltimore: Johns Hopkins University Press, 1985.

Rieger, James Henry. "Erasmus, Colet, and the Schoolboy Jesus." *Studies in the Renaissance* 9 (1962): 187–94.

Romans. In Anchor Bible, vol. 33, translated by Joseph A. Fitzmeyer. New York: Doubleday, 1992.

Rummel, Erika. *Erasmus as a Translator of the Classics*. Toronto: University of Toronto Press, 1985.

———. *Erasmus' Annotations on the New Testament: From Philologist to Theologian*. Toronto: University of Toronto Press, 1986.

———. "Erasmus and the Valladolid Articles: Intrigue, Innuendo and Strategic Defense." In *Erasmus of Rotterdam: The Man and the Scholar*, edited by J. Sperna Weiland, 69–78. Leiden, 1988.

———. *Erasmus and His Catholic Critics (1515–1522)*. Vol. 1. Nieuwkoop: De Graaf Publishers, 1989.

———. *Erasmus and His Catholic Critics (1523–1536)*. Vol. 2. Nieuwkoop: De Graaf Publishers, 1989

———. "New Perspectives on the Controversy Between Erasmus and Lee." *Nederlands Archief voor Kerkgeschiedenis/Dutch Review of Church History* 74, no. 2 (1994): 226–32.

———. *The Humanist-Scholastic Debate in the Renaissance and Reformation*. Cambridge, MA: Harvard University Press, 1995.

Schmidt, Charles B. *Cicero Scepticus: A Study of the Academica in the Renaissance*. The Hague, 1972.

Schoeck, R. J. *Erasmus of Europe: The Making of a Humanist, 1467–1500*. Edinburgh: Edinburgh University Press, 1990.

Schoof, Mark. *A Survey of Catholic Theology, 1800–1970*. Translated by N. D. Smith. Paramus, NJ: Paulist Newman Press, 1970.

Screech, M. A. *Laughter at the Foot of the Cross*. Boulder, Colo.: Westview Press, 1977.

———. *Erasmus: Ecstasy and The Praise of Folly*. London: Penguin, 1980.

Schweiker, William. "Humanity and the Global Future." *Responsibility and the Enhancement of Life: Essays in Honor of William Schweiker*, edited by Günter Thomas and Heike Springhart, 13–33. Leipzig: Evangelische Verlagsanstalt, 2017.

Seidel-Menchi, Silvana. *Erasmus als Ketzer: Reformation und Inquisition im Italien des 16. Jahrhunderts*. Leiden: E. J. Brill, 1993.

Seneca. *Seneca ad Lucilium Epistulae Morales*. 3 vols. Translated by Richard M. Gummere. Cambridge, MA: Harvard University, 1934.

———. *Seneca: Moral Essays*. 3 vols. Translated by John W. Basore. Cambridge, MA: Harvard University Press, 1935.

Spitz, Lewis E. *The Religious Renaissance of the German Humanists*. Cambridge, MA: Harvard University Press, 1963.

Stauffer, Richard. "Lefèvre d'Étaples, artisan ou spectateur de la réforme?" In *Interprètes de la Bible*, 11–29. Paris: Beauchesne, 1980. Original article from 1967.

Stavru, Allessandro. "Socrates' Physiognomy: Plato and Xenophon in Comparison." In *Plato and Xenophon: Comparative Studies*, edited by Gabriel Danzig, David Johnson, and Donald Morrison, 208–51. Leiden: Brill, 2018.

Steenbeek, Andrea W. "Introduction." In *Opera omnia: Desiderii Erasmi Roterdami*, IX – 3, edited by Andrea W. Steenbeek, 1–77. Amsterdam: Elsevier, 1996.

Stegmann, A. "Érasme et la France (1495–1520)." In *Colloquium Erasmianum*, 285–88. Mons: Centre Universitaire de L'Etat,, 1968.

Terence. *The Comedies of Terence*. Translated by Frank O. Copley. Indianapolis, IN: Bobbs-Merrill, 1967.

Thompson, Craig R. *Inquisitio de Fide: A Colloquy*. Hamden, CT: Archon Books, 1975.

Tracy, David. *Plurality and Ambiguity: Hermeneutics, Religion, Hope*. San Francisco: Harper and Row, 1987.

Tracy, James D. "Erasmus and the Arians: Remarks on the *Consensus Ecclesiae*." *Catholic Historical Review* 67 (1981): 1–10.

———. "Humanists Among the Scholastics: Erasmus, More, and Lefèvre d'Étaples on the Humanity of Christ." *Erasmus of Rotterdam Society Yearbook* 4 (1984): 30–51.

———. *Erasmus of the Low Countries*. Berkeley: University of California, 1996.

Tyrrell, George. *Christianity at the Crossroads*. London: George Allen and Unwin, Ltd., 1963.

Van Herwaarden, Jan. "Erasmus's Doctorate in Turin, Free Thought and Rotterdam, 1506–1876." In *Between Saint James and Erasmus: Studies in Late-Medieval Religious Life: Devotions and Pilgrimage in the Netherlands*, translated by Wendie Shaffer and Donald Gardner, 736–62. Leiden and Boston: Brill, 2003.

Van Unnik, W. C. "A Note on the Dance of Jesus in the 'Acts of John.'" *Vigiliae Christianae* 18 (1964): 1–5.

Vessey, Mark. "The *Ratio* in Erasmus' Life and Work to 1519." In *Erasmus on Literature: His Ratio or "System" of 1518/1519*, edited by Mark Vessey, 21–47. Toronto: University of Toronto Press, 2021.

Virgil. Translated by H. Rushton Fairclough. Cambridge, MA: Harvard University Press, 1942.

Walker, D. P. "Origène en France au début du XVI siècle." In *Courants religieux et humanisme à la fin du XVe et au début du XVIe siècle*, 101–19. Paris: Universitaires de France, 1959.

Waltke, Bruce K., James M. Houston, and Erika Moore. "Psalm 39: The Lament of Silence in the Theology of Erasmus." In *The Psalms as Christian Lament: A Historical Commentary*, 149–55. Grand Rapids, MI: Eerdmans, 2014.

Whitfold, David M. "Yielding to the Prejudices of his Time: Erasmus and the Comma Johanneum." *Church History and Religious Culture* 95 (2015): 19–40.

Wood, Anthony. *Athenae Oxonienses: An Exact History of All the Writers and Bishops Who Have Had Their Education in the University of Oxford*. Vol. 1. London, 1815.

Xenophon. *Xenophon: Anabasis, Books IV–VII and Symposium and Apology*. Translated by O. J. Todd. London: William Heinemann, 1932.

INDEX

Academic skepticism, 10, 191
accommodation: in interpretation,
94n12, 132–33, 149, 166n45; toward
others, 80, 132, 141, 149; rhetorical
principle, 58n122, 79–80, 247n6;
in the theology of Erasmus, 11, 14,
33–34, 79–80, 90. *See also* incarnation; philosophy of Christ
Aelian, 60n2
allegory: balanced use, 94, 95n15, 105;
elasticity of wording, 109–10, 113;
excessive use, 95n15, 102, 105; in
interpretation, 90; and irony, 93–94;
and literal sense, 93–94; spiritual
sense, 92–94; springboard for, 92,
94–95
Ambrose, 44n65, 95n15, 132, 137, 143,
171, 173, 204
annotations: on biblical books, 6; on
biblical passages, 121–22, 128–29,
131, 136n68, 137n71, 138n74, 142n85,
144–45, 148, 183–85, 196, 206n89;
exegetical resources, 119, 153; not
doctrines, 6, 9n25, 147, 189–90;
meant for the learned, 158, 162, 164.
See also Bible
Aquinas, Thomas, 172, 220n23, 234n75
Arian: as heresy, 124–25, 130–31, 143,
150; their impressive scholarship,
125–26; proximity to orthodoxy,

132–33; their reasonableness, 135–37,
139–41, 146, 148. *See also* Arius
Aristotle, 62, 63n15, 89, 91, 186n10,
198n62, 224
Arius, 26, 90, 114n90, 124n22, 125,
132n56, 144n94
Asso, Cecelia, 121n9, 152
Athanasius, 85n92, 148
Augustine, 21n66, 75n15, 48, 92n3,
96n19, 117, 135–36, 145, 166, 167n48,
170, 171n60, 174–75, 184n5, 200, 204,
206

Backus, Irena, 189n23
Baechem, Nicolas, 155n3, 174n70
Baker-Smith, Dominic, 93n8,
Barker, William, 51n98, 58n120, 73n50
Bateman, John J., 144n94
Béda, Noël, 3, 5
Bedouelle, Guy, 26, 185n9, 186n11,
186n13, 187n16, 187nn18–19, 189n23,
194n49, 198n62, 208n95, 211nn108–9
Bentley, Jerry H., 143n89
Benz, Ernst, 72n48, 76n63, 79n75,
83n87
Bible: authority, 20, 27, 91, 124, 134,
140, 142–43, 156; clarity and ob-
scurity, 10n29, 91–92; difficulty of
interpretation, 91–92; as historical
document, 20–21, 124n 126, 142;